EDUCATION IN
PARAPSYCHOLOGY

PROCEEDINGS OF AN INTERNATIONAL CONFERENCE

HELD IN SAN FRANCISCO, CALIFORNIA

AUGUST 14–16, 1975

EDUCATION IN PARAPSYCHOLOGY

PROCEEDINGS OF AN INTERNATIONAL CONFERENCE

HELD IN SAN FRANCISCO, CALIFORNIA

AUGUST 14–16, 1975

Edited by
Betty Shapin and Lisette Coly

PARAPSYCHOLOGY FOUNDATION, INC.

NEW YORK, N.Y.

ISBN 0-912328-28-2
Library of Congress Catalog Card Number: 76-19467

Manufactured in the United States of America

The opinions expressed herein are those of the individual participants and do not represent the viewpoints of the editors nor of the Parapsychology Foundation, Inc.

PARTICIPANTS

John Beloff	University of Edinburgh Scotland, U.K.
Irvin L. Child	Yale University New Haven, Connecticut, U.S.A.
Frederick C. Dommeyer	San Jose State University San Jose, California, U.S.A.
Wilbur Franklin	Kent State University Kent, Ohio, U.S.A.
Martin Johnson	State University of Utrecht Utrecht, The Netherlands
Stanley Krippner	Humanistic Psychology Institute San Francisco, California, U.S.A.
Robert L. Morris	University of California Santa Barbara, California, U.S.A.
James E. Morriss	Division Avenue High School Levittown, New York, U.S.A.
Enrique Novillo Pauli	Universidad Catolica de Cordoba Cordoba, Argentina
Brenio Onetto	Universidad de Chile Santiago, Chile
K. Ramakrishna Rao	Andhra University Visakhapatnam, India
J. B. Rhine	Foundation for Research on the Nature of Man Durham, North Carolina, U.S.A.
D. Scott Rogo	Reseda, California, U.S.A.
Gertrude Schmeidler	City College of the City University of New York New York, U.S.A.

Rex G. Stanford
St. John's University
Jamaica, New York, U.S.A.

Rhea A. White
East Meadow Public Library
East Meadow, New York, U.S.A.

American Society for Psychical Research
New York, New York, U.S.A.

OBSERVERS

John Bisaha
Mundelein College
Chicago, Illinois, U.S.A.

James Bolen
Publisher, *Psychic*
San Francisco, California, U.S.A.

Douglas Dean
Newark College of Engineering
Newark, New Jersey, U.S.A.

Arthur Hastings
Hastings Associates
Mountain View, California, U.S.A.

Gerald Jampolsky
Child Center
Tiburon, California, U.S.A.

David McKnight
Blue Ridge Community College
Blue Ridge, Virginia, U.S.A.

Marian Nester
American Society for Psychical Research
New York, New York, U.S.A.

John Palmer
University of California
Davis, California, U.S.A.

Milan Ryzl
San Jose, California, U.S.A.

John Saloma
University of San Francisco
San Francisco, California, U.S.A.

Charles T. Tart
University of California
Davis, California, U.S.A.

Alan Vaughan

Editor, *Psychic*
San Francisco, California, U.S.A.

PARAPSYCHOLOGY FOUNDATION, INC.

CONTENTS

INTRODUCTION
Allan Angoff, Eileen Coly   xiii

A REVIEW OF CURRENT NEEDS AND EXPECTATIONS
J. B. Rhine   1

THE STUDY OF THE PARANORMAL AS AN
EDUCATIVE EXPERIENCE
John Beloff   16

RECRUITING FOR RESEARCH
Gertrude Schmeidler   30

EDUCATION IN PARAPSYCHOLOGY: SYSTEMATIC COURSES OR
FREE EXPERIMENTAL RESEARCH TRAINING
Brenio Onetto   47

PARAPSYCHOLOGY IN THE SECONDARY SCHOOL CURRICULUM
James E. Morriss   58

PARAPSYCHOLOGY IN THE LIBERAL-ARTS CURRICULUM
Irvin L. Child   87

TEACHING OF PARAPSYCHOLOGY IN INDIA AND THE
ANDHRA EXPERIMENT
K. Ramakrishna Rao   107

PARAPSYCHOLOGY AND EDUCATION
Martin Johnson   130

SOME CRITICISMS OF EDUCATION IN PARAPSYCHOLOGY
D. Scott Rogo   152

PARAPSYCHOLOGY AND HUMANISTIC PSYCHOLOGY: THE
EDUCATIONAL INTERFACE
Stanley Krippner   169

PREPARING FOR A CAREER IN PARAPSYCHOLOGY
Rex. G. Stanford   192

PARAPSYCHOLOGICAL EDUCATION IN ARGENTINA
Enrique Novillo Pauli   212

THE ROLE OF PARAPHYSICS IN PHYSICS EDUCATION
Wilbur Franklin   229

PARAPSYCHOLOGY AND THE TEACHING OF PHILOSOPHY
Frederick C. Dommeyer   249

THE ROLE OF THE LIBRARY IN EDUCATION
FOR PARAPSYCHOLOGY
Rhea A. White   273

THE RESPONSIBILITIES OF INSTRUCTORS
IN PARAPSYCHOLOGY
Robert L. Morris   300

INTRODUCTION

ALLAN ANGOFF: Good morning, ladies and gentlemen. For the officers and trustees, I am glad to open this 24th Annual International Conference of the Parapsychology Foundation. Our theme is "Education in Parapsychology," and it is a theme that represents a culmination of the Foundation's objectives.

The Parapsychology Foundation was established almost a quarter of a century ago, to encourage research, study, and experiment in the psychical aspects of human behavior. Eileen Garrett, founder and first president—a great friend of learning, and a noted psychical researcher, who participated in some of the landmark experiments in parapsychology in the United States and England—felt there was a need to support in substantive fashion scientists and others studying the paranormal in laboratories, universities and classrooms.

It should be noted here, also, this morning at this Conference, that Mrs. Garrett said, "The organization would constantly seek to encourage parapsychological research within universities among scholars of firmly established reputation. At the same time," she added, and these are her words, "The Parapsychology Foundation does not endorse any specific technique of study or research, but encourages activities in areas that would appear to offer possibilities of serious achievement within our area of inquiry." That was, and that remains the continuing objective approach of this organization, and this conference was organized accordingly.

I pause now to present Mrs. Garrett's most worthy successor, our second president—Mrs. Eileen Coly.

EILEEN COLY: Good morning, everybody. I just want to say "Welcome again." We won't waste any time. We'll go right to work because we have a great deal to do on this very vital subject of education.

A REVIEW OF CURRENT NEEDS AND EXPECTATIONS

Joseph Banks Rhine

We can all agree, I think, that the topic of this conference is a most important and timely one for the present stage of parapsychology. The opportunity thus given to a number of us for a meeting of minds on this problem area could have great value for our field.

In choosing to discuss the needs and expectations of education in parapsychology I intend to put more emphasis on needs partly because I have personally been especially conscious of this aspect for a very long time. On the other hand I am not as yet nearly so well prepared on the side of expectations. But even a half century ago I was keenly concerned about the need of educational preparation for what we now call psi research, primarily then my own personal need. It was uppermost in my mind as I found myself drawn into trying to make a thorough inquiry into psychical research. My wife too was in very much the same state of mind as I, both of us then being at the postdoctoral stage, and together we considered and developed such plans as we could for educating ourselves for this objective.

We found ourselves confronted by two main requirements; first, we wished to pursue the best scholarly approaches we could find to the claims of psychical research, and second to discover the best institutional entry point at which in due course to move across the border into that research. After we had some years of informal study and consultation while pursuing full-time academic work in another field, we felt ready to seek the "institutional entry point" and to plunge into giving primary attention to the study of psychical research as a possible career field. This first bridge-burning move took us first to Harvard University in 1926 and a year later to Duke. While at both universities we divided our main attention between departments of psychology and philosophy, emphasis was also given to the formal and informal study of the history of science and what was known at the time of the history of psychical research itself. Some years of practical experience were gained on the problems of mediumship; much attention was given to the analyses of mediumistic records bearing on the major question in the psychical research of the day—post-mortem survival. After a year of this study program at Duke on a fellowship basis and as a research assistant to Professor William McDougall, I was given an instructorship in psychology and philosophy with the express freedom to pursue the independent study of psychical research. I was even allowed to choose certain special courses as part of my teaching load—courses that served my purpose of preparation for working in psychical research. Among these courses were logic, the history of science, hypnosis, personality and eventually a course in psychical research itself.

The main point of this prefatory review of my own educational preparation for parapsychology in the 1920's is that it helps me, if only by contrast, to think of what such education ought to be today. But while I was most appreciative of the opportunities that were given me then, I am not much disposed to recommend such a course of preparation to anyone at the present stage.

Rather, in looking back over the long, slow decade of search for what I thought I needed most to know in considering a research career in PR, I think now of its inefficiency, of the absence of the essential evaluative methods and standards which good schooling normally provides, the lack of any comparative appraisal of my own progress and of all those guiding judgments which term papers, examinations and other class requirements normally furnish the student. Missing too was the critical stimulation and counsel of a qualified teaching staff in surveying my successes and my frustrations. In reflection now I can appreciate something of what I was missing and why it took so long to make important decisions, to advance my program, discover my own relative capabilities and especially what was faulty in my preparation, the omissions that were to be discovered later when it was too late to digress enough to correct them.

This sketch however is intended neither as a confession of comparatively poor preparation nor a complaint of limited opportunities. My wife and I were deeply grateful for the generous assistance we received, and especially appreciated the unusual freedom to choose our own way and extend our scope of exploration at our own rate. Our greatest advantage was in the close relations we had with the two leading figures in American psychical research at the time, Dr. Walter Franklin Prince and Professor William McDougall. They were not only our informal tutors and friends but our sponsors as well. But we could however have had just as good relationships with these men along with an organized and institutionalized program of preparation had there been one.

It is of course quite understandable that at our period of training no American university could have managed a formal educational program in psychical research as we think of it today. It would have been quite premature then to have offered enough of a course program to prepare students for entering this field in a professional way. Rather it was at about that time (1926) that Professor McDougall gave his well-known lecture entitled "Psychical Research as a University Study;" yet even he did not have in mind the more ambitious study program he would have, I think, if he were living today. For 1976, a half century after the bold proposal in his Clark University address, the plan he would propose, I should like to think, would be much like the outline I shall present here today, with all due acknowledgments of his influence.

And now, after briefly surveying next what the educational needs are that seem most pressing, I will go on to ask what kind of program could best provide for them; and finally then consider what the prospects are for bringing about such a program.

EDUCATION FOR WHAT?

Just what is it for which educational advance is required and intended? It is obviously necessary to be clear about this, right from the start, as I have learned by experience. When in the 1930's I hopefully introduced a course in psychical research in the Department of Psychology at Duke, I completely overlooked this primary question; but I soon discovered it when for every student in my class who wanted to take psychical research as seriously as I did as a coming science, even for a possible career field, I found there were ten others who had no such serious order of interest. While of course I did not disapprove the action of these other students taking the course for their own proper enough reasons, it did make quite a difference in the value I could put on my own time and efforts in giving the course.

Fortunately I found still other students who were not taking the course but who wanted to participate in our experiments. In many cases these young people quickly fell into an independent study program which I encouraged as their interest grew. After a few years of seeing the success and efficiency of this informal sort of collaboration I gave up the formal course. Instead I gratefully accepted all the student participation that was volunteered and considered it a fair exchange for the educational benefit the students received. This of course is the old method of education by learning on the job. It was operating unofficially and yet quite satisfactorily for all concerned.

Conferences, seminars, and discussions of research reports by staff and visitors, all further enriched the active experience of the students in the laboratory.

Naturally I have thought many times during the 40 years since about this decision not to continue my own psychical research course, especially as other academic people, mostly psychologists, have indicated their interest in giving a course in parapsychology. I would in fact often be asked why I was not giving one myself. My reply usually has been that I just did not have time. I did agree, however, to write (with my colleague, Dr. J. G. Pratt) what was intended to be a textbook. But even as I worked at it, around 1957, I had its other uses as a handbook of research primarily in mind.

I do indeed recognize the need for an intelligent public to be educated on what is going on in this branch of scientific study and know of no better way they can be informed about it than by a course on the academic level. So I welcome the rather strong trend towards the introduction of such courses, especially when teachers with some training and background in parapsychology can be found to conduct them. However, I have not been generally promoting these courses, mainly because of the shortage of qualified teachers, the need for more literature of good quality to help students and teachers, and more serious consideration of the scientific standards and perspectives by which the field should be judged and studied. Yet the number of courses does continue to increase and the time will doubtless come, perhaps before many years, when every college and university will offer (preferably in its department of psychology) at least one course on parapsychology. This, however, is still not a matter I can get primarily excited about just now.

What does stand out as a timely and urgent need of the field at this point is for the kind of parapsychological education required to train, select and qualify the future researchers and the necessary teachers to sustain an adequate research program for the field. Above all, research personnel in parapsychology do need to know at the outset, much better than most of them do, about this field they are attempting to enter and how best to go about it. Moreover, they need to know all this at the start of their research careers so as not to have to spend years in the difficult and often discouraging efforts of undirected independent study to acquire the essential basis for a fair expectation of success.

Parapsychology has existed much too long, especially in this country, without an available professional training school to educate the many young people and the few of their elders who cross the border to participate in psi research. Too often they do not know even what it is they are bypassing as they move right up to the front lines, where naturally the greatest interest and action are to be found, unavoidably skipping over those many years of basic preparatory studies such as other branches of research require, and often even misleading themselves with superficial quick-spun theories, which a wider knowledge of the field would warn them to take less seriously.

Much more than the essential training, however, is being missed through the lack of a properly organized educational system. In any department of science staffed to give a well-planned approach to professional status several other important educational services are contributed along with the acquisition of knowledge. One of these is the "natural selection" of the most qualified individuals among those participating in the program, a process that goes on incidentally in the course of study and the training in research methods. This selection effectively eliminates the potentially less capable and undermotivated students. The setting ideally allows the student to put his own qualifications to the test while he is under the helpful observation of the staff. It is also his opportunity to acquire the habits and values needed to cope with the strains and challenges which psi research is likely to impose upon him. All other sciences and disciplines need and require screening and training programs extending over many years. Parapsychology, now perhaps in its most critical stage, can hardly continue without these well-established educational benefits. With this thought in mind I turn now to the question of what sort of education it will take to provide the best possible selection and training of psi research personnel.

THE KIND OF EDUCATION NEEDED

Without being narrowly exclusive the first educational emphasis in parapsychology should be much the heaviest on the preparation of the student for successful experimental research. With the field at its present stage the first aim of the teaching itself needs to be in the furtherance of basic research, from its rational conception and planning of projects right on through the production stage and into the final interpretation and meaning of results. Today and for the foreseeable future primary recognition must also be given to the preparation and selection of the individual research worker so as to enhance his capacity to conduct successful exploratory tests; these of course are the tests that register adequate evidence of psi ability.

The field should not, however, be permanently unbalanced by over emphasis on any one step or stage of research. In the long view the writer, teacher, administrator, technician, consultant and editor (among others) all have their more or less essential roles to play. Eventually, their participation, too, will require a high order of preparatory training, with much of it being the equal of the education required of the research staff itself. But as of now the prime limiting factor is expertise in the productive elicitation of psi effects under adequate test conditions. This critical necessity—so long as it lasts—must accent the educational policy of the field.

Obviously this primary requirement makes a great difference in a number of ways; one of these is that psi-testing (one might as well say psi-finding) calls for certain gifts (as far as we can now judge) in the experimenter's personality. The personal qualities that may be helpful in evoking psi evidence and in keeping the ability in operation during an experiment are recognizably most important. At the same time that this is a legitimate emphasis, it is not an exclusive consideration; that is, good testers are not the only people needed and the present high priority requirement of the testing capability will almost certainly pass with time. Even now the growing complexity of test methods and equipment, and the continued emphasis on experimenter teamwork, promise to make the field increasingly diversified in its need of various skills; if so it should in the future lose few people because of limited gifts as psi testers. (And if we try we may even learn eventually how to *train* good testers.)

The most immediately urgent need, however, of the training program I am discussing lies in the selection of "good testers" in the course of a well-developed training process. In an adequate school situation the individual who finds himself under a handicap is naturally self-eliminating. The system should of course help him to test himself in the actual testing practice. Whoever encounters comparative difficulty in this, as in any other field requiring special skills, is automatically made aware that he should not enter such a field with hopes of making a successful contribution. Thus he would normally be spared the agonizing experience of a tardy discovery of his limitations after he had already committed himself and burned his bridges. This embarrassment has unavoidably happened all too often in the history of parapsychology. The schools that train professional workers in other sciences have long since been able to combine selection with training in preparing their personnel.

With still another, and an equally important, problem the school for parapsychology would have a unique role to play—one that relates to the now active issue of experimenter deception. In a proper training program for his education the individual would be expected, as I have been saying, to find out during his schooling whether he could properly achieve success in psi testing. He would do this still in a period when transfer to another branch of study would be easy should he find out that his capabilities did not well qualify him for the field of psi research. Such a decision then would spare him the temptation of making up for his lack of ability by recourse to unacceptable practices.

The most elemental purpose, then, of such a school at present would be to enable the student, as he goes on to acquire a thorough scholarly acquaintance with this branch of science, to discover also the degree of his fitness for it. His training should prepare him to judge his own ability as an experimenter and give him the confidence he will need in facing the inevitable requirements of objective reliability.

However, as I have hinted, there may be more to be done on the sensitive question of who can become a good psi-tester. Little effort has been made so far to explore the trainability of capable experimental testers. Yet it would quite obviously be a project of great potential to combine with the general training program itself—that is, the study of how best to help psi testers to improve their skills.

Surely the time has come for this field to provide for its students all of the combined training and services that are now potentially available and to attempt to give every psi worker at the beginning whatever advantages such educational preparation can offer. In fairness to the individual himself as well as to the field as a whole, it is important that this be given high priority.

It would be a bit premature at this time to outline a proposed program for a university department (or sub-department) of parapsychology from an undergraduate beginning to the doctorate. But some general considerations can be suggested that would likely apply to a wide variety of situations that might occur.

For the best preparation for a career in parapsychology I would suggest biology as the major field of concentration on the under-graduate level, with psychology receiving first rank in emphasis at the stage of work for the M. A. degree. Also enough psychology should be taken by the undergraduate to qualify for graduate entrance in that department for the Master's degree.

The formal study of and introduction to research in parapsychology itself should most suitably come in the junior and senior years, and may wisely be kept secondary even then to the emphasis on biology and psychology. However, independent study and research can well be encouraged in earlier years if time permits without any neglect of the formal course work. It is important to fulfill the other scheduled commitments and restrain special enthusiasm for parapsychology in order to avoid the threat of unwelcome competition with other branches of study.

The M. A. emphasis can well be primarily on psychology with the aim of broadening the training program with some of the many useful techniques and skills the field offers. The M. A. thesis research can perhaps best be done on lines of training in psychology that are readily transferable to psi problems of adjacent character. Research in parapsychology may, but need not, be identified with the thesis. The more advanced studies in parapsychology can still be given second place to psychology and other courses that should be helpful in psi research itself in the years ahead.

For the Ph. D. program, however, emphasis should finally be given to parapsychology itself, in study, and in laboratory practice, as well as in thesis research. With the more basic training on the general requirements already completed by this time, a thorough historical grounding in the literature of parapsychology should be required and well certified by examination and review. Without his basic preparation in the field itself parapsychology would be admitting not just a blind man, but one who knew not that he was blind.

At the same time the study of parapsychology should always be kept in the larger setting in which it belongs. For example, the history of parapsychology should be integrated with the history of psychology and a broad program developed around the general history of science. The training should lead on to a convergence of studies (philosophy, psychology, biology, anthropology, sociology, history, statistics, etc.) upon the resulting conception of the nature of man. The course work should be accompanied by research training appropriate to each stage of progress on through the doctorate.

Throughout the training of a parapsychologist it is of prime importance not only to keep an eye on the distant goal of effectively dealing with *psi-testing*, on the one hand, but of relating this aim at every step to the ultimate objective of the understanding of psi. Both perspective and direction are essential. Scientific outlook as well as research capability is needed.

PROSPECTS

I have tried to point up the well-defined educational needs we face in parapsychology and to indicate, in outline at least, what will be required to meet these needs. This brings me to the question as to what reasonable prospects there are in our field that these steps can be taken and that the educational program required can be carried through. At this point there are naturally many uncertainties, but some of these can be greatly reduced by extending our acquaintance with the facts we face and the situations that exist. In fact I expect from these exchanges at the conference that there will be both corrective judgments and supplementary information that may help in the development of a stronger program than has been available.

As a first and immediate step I am inclined to propose a well-directed evaluative survey of parapsychological education, not only as it is at the current stage but in all the principal successes and failures of the past. I do not think of this as something to complete before doing anything else; rather, this survey should be a source of supporting information for policies that I hope will soon be under active consideration.

Let us concede at the beginning that generalizations from the report of such a study must necessarily be limited. But even at the current stage we can still learn much from the problems, progress and conditions at Freiburg, Andhra, Edinburgh, and Utrecht, even with all the allowance for cultural differences that would have to be made. Likewise in going back through the past to some of the premature efforts at earlier educational programs in the universities the difficulties and relative failures at Stanford, Harvard, Duke and elsewhere may have considerable pertinence to policy making in American universities today. At least we cannot know in advance that they do not pertain.

Even the wave of interest spreading through the collegiate world of the U.S.A. in recent years in the introduction of courses of various types dealing with parapsychology, with or without some accompanying research effort, might furnish some illumination. Here and there, an encouraging innovation can be found that may be especially instructive, cases such as the Eileen J. Garrett Lectureship in Parapsychology, set up by the Parapsychology Foundation at the University of California at Santa Barbara, and held by Dr. Robert Morris.

This educational survey should make it much easier for the necessary judgments to be made as to what beginnings would be feasible, what support might be expected, how confident we can be that sufficient interest will be sustained, and even what the most probable sources of financial support are likely to be. The project should be of short-term duration in order to make the facts promptly available. Other larger surveys of parapsychology are, as most of you know, being contemplated, and histories and other appraisals are being made of the field as a whole; this educational program however should not be made to wait for anything as time consuming as these. It has, in effect, been waiting something like 25 years too long as it is.

In the meantime another type of educational exploration could well be made concurrently, and there is no need of which I know for making it entirely independent. The two could be a single mission. What I have in mind is the present interest among some academic institutions in having scientific parapsychology represented on their campuses. There is some reciprocal interest, too, on the part of some parapsychologists and a few research centers in these possible university connections. While on the one hand it should help to know how well the psi research activities are getting along where they already have campus connections, there is still no need to wait for the completed survey to explore these new openings to possible application. At any rate such considerations are receiving serious attention today in a number of instances, with the initiative shared by both sides.

One comforting fact about these negotiations (for an educational program for parapsychology on a university campus) is that the matter can be discussed, at least on a fair number of campuses, with a degree of detachment that allows the real problems to be considered. Today it appears that these problems are much the same as they would be with any new branch of inquiry. There is no serious likelihood of unacceptable discrimination against the new subject. The administrative concern spells out the decisions for which the university would have to assume responsibility. Those concerned with parapsychology have to concede such authority and at the same time to require the assurance and commitment that the new subject will receive the treatment that any new scientific program would have to have. Quietly and gradually the time has come when parapsychology has, to that extent, been accepted—not everywhere of course; but, for the present, only one such place is really essential, and yet it is for such a start that, if the program is a proper one, parapsychology is in great and urgent need.

We need indulge in no illusions that there are no risks in depending upon an academic program for the education of parapsychologists. Some of the poorest education I have ever seen was on university campuses. There can be much about the academic system to dull the enthusiasm of study and research. In fact some of the freedom the research explorer (and director) enjoys in a nonacademic research center would have to be surrendered in a university department. However, there will probably always be a place also for the nonacademic research institute in this branch of science, just as there is in most of the others. Even so, I am convinced we shall have to depend on the university system for the educational preparation of psi research personnel, as the other branches do.

Where should parapsychology be centered in the university? The answer should obviously be, close to psychology, of course, but only if the latter accepts the proximity; happily, the trend is now more favorable to that relationship. Naturally much depends on the individuals most concerned on either side. Similarly the question of how closely the parapsychological branch is to be affiliated is a sensitive one. It appears to be most efficient to make it a subdepartment of psychology, but on some campuses it may be of advantage to be autonomous, at least as a beginning. In either case, the advantage of a separate laboratory or even a semi-independent research institute would be considerable. Models of the various possibilities may well be studied for guidance in decisions.

It could well be an unfortunately long time to wait for the "group mind" of parapsychology to mature to the stage of a coordinate move ahead to fill this crucial need. Almost certainly the original step will have to consist of action taken by one of the philanthropic agencies that have largely generated the bolder initiatives of this field in the past. It can however be brought on by a modest series of cautious steps, starting with such a survey of the educational situation as I have suggested. This may logically lead to a decision as to the next step and even show what that should be. Or a beginning already made, such as that at Santa Barbara, may well serve in due course as the grafting stock for a still more fruitful and permanent cutting.

Conceivably one of the more experimental graduate schools may go far enough to furnish some challenges to the field as to adequacy of educational preparation. But in this field the advantage of compliance with existing practice in its academic debut is well beyond argument. Yet at the same time there is ample room for many types of approach in so new an undertaking. We know too that education itself has its limits; that individual differences can range widely beyond the extremes of educational influence. Accordingly, much as we need the best possible educational program, we must not exaggerate its potential or be overconfident about its effectiveness.

It is fair to say, I think, that the step represented in this conference is itself the most concrete assurance we have that there will now be a growing interest in this great problem and that the stir it makes in our minds will not subside until some firm advances will have been made as a consequence.

DISCUSSION

RAO: From what you have said and from what we ourselves have been feeling for quite some time, not only are the facilities for training parapsychologists inadequate, but a number of parapsychologists who are involved in publishing papers in the field, themselves need training for further development. Do you foresee any possibility of organizing at least a one-time long program, say, six months or one year, for these people, that would make them truly professional?

RHINE: Yes, I do. I think that it is very important that we do not wait for any kind of an ideal, far-off development. It should be possible to arrange for extramural courses of that kind, probably extension courses. The only thing we've tried was short courses of a month or two, in the summer, and they've been worth the effort (and the effort *is* great). But we can do much more, and a course or a semester, or something like that, would be very desirable.

FRANKLIN: Dr. Rhine, I wanted to ask about the interplay with physics. I'm a physics professor and I was wondering whether or not, with your background and experience, you think there should be a great interplay between parapsychology and paraphysics.

RHINE: I haven't been able to find a dividing line, so excuse me if my geography in that isn't very good. I once attempted a somewhat ambitious classification and in my monograph (1934), in the first chapter, you will see the rash attempt I made to organize the field. I think it did some good. I don't find that it all needs to be changed or forgotten. In relation to a physical effect, that would be "para-psychophysical" because the "parapsycho" part identifies the psi function in so far as it transcends the sensorimotor range. The parapsychophysical would be that. My wife has subdivided these in a new way which she and I are going to describe a little more one of these days. She says that the psychokinetic effect, which is the way psi interacts with the physical world, is the direct action of psi. Other psi responses of the individual are intermediary, as through dreams, intuitions, hallucinations, compulsive movements, compulsions, etc. The direct parapsychophysical operation is what we've just been calling psychokinetic. I don't think these terms are going to wear unduly long. I think we'll have some kind of a meeting—I hope a harmonious one some time—in which this will all be taken up. The time for something like that would be at one of these programs the Parapsychological Association is considering for a state of the art review.

FRANKLIN: Will physics have a more important role in parapsychology in the future?

RHINE: Than it did in the past. . . is that your question?

FRANKLIN: Yes.

RHINE: I think it will. You see, the first thing we had to do was to show whether or not, as people believe, psi is something nonphysical. That's the heritage of this from the past. People meant nonphysical when they used the term "spiritual" and it meant a great deal to them to make the distinction. It still holds even though we have largely abandoned the term supernatural. Now we're dealing with something that is superphysical; that is the part of parapsychology that has been the most firmly proved.

On the other hand, we have never said that psi has nothing to do with physics. To say it is nonphysical, meaning it doesn't follow physical principles, is one thing. To say it has nothing to do with physics is another and we wouldn't dare say that. It is much the same problem as that of consciousness. How can the experience of consciousness be related to the physical order of things? We already have that problem and right there a knowledge of physics is needed too; in fact, it would be best if physicists would take some of the initiative. If I were a physicist, I would be tempted now to try to discover how it is that these interactions in the PK field can occur, since they do so without any known relationship to the physical properties (e.g. mass) of the objects affected.

Take the recent experiment by W. E. Cox in 1971 just to illustrate. (Not for a final conclusion; it needs repeating.) It was an experiment with two weights of dice. The subjects did not know there were two, but they nevertheless unconsciously distinguished between them. Cox got *the same amount* of psychophysical effect (PK) on the two kinds of dice but it registered as deviations from chance in opposite directions. His subjects scored above chance on the light dice; below chance on the heavy ones.

TART: I'd like your reaction to a slight modification of your proposal, based on the idea that perhaps training from almost an undergraduate level is too ambitious. I get a lot of letters from people who believe I have a Ph. D. program in parapsychology. I send them discouraging form letters; but one of the first things I always emphasize is that, unless they're independently wealthy, they shouldn't even try to be identified as a parapsychologist at the initial stages of their training. There's no guarantee that jobs will ever be available.

RHINE: I like your candor with your correspondents. We would not want a program of parapsychology without a great deal of other study in it, preferably psychology to provide a basis for an alternative vocation. Now how are we going to manage that in proper proportions? I think we must begin slowly and explore the existing possibilities. If we begin with a general course in parapsychology on the undergraduate level, we should, after a couple of years, be able to see if it is working out successfully. We might then go up to the graduate level for a similar trial run; or if anybody is ambitious enough and well enough situated, he could begin on the graduate level in place of the undergraduate. I think experience will be the best answer to many of the questions that we're going to have to face.

I think it should be part of the policy of the Parapsychological Association to help to develop, perhaps through standing committees, the kind of training program that would best integrate the needed background courses. I'd want heavy emphasis, of course, on the actual testing opportunities and training—the field work, the actual experience in a variety of experimental projects; it could all be incidental to the course work and the research program of the department as well.

Now, as you suggest, the question of jobs *has* to be faced. There are very few permanent jobs. Most of us who have positions had to help to make them! And that's going to continue to be the case for some time. Of course, that's been true of all beginning sciences. Parapsychology is not yet very applicable, as you know, and it's applicability is not even being made the subject of study as yet. Your question has to be considered when we do start talking about a proper training program: What *are* we going to do with these people when we give them graduate training and they haven't any opportunities to use it? I think the people who go through the training program would know long before they finished what they were up against. They would all be working part time in related branches and getting experience and qualification as teachers. Many such parapsychology teachers are going to be needed in the universities and colleges. Most of all, however, there will always be the need for the capable psi tester, one who knows his field well and at the same time can obtain significant test results in well-designed experiments.

TART: I'm proposing a more specific alternative. We will have some undergraduate courses, anyway, because of student demand, but in a sense we can say that's not our really serious work. What we need to do is take people who already have a professional degree in another field and do something like Dr. Rao proposed. Train them starting from the professional level they are at, similar to the way hypnosis people generally use traveling seminars for already accredited professionals, rather than an attempt to work through the whole university system. That's what I'd like your reaction to. In a sense we can't seriously train that much at the undergraduate level, so we shouldn't put emphasis there, but work at the post-graduate level.

RHINE: You are right that the educational problem is different for the mature scientist who decides to transfer into parapsychology; it is a different situation even for *each one* of these. They all need special help and provisions, but a good graduate department ought, to some extent, to accomodate its program to their individual requirements. Also a period of work at a research institute could greatly help these people.

The transfer scientist, coming into parapsychology from whatever scholarly profession, can best be prepared by being actually brought into a situation in which he is exposed to the level of knowledge which he needs to be able to match; one where courses in the history of psi research are available and where his skills in psi testing can be tried out as he becomes ready for such practical exploration. It is better to provide the right sort of place for him (or her) to prepare, train, and practice—at the best advantage to him. A good university graduate school should do all that.

THE STUDY OF THE PARANORMAL AS AN EDUCATIVE EXPERIENCE

John Beloff

The question I want to raise in this paper is a very basic one, namely: What justification can we offer for the teaching of parapsychology at the university?

I presume that no similar defense is called for with respect to parapsychological research. If there *are* paranormal phenomena—and I take it that we are all agreed that there is an overwhelming case for supposing that there are—then, clearly, someone ought to be studying them and where better than at the university? In short, the pursuit of knowledge, the quest for truth is one of those unconditional values of our culture that requires no extraneous justification.

The same cannot be said, however, when it comes to our educational policies. We cannot teach everything and it is a matter for debate as to which options deserve a place on the undergraduate curriculum. Basically, two reasons can be advanced for the teaching of any particular topic: the one social, the other purely intellectual. The social reason is that there are certain sorts of knowledge and certain skills that a student needs to equip himself for his future profession. Hence the prominence we give at the university to such faculties as those of law, medicine or engineering. Since parapsychology can scarcely be described as a profession—the number of those who make it their career, in your country, is still negligible—we can hardly justify the teaching of it on vocational grounds.

The intellectual reason is the one that is presupposed in the idea of a liberal education. Philosophy, logic, pure mathematics, no less than history, literature and the study of dead languages and defunct civilizations have few social applications and they have vocational value only to those who will in turn be teaching them to others. Yet only the most hardened philistine would dare to suggest that we banish them from our seats of learning!

Could a case be made for parapsychology on the grounds that it contributes to a liberal education? We must admit that it seems sadly lacking in many of the qualities that we expect of those disciplines that are cultivated for their own sake. It lacks that majestic edifice of theory that has been the pride and delight of the physical sciences; it lacks an agreed body of facts such as gives the historical, geographical or social sciences a firm consensual basis; and it lacks, finally, both the aesthetic appeal and the cultural significance that attaches to the arts and the humanities.

Nevertheless, there are, I am going to suggest, three possible lines that our defense may take. First, we may argue that the demand for it already exists. That the young are eager to learn more about the paranormal and that, if we fail to satisfy this demand in a responsible academic manner, there are charlatans and vulgarizers enough to whom they can turn who will be only too willing to satisfy it in an irresponsible, commercial manner! Secondly, we may argue that, whether or not parapsychology has any intrinsic educational merit, it has by now shown itself to have suffcent relevance to other disciplines whose importance is not in question: to psychology, psychiatry, or anthropology, to philosophy and theology and finally to physics itself. Then, thirdly, we may argue—indeed I shall argue—that, over and above any relevance which it may have to these other disciplines, the objective study of the paranormal (which is how I would define parapsychology) may be credited with certain unique virtues as an educative experience in its own right. In what follows, I shall consider each of these arguments in turn before trying to draw some general conclusions.

Let us start, then, with the argument that, since the demand exists, it is incumbent on us to try and meet it. This is a recent development and it is still only marginally relevant to the situation that obtains in my country. Its urgency arises from growth of the so-called "counter cul-ture" in the United States during the 1960s and, more particularly, of the "occult revival" which was one aspect of it.

I am not here concerned with the causes of the particular episode of our recent social history. It may be, as some have suggested, that too many people these days are educated beyond their intellectual means. When they find that they are incapable of grasping genuine scientific ideas or are bored by genuine scholarship they turn instead to the pseudo-sciences which, at the cost of a modicum of intellectual effort, enable them to enjoy the seductive feeling of being the possessors of a hidden knowledge and a superior wisdom. It is also the case that we are witnessing today a widespread disenchantment with official science, which is often blamed for the crisis through which our civilization is now passing. Anything, therefore, that serves to cast doubt upon the validity or at least the sufficiency of the accepted scientific world view is bound to be welcome to those who are struggling to promote an alternative world view. In these circumstances we have to think carefully before lending ourselves to what is essentially an anti-rational, anti-intellectual revolt.

Our traditional antagonist was the hard-headed skeptic who clung tenaciously to a dogmatic materialism. It was against his opposition that we strove to produce some small dent in the carapace of scientific orthodoxy. We were less concerned about those who believed too much too readily; we thought of them as the lunatic fringe whom we had to learn to tolerate. In the present intellectual climate, however, when the universities are no longer peaceful havens of reason and learning, we have a positive duty to restrain the credulity of the young and to counter the mass of misinformation to which they are exposed, and to which they are so pathetically vulnerable. For, after all, is not one of the chief aims of all education that of helping the learner to distinguish between well-founded and ill-founded claims to knowledge? It is, I may say, unfortunate that, at such a time, too many among us who should know better are themselves being seduced by the ideals of the counter-culture and are willing to lend countenance to the nonsense that is purveyed under its aegis, but it is all the more vital that the rest of us should not weaken in our resolve to uphold the highest critical standards.

We come now to our second line of defense, namely the relevance of parapsychology to established fields of inquiry. Here the two most promising openings are those afforded by (a) psychology and (b) physics. How you propose to integrate parapsychology with either of these two fields will depend, in the first instance, on what you conceive a paranormal phenomenon to be. If, like the late Sir Cyril Burt, or like J. B. Rhine, you believe that psi is essentially non-physical, even though it may have physical manifestations, you will be more likely to want to assimilate parapsychology to psychology than to physics. If, on the contrary, like a number of parapsychologists of a new generation, you believe that everything that happens must ultimately have a physical explanation, you will look for an understanding of psi phenomena, not to the mind but to the brain conceived as a purely physical system and to the possibility that it may possess certain novel and unsuspected physical properties which we had not previously allowed for.

Physics, in any case, can never be left out of the equation if only because PK is, in effect if not in origin, a physical phenomenon. Today, in the post-Geller phase of parapsychology, when PK effects of a directly observable kind have once more come to the fore, we again find that physicists, in America, in Britain and in the Soviet Union, are being drawn to parapsychology in the hope that it may enhance our understanding of fundamental physical processes. There is some difference of opinion, however, among these physicists as to whether psi phenomena can be explained in terms of known physical principles or whether physics itself will have to undergo another transformation before it can encompass them. Only a little while ago it looked as if nothing could be more discredited than the idea that parapsychology could be reconciled with physics as it now stands. Yet, no less an authority than Gerald Feinberg, in his foreword to Edgar Mitchell's compendium *Psychic Explorations*,[1] ventures the opinion that psychic phenomena may not, after all, be found to contradict "known physical laws" and may prove explicable "within the existing body of physical principle."

Again, it looked until quite recently as if nothing could well be more futile than to attempt an electromagnetic theory of ESP. Yet, today, we find several theorists independently coming forward with the suggestion that telepathy at least might turn out to be a form of telecommunication based on extremely low frequency electromagnetic waves, the idea being that this type of transmission is exceedingly penetrating and so cannot be arrested by faraday cages, long distances or other obstacles that interfere with other types of radiation. John Taylor,[2] a theoretical physicist of King's College, London, Michael Persinger,[3] of the Psychophysiology Laboratory of the Laurentian University, Canada and I. M. Kogan[4] of the Society of Radio, Electronics and Biocommunication of Moscow, have each, in their various ways, been toying with this idea. Taylor has gone further and suggests that this kind of radiation can explain the metal-bending performances he has observed with Geller and a number of mini-gellers.

Personally, I do not take very seriously this line of speculation. It seems to me that if psi phenomena are ever reconciled with physics it will only be when physics has been transformed and extended out of recognition. But, of course, I am not a physicist and I may well be mistaken. Meanwhile the critical test of the physicalistic approach to psi, I suggest, will be whether the phenomenon can be simulated artificially. Thus, if low frequency electromagnetic radiation of the sort which the brain can emit can carry information of the sort that has been demonstrated in telepathic experiments, then it should be possible to design apparatus that can pick up this information in lieu of a living subject. Similarly, if such radiation is responsible for releasing stresses in metals so as to create bending, as Taylor suggests, it should be possible to design a gellerizing machine that would render Geller redundant. After all, we can, to a large extent, simulate artifically in this way the functions of our sense organs. We can even design artificial intelligences. We surely have a right to demand from those who believe that psi is physical, an artificial psi subject!

But, whatever the future may hold, there can be no doubt that the most concerted attempt so far to bring parapsychology into the academic fold has been via psychology. This is hardly surprising since, whatever else may be said about psychic phenomena, they seem only to occur in the presence of, or at least in connection with, a living subject, normally a human being. Hence, so long as we are content to ignore the question of the mechanisms by which information is acquired or transmitted, the only questions we can ask about psi are psychological ones, questions relating to the psychological conditions under which they occur and the characteristics of the individual who manifests them.

Historically speaking, the most famous attempt to domesticate parapsychology, with a view to affiliating it to academic psychology, was that associated with William McDougall and his disciple J. B. Rhine at the Duke University Parapsychology Laboratory. They were inspired in their endeavor by three ideas in particular: first, the idea that ESP was a universal property of mind, not just the freakish gift of a few exceptional individuals; secondly, that a statistical methodology would enable us to reveal even the small degree of ESP ability that ordinary individuals may possess; thirdly, that by making the test-procedure simple and rigorous it could be readily copied as a result of which independent confirmations would be forthcoming that would put an end to any lingering doubts about the question of authenticity. The same reasoning, of course, was applied to PK which entered the picture somewhat later. We may note here that, by introducing the term "parapsychology,"McDougall hoped to delineate this quantitative and experimental approach from the broader field of psychical research which would continue taking care of spontaneous cases and uncontrolled phenomena but could not so readily be brought within the academic purview.

These were splendid ideas and by no means unreasonable at the time they were conceived. Yet, I do not think I am being provocative if I say that none of them has been fulfilled. Positive results still largely depend on having the right subject, and a good card-guesser is no less of a rarity than a good medium in the bad old days of psychical research.

Independent corroboration is still the exception rather than the rule, and it is now beginning to look as if we need not only the right subject but even the right experimenter. Rhine, I gather, discourages young aspirants from embarking on a career in parapsychology if they cannot first demonstrate that they are the right sort of experimenter, that is one who can get positive results! In the event, so far from skepticism dissolving under the weight of accumulating statistical evidence from the laboratories, few other universities have felt encouraged to follow the example of Duke, which, on Rhine's retirement, itself severed its connection with parapsychology.

Yet, despite these setbacks, the aim of bringing psychology and parapsychology closer together is still very much alive. It is notably exemplified in the work of Gertrude Schmeidler and Ramakrishna Rao, who have done much to link parapsychology with personality theory, using unselected subjects. It is the point of departure for the work of Rex Stanford. His PMIR (Psi Mediated Instrumental Response) model of psi is based on the premise that, without knowing it, we utilize paranormally acquired information in the satisfaction of our immediate needs.[5] Stanford has pioneered what I like to call the "surreptitious" approach to psi. That is to say, the subject is kept in ignorance of the fact that psi is involved in the ostensible task that he is required to undertake. In recent years at least three researchers have independently adopted the surreptitious approach with positive results: Stanford himself, using a pseudo-memory task,[6] the Kreitlers of Tel-Aviv University using a pseudo-subliminal perception task[7] and Martin Johnson using a pseudo-examination task.[8]

Others have sought a meeting point between psychology and parapsychology not in these everyday acts of cognition but rather in certain special states of consciousness. Perhaps the most notable exponent of this approach at the present time is Charles Honorton, currently president of the Parapsychological Association, but the approach has been so widespread that it may seem invidious even to single out any particular worker. An enormous number of different techniques and different states of mind have been explored from this angle and, although success has been sporadic, this approach continues to attract adherents.

Yet another avenue towards a rapprochement with academic psychology has been to explore the physiological substratum that may be assumed to be common alike to psychological and parapsychological phenomena insofar as both are mediated by the psychophysical organism. Here, again, many names could be cited, but I do not need to look any further than our own laboratory at Edinburgh. Thus, Richard

Broughton has been investigating the possibility that our ESP function may be mediated by the right hemisphere in the sort of way that language and, more generally, logical and sequential thinking seems to be mediated by the left hemisphere. Brian Millar is pursuing an even bolder hypothesis. He is attempting to replicate the so-called "Lloyd Effect,"[9] namely, that if you stimulate the agent, in a telepathic set-up (Millar uses a stroboscopic lamp for this purpose), an evoked potential should be discernible in the subject's EEG record, if this is analyzed by a computer which averages the brain-responses on each trial. Both Broughton and Millar will be reporting on their work to the forthcoming Parapsychological Association Convention so I will not say more about it now and I mention it only to illustrate the new psychophysiological approach to psi. Perhaps, however, I should add that, in the best Edinburgh tradition, Millar got only chance results.

As a psychologist myself, as well as a parapsychologist, I naturally welcome these attempts to bring parapsychology into the psychological arena. Psychology is, in any case, far from being a unified science and I have myself elsewhere attempted to present parapsychology as one of the many distinct psychological sciences.[10] Yet, for all that, I am bound in all honesty to admit that so far the influence which parapsychology has had on any of the other psychological sciences has been minimal. The one area where parapsychology has undoubtedly made a difference is that of philosophical psychology. It no longer seems possible to discuss the nature of mind, or the mind-body problem, as if the parapsychological evidence did not exist, although, amazingly enough, there are plenty of philosophers who are so purblind that they go on writing as if they were still living in the eighteenth century, when commonsense could always expect to have the last word!

But, if, as we have seen, the relevance of parapsychology to physics is still so controversial and its relevance to psychology is at best marginal, where does this leave us with respect to the question of justification that we set out to answer? I think that one thing we have got to recognize is that our field is much more erratic, anarchic and basically subversive than we like to admit when we are engaged in one of our public-relations exercises. It is only by arbitrarily restricting the scope of parapsychology, as McDougall and Rhine attempted to do in their justly celebrated program, that we can give it even the semblance of being like any other conventional science. If there are any of you who are ever tempted to play down the sheer unruliness of our data, I would recommend the following salutary excercise to be performed once a day before breakfast until further notice: try repeating over to yourself the names of some of the more colorful psychic personalities who have left their imprint on our turbulent history: Daniel Home, Eusapia Palladino, Franek Kluski, Eileen Garrett, José Arigo, Ted Serios, Uri Geller. . . you may add or subtract as you please. I am not asking you to accept any or all of these at their face value, merely to acknowledge that they represent so many prodigious question-marks. To contemplate the careers of these, or others like them, is to be confronted with the sheer impenetrable mysteriousness of the world which makes a mockery of our scientific pretensions.

This brings me to my final point, namely, what *I* conceive to be the most distinctive contribution which parapsychology can make to a liberal education, and the chief lessons that we can hope to learn from it. It teaches us, I suggest, not only that the world is a stranger place than we would otherwise suppose, but also how difficult it is to arrive at any definite conclusions about it. It raises for us, in its most acute form, the eternal question: "What can I believe?" This question is one that we encounter all through life whenever we are forced to consider some creed or religion that makes far-reaching claims on our credence. Unlike these other creeds or religions, however, parapsychology spurns any resort to propaganda or appeal to faith. On the contrary, it deliberately fosters skepticism by being hypercritical of every claim which it is called upon to adjudicate and so keeps us in a perpetual state of uncertainty. At one instant it will open up for us exciting vistas of new worlds to be conquered; at the next, it will cause them to vanish again in a haze of doubts. It forces us to reckon with the almost bottomless duplicity of our fellow creatures, and yet it forbids us to take refuge in any easy cynicism no matter how fantastic the case under consideration. In a word, it plays tug-of-war with us so that we can enjoy neither the peace of mind of the committed believer nor the complacency of the skeptic.

From one point of view we have much in common with the lawyer, or even the historian, who is likewise concerned to reach a conclusion about some episode that can only be reconstructed on the basis of human testimony or, at most, documentary evidence. We, however, are in a much more perplexing situation than they are, in that we lack the canons of plausibility based on commonsense experience to which they can appeal. One can see this when the law is called upon to pronounce on some paranormal claim that comes before the courts. The result is usually farcical. As we know, it is not easy to prove that an accused person is insane, but to convince a judge that an accused person has paranormal powers is almost beyond the wit of man! A celebrated trial took place in London, at the Old Bailey, during the last world war, of the notorious materializing medium Helen

Duncan, who was indicted for fraud under the "Witchcraft Act."[11] Her defense counsel offered to stage a séance for the benefit of judge and jury in order to demonstrate their client's authenticity. The judge, however, declined the offer on the grounds that it would be demeaning to the dignity of the court! In spite of a score or more of witnesses who testified to the marvels which she had wrought, it took the jury only twenty minutes to return a verdict of guilty. Perhaps the jurors were all earnest disciples of the philosopher David Hume who, you will remember, argued that it was always more rational when in doubt to suppose that those who testify to a miracle are either lying or are deluded than that the miracle really happened as alleged. And, in the case of Mrs. Duncan's miracles, this may well have been the wisest maxim to adopt.[12] Unfortunately, the parapsychologist cannot settle for this simple Humean rule or for any other *a priori* principle of rationality. Or, perhaps, this is not a misfortune after all, perhaps it is this very absence of any rule or precedent that makes the study of the paranormal such a unique educative experience. There is no other discipline that I know which engages at the same time a person's critical faculties and his imagination and then stretches them both to a comparable extent.

REFERENCES

[1] Mitchell, E., et al.: *Psychic Exploration.* Edited by J. White. New York: G. P. Putnam's. 1974.

[2] Taylor, J.: *Superminds.* London: Macmillan. 1975.

[3] Persinger, M.: *The Paranormal: Part II.* New York: MSS Information Corp., 1974.

[4] Kogan, I. M.: "The Informational Aspect of Telepathy" (Paper presented to the UCLA Symposium "A New Look at ESP," 1969). Unpublished.

[5] Stanford, R. G.: "An Experimentally Testable Model for Spontaneous Psi Events, Part I, Extrasensory Events," *J. Amer. S. P. R. 68,* 1974, 34–58. Part II Psychokinetic Events. *Idem* 321–357.

[6] Stanford, R. G.: "Extrasensory Effects upon 'Memory,' " *J. Amer. S. P. R. 64,* 1970, 161–186.

[7] Kreitler, H. & Kreitler, S.: "Does Extrasensory Perception Affect Psychological Experiments?" *J. Parapsych. 36,* 1972, 1–45.

[8] Johnson, M.: "A New Technique for Testing ESP in a Real-Life High-Motivational Context." *J. Parapsych. 37,* 1973, 210–218.

[9] Lloyd, D. H.: "Objective Events in the Brain Correlating with Psychic Phenomena," *New Horizons, 1,* 1973, 69–75.

[10] Beloff, J.: *Psychological Sciences.* London: Crosby Lockwood Staples. 1973.

[11] Becchover Roberts, C. E. (Ed.): *The Trial of Mrs. Duncan.* London: Jarrolds. 1945.

[12] West, D. J.: "The Trial of Mrs. Duncan," *Proceedings of the S. P. R. 48,* 1946, 32–64.

DISCUSSION

FRANKLIN: In the reference that you made to the physical sciences, have you seen any developments of theoretical approaches which are appealing to the mind as well as to students in the area, which are not within the realm of accepted things? In other words, it looks as if there is a step towards new approaches and have you seen anything that is satisfying there?

BELOFF: I assume that you are referring here to what's coming under the heading of "Paraphysics," and that sort of thing. . . these sort of speculative theories. . .

FRANKLIN: I'm certainly not sure. There are many advances in psychology that I have very high regard for, but I'm a physicist and look principally at that area. My question is, "Why hasn't there been much new?"

BELOFF: Why is this question directed at me? I'm not a physicist. If physics has something to say about parapsychology, you, sir, should be the one to enlighten us.

FRANKLIN: Well, you reviewed the work of John Taylor and of others and made reference to them. That's why I asked.

BELOFF: Yes, indeed. I mean, such theories as these that I have studied and insofar as I can comprehend them, have failed to impress me at all as a solution to the problems of psi. But this may be my own shortcoming.

JOHNSON: I would just like to follow up the question. As far as I know, one of the difficulties is that I wouldn't call them theories—just surmises or assumptions and these usually don't have very much of test implications. Secondly, we still have the tremendous problem to overcome regarding repeatability within parapsychology. Is that some of the reasons why you don't feel impressed by the theories or the hypothesis from the physical side, so to say, or why don't you feel impressed by them?

BELOFF: I think you put your finger here on a very important point. I mean, if they could make predictions that we could test empirically and these predictions or hypotheses are confirmed, we should have to pay much more attention than when they are simply at a speculative level and one is really dealing in analogies and possibilities of a rather fluid kind.

DOMMEYER: It has occurred to me that there seems to be a tendency to associate parapsychology rather constantly with psychology. Maybe this ought to be done, but I wonder whether there are not some unfortunate features connected with that association. Doesn't one sometimes drag all the prejudices of psychologists into parapsychology? I think, for instance of the experience of Stanford University with the Thomas Welton Stanford Psychical Research Fellowship. The psychology department, in general, was not very favorable to the use of the fellowship in the way in which this organization would like to have it used, so I wonder whether it might not be better ultimately if parapsychology were simply to disavow connections with any of the established fields. I wonder whether it would not be better to have parapsychology set itself up on an independent basis and rather than taking the psychological approach, perhaps taking a multi-disciplinary approach because obviously some physicists and people from other disciplines are interested in this area. So I wonder why we should associate it so often with psychology, and whether that doesn't constitute a handicap.

BELOFF: Yes, I have considerable sympathy with your question because, although, as a psychologist, naturally, I have a certain interest in bringing the two together, I have come more and more in the course of time to recognize the sort of unique nature of parapsychology. I quite agree with you. I don't think it can be simply brought into any other single discipline. On the other hand, we have to recognize as a practical fact that we are hardly yet strong enough to stand alone and I can't quite see how we would make our entry into the university, which I think is very important because this is where important research will be done. I can't quite see how, you know, simply calling ourselves "interdisciplinary," we are going to make a stand, but maybe these practical difficulties can be overcome.

RAO: You pointed out two possible areas of relevance with regard to parapsychology finding a place in the university curriculum—the social relevance and the intellectual relevance of the field. You apparently felt that you can hardly claim a justification for social relevance. Don't you agree that many cultures in the world have built-in belief systems that border on the acceptance of the paranormal, and that any inquiry or investigation into these assumptions with a view to find factual evidence bearing on them is an important social function to perform? I personally believe that a scientific inquiry which will throw light on our assumptions and belief systems is a legitimate function that has an important social relevance. This is one comment.

The second one is with regard to the greater emphasis on or justification for having parapsychology in a university teaching situation for intellectual reasons. Now, I have a feeling that for anyone who is undergoing training for a research career in psychology, judicious training in parapsychology could be very useful. Parapsychology is a discipline which deals with problems replete with conceptual ambiguities and uncertain variables that can easily trap a less sophisticated investigator into committing errors of design and inference. The history of the progress of parapsychology, I think, is a story of the development of methods and techniques to tame and control what one time appeared to be uncontrollable behavioral variables. As such, a study of parapsychology should prove to be an enviable asset for any student of human nature.

BELOFF: Yes, Dr. Rao, I really am in agreement with both the points you've raised, but I feel the first one about social relevance. . . I mean, obviously parapsychology does have social relevance because it enters into daily life and into people's culture, but I think there would be more of what I could consider a justification for research into the field rather than the actual teaching aspect, but that's a small point. In the other case—I bring that under my heading of being connected with psychology. Certainly if parapsychology is, as I think, a psychological science, then no psychology student is complete without some knowledge of it. Although I don't give courses at the undergraduate level in parapsychology, I always in my general courses try and make them aware of the fact that there is parapsychology as well as the other things that they have to learn.

KRIPPNER: I would like to pick up on the comments that Dr. Dommeyer and Dr. Rao just made about the place of parapsychology in the curriculum. It seems to me that this is another piece of evidence that the universities, by and large, are behind the times. We are now getting to the point where we realize parapsychology, at its best and at its truest, is interdisciplinary and covers psychology, physics, anthropology, philosophy, biology, etc. Some universities are finally starting to open up a little bit by admitting parapsychology into a few psychology departments. What these universities are doing is very gratifying but might be passé, in terms of the standing the field will have in the near future.

BELOFF: I don't have very much to add to that because I am basically in agreement with it—that it is an interdisciplinary study and that some of the people making some of the most important contributions today certainly aren't psychologists by background. They often come from physical sciences or elsewhere. We shall hear something more from Bob Morris, because I understand that his position is something of an interdisciplinary situation, and he will have more, perhaps, to tell us about how it's working out. My misgivings were how we would convince universities of our relevance, you see—if they acknowledged us, there would be no problem. We would then have a department of parapsychology which could draw upon all these other ongoing disciplines.

RYZL: I want to address myself also to this interdisciplinary feature of parapsychology, and I think in California we have good examples. Several universities or colleges have accepted parapsychology on this interdisciplinary level. An example is the Tutorial Department at the University of California in Santa Barbara and I would suggest that Bob Morris tell us more about it. For another example, the San José State University has had successful courses in the cybernetics department; this is another case of an interdisciplinary approach; and now there is a program being prepared in John F. Kennedy University which plans to offer parapsychology in a department related to religious studies, but not only on a philosophically-oriented level, but experimentally-oriented. So this is an example of the fact that parapsychology is transcending the limits of one single field.

BELOFF: Yes, thank you, Dr. Ryzl. I'm glad to hear you tell me of this because I think it's a healthy development that this should be coming about.

HASTINGS: I have two observations. One is that there is sometimes an advantage in doing an interdisciplinary program instead of an internal departmental program, simply because you have more access to the different contributions form various academic areas. Secondly, in some cases we are handicapped as a profession by having to fit into the traditional and current university and college departmental programs. In order to gain status and legitimacy, we sometimes find it necessary to justify ourselves as philosophers or cyberneticians or psychologists or physicists, when research is coming from all these areas. This does not mean that parapsychology is subordinate to any of these, but that it is more than any one traditional field. We may want to look at ways the research concepts can be opened out so as not to exclude the many areas that are contributing. Psychologists may have to understand ways of research that are quite different from their familiar ones. Physicists may have to learn psychological ideas that are quite foreign to their discipline. So I think we should consider how we can incorporate diverse approaches as we move into a coherent education program.

MORRIS: I guess I should mention some of what's going on at the University of California at Santa Barbara now. The only reason that UCSB was an acceptable campus really for parapsychology was because of the existence of an interdisciplinary undergraduate major called the Tutorial Program; because of this, I teach all three of my courses in the Tutorial Program. They do not threaten anybody. They do allow a fairly natural kind of interaction. The contacts that I've had at the University so far have been drawn primarily from electrical engineering, physics, geology, and religious studies. My boss is a professor of Italian, and I am also overseen by a professor of English and a professor of religious studies.

TART: Let me make an exteme statement, though. I'm all in favor of interdisciplinary studies, but as I think about the parapsychological literature, the only variables that significantly and reasonably consistently correlate with psi performance are psychological ones. While I would like to know of other variables that correlated with psi, I think that in practical terms, psychology is still by far the most relevant discipline for working with psi.

BELOFF: I would endorse that opinion, certainly.

BISAHA: I agree with Bob on that matter. I attended a few education conferences, and the tendency is now for the programs to be inter-disciplinary-related. The fact is we're no longer departmentalizing in the departments, but making programs that are communications which encompass a whole section of college courses. Previously we called it *liberal arts*, but recently it's called *general education*. We are under the illusion that if a student goes to college, we expect him to get a job, but that's no longer the case. They're going there for an education, and the specific purpose, of course, is to develop a new educational principle. Maybe the fact is that education is meeting our prerequisites for parapsychology in this line right along with what we've been speaking about this morning.

RECRUITING FOR RESEARCH

Gertrude Schmeidler

In parapsychology, research is the name of the game. This was explicit when the area was called "psychical research" by those who first set it apart as a field of study; and it is implicit even now, after J. B. Rhine has renamed it. The "ology" ending of our modern term "parapsychology" stands for science, and science is defined by its methods of investigation.

But aside from semantics, I will argue that we need to center our educational as well as our other activities around research—or at least to aim our activities toward furthering it—partly because of moral reasons and partly because of the simple, eminently practical reason that we do not yet know enough to be effective in doing more. You may differ with me on this point, and if you do I hope you'll try to convince me otherwise in the discussion after this paper. But now, while I have the floor, let me state and defend the position.

The strength of my own conviction on this point was brought home to me just last May, when someone from a well known publishing house asked me to write a book for them on "How to Develop Your ESP." My immediate response was tactless, I suppose. I said, "No! It wouldn't be ethical." But thinking about it afterwards, it seemed to me that the conviction was sound, even though the phrasing was on the crude side. The arguments go along these lines.

In the first place, we have no infallible technique for ESP (or PK) development. Training techniques that have worked well for one investigator have not, so far, shown consistent success when they are tried by others. We have no cookbook formula that can be guaranteed to improve anybody's ESP performance if its directions are followed. A "How to—" book would promise more than it could fulfill; the title would be a kind of false advertising.

In the second place, I put to you a different hazard in overselling, familiar but still worth stating. Probably all of you have often heard someone talk about what he was sure were ESP experiences although you, listening critically, felt uncertain that they were. The various incidents were perhaps attributable to normal inference, or else to disregarding negative instances and therefore overweighting the positive ones, or even to the person's assuming that hallucinations or delusions had a basis in reality. Any onesided emphasis in "How to Develop—" or even in educating about the fact that ESP and PK can occur might unhappily encourage overdependence upon wishful thinking, or even neurosis or psychosis. Perhaps an ethical and needed book would be one called something like, "How to Recognize When You Are NOT Using ESP."

And in the third place, more remote but troublesome, are ethical issues of invasion of privacy, or of undue power. At the present stage of our knowledge, if ESP were a readily trained ability accessible to anyone no matter what his motives were, it might be misused to do harm instead of good. And the same principle applies with even greater force to PK. Anyone concerned with application or with general education should, I think, give as much attention to the question of how to shield from the undesirable use of telepathy or PK by others as to the question of how to facilitate the use of either.

This leads back to my initial point, the need for further research. The basic problems of parapsychology were set before us generations ago by the early members of the London Society for Psychical Research. The work of the nearly hundred years since the SPR was founded has told us that the problems are worth study and can yield answers; but we have only the roughest approximation of what even our firmest answers are. By the scientific standards which we are surely all glad to accept, we should not be content until we can make accurate, quantitative predictions about what will occur under given sets of conditions. But I think there are none of us (and feel sure there are few of us) who can state confidently and correctly, in numerical terms, what the results of any investigation will show.

We have the problems, and have had them for a long time. How do we work toward the solutions? From a broad perspective there are many possible routes toward contributing usefully. The most direct, of course, is to do the research: to try to find the answers ourselves. Another is to encourage members of the scientific community to be alerted to and interested in these problems, in the hope that others will turn to them and do the work. Another is to build the broad base of academic support which will let scientists who are already interested feel that they can work on parapsychological problems without jeopardizing their own careers—or even feel that it will further their careers to work on such problems. Another is to build an even broader base in the business and governmental organizations that help to fund the scientific community. And another is to work toward the broadest base of all: general public acceptance of the legitimacy and importance of the issues.

We might think of all this as a pyramid, where the broad public acceptance provides the foundation and the other layers rest progressively upon it. All are useful, but my own paper will be addressed to only two levels of this total structure: the parts near the apex, closest toward providing the research cadre we so need, where I have had a fair amount of experience. It will deal with the encouragement of research in the academic or scientific community, and especially with the possibility of encouraging parapsychological research among advanced undergraduates or graduate students. Its topic is the attempt to recruit and train scientists to work in parapsychology.

You may have noticed that I told you about having had a fair amount of experience with this. The sad truth is that my experience is rather substantial but its success rate has been low. Let me start with an analysis which seems to show that in one subset of my efforts the success rate has been zero or near zero, and that whatever successes there were cluster in another subset.

The formula for training scientists to work in parapsychology surely must begin like the recipe for rabbit stew: first catch your scientist. The obvious way to do this is to go where the scientists are: to research organizations and colleges and universities. Then, in the ideal if not the real world, you alert the scientists to the research issues; you show the relevance of these issues to the problems that already interest them; and you thus direct them to integrate those issues into their own ongoing projects.

This is what I've tried again and again, but—at least when I try it—it doesn't work. Scientific groups to which I lecture seem attentive; they ask good, research-oriented questions; they show interest by staying after the session is over to keep on with the discussion. They give every evidence of being stimulated and concerned—short of the only evidence which is important: doing something constructive about it on their own, after the lecture is over. And this has been true both for specialized groups actively involved in ongoing research, such as engineers and Ph.D.s at NASA or at Bell Laboratories, and for doctoral students at places like Harvard and Columbia, and also for adult groups with a sizable proportion of trained professionals, like Mensa.

Why so? My guess is that by the time research people have grown set in their profession, most of them find security in their own field of expertise. They know how long it takes to become an expert; and from the point of view of safeguarding and advancing their own careers, they know they have to keep on running to stay in the same place. If they shift to a different area, they recognize that they will have to devote a very large number of hours to familiarizing themselves with its prior findings and with its new techniques. But if they spend so much time on the new area, there will not be hours enough to keep on their old one; and this means a hiatus in publications and research output—a hiatus that the effective worker has learned to avoid. (I omit here a discussion of any fear that becoming a specialist in parapsychology means working themselves into a corner where job opportunities and research grants are scarce, because this applies across the board to young people who have not established themselves, as well as to the older ones. It is the special difficulty of recruiting experienced scientists that I am discussing now.)

The preceding argument may be only rationalization: an attempt to justify to myself my repeated failures at recruitment with the trained scientists who would make the best recruits of all. But if it were only a personal failure, I would expect to hear of others who are better lecturers having a great deal more success—and there have not been many reports along these lines. Two exceptions need to be noted, but neither (I think) affects the general argument. The less interesting one is that if research money is available, members of the lecture audience who need money will apply for the position, just as they might answer a classified advertisement. But this seems like recruiting a technician, not an independent scientist. The other exception, a pleasant but rare long shot, comes when someone who has developed his own interests will utilize the occasion of the lecture to make them known and then begin the work toward which he had been heading before the lecture began. Here what happens is less recruitment than internally controlled self-starting, and the lecture merely provides a convenient opportunity for what would have occurred without it.

I therefore put to you my second proposition, one which I would be very pleased to have you refute in the discussion that is to follow this paper. My proposition is that, with the two exceptions stated above (job applicants and self-starters), working scientists who already have their research degrees are too well set into their own specialities to be good prospects for recruitment into another area such as parapsychology. They may feel the allure of working on its problems, but they are well able to resist it.

Where, then, is it worth directing our educational efforts so as to recruit the research workers we need? Not among adults who are set into their own careers. Should it be among young people who have not yet decided on a vocation? Perhaps; but few young people have the temperament for scientific training and its peculiar disciplines. My guess is that attempts to recruit at the high school level or below will spark short-burning fires that soon die out. I therefore suggest to you that the best possibility lies in a middle ground between these extremes: with young people who have already exposed themselves to scientific disciplines and who find them congenial, but who have not committed themselves as yet to the long course of training which will make them expert in some other highly specialized area.

And where do we find this most favorable group? My suggestion is that it is among the advanced undergraduates who are science majors, or among the first or perhaps the second year graduate students in science at a university. They will have already gone through the preliminary hazing that science programs demand: the required techniques courses in laboratory methods and in statistics or other mathematics—courses notorious at most colleges for having stringent requirements but being low in interesting content. Students who have survived these courses without changing their majors are outstandingly our best candidates for education in parapsychology. It is to them, I think, that we should direct all possible educational efforts.

The reason I consider this group so promising comes only secondarily from the logical arguments I have been trying to present. The primary reason is experience. And here, again, it seems appropriate to tell you the kind of experiences that have predominantly led to failures on my part before recommending that you as well as I should emphasize the other kind that has been more successful.

Over the years a very large number of people have written to me or spoken to me about wanting to do parapsychological research. My natural response has been to encourage them and try to help. We first specify together the particular questions which make them most enthusiastic, state the hypothesis they will examine, and then work out together the details of method, recording, finding appropriate subjects, and so on. And I assure them that after they have their data, I will help with—or perform, if they choose—the data analysis. They seem eager and active: good research recruits.

These preliminaries take many letters—long letters!—if the people are some distance away, or many interviews if they are in the neighborhood. A lot of their time and mine goes into it, but from my point of view most of the efforts are wasted. Typically, if the persons had no prior research background, the data-collecting stops with a pilot study, which satisfies them but not me. There have been a few occasions when the person will go on to complete useful work, and these exceptions have been encouraging enough so that even now I cannot help responding enthusiastically to enthusiasm and spending hours trying to think through problems with the scientifically untrained. But dispassionately, looking back over the years, it seems that time spend this way is not well spent. If our primary goal in advancing parapsychology should still be the research that adds to our information about it, then it seems more useful to direct our efforts to those trained in research than toward even the most enthusiastic of the untrained.

Now let me speak to the efforts that have been more productive. Occasionally undergraduates have come to me for an honors project, or some similar plan which could fit into a unit of the college curriculum, in parapsychological research. They would normally have had basic experimental and statistical training before they felt themselves ready for it. I've taken them on, of course; and fairly often the research that they did merited publication. Some stopped there; others stayed with the field for a short time after commencement; but in either case the work seemed useful. For an area as short of manpower as ours, even a one-shot published research report or a few productive years are likely to be helpful.

First or second year graduate students fit into the same general category, and recently there have been many more of these. With such students, little effort is wasted. As we work out the particular problem they want to cope with, and the appropriate way of going about it, these trained people recognize quickly how much hard work it will entail. With this recognition, they soon reach either the decision to drop it or else the decision to continue. They know where they are. And of course anyone who has served as apprentice in a parapsychology laboratory, and gone through the laborious process of data collection and data analysis, has a background comparable to what is gained from statistics and laboratory courses. He knows where he is, too.

From the point of view of research outcome, then, working with trained people is rewarding. Often it results in good research; and when it does not, little time has ordinarily been lost. But there is another further reward, which might in the long run be even more meaningful. These trained people are likely to go forward to professional work, if not in parapsychology then in their own scientific fields. They often end up in university teaching positions. They are thus, after a parapsychology project, our emissaries to the academic world. They will have had enough background in our area to vote favorably for the introduction of a parapsychology course if the question comes up in a faculty meeting, or probably to bone up for and then teach such a course when it is offered. Training future professionals is, probably, our best long term investment.

More recently a different way of reaching the same population has become possible for me. Instead of merely letting it be known that I was willing to sponsor research in parapsychology, I have twice been able to offer a parapsychology course, and it looks as if next year I will teach two more, one undergraduate and one doctoral. The doctoral course will of course be research oriented and therefore needs no discussion here. But it may be worthwhile to tell you about the undergraduate ones, because they have produced what seem promising results: three active members of a working team in parapsychology. Though two courses are obviously a small sample from which it is unsafe to generalize, we might share the unsafe hope that what worked well twice will work again if it is tried, at City College or elsewhere.

What seems to have been the most important factor in their working well is something that was put into effect before enrollment: the decision to limit matriculation to qualified students. The particular qualifications that the registration desk demanded were, as by now you of course expect, that psychology majors should have statistics and experimental laboratory courses as prerequisite or corequisite, and that students not majoring in psychology should have the equivalent in their own fields. It seems to me that there are two useful functions of this requirement. One is that it brings together a group that knows the ground rules. The other is the converse: it warns away the students whose interest is only in personal discussion. They are shown a red flag, as it were, telling them that the road ahead is a bumpy one where they have to go at low speed.

One further part of the course seems to have been useful, and since it is perhaps unusual, I will tell you about it in some detail. That was the option, offered early, between writing the usual kind of library term paper or doing an experimental project instead. The choice (rather than requiring an experiment) seems to me to be necessary so that students will not feel they are being drafted as unpaid assistants in what, after all, is more my interest than theirs. And making the research project equivalent to a term paper means that a substantial block of time will be devoted to it, far more than if data-collecting were only a part of the regular course assignments.

For a laboratory project, it's long been my feeling that students should be advised to do a replication of published research. Both in the experimental psychology courses which I have taught our graduate students for many years and here, I urge them to choose for replication either of two types of research. One type is the kind that leads to a conclusion which seems so natural and "right" to them that they are willing to accept it as a basis for their further thinking. Redoing it will show if it is as dependable as the published report seems; whether they should continue to accept it or should look elsewhere for stability. The other type is the kind that seems to them incredible and bizarre, contrary to their preconceptions. If the reported results work out for them too, they may need to change their preconceptions; and if the results fail to replicate, they may be able to publish a refutation which will keep others from falling into the error of accepting the original author's contention.

For students who feel insecure about research, advice to replicate, I find, alleviates anxiety. It gives them guidelines to follow; it makes them secure enough to take that crucial first step into the laboratory. But the best part of such advice is that bright students don't take it. What happens again and again is that someone will start with an article which he or she intends to copy exactly, but then says, "What would happen if. . ?" and proposes a change in the method. Ideally, then, they would split up their subjects and collect half the data with the old procedure and half with the new. More often, because there is not time to do the whole job, they will (with my encouragement) try out their own idea, and find themselves doing original research when they had not realized they could. Attempting to follow often turns into leading instead. And of course advising rather than requiring replication permits sufficient freedom for a student who prefers to investigate some radically novel idea, if that idea seems practical; it leaves options open.

There are two other advantages in it, I think: one technical and one fundamental. The technical one is that attempting to follow someone else's published method results in more careful reading than usual—reading which all too often shows that important points were not adequately described. This not only makes for healthy skepticism about the generality of the conclusions but also for the equally healthy resolve that when the reader writes up his own research for publication, he will do a more complete description of factors like subject selection, experimenter attitude, subtleties of instructional wording, and others which could determine the outcome of the research.

The more fundamental point deals with research values. Naive students, and unfortunately some professionals, feel that the research most worth doing is something that will lead to a sensational breakthrough, something radically original. And of course this would indeed be valuable, if it stands up to later replication. Too often, as we all know, the sensational claims go up like a rocket but come down like a stick. Much more important, as Gardner Murphy kept telling me years ago, is any finding—even a small, pedestrian one—that will stand up to replication by oneself and then others. This seems to me a basic attitude to inculcate, for a research worker in any field. Unless his values are true, he may become a liability instead of an asset. Emphasis on replication therefore serves the further purpose of showing the potential research worker subtly and indirectly, as well as telling him directly, that there would be no point in publishing work unless the results are stable enough that others who try for them will find them, too. Overstating one's findings, or failure to specify the particular conditions which led to successes, will not go uncorrected for long. It is the results which stand up in other laboratories for which even the beginning research worker should aim.

This is where I planned to end my paper, but as I reread it, it seemed to me that some of you might want—since this is an educational symposium—to hear more detail about the formal courses in parapsychology which our conservative university has recently put into the books. Impetus for them came from two sources. The more important one was student demand: the groundswell of interest that we see almost everywhere. The other came from having available a member of the college community (myself) who was able to propose a course which seemed appropriate for academic learning, which emphasized the critical appraisal of published research, and in general spoke the approved academic jargon. My estimate is that we do well if we work from within rather than from the outside; that we can best take advantage of student demand if conventionally qualified instructors are available. Training in parapsychology alone may be counter-productive; it may make the college departments which consider including a parapsychology course refuse to hire someone who seems alien to them. I recommend rather a sort of gradualism: that someone with an orthodox degree in physics or philosophy or psychology or some other standard discipline be, in addition, trained in parapsychology.

On this basis, if a course is approved within a college department rather than being relegated to the limbo of adult education or a nondepartmental offering, library and laboratory facilities offer no problem. Any college library will ordinarily have a budget item for new courses, and be able to buy most or all of the journals and books needed, or perhaps at worst require a very small supplemental grant. The college laboratory facilities will similarly be open; with them as a base, only small requests will be needed for specialized equipment. The library and laboratory changes will be smooth, instead of seeming to be a foreign body grafted on a dubious or rejecting host.

The single need which I have felt most pressing is for a suitable textbook. Texts in better established specialties are usually so good that student standards are high: they demand careful and full coverage, a conservative but interesting writing style, and so on. We have nothing that is both appropriate and up to date as a text, though we abound in excellent supplementary readings. A text that is modelled after the good introductory ones in the usual academic areas would not only be a help to both instructors and students but would also, I think, if scanned by university professors, add to parapsychology's prestige.

Let me summarize. I have been trying to put three more or less controversial theses to you. The first is that at present, educational efforts in parapsychology should center, directly or indirectly, on furthering research rather than on application or popularization. The second is that the best way of encouraging research is to recruit among advanced undergraduates or else students in the first years of graduate work in a science. The third is that the primary goal to be put forth to the new recruits is that their work should be so careful and so clearly described that it will stand up to replication. This last is a demand for dullness, in a sense; but I think it would be easy to defend the contention that even the most quick and brilliant person must sometimes change his pace and work out his ideas in a pedestrian, careful, plodding way if he is to make scientific advances.

DISCUSSION

ONETTO: I would like to ask you a question about the three people you say were working with you. Did they really come from undergraduate courses or levels, or from other sources?

SCHMEIDLER: There are about seven people who meet regularly with me every week in a noncredit seminar, and of that number, three came from undergraduate courses. It's a serious discussion group, research-oriented.

ONETTO: In other words, you have a higher percentage than you usually get from a group of students from the regular courses.

SCHMEIDLER: You're comparing it to my regular courses?

ONETTO: Yes. The percentage is much higher—practically forty per cent—from seven, you say three.

SCHMEIDLER: It's a special kind of group—doctoral student, M.A.s and two undergraduates, one from a different university.

ONETTO: The point I want to sustain is that perhaps it's not so bad as you say; that sometimes professional people also have graduate courses in parapsychology, say, clinical psychologists or a physician or an engineer. They don't need parapsychology. So if they come to your courses, I would expect that you have a higher percentage. You will find people who are really interested, because they don't need it.

SCHMEIDLER: Yes, that's true. But I think that if, instead of an undergraduate course, I had been giving a graduate or a post-graduate course, then more than three out of forty would have come.

ONETTO: Three out of forty. . .

SCHMEIDLER: Well, enrollment in those two courses was officially limited to twenty. It seems to me that the proportion of students who turned into actual workers is rather low. It would be interesting, I guess, to get some statistical comparison of how many students and how many courses started at each level and at what level did more published research projects come.

TART: Gertrude, I agree with you about recruiting of the early graduate student level, but maybe I'm more conservative than you. I tell them to read up, get their interest going, but for God's sake, don't do their dissertation on parapsychology if they want to get a job! Do you have that problem?

SCHMEIDLER: Well, what I keep telling them is we need to tie things in, and you can be working on an orthodox psychology problem and parapsychology at the same time.

TART: Especially if it's something that will give you tools that you can later use in a parapsychology study.

SCHMEIDLER: Yes, the tools are the same for psychology and parapsychology. I'm kind of worried about the young man who is doing a doctoral dissertation with me now in straight parapsychology, without investigating any psychological problem at the same time. One reason that I went ahead with it was that he wouldn't have it any other way, so I didn't have a choice. But the reason that it seemed all right to me was that he had already been supporting himself by psychological work for years, so he knew how to function as a psychologist. He knew what reality was. I don't think it's quite as bad in the job market now as it was a few years ago, to be labeled as interested in parapsychology; but it still isn't good.

Rogo: I'm wondering, really, how eager we should be to recruit students for research. Having conducted some seminars and having taught in seminars such as Bob is doing in the University of California at Santa Barbara, I think that students coming into our field are much too eager to do research. They don't have that same level of eagerness to sit down and really learn the background history and literature of the field before they do that research. I'm wondering if it really serves the students to encourage them right off the bat to get into experimental research before they really have sat down and gotten a good grasp of what other people have done, what the whole history and literature on experimental parapsychology is, and what the history and literature of non-experimental parapsychology is before they try to embark on something that really might be over their heads completely.

Schmeidler: That's a very difficult point, and I think not just in parapsychology. It's true in psychology too, that if you get a really conscientious person who wants to work on some special area and decides to read everything in the *Psychological Abstracts* that have been published in that area, he spends so much time reading that he never gets his thesis done; and of course, if he goes in blind, all he does is replicate in a weak way what somebody else has already done well and what he's ignorant of. So I think what you did was correct. My tendency is to overstate one side of a difficult issue. . .

Rogo: I'm actually thinking more in terms of the undergraduate students than students at the graduate level who do have thesis requirements.

Schmeidler: Well, maybe a compromise there—that is, when a person says that he is interested in this particular project, you say, "Read these two articles, or those three. They're short. They're in your journals; they're on your topic. Then see if you want to do something along those lines. . ." and then maybe let him do some selective reading besides.

Krippner: I'd like to comment on Dr. Schmeidler's advocacy of the replication of past research studies. Frankly, I feel that this is one of the great problems in our field; that people are so eager to attack the thousands of hypothetical research experiments that they don't try to replicate what has already happened, to check on the conditions, collect more data, start to look into the variables that can be manipulated, and build up a much more solid body of evidence. It might not be as glamorous or exciting to repeat somebody else's experiment, but I think in the long run for the field it will be more helpful.

We have an observer sitting in back of me—Henry Dakin—who has a laboratory here in San Francisco where a number of researchers are doing some interesting work. It is to his credit that he has emphasized repeating work that's been done, especially replications of the early Grad experiments. Once they find out if Dr. Grad's work on seeds and plants can be replicated, they might go on from there. There are all sorts of interesting research studies lying around in the journals which nobody has done since they were reported by the original experimenter.

SCHMEIDLER: I wonder if Mr. Dakin would like to say whether his students, too, find that when they start working on a replication they keep being allured by wanting to introduce this change of procedure or that change of procedure, so they compromise between original research and replication research and do both at once.

DAKIN: We haven't finished analyzing the data on that.

KRIPPNER: What's the process that your assistant has gone through with the seeds exposed to water treated by a "psychic healer?" Has he been sticking very closely to the Grad work or has he attempted to veer off on his own?

DAKIN: I think he's trying to follow it as closely as he can.

SCHMEIDLER: That's virtuous. That's the way it should be.

STANFORD: I don't want to disagree with what you say about the value of the approach that you've advocated in training persons to do research. I see no problem with that. I do want to point out that some other kinds of approaches are being tried in some places and I think are having some usefulness. Now there was a program for undergraduate psychological research instituted at St. John's University some time before I came there, which seems to have resulted in an undergraduate program of laboratory experimental courses where the students seem to have a higher level of morale than in any other undergraduate program that I've ever personally encountered. Now the way that this is done is that even in undergraduate labs, let alone graduate labs, *every* experiment that a student undertakes, even in a group lab, is never an exact replication of anything that is done. The students seem to derive from this the feeling that there is a possibility for them to contribute in some way to our knowledge. I have had the experience, and many other teachers have also had the experience of students being utterly bored with doing standard textbook type experiments over and over again. One of the results of that boredom is

"I really don't want to do that," and some students lapse into cheating; some expect that if this was gotten before, it's got to be had again—we've got to produce those results.

Now I'm not pushing this paradigm as an ideal one either, but I am saying that in training and education I think we ought to benefit from learning theory and recognize that if what a person does, if he's doing it right and if it's rewarding to him, this is a valuable educative experience. What you're proposing, Dr. Schmeidler, could be rewarding to certain students. My own feeling about this is that when I work with students, I find I try to feel out the inclinations of the individual student. There are some students who seem to be inclined toward doing exact replication or a slight modification; there are others who want to go way off into outer space, and usually with a little talk you can tone that down, or you can get them to tone that down a bit, but I think that in trying to get an individual trained for research, one needs to consider the inclinations of the individual. We know that there are some scientists whose forte really is in doing the small step-by-step research and others, the bolder, leaping type of thing, and if we can train our students with regard to their individual inclinations yet with plenty of discipline, I think that we may turn out a quality product.

SCHMEIDLER: I would be interested to know how you introduce the replications into your students' plans. Do you let them work out their own variations, or do you impose the variations on them?

STANFORD: Well, it would depend to some extent on the circumstance of the individual student, but one of the things that I would certainly always try to do is to make sure that they first of all really understand what was done in the original experiment, and that is really a problem, because I've seen people try to replicate things where they didn't understand it. They made a horrible mess of it.

JOHNSON: I would like to add that very often it's impossible to replicate because the way the articles are written and published there isn't enough information given, and I think that has an educational impact.

SCHMEIDLER: I agree, fully.

MORRIS: I'd like to follow up on just that last point because I think one of the most valuable things in Dr. Schmeidler's talk was the whole business of having people read a journal article in detail, to try to understand what was done in order to repeat it. It's been almost a uniform experience that articles are not well written, such that we don't get the wealth of procedural details that seem to be necessary in parapsychology, especially with all the variables involved. One strategy I use to get this point across to students is to require Hansel as a text for our research methods course, since many of the criticisms that he comes up with simply involve the lack of experimental procedure description and precision. He's always saying, "Well, now thus and so might have happened. The author doesn't let us know," and that leads students to question the details of any study. I also think that this problem is not going to be completely solved until and unless we find better ways of writing up our procedures and finding techniques for compressing the space that it takes, because we could blather on for hours describing what we wore and what our attitude was at the moment, etc. We do need to solve a problem here.

WHITE: Maybe one possible solution to that problem would be to write up a very thorough description of what you did, and even though it can't be published in a report, you could put a footnote, as sometimes people do, stating that anybody interested in further information could write for the complete protocol. Or we could even have the Parapsychological Association or some other organization deliberately keep this sort of thing on file so the individual wouldn't have to be involved with paper work.

SCHMEIDLER: That sounds like a very good idea.

RAO: How does it compare with the published psychological experiments? My own feeling is that the procedural details that are given in the reporting of parapsychological experiments are far more extensive in comparison to a number of psychological studies that are published. I think the failure of repeatability in obtaining the same results is very much in the nature of the subject matter we are investigating rather than the lack of appreciation of the test procedures involved. Even if there is the desired appreciation, I think, I can safely bet on failure of repeatability rather than successful repetition. I think it is in the very nature of the subject matter with which we are dealing rather than in the lack of communicating the proper procedural details. The way we handle our subjects is extremely crucial and this cannot be easily communicated in words.

SCHMEIDLER: My impression is that psychology and parapsychology are just about parallel there. In psychology experiments, too, you often find people from one university getting one result with the procedure, and others who claim to be using the same procedure getting different results, until the two visit each other and find out the things that each has omitted in the writeup; and then when they try varying those previously unstated factors, their results begin to converge. As far as the box score of replications in psychology is concerned, there are many well-established areas where the percentage of replicated results is just about comparable to what we get in a lot of parapsychological areas. And this teaching method that I've been suggesting for parapsychology is the one that I've been using in psychology and that students seem to like. It starts them toward dissertation research. So I agree with the tenor of your remarks. When your question is "How different is parapsychology?" I'd say, "Not very."

NOVILLO: Some researchers in the field of parapsychology want to replicate the investigations performed in other research centers, but obtain different results. I am talking about replication in my country. I think the results are different because the researchers don't pay attention to different conditions when they are testing the subjects.

Good subjects are children at elementary school level, but it is necessary to know beforehand the psychological situation of the students in their family and social life and their relationship with their teacher. If the researcher wants to interpret correctly the results of his tests, he must know the psychological environment of the subjects from talking with great prudence to the director and the psychologist of the school in order to get information about teacher and students as well. On the other hand, if the students dislike the teacher, the researcher or the tests, then the results would be very different. It would be a totally different research work and not a replication of the former experiment because of the changed conditions.

SCHMEIDLER: So you're suggesting that a lot of us are working in problems of social parapsychology without knowing it and that this ought to be stated too.

NOVILLO: I don't want to say that all researchers don't consider this social parapsychology, if you want to call it that. What I am trying to explain is that we need to know very precisely the psychological environment where the research work will be done.

I have got good results when there was good relationship between students and teacher, and where the teacher explains and encourages the research work; and other times negative or chance results where the teacher does not properly handle the students.

SCHMEIDLER: It sounds like a brilliant way of handling research, but you might make yourself so unpopular with all the teachers who lose the contest that you'd have to leave that town quickly when you got your experiment done.

TART: I understand the importance of replication as we've talked about it, but I think to some extent we're a little bit too taken with it. Replication is very important in a science when you're in a paradigmatic stage and your results are cumulative in a very real sense. To take the devil's advocate position, let me make the extreme statement that the level of results we generally get in parapsychology represent such a low absolute level of the phenomena, that why bother to repeat them? Maybe we'd be better off just trying this, that, and the other thing in the hope that we'll stumble on something by luck or some unknown unconscious psi process that will give a much higher level of results, and that's what we need. So, yes, replication, but maybe we're better off stumbling around to some extent at this point.

SCHMEIDLER: Well, as to that, I do think I have a response. And that is, not everybody is brilliant; that people can make useful contributions along a whole gamut of intelligence; that offering replication or even suggesting it as one worthy possibility, alleviates anxiety and brings in the worthy but more pedestrian thinkers. I'm suggesting it as a weak possibility which offers an option to the bright innovators. If they say, "Well, replication is okay but I don't want to," then they can do their own thing. I do try all the way through to advise but not to require.

TART: It's really a mixture of both things and depends very much on the personality of the experimenter. Some people like to do careful replications and build steadily, and others hop around.

BELOFF: Could I ask you simply, what is your policy with regard to publication of any findings that come out of these replications, whether positive or negative?

SCHMEIDLER: I've been thinking about that lately, especially since Bob McConnell has been circulating his questions about suppressing results, and it seems to me that I just have no policy. Students vary so much. Some of them give me the impression of doing extremely careful work. When the careful students are done with an experiment—whether the results are positive or negative—I urge them to write a report and submit it. But other students don't impress me as being so rigorous and with them, no matter what the results are, I'm likely to say "Very interesting," and let it go at that. That's really not a policy at all, is it? That is, I treat some students as colleagues, but others just as beginners.

BELOFF: Well, I think it's a very excellent policy. In other words, it's merit that decides whether you push them to publication, not whether it's positive or negative.

SCHMEIDLER: Oh, sure.

SYSTEMATIC COURSES OR FREE EXPERIMENTAL RESEARCH TRAINING

B. Onetto Bachler

In what will be a really "condensed" framework I shall try to synthesize my personal experiences in five years of teaching parapsychology courses at the university level. As I have been teaching since 1962, I shall mostly exclude all kinds of conferences, T.V. or radio programs, interviews, other conferences or courses under the aegis of a private parapsychological society and yearly "season" courses, under the direction of the Extension Department of our university. On the contrary, I shall comment here briefly on a postgraduate course which was given in 1971-1972 to a dozen or so of "professionals" and I understand, for the first time in a Latin American university, with the rather ambitious purpose of "producing researchers in parapsychology."

Let me first begin with some general considerations about this experience. From a statistical point of view, the five courses have been given to 330 students with a mean of 66 students per annum and per course. But since the distribution was not homogeneous, we can criticize on a dispersion of 15 to 150, something that may be interesting for the didactic purpose we had in mind, and also of course, for results. We can rule out any course of, say, more than 30 pupils. There is no good way to work with more students, unless we can get an idea on how to handle parapsychological "testing"—which we consider a *conditio sine qua non* matter for every parapsychological course—with a large number of people, since we all know the negative trend in practically all mass experiments. (We shall return to this "psi-missing" of groups when we give a short resume of the results in our protocols of GESP, precognition and clairvoyance).

Our course is subtitled "Introduction to Parapsychology." This covered mainly the so-called "crucial" experiments for psi and PK phenomena. In other words, ours was the type of course that D. Scott Rogo[1] would call his C group of "Parapsychology as an Experimental Science." We have to be aware of course of the "local" varieties due mainly to differences in language, laboratory facilities and perhaps something we had unconsciously in mind: medical students were rather worried about the value of this new science for a future medical practitioner. We gave therefore, whenever it was possible, examples concerning physiological studies, like those of EEG, GSR, and other types of laboratory measurements; chemicals, drugs etc.

This was important per se because it served as a kind of introduction to the experimental point of view. For the same reason, at least one class was devoted to hypnosis, and another two classes were given to explain some of the theories. We actually feel more and more that a very strong emphasis must be given to audiovisual materials, slides or films, and that they certainly should dominate over their theoretical counterparts.

Now some words concerning the distribution of the qualitative versus quantitative approach. We ought to be as eclectic as possible in the way of a synthesis of both approaches, as proposed by C. G. Jung and realized in Tenhaeff's "Anthropological Parapsychology." And we can do that if one can wisely combine the statistical method (which is usually an indigestable nut for younger students), and the certainly more attractive "spontaneous cases." About this most important source of parapsychological information, we still lack thorough epidemiological and demographic studies.

Nonetheless we quote in our classes the only two approximate classifications today available, the five tentative groups of Louisa E. Rhine and the Bender-Hanefeld percentages, although both lack "control groups" for comparison purposes. But in my opinion, students can help here very much and we are actually doing a first approach to a possible 1000 Chilean population[2] pilot study using the only combined possible method of questionnaires and personal interviews (for reasons I shall not enter into here we cannot rely very much in Latin American countries on "mail" cases; we would not get more than a good 15 percent). Another typical and useful (and I should say "lawful") classification we enter into is the one of "sheep-goats." Since in the sixties we encountered Dr. Schmeidler's psychological testing with the Rorschach, etc., using larger groups and after Dr. K. Ramakrishna Rao subdivided in his book[3] the two original groups into six with scientific, emotional and dogmatic subgroups, we try to explain to our students in what sense we can help our young scientific discipline with this illuminating tool. Because of our background in psychology as well as psychiatry, we feel that an important effort must be dedicated to show the inner relationship of parapsychology and psychology. Two chapters in Rao's already mentioned textbook can certainly be recommended here, too.[4] The useful didactic triangle of experimenter-subject-object can and should also be treated from the point of view of psychological studies. Again, here we lack literature concerning the first and last part of this triangle, a fact that will be a sort of handicap for teachers, but any evolving science may show these trends that slowly begin to disappear.[5]

Allow me, before coming to the most difficult part in a parapsychological course, that of the theories, a small digression about a general position I wish to roughly express as follows: In parapsychology, we have a number of points of view and parallel ways of consideration, usually justified per se, that complement each other, and in my opinion, do not mutually exclude themselves. Therefore we divide some dozen or so possible explanations into mainly three groups: psychological, psychical, and parapsychical or "mixed" theories. We are of course aware of the insufficient background for such "forced" placement of the sometimes very sophisticated points of view of our fellow scientists theorizing on parapsychology. But when we come to explain something like C.G. Jung's synchronicity theory, we expect perhaps a rather optimistic desideratum from our students, but should not a good teacher work only for the most dedicated students and "force" them to the level of science? We are aware of the perhaps difficult pedagogical bridge we have to cross, to be able to arrive at the next one.

One important factor in any course, is the one concerning the bibliography.[6] The only standard textbook available in Spanish is the Rhine-Pratt.[7] You may want to complement the statistical with the "qualitative" approach. And we would like again to underline the word *"complement."* For this purpose of course, all studies on spontaneous cases would be useful, but perhaps a small study like the one by W.H.C. Tenhaeff[8] now also available in English, and some of his new "Introductions," which we all hope will some day be translated. I feel it a necessity, and also having in mind a sort of "brainwashing" of most conceptions, to give to my students a list of the actual 60 titles we have in Spanish, not with the purpose that they should get "indigestion" trying to read all of them, but with the hygienical intention that they "avoid" occultism and the like. This of course I realize is difficult to achieve, as also pointed out by R. McConnell[9]. I shall not mention here books in other languages, because any thorough parapsychologist knows that we still have no "complete" parapsychological anthology such as Professor Bender's who provides one for German-speaking students. It is already, I guess, in its third edition.[10] We do not mention handbooks for testing, which are as scarce in Spanish as they are in English. Others, like D. Scott Rogo and the already mentioned Dr.

McConnell have devoted some paragraphs to parapsychology as treated in psychological textbooks, but since in Spanish (with the exception of Katz and Eysenck) we have no parallel treatment of equal importance of some of them, we can not comment on this. On the contrary, some parts of the theories are already translated; may we cite here the important book by C. G. Jung[11] and the new physical approaches presented by Arthur Koestler's "Roots of Coincidence." We should add, here, something that of course, any western parapsychologist feels actually as a necessity: a contact with an eastern colleague. Some books such as those of Vasiliev,[12] Martin Ebon,[13] and Ostrander-Schroeder[14] can be very useful. This last one must, of course be handled carefully because of the way the facts are presented, and it will be useful to present at least two parallel criticisms, one pro and one against. Reference to the historical Bechterev experiments with dogs will help to provide our course with a more contemporary approach to the field of anpsi, in which we still await a more comprehensive study such as the one given by Louisa E. Rhine[15] for the experimental developments in PK.

We come now to the problems of drugs and their use with "parapsychological" intention. We believe it is useful for younger students to recognize some common misconceptions. A good presentation will contrast stimulant versus depressive pharmacological agents already known to physicians: e.g., alcohol, beginning with H. J. W. Brugmans, who was one of the first to use it in 1921. We also mention Warcollier, and Rhine-Averill of the middle forties. We still have to wait for a good contribution about ethanol. On the list of stimulants we note at least two more: a) peyote or mescalin; already mentioned in 1886 by the German pharmacologist Ludvig Lewin, but later by the Frenchmen, Alexander Rouhier (1924-1927) and René Desoille (1928). As a kind of digression, the more literary descriptions of Aldous Huxley are sometimes already known to students. b) LSD or the "phantastika" described by the Swiss authors Hoffmann and Stoll (1947), and available in a standard monograph by Emilio Servadio and Roberto Cavanna (1964); still more studies are awaiting publication about the use of so called psychedelic substances. As depressive drugs one can mention the standard study done by Remi Cadoret 1953, with sodium amytal but using placebo and dexedrine for the controls.

We actually consider a "double blind method" a sine qua non condition for any pharmacological study, with any type of drug, be it a stimulant, e.g. Ritalin (which we tried in the sixties with several members of my family as well as with Mr. Arthur Koestler, indeed a very "tolerant" friend of parapsychology); or even hormones. These last have been very recently studied in connection with anpsi. We mention the Janik-Klocek studies with noradrenalin (1970) in rats, and also with a cocktail of thyroxin and adrenalin or noradrenalin, which gave apparently very good results.

We realize of course that this list of drugs can not pretend to be exhaustive but it has two purposes in mind: first, to teach students a good methodology and the placebo and control factors in science, and second, the knowledge of the so called "double blind" method.

In the same line of thought we consider it necessary to cite some experiments done by Robert Rosenthal to see the possible influence of the experimenter in his experiments, although we are aware of the unavoidable difficulty from the point of view of methodology of applying some of these concepts directly in parapsychological experiments, and this, we believe, is the main reason why we do not have available studies of this type.

Most psychologists and psychiatrists today consider dreams a sort of "royal road" to the unconscious, i.e. parapsychological level. Nobody can actually deny the importance of the dream studies done by the Dream Laboratory of Maimonides Hospital in New York (Ullman-Krippner) and other dream laboratories that sooner or later followed the new trend in the neurophysiology of dreaming that started with Kleitman-Dement in the fifties (few parapsychologists know that the Argentinian Dr. Orlando Canavesio did some preliminary studies with the EEG and some special "trance" states as early as 1951. Unfortunately there are only seven cases in his thesis, which could not be continued later on because of his premature death). The EEG line of research is still at its beginning in parapsychology, but we believe some of the findings in alpha rhythms can be quoted in classes, as well as the limitations and possibilities of this type of "measurement." Also in physiological quantitative methods we mention at least a few more that are important: GSR (Figar and Otani) polygraphic inscriptions for several measurements together, as are done by Charles T. Tart and colleagues (1969), H. Motoyama (1972), etc.

As we come to some special type of altered states of consciousness, we present some of the more specialized studies referring to out-of-the-body experiences by Celia Green, Charles Tart and Karlis Osis, but all these studies are in my opinion in their preliminary state and still not clearly detached from the atavistic "astral body" and the like. One can describe this area of parapsychology as a characteristically neglected one.

We make a brief excursion into so-called anpsi, referring to some of the Remy Chauvin studies, and of course the interesting and sophisticated but very readable chapters in J. G. Pratt's lucid book.[16] As an historical illustration, one can also note the dog studies by Vladimir Bekhterev whom we do not hesitate to call the father of Russian parapsychology. And last, but not least, we are perhaps not over-stating the case in saying that all parapsychologists still await the publication of Louisa E. Rhine's forthcoming "opus 5"!

While I was writing these lines, two illustrative parapsychological "matters" came to my attention: a) a book for review by Dr. Michael A. Persinger from Laurentian University, Sudbury, Canada.[17] b) Too late perhaps, a curious paper by Dr. R. A. McConnell on the academic future of parapsychology, published last year in the JASPR.[18]

Let me confess that for educational purposes on the actual level of teaching parapsychology in universities and colleges, Persinger's book is a big failure or a premature experimental design for *physical* parapsychology which as every one knows is still in its developmental phase. To be fair in my criticism, I must state here that only Volume II, "Mechanisms and Models," of Dr. Persinger's work has come to me for review. Perhaps his Volume I, "Patterns", is a bit more "parapsychologically" worked out! The experimental hypotheses and proposals of this rather unusual book are too sophisticated for the students in our introductory courses. In my opinion they are mostly appropriate for established experimenters, to stimulate their imagination in the area of "physiological measurements." At any rate, the book mentioned deserves a more detailed review which can not be given here.

Dr. R. A. McConnell, of Pittsburgh University, proposes, under a rich mass of ideas and practical "suggestions" for academic authorities, that old argument against a parapsychological chair which we heard also years ago from J. B. Rhine—they are not worth the effort given to them, etc. He goes even further to propose a professional chair of say 5 years, which is in my opinion a complete misunderstanding of the "status" that is needed at the University level for fully qualified teachers of any particular science. A good balance between research and teaching is always welcomed, but I do not understand how Dr. McConnell intends to give some perspective or "stability" to anyone whom he promises a "skeletal" five year period.

I promised at the beginning of my paper a short comment on graduate courses. This is certainly a very high and ambitious level and according to my understanding this type of course has to be a qualified seminar trying directly to teach research methods and with, if possible, field work with spontaneous cases. Although my own experience is until now very poor, I feel that a very precise lesson can be drawn from it. These are the people who are going to be the future parapsychologists, although I do not deny the possibility that also some good elements will originate from bigger groups. But in our Chilean team we have, from a group of ten professionals, three who are already joining in a recent research project we are actually signing which we have called "Inter University Psychotronic Area Project." This is being conducted at the University of Chile, Parapsychological Laboratory and the Technical State University, Department of Physics. Actually the total number of academic people involved in the project amounts to seven under my direction. This is of course a high percentage that can be attributed to the fact that these were professionals, mostly "old" friends of parapsychology.

A few final words concerning the results we had with our students using parapsychological *tests* covering the years 1967–1975. The complete analysis of the protocols involved in our experiments will be published later on elsewhere due of course to pressure of time and the amount of material under consideration: about 3,500 protocols! (Some 200 protocols of mass "down through" technique were disregarded in total amount of data given.)

We begin with precognition, a work already partially published.[19] The mass precognition (with lottery digits) has actually a total of 789 protocols with a total of 7,890 trials. Result was negative as expected, but still gives a good 1% of significant subjects (9 with a good level of divination). We shall come in a later communication with a control group using enough "goats" for the possibility of confirming or not Schmeidler's hypothesis, in a sort of indirect way, so to speak. Curiously enough, precognition done at home, using ESP standard cards and protocols gave much better results than we expected. A total of 600 complete standard sheets with 150,000 trials gave an arithmetic mean of 49.35 which is a little bit below chance.

The GESP protocols (in experiments done in classes in which the teacher usually acted as a telepathic agent) also gave very curious results. The total number of $234,750$ trials (939×250) is here overwhelming and we only give the big times: MCE = 46.95; D = -4.619; M = 45.08.

Pure clairvoyance which was usually done with the STM technique (also with instruction in this type of procedure), gave very poor results. A total of 357 sheets with a MCE of 5×6 (=30 hits) gave only a total of 28 hits (2 points below MCE).

PK in a total of 510 protocols (220320 trials) was done with standard procedures: 12 times 2 dice alternating faces: every pupil did 216 times 2 throws or more, which amounts to 432 trials for each complete sheet. Surprisingly enough some subjects got very high results (with CR over 5 and 6 and at least 2 or 3 on the 10 level), and according to this, we highly recommend the PK experiments for use in classes. Sensitive subjects should be "selected" for further experiments to get a real idea of their capacities.

The literature concerning experiments with students is scarce and we can only say that in the small group of students (apparently only 48) used by Timm in his paper[20] we can have only a proportional but significant idea of the sometimes unusually high results that are obtained if students are well motivated to work even with "dry" testing.

Some general ideas concerning the peculiarities of methods and the specificity of areas concerning scientific parapsychology leave no doubt of our negative position concerning the use of too many professors for our courses. We do not pretend to dominate the whole field of this science that has every day more border lines we would like to get rid of, but we also do not need a rather "wild" dispersion of our ideas on a good pedagogical purpose which has to give a somewhat fruitful amount of results and not a group of eclectical "monsters"! In other words, although we feel that at this moment we have no good orthodox assistants yet, we are hardly trying to have "parallel" peers and "complementary" colleagues to help in our classes. As a matter of fact during this present year we have given four of our classes to a specialist in psychotronics (Kirlian photography and the like), and one to a hypnotist (although I still consider them both only on a tentative level until we have a better idea of the real parapsychological factor of these techniques).

Paraphrasing Jaspers, we may tentatively say that "it is dangerous to learn only our matter in parapsychology," we ought not to learn only parapsychology as such, but we rather should observe, we should ask and we should analyze parapsychologically. In other words: we ought to learn *to think* parapsychologically.

REFERENCES

[1] D. Scott Rogo: *Methods and Models for Education in Parapsychology*. Monograph No. 14, Parapsychology Foundation Inc. New York, 1973.

[2] We feel it is an impossible task to use in Chile questionnaires like the "Virginia ESP survey" (by J. Palmer et al.) or similar ones because they are too long and of course some of the questions would have to be "locally" adapted.

[3] K. Ramakrishna Rao: *Experimental Parapsychology*. Charles C Thomas Publisher, Springfield, Illinois, 1966.

[4] op cit. Chapters 4 and 5.

[5] It is perhaps useful to mention here some of the uncertainty principles, such as Heisenberg's and the relativity of information and intensity in parapsychology, as was shown in 1940 by the mathematician B. Hoffman.

[6] Rhea A. White and Laura A. Dale: *Parapsychology: Source of Information*. Scarecrow Press Inc. Metuchen, N.J. 1973.

[7] J. B. Rhine and J. G. Pratt: *Parapsychology*. Charles C Thomas Publ. Springfield, Illinois, 1957.

[8] W. H. C. Tenhaeff: *Clairvoyance and Telepathy* (1965, 1973)

[9] R. A. McConnell: *ESP Curriculum Guide*. Simon and Schuster, New York, 1971.

[10] Dr. Hans Bender: ed. *Parapsychologie. Entwicklung, Ergebuisse, Probleme*. Wissenchaftliche Buchgesellschaft, Darmstadt, 1971.

[11] C. G.Jung: "On the Nature of the Psyche," in *The Structure and Dynamics of the Psyche*. 2nd ed. Princeton University Press, 1969. Collected works, vol. 8.

[12] L. L. Vasiliev: *Mysterious Phenomena of the Human Psyche*. New Hyde Park, New York. University Books, 1965.

[13] Martin Ebon: *Psychic Discoveries by the Russians* New York, New American Library 1971.

[14] Sheila Ostrander and Lynn Schroeder: *Psychic Discoveries Behind the Iron Curtain*. Prentice Hall Inc. Englewood Cliffs, N. J., 1970 (nine translations available).

[15] L. E. Rhine: *Mind Over Matter*. MacMillan & Co, New York, 1970.

[16] J. G. Pratt: *ESP Research Today. A Study of Developments in Parapsychology since 1960*. Scarecrow Press Inc. Metuchen, New Jersey 1973.

[17] Michael A. Persinger: *The Paranormal. Part II Mechanisms and Models*. MSS Information Corporation, New York, 1974.

[18] R. A. McConnell: "Parapsychology. Its Future Organization and Support". JASPR 68: 2: 169–181 (April 1974).

[19] B. Onetto-Bächler: "Mass Precognition and Schmeidler's Classification". First International Congress for Parapsychology and Psychotronics, Prague, June 1973 (*Proceedings*, v.I pp. 120–24 edit. by Z. Rejdak. Also: Revista de Parapsicologia Nr. 4:3–6 (March 1975).

[20] Ulrich Timm: "ASW-Experimente mit Studentengruppen." *Z.f. Parapsychol*. XI 1, 1–22 (1968)

DISCUSSION

Rao: Dr. Onetto, do you give your course to all medical students or do they elect to take your course? Is it a compulsory course for all medical students? Does every medical student have to take the course to get his degree?

Onetto: No. In the first semester, they have to elect. They can make an election usually between anthropology, parapsychology and medical history.

Rao: What percentage of your medical students choose parapsychology?

Onetto: Well, I must say, usually I have a lot of students. I don't know the percentage. I have much more than my two colleagues.

White: You mentioned in PK tasks that you were getting CRs of five and seven for the girls. What happened with the boys? Nothing with the boys?

ONETTO: Well, I don't know. As I said before, I have still to analyze about 3,000 protocols and I didn't have too much time, but I don't think they have negative results.

WHITE: But you specifically mentioned the girls.

ONETTO: . . . Well, I was surprised with the results with the girls. They were really very surprising because some people say that usually PK tests are more difficult to get with them, but this was not the case.

NOVILLO: Were the children, boys and girls, working together in your PK research or was this an individual test, one boy and one girl? How did you conduct these experiments?

ONETTO: I gave them usually the explanation for both together, boys and girls, but then they did it privately at their homes and then they were individually girls apart from boys—not together.

NOVILLO: A group of boys, or one boy?

ONETTO: No, usually two. One was an observer and another was making the test himself. We took that measure because if not you have the possibility that they would cheat too much.

NOVILLO: Do you have the results of the experiments when the boys and girls were working together?

ONETTO: No. Usually they did that in classes, but this was only a few experiments and I couldn't evaluate that.

NOVILLO: Dr. Onetto, what kind of experiments in ESP were you conducting?

ONETTO: Well, telepathy, usually.

NOVILLO: With Zener cards?

ONETTO: ESP cards.

NESTER: Just in passing, about needing audiovisuals, I was wondering what kind of audiovisuals you had in mind, whether it would be tapes or pictures or films or anything that you'd find useful. I would be very interested in that.

ONETTO: I would say all of them.

NESTER: All of them? Are tapes useful to you mixed in with your own speaking?

ONETTO: It depends. I wouldn't think of tapes very much. More on the kind of visual things.

NESTER: Like slides.

ONETTO: Yes, slides, films, and that sort of thing.

NESTER: Showing the kinds of things that are involved in the experiments?

ONETTO: Yes. As a matter of fact, when we speak about PK we usually like to see people acting on PK experiments and things like that.

JAMPOLSKY: Did you discuss the use of clairvoyance in medical diagnosis with your medical students?

ONETTO: Only as a possibility. They usually ask very much about Arigo and healers that have done some diagnoses and we discussed that too as a possibility.

PALMER: Did you find, with your medical students, that they were very concerned with practical applications of psi? Whether something can be applied seems to be a very common concern of medical students in the United States, perhaps more than other kinds of students, and I was wondering whether that was also true in Chile.

ONETTO: Well, they are usually very much concerned about this possibility, but along these lines, they usually ask for EEG or neurophysiological studies and things like that. They are interested in knowing how this field relates to their studies. They ask, "Why do we study parapsychology in medicine?"

BISAHA: I was just wondering what is the attitude of the physician towards parapsychology in your country? Did you meet with opposition when you initiated this course with medical graduates when previous students had never had this?

ONETTO: Well, I believe it's like in other countries. There are physicians pro and con. There were more against, but I wouldn't say that of the last four years generation. There may be more pro.

PARAPSYCHOLOGY IN THE SECONDARY SCHOOL CURRICULUM

JAMES E. MORRISS

When I was growing up there were three subjects of considerable concern to teenagers that, in our society, were not considered appropriate for polite conversation. They were sex, death, and the supranormal. I suspect many maturing minds have grappled with the troubling questions these subjects raise without much help or guidance from their elders. These were uncomfortable topics that were seldom discussed in the home, and subjects that were considered far too delicate or personal in nature to be covered in the classroom. For the most part children were left to find answers on their own.

A decade or so ago the idea of including any of these topics in the school curriculum would have been unthinkable. Today, however, sex education is rapidly becoming accepted in the schools. More recently, with the considerable attention that is being given in the media to the problems of aging and death, courses in thanatology are becoming popular in colleges and some high schools are even beginning to include this subject in the curriculum. As for the supranormal, media coverage has increased to an all time high and youth's growing interest in the "occult" sciences has forced the buyer's market of education to give serious attention to the possibility of including this subject in the curriculum. Today over 100 colleges and universities offer courses in parapsychology and some high schools are beginning to follow suit, but, due to a lack of guidelines, schools are reluctant to embark on a course of study for which there is no clear direction. The information explosion in this field has far outstripped the few meager efforts that have been made to offer some kind of educational guidance to the inquiring young minds that are often confused by the great variety and quality of information with which they are confronted. "There can be no doubt that the so-called 'occult explosion' of recent years has proven a very mixed blessing for parapsychology. While it has certainly led to great interest in the parapsychologist's work, and a larger audience for his worthwhile books, it has also led to a spate of shallow literature disseminating misinformation."[1]

As Charles Honorton has pointed out, "One of the most difficult problems encountered by persons wishing to become familiar with parapsychology is distinguishing between reliable and unreliable reading material. It is only too obvious that in the 'psychic' book area, the signal-to-noise ratio is very low."[2]

It is disturbing to note that a study by McConnell and McConnell showed that in one college bookstore, while "occult" books ranked very high in sales, the quality of books most frequently purchased was rather low, with books on mainline research in parapsychology being almost at the bottom of the list of the books sold in this category.[3] Similarly, sources of information high school students commonly use are insubstantial and of questionable quality and content. Since sensationalism always attracts the attention of youth it was not surprising that a recent survey (included in this paper) revealed that high school students found the TV show *Kreskin* and the *National Enquirer*, a tabloid billed as the nation's largest selling newspaper, their most commonly used sources of information on the supranormal.

The confusion between fact and fable in parapsychology and the difficulty students have in separating serious scientific research from superstition create a real need for a sound carefully structured educational program that addresses itself to these problems. A curriculum is needed that offers the kinds of information and experiences that will help students develop the kind of healthy skepticism and critical thinking they need to deal with the media explosion in the occult and the bombardment of information they are receiving on the supranormal. Such an educational opportunity recently occurred: In January, 1974, the American Psychological Association received funding from the National Science Foundation to develop a curriculum in human behavior for secondary schools. One of the 30 topics recommended for inclusion in the curriculum was: "Parapsychology and the Supranormal: Belief and skepticism in a legitimate area of research."[5] Each topic was to be covered in a two-to three-week instructional unit or module. The module on parapsychology was described as one that: "Establishes the legitimacy of such areas for investigation; examines the present evidence and the skepticism of many scientists; concludes with the psychology of belief."[4]

The plan was for each module to be designed in the field by teams composed of a specialist in the subject area and one or two high school teachers and students. In the summer of 1974 the American Psychological Association announced that the Human Behavior

Curriculum Project (HBCP) for secondary schools was accepting proposals for individual module topics from qualified teams.[5]

For the past few years I have been teaching a course in behavior, offered as a science elective for high school juniors and seniors in Division Avenue High School in Levittown, N. Y. I was asked to develop the curriculum for this course as a result of three books in comparative psychology I had co-authored for young adults. The course, which was based in part on these books, included a unit in parapsychology. Since I had begun research on another book for teenagers which was to have several chapters on parapsychological research, development of a module on parapsychology for the HBCP would complement the work I had already begun and would allow me to concentrate my effort in one area.

The first step in developing a module proposal was to organize a team which, according to the HBCP guidelines, should include a high school student and a specialist in the field. For advice regarding the selection of a specialist, I contacted Dr. Robert Van de Castle, information officer for the Parapsychological Association (PA). Dr. Van de Castle suggested that the Council of the PA be asked to recommend someone to work with me. During their meeting at the 1975 APA convention last September, the Council designated Joanna Morris as the team specialist. Her husband, Dr. Robert Morris, was then President of the PA, and Joanna had for the last several years been editing the *Proceedings of the Parapsychological Association.* To complete the team a high school student was chosen from several outstanding seniors in my behavior class who had expressed interest in working with us. In addition to the team, Dr. Irvin Child of Yale University and Dr. Gertrude Schmeidler of City College of the City University of New York agreed to act as consultants to the project.

In an effort to enlist input from the many scientists and educators who are members of the PA, a letter announcing the preparation of a module proposal in parapsychology was sent to all members. Included with the letter was a questionnaire which invited opinions and suggestions for module content.

HIGH SCHOOL SURVEY CONFIRMS STUDENT INTEREST IN PARAPSYCHOLOGY

Before beginning work on the module proposal I felt it would be useful to determine the knowledge, attitudes and interest in parapsychology among high school students. With the help of several of my students and colleagues, a questionnaire was developed and given to 130 high school juniors and seniors in my school. In order not to influence student responses, the content and purpose of the questionnaire were not discussed prior to the administration of the survey. The same survey was given to 130 students in a high school in Decatur, Illinois, and 30 students in the Tam High School District in the Bay area of Northern California. Following are the questionnaire and the results from each of the three schools in which it was given:

QUESTIONNAIRE

Please answer each question in the order in which it appears. If you don't know the answers to the first two questions make a guess. Do not change any answers.

1—Parapsychology is a branch of science that studies_____

	Acceptable definition	Unacceptable definition
N. Y.	23%	77%
Ill.	24	76
Calif.	39	61

2—What kinds of experiences would you describe as ESP experiences? _____

	Acceptable definition	Unacceptable definition
N. Y.	91%	8%
Ill.	86	14
Calif.	87	13

3—ESP stands for Extrasensory Perception. Such phenomena as mind to mind communication (telepathy) and correctly predicting events before they occur by hunches (precognition) are examples of ESP. There is no satisfactory scientific explanation of how people could receive information other than through their senses. Therefore, ESP is a controversial subject. Many people deny it exists.
Do you believe ESP does exist?   YES   NO

	YES	NO
N. Y.	96	5
Ill.	86	14
Calif.	90	10

4—The following list of phenomena are associated with ESP. Please indicate your feelings about them.
Telepathy (mind to mind communication)

	YES (Believe it is possible)	NO (Do not believe it is possible)	MAYBE (Am not sure)
N.Y.	60	12	28
Ill.	67	12	21
Calif.	74	13	13

Clairvoyance (perception of physical objects and events not available to the senses)

N. Y.	48%	17%	35%
Ill.	53	25	23
Calif.	58	23	19

Psychokinesis (influencing the movement of matter mentally)

N. Y.	44	32	24
Ill.	22	51	27
Calif.	39	29	32

Precognition (knowing about the future without any clues from the senses)

N. Y.	70	9	21
Ill.	57	19	24
Calif.	65	13	23

Paranormal healing (the ability of one person (the healer) to produce a "miraculous" cure in another)

N. Y.	24	43	33
Ill.	22	57	21
Calif.	23	10	68

5—You have probably heard about ESP from some of the following sources. Using the numbers from 1 to 3 please indicate the sources from which you have received information.

1 — Most information   2 — Some information
3 — No information

Source of Information		Most	Some	None
TV	N. Y.	10%	43%	46%
	Ill.	34	60	6
	Calif.	41	43	26
Radio	N. Y.	60	29	12
	Ill.	7	34	59
	Calif.	5	27	68

Books	N. Y.	24	40	36
	Ill.	41	43	16
	Calif.	46	46	8
Magazines and	N. Y.	31	50	19
Newspapers	Ill.	32	54	13
	Calif.	29	63	8
Personal Experiences	N. Y.	41	41	17
	Ill.	10	38	52
	Calif.	20	64	16
Experiences of	N. Y.	31	52	17
People you Know	Ill.	12	54	34
	Calif.	24	60	16
Word of Mouth	N. Y.	20	40	40
Discussion with	Ill.	36	46	18
Others	Calif.	57	43	0

The students were asked to list any specific books, magazine articles, TV shows etc., from which they had learned about ESP and give their reaction to the information they received from the sources listed. While the sources were quite varied the responses they described to the information they had received were characterized by interest, amazement and credulity.

6—Have you ever had an experience or known someone who has had an experience you believe can *only* be explained by ESP?

	YES	NO
N. Y.	55%	45%
Ill.	38	62
Calif.	39	61

Students who felt they or someone they knew had had an experience that could only be explained by ESP were asked to describe the experience. The experiences they described were classified in one of the following categories:

	Telepathy	Clairvoyance	PK	Precognition
N. Y.	33%	27%	4%	36%
Ill.	26	29	0	46
Calif.	16	34	0	50

7—Do you believe scientists should investigate ESP?

	YES	NO	NOT SURE
N. Y.	82	3	15

| Ill. | 63 | 11 | 26 |
| Calif. | 71 | 13 | 16 |

8—Scientists are investigating ESP and recent research indicates that most people probably have some ESP abilities. Would you be interested in finding out about your own ESP abilities?

	YES	NO	NOT SURE
N. Y.	84%	4%	12%
Ill.	69	18	13
Calif.	77	13	10

9—Many colleges and universities are now offering courses in ESP. Do you think there should be a high school course in this subject?

	YES	NO	NOT SURE
N. Y.	80	7	13
Ill.	60	21	19
Calif.	71	6	23

10—Would you like to take a course in ESP if it was offered in your high school?

	YES	NO	NOT SURE
N. Y.	75	8	17
Ill.	60	21	19
Calif.	74	19	6

11—Here are some topics that might be explored in a high school course in ESP. Please use numbers from 1–3 to indicate your interest in these topics.

1—Great interest   2—Some interest   3—No interest

a)   The History of ESP

	1	2	3
N. Y.	18	58	24
Ill.	14	63	23
Calif.	14	59	28

b)   Case studies of famous psychic (ESP) subjects.

	1	2	3
N. Y.	13	39	47
Ill.	50	37	13
Calif.	28	59	17

c)   Exploring reasons for belief or disbelief in ESP.

	1	2	3
N. Y.	11	45	44
Ill.	38	42	20
Calif.	24	52	24

d) Experimental techniques used in ESP research today.

N. Y.	16%	49%	36%
Ill.	41	38	21
Calif.	39	54	7

e) Dangers of fraud and deception and how they can be avoided in ESP research.

N. Y.	23	43	34
Ill.	32	45	23
Calif.	31	41	28

f) What investigators have discovered about ESP and related phenomena.

N. Y.	14	44	42
Ill.	51	34	15
Calif.	48	34	17

g) Classroom projects and experiments in ESP.

N. Y.	16	41	43
Ill.	52	31	18
Calif.	48	41	10

h) College courses in ESP (what is offered and where).

N. Y.	22	42	35
Ill.	18	47	35
Calif.	31	48	21

i) Career possibilities in ESP research.

N. Y.	29	37	34
Ill.	13	40	47
Calif.	7	52	41

j) Possible applications of ESP.

N. Y.	15%	51%	34%
Ill.	42	38	20
Calif.	25	46	29

k) Implications of ESP research for science and society.

N. Y.	19	52	30
Ill.	33	45	22
Calif.	25	43	32

Listed below are some of the areas in which research is being done. Which of these areas would you be interested in?

l)   Telepathy, mind to mind communication.

N. Y.	17	34	49
Ill.	64	20	16
Calif.	69	24	7

m)   Clairvoyance, information about objects and events not available to the senses.

N. Y.	18	38	42
Ill.	36	38	26
Calif.	41	30	30

n)   Psychokineses, influencing the movement of matter mentally.

N. Y.	27	43	55
Ill.	36	30	34
Calif.	30	48	22

o)   Psychic Healing, the ability of one person (the healer) to produce a "miraculous" cure in another person.

N. Y.	32	35	33
Ill.	17	31	52
Calif.	23	46	31

p)   Precognition, predicting future events.

N. Y.	17%	32%	51%
Ill.	49	29	22
Calif.	66	21	14

q)   How ESP is affected by altered states of consciousness such as meditation, hypnosis, dreaming, drugs etc.

N. Y.	23	34	43
Ill.	38	34	28
Calif.	32	50	18

r)   ESP in animals, what present research indicates.

N. Y.	30	35	36
Ill.	23	42	34
Calif.	30	44	26

HIGH SCHOOL COURSE IN PARAPSYCHOLOGY OFFERED AS A SCIENCE ELECTIVE

To prepare a testing ground for the HBCP module, should it be funded, I decided to write and submit to my own school district a syllabus for a course in parapsychology. The course, which I titled *ESP–A Challenge for Science,* was to be a ½ year science elective for juniors and seniors.

Although inclusion of parapsychology as a unit in my behavior course had not met with any objections, I was a bit apprehensive about the administration's approval of a course offering in a subject that is not only considered controversial, but is, in the minds of many people, still confused with magic and superstition. This attitude was reflected in a comment by one of the administrators when my syllabus was presented for approval at a meeting of the District Principal's Council. "The next thing you know", he said, "we will be teaching astrology and phrenology." I recently came across a syllabus for a high school course in experimental psychology proposed for the New York City public schools which indiscriminately lumped parapsychology with witchcraft and magic in a kind of confused potpourri, with no attempt made to distinguish between serious scientific research and the occult's lunatic fringe. Perhaps the authors of this syllabus thought they could make parapsychology more palatable by not taking it seriously.

Youth are attracted to the occult, and with increased media coverage of the paranormal, there is a growing need for an educational program in the secondary schools that would not only give serious treatment to the sound research in parapsychology but would also offer the kinds of information and experiences that would help gullible adolescents to differentiate between serious scientific research in this field and the superstitious and pseudo-scientific claims of various cults. I wanted to structure my syllabus in such a way as to minimize objections, but at the same time present material on this subject that would be not only accurate and up to date, but would be recognized for its broader educational value. R. A. McConnell's *ESP Curriculum Guide* provided excellent guidelines.[6]

McConnell suggests that "We can learn much about science in general from the study of ESP," and that the educational challenge of ESP lies in its elucidation of "the use of scientific method in the nature of scientific controversy." For example, "While scientists welcome minor changes in their thinking they vigorously oppose major changes." The history of science, from William Harvey to Albert Einstein, is honeycombed with dramatic examples of the scientific communities' opposition to significant change. McConnell stated that "The wide acceptance of a revolutionary scientific idea will depend primarily upon philosophic belief or practical application, but scarcely at all upon laboratory evidence." This has certainly been true of acupuncture, aspirin and electricity. Their practical application in society has far exceeded any laboratory evidence elucidating the nature of their function. Our understanding of psi may also be preceded by its practical application in society if the lightning flashes of spontaneous phenomena and the static discharges derived from statistical analysis of laboratory data can be harnessed in some yet to be discovered generator.

I was impressed with McConnell's approach. The possibility of exploring parapsychology in the context of scientific history and methodology was appealing. This approach would give wide-eyed but restless youth an opportunity to learn something about the processes of science. They would also learn, as McConnell suggested, that while "the research problems seem limitless, research is restricted by present understanding and techniques upon which we must build" and "revolutionary scientific research is often slow and unexciting, requiring painstaking attention to detail."

The study of scientific research and methodology, not to mention history, is as much an anathema to most high school students as I expected parapsychology might be to the administrators who would have to approve my course. However, when I submitted the syllabus for approval, the administration was pleased to see a controversial subject, of obvious interest to the students, presented in a framework they found acceptable. Once the syllabus was approved, the title *ESP—A Challenge for Science*, was enough to bring the students flocking to sign up for the course. When the course is offered, some of the students may be surprised to find that in addition to learning about ESP they will also learn something about science.

The preparation and approval of the syllabus in parapsychology for my own school's science curriculum gave impetus to the development of the module proposal for the Human Behavior Curriculum Project. With the assistance of Joanna and Bob Morris and the many helpful suggestions of the PA members, the proposal was completed and submitted to the Curriculum Project Headquarters on February 1, 1975.

A PROPOSAL FOR THE HBCP's MODULE IN PARAPSYCHOLOGY

In a letter to the HBCP director which accompanied our proposal, the reasons for the importance of this module were stated as follows:

First, it deals with an area in which the need for careful experimentation is paramount and can thus serve as a tool for teaching principles of scientific methodology and statistical inference, as well as the dangers of ignoring them. Second, it attempts to fill a need for information which is not now adequately met in the schools or society at large.

We pointed out that recent media coverage of parapsychology, usually intermixed with other "occult" topics, has increased the necessity for providing guidelines to educators. High school teachers interested in answering their students' need for information in this area are groping for guidance and asking for help in selecting materials which will present a balanced view.

We indicated that most parapsychologists are aware of the problems created by increased public interest in the field and pointed out that psychologists and other professionals are being offered a more informed treatment of the field through parapsychological symposia that have been presented at the last two APA conventions and at four recent AAAS conventions and by increased publication of articles in reputable scientific magazines, books and journals.

Though space does not permit the inclusion of the module proposal in its entirety some of the main features are described below: In our description of the Module topic, we stated that: "besides dealing with the research in parapsychology, the module would attempt to use parapsychology as a vehicle for illustrating the importance of careful experimental design and statistical methodology in the behavioral sciences, and the necessity for critical judgment in the student's daily life."

Some of the objectives of the module were:

1. To create an understanding of the need for scientific investigation of any poorly understood or unexplained phenomena by a brief look at the history of the development of new concepts in science.

2. To acquaint students with the methodological requirements for scientifically sound research and the qualities of a good investigator (curiosity, open-mindedness, critical judgment, and the ability to suspend judgment).

3. To increase the students' openness to the possibilities of new discoveries about human behavior, while at the same time helping them develop the tools of thought they need to make cautious evaluations regarding the evidence and claims for the paranormal.

4. To identify the kinds of phenomena being investigated by parapsychologists and to distinguish between these phenomena and those popularly believed to be paranormal for which there is no scientific evidence.

5. To summarize the methods, findings, and implications of current experimental parapsychology, emphasizing that psi effects in the laboratory have typically been slight, transient and often difficult to interpret.

Some of the specific points that would be made in the presentation of this instructional unit were described in the module proposal as follows:

1. Phenomena claimed to be instances of psi do not seem to be rare or isolated. They have been reported in many cultures throughout history, and therefore deserve careful and critical scientific attention.

2. Scientists involved in parapsychological research do not necessarily endorse all the claims of cultists, faddists, and other popular proponents of the paranormal. This will include a clear definition of psi phenomena with a distinction between those kinds of phenomena that are lending themselves to investigation and those that are not.

3. We need to be open to the possibilities of different ways of perceiving the world. New conceptions of reality, from Copernicus to Einstein, have been the result of exploration beyond the boundaries of conventional interpretation of reality.

4. Science is not a monolith pronouncing truisms, but an ongoing process of disagreement, discovery, synthesis and resolution of conflicting positions and ideas. Controversy thrives at the frontiers of knowledge, and controversy stimulates research to satisfy the need for evidence to support, modify or correct hypotheses.

5. Since we filter and structure incoming stimulation, it is important that we be aware of the many factors that influence our perception and interpretation of information, including expectations, needs, cognitive sets, and previous experiences.

6. Parapsychology has had difficulty being accepted as a legitimate area of scientific investigation for a number of reasons that are important to understand. These include, among others:

   a) Lack of an acceptable theory that will harmonize its apparent findings with known facts.
   b) Lack of a consistently repeatable experiment.
   c) Reputation for irresponsibility brought about by its association in the minds of many people with the occult and unscientific groups.

7. Today new concepts and techniques are enabling investigators in this field to explore the parameters of psi and study the possible channels of transmission in relation to psychological and physiological variables.

In introducing the activities in which the students might be engaged, we stated that:

Activities are envisioned as the core of this module. They will be designed to fulfill the objectives and illustrate and elucidate the main points. In the module, there will be a sufficient selection of activities covering a broad enough range to enable a teacher to adapt the material to the diverse needs and interests of various groups of students. Some of the activities we suggested for inclusion in the module were:

1. As a way of making students aware of their susceptibility to deception we suggested the use of stage magic in the classroom and included descriptions of several demonstrations of pseudo-telepathy.

2. In order to give the students the opportunity to experience being both subjects and experimenters and deal with the problems of executing a carefully controlled experiment, we suggested the replication of a few fairly simple ESP experiments using both standard ESP cards as well as pictorial material.

3. Since many high schools offer computer courses and have computers available for student use, a number of computerized ESP games were recommended.

4. It was also suggested that the module packet include a tape cassette designed to assist the students in relaxation techniques which could be used with interested groups during the course. ESP scoring could be measured before and after several weeks of daily relaxation sessions and students could be asked to give a report of their subjective reactions to the relaxation experiment as well.

5. Since it is necessary for students to have some knowledge of the concepts of chance and probability in order to know whether an apparent correspondence between two events is sufficiently meaningful to be labeled psi, we suggested the inclusion of activities such as coin tossing, dice throwing or use of a commercially available hexastat which dramatically demonstrates normal distribution patterns.

6. Since personal reports of ESP are often criticized as examples of inaccurate reporting, we suggested that students be given activities that would enable them to experience how our memory of information and events often suffers from selection and distortion. One suggestion was the staging of an "accident ruse" in which unsuspecting witnesses to a dramatic event are polled for their description of what happened.

7. Library research would provide an excellent activity for individuals who are interested in exploring specific topics in greater depth. The module could be enriched by students presenting research findings for class discussion. Suggested topics accompanied by

provocative questions and a bibliography of suggested resources would be included in the module handbook.

8. Surveys conducted by students to discover the attitudes and opinions regarding psi; frequency of psi experiences in a population, or the kinds of phenomena most commonly reported would provide an excellent activity for individuals or small groups. The module would provide guidelines for compiling and administering such a questionnaire effectively.

In addition to the teacher's manual and the student handbook another instructional component we recommended for inclusion in this module was a standard tape cassette containing interviews with leading scientists in the field. The tape, prepared specifically for this module, would focus on topics relevant to the students' educational experiences. We were also asked to include a statement on instructional strategy. One of the problems we addressed ourselves to in this section was the teachers' probable lack of training or experience in teaching both parapsychology and scientific methodology. We feel it would be necessary to structure the module in such a way as to minimize this problem and to provide the kinds of information and guidelines that would make a teacher feel comfortable with the subject area.

The "Instructional Strategies" section states that:

"Since the material contained in this module may be unfamiliar to most teachers, their role should be viewed as that of participants in the learning process. They should function not as teachers in the traditional sense but as learning catalysts, facilitating and orchestrating a meaningful educational experience." Though carefully structured, the module would be open-ended and while the material itself is intriguing enough to hold interest, student involvement in the suggested activities, experiments, and library investigations would enhance the module and assure a high degree of motivation and participation by all involved.

The guidelines for preparing the proposal also suggested that we include a reference to the "Principles of Human Behavior on Which the Module Will be Based." Two points made were:

1. A module on parapsychology provides an excellent forum for discussion of the need to achieve a cognitively coherent world view. Purported psi phenomena have in the past been either rejected a priori, reinterpreted in religious terms, or uncritically embraced, depending on how well they fit into the belief systems of the society or individual.

2. Motivational and situational factors as well as personality variables are known to affect subject performance in psi experiments just as they do in other experiments in the behavioral sciences.

This proposal included a list of audio-visual materials, a well balanced bibliography which included resources critical of research in parapsychology, a statement of the qualifications of the team's personnel, and a budget that was well within the guidelines given in the Module Design Handbook.

Appended to the module proposal were: 1. a copy of the survey of the student attitudes, knowledge and opinions along with the results obtained; 2. the syllabus for the course, ESP—A Challenge for Science, which had been approved for inclusion in my school's science curriculum; and 3. three sample responses from PA members with their suggestions for module content (included were the responses of a well known psychiatrist, a physicist and the much appreciated response we had received from Dr. Gardner Murphy).

CONTROVERSY

Subsequently we received a letter from the Director of the project in which he detailed the reviewing process that all proposals would undergo. The proposals were first to be reviewed by the project director and his staff. Some proposals would be rejected and others that were potentially acceptable, but found to need further work, would be returned to the authors for revision or modification. When this occurred, the rewriting would become a joint effort of the module team and the staff at project headquarters, involving a cooperative effort designed to put the proposal in what was described as its "Sunday best" before it was sent to the Steering Committee for final approval. The Steering Committee was made up of 15 leading authorities in the field of psychology and included such men as Donald O. Hebb, Ernest R. Hilgard, Jerome Kagan, and others. It was the Steering Committee itself that had suggested the 30 module topics for the Human Behavior Curriculum, including the one on parapsychology.

A proposal was not ordinarily sent to all members of the Steering Committee. Usually only two of its members were asked to approve a particular proposal. Considering the careful and thorough work of a competent staff at project headquarters whose stated job was to work with the teams to polish the proposals and put them in an acceptable form, it was unlikely that the Steering Committee would receive many proposals they could not approve.

Funding for module development was to be forthcoming in June and the modules were to be developed during the summer. Our proposal was not returned for revision or modification. At the end of April, we received a letter from the project director stating that our proposal had been reviewed favorably by Project Headquarters and "sent to the Steering Committee for review" and that they were hopeful "that a decision (on funding) could be made within two weeks." In regard to funding he stated that "There appears to be no need at the moment for pessimism."

Though a decision had been promised within two weeks, a month passed without further word from project headquarters. In early May, when we contacted the Director by phone, he indicated that some problems had developed regarding the funding of our proposal: the Steering Committee members who had received our proposal for review had decided to solicit the comments of a reviewer not associated with the HBCP. This independent reviewer had reacted to our proposal "less favorably" and though the HBCP guidelines for proposal development had specifically requested a specialist in the field for each module topic, this reviewer had recommended that the module on parapsychology be written by someone *outside* the field of parapsychology. The project director was assured that if this was a real concern, our team would be happy to work with any objective and informed consultant whom the Steering Committee might wish to recommend.

Shortly thereafter we received a letter from the Project Director which stated that "because of disagreement among the Steering Committee members about the advisability of funding the proposal on parapsychology . . . it would take some time before a decision could be made." He went on to say that what he wished to do "was to contact other members of the Steering Committee to get their views [and that] this might take as long as three weeks." As will be noted "he did not see his way clear to funding the proposal very quickly." Realizing the committee concern that the module should receive critical and objective guidance during its development, we forwarded papers written by our consultants that would familiarize the Committee with the high quality and critical nature of our consultants' work. The papers included an address delivered by Dr. Morris at a 1975 AAAS symposium which was devoted entirely to the dangers of fraud and deception in a field in which the strictest controls and most careful experimentation are of acknowledged importance. Also included was a paper delivered by Dr. Gertrude Schmeidler, at the same symposium, in which she debunked the claims of a popular mind control group that has grossed millions from gullible youth who are easily enticed by promises of expanded mental powers. The paper detailed the carefully controlled double-blind experiments that supported her criticism. Also included was an unpublished manuscript by Dr. Irvin Child which described his own quite recent encounter with research in this field.[7]

This paper reflected the kind of cautious, critical open-mindedness that would be expected from a man of his stature in the field of psychology. It is important to note that with the papers a letter was included in which we restated our willingness to work with any outside consultants the Steering Committee might wish to recommend, including critics of the field.

On June 25, 1975 we received the following reply:

June 23, 1975

Mr. James E. Morriss
P.O. Box 292
Babylon, New York 11702

Dear Mr. Morriss:

I am at last able to report that a decision has been reached on the support of your proposed module on *Parapsychology*. I am sorry to report that the decision is not to provide the necessary funds.

You are aware, I know, that the decision has not been an easy one. Indeed, the proposal was more extensively reviewed than any other we have received to date. I shall try to explicate the reasons for the decision in the remainder of this letter.

While your position on psi is apparently not that of a believer, the members of your team and the consultants which you have selected must be so described, and their papers which you sent me confirm that description. Given the goals of the project, it would appear that at a minimum the module should be developed by those who are open-minded on the phenomenon. Neither believers nor non-believers can make that claim. To extend that thought, what the student would appear to need, based even on your data, is at least the amount of skepticism that the scientist usually has, particularly if he is to become more sophisticated about the care and caution required in arriving at any conclusion. The high school student would appear to accept beliefs uncritically, and several reviewers saw a need to try to change that tendency.

A second concern is that there are areas of behavior in which there is considerably more understanding and which appear as well to have the potentiality of considerably more impact on the lives of students, particularly in their social interactions. It was perhaps this that the Steering Committee had in mind at their last meeting when they decided not to include this topic in the 25 which had the highest priority for development.

Finally, some reviewers felt that some of the methodological issues would be too difficult for the target audience. One that comes to mind is whether one can talk about separating out the treatment from the error variance in the absence of a treatment.

I am sure you will be disappointed and I hesitate to consider the opinions that this decision will engender in some. Our decisions, necessarily of a go, no-go kind, cannot easily reflect the variety of considerations that enter into them.

Sincerely,

In our letter of response we thanked the project director for his effort is seeing that our proposal had received such an extensive evaluation, and pointed out that our experience with high school students had convinced us of a profound need for an educational program that would offer the kinds of experiences that would help youth develop a healthy skepticism, and give them some insight into the ways in which their belief systems are structured without "turning them off" or nurturing a negative attitude toward science by a closed-minded approach to a subject they find exceedingly attractive, and expressed our belief that with his advice this could have been accomplished in the module on parapsychology.

We pointed out that the potential problems he had mentioned, such as "methodological issues too difficult for the target audience" could have been resolved during field testing and revision. As for their objection to our consultants, we reminded him that we had offered to include as advisors any objective and informed "outsiders" the Steering Committee might wish to recommend and pointed out that the Steering Committee's description of the module topic was misleading, since it indicated that they believed parapsychology was a legitimate field of research. If this were the case, the only difference between the Steering Committee and our consultants, derisively characterized as "believers," was that our consultants had acted on their belief in the legitimacy of this field by doing research in it.

We expressed our shock at the Steering Committee's lack of commitment to a topic they themselves had recommended. Had they ever seriously intended to fund this module, or had they included this topic as a ruse to detract from their bias against a burgeoning field of research they felt uncomfortable with but were unable to ignore?

We suggested that it was not the module that had been submitted, but the whole field of parapsychology that was being rejected as too threatening for inclusion in the Human Behavior Curriculum for Secondary Schools. Since our proposal had been found acceptable by project headquarters and had even caused disagreement among Steering Committee members, their solution had apparently been to eliminate parapsychology from the list of topics in line for funding by tardily relegating it to a position of low priority. However, parapsychology was not alone in being designated as a low priority project. Fourteen other topics that appeared on the original list or were being considered for inclusion were not among those the committee felt would be the most important to include. The list of topics to receive funding had been reduced in apparent anticipation of possible cuts in National Science Foundation funds during the coming year.

It is perhaps inappropriate to search for blame, for, as the Project Director pointed out, "it frequently lies, often hidden, in the world of human interactions."

CONCLUSION

With the rapid expansion of research and increased public interest, it is inevitable that parapsychology will find an acceptable gateway into public education, but, until this occurs, nothing is gained by becoming discouraged with the roadblocks that seem to inhibit progress. While we may disagree with the gatekeepers who guard the doors of education and protect the citadel of scientific tradition from sudden change, we must realize the importance of their role. Perhaps the time was not yet right.

The forces that shape policy in both science and education are far more complex than they might appear. In the confluence of events there is a time for everything and everything is fulfilled in its time. One possible reason for our failure to receive funding concerns timing, and may reflect more favorably on the Steering Committee's decision. A few days after I had replied to our letter of rejection I became aware of the running controversy that was reported in several articles in the *Monitor* (the newsletter of the American Psychological Association).[8] The articles described a storm that was raging in Congress over government funding of educational programs that were said to have a questionable effect on the minds of our youth. The curriculum in question was the widely publicized and increasingly popular innovation in social studies called *Man, A Course of Study*. This curriculum had been designed for elementary schools by a Harvard University team headed by Dr. Jerome Bruner, a leading figure in psychology and education. In the heated debate over this issue, some Congressmen were criticizing the National Science Foundation for funding a program that was said to be causing serious psychological problems for some students, problems that apparently ensued from the way this course openly and vividly exposed children to the customs, ideals and morals of other cultures. This encounter with mores that often conflicted with those of our own society, had apparently caused some of the youngsters to question the validity of parental authority and the belief systems of our own culture.

It doesn't require much imagination to see the scenario that might have developed if parapsychology had been included in the Human Behavior Curriculum for Secondary Schools. A Congressman caught up by the fears of a conservative constituency could, in a fire of political oratory, burn at the stake the American Psychological Association and the National Science Foundation for having funded the development of a controversial instructional unit that would cast spells of enchantment on the minds of innocent youth. He could flail, with well chosen words, the reputation psychologists have, which is already shaky in the minds of some people, accusing them of trying to poison our children's education with what he might mistakenly but effectively portray as a module on magic and superstition.

Public interest in parapsychology and a general awareness of progress in the field during the past few years has been considerable.[9] However, it takes only a few firebrands to ignite a conflict, and many people are confused by occult propaganda and are still ignorant about what constitutes science. Unfortunately, parapsychology still suffers from its identification in the minds of many people with pseudo-scientific cults and the "lunatic fringe." This is clearly demonstrated in almost any book store or library where serious research in parapsychology is still shelved with esoteric titles under the general category of "OCCULT." Perhaps the Steering Committee felt they had no choice. The stakes were too great to chance another Scopes trial in the House or Senate chambers where science education, already 20 years behind the times, could be set back another decade or so. Could this be the real reason that a possibly well intended recommendation by the APA for the inclusion of parapsychology in the secondary school curriculum was rescinded in the final hour? We do not know for sure, but, if the political implications were a consideration, their decision is a bit more understandable. However, considering the rapid rate at which new knowledge is increasing in all fields, particularly in parapsychology, their decision was unfortunate. It has been calculated that "by the time a child, born today, graduates from college, new information will be four times as great . . . and by the time the same child is 50 years old . . . 97 percent of everything known in the world will have been learned since the time he was born."[10] We have not yet felt the full impact of the information explosion, and man has no precedent in his history that can forecast its effects on society, but as Margaret Mead has said, "We must educate people in what nobody knew yesterday and prepare people . . . for what no one knows yet, but which some people must know tomorrow."[11]

Today our young people enjoy few of the old certainties. There is no longer a stable order of things to provide them with a sense of security.

Everything is changing around them. The old social ideals, the old religion, the old matter-of-fact assumptions about how to live are not enough. Today's youth are keenly aware of the possibility of atomic holocaust or ecological disaster in their lifetime. They face far more questions and uncertainties than they should have to face on their own, but today's education offers few answers and little guidance. However, in some vague intuitive way, our youth are catching fleeting visions of a better world. They are interested in exploring consciousness and probing the varieties of human experience which our society had previously ignored. From the drug culture of the 60's, with its communes and mystical unions of cults, today's youth are moving in a new direction. They are still in search of a new paradigm for life, but they are seeking answers that will provide a touchstone with reality, answers that may alter our image of man and offer new hope for the future of humankind. Our challenge and responsibility as educators in parapsychology is to help them ask the right questions.

REFERENCES

[1] Robinson, Diana, "Planning a Course in Parapsychology" *Parapsychology Review,* Nov.– Dec. 1973.

[2] Honorton, Charles, "Parapsychology and Education—Circa 1972. An Appreciation of R. A. McConnell's ESP Curriculum Guide." *Journal of the American Society for Psychical Research*. Vol. 66 October 1972—November 4 p411.

[3] Rogo, D. Scott, *Methods and Models for Education in Parapsychology* Monograph No. 14, 1973 by Parapsychology Foundation, Inc. pp14–15.

[4] Module-Design Handbook, Human Behavior Curriculum Project for Secondary Schools, HBCP Publication 74–2 July 1974 Carleton College, Northfield, Minnesota

[5] "High School Psychology Project Seeks Curriculum Proposals *Monitor,* American Psychological Association, Aug. 1974.

[6] McConnell, R. A. *ESP Curriculum Guide* Simon and Schuster 1970 pp11–12.

[7] Child, Irvin L., "Parapsychology and the Rest of Psychology: A Mutual Challenge." To be included in a book edited by Schmeidler titled *Parapsychology: Its Relation to Physics, Biology, Psychology and Psychiatry* (Scarecrow Press Inc., 1975)

[8] "Macos Controversy," *Monitor,* American Psychological Association June 1975, July 1975.

[9] Vaughan, Alan, "The Media and Parapsychology," *Psychic*, June 1974 pp44–48.

[10] Toffler, Alvin *Future Shock*, 1970 Random House, N. Y. p157.

[11] Barnes, Ron *Learning Systems for the Future* 1972 The Phi Delta Kappa Educational Foundation—28.

DISCUSSION

SCHMIEDLER: This is a sophisticated module which you are going to have taught, which is going to inculcate skepticism without rejection and openness, etc. How would you prepare teachers to teach this sort of thing?

MORRISS: When the teachers of my district heard that I was developing a syllabus in parapsychology a number of the teachers in our teachers' union came to me and asked if I would be willing to offer parapsychology as an inservice course. Well, I was very busy but I thought it was a good idea, and so I did. The course was titled "New Frontiers in Mind Research" and our main focus was on parapsychology.

We had thirty teachers in the course, and a local university which worked with us, gave three graduate credits for the course. Many of the teachers told me the course was the most exciting experience they had ever had. "We'll never be able to teach the same," they said, "you've opened new doors for us, expanded our horizons." I would like to explore the possibility of packaging such courses on video tape so that they could be made available for a wider audience.

SCHMEIDLER: In pre-testing this program, you'd need to get the second generation's response—the response of your students' students in order to find out whether what seems so exciting is objectively effective.

MORRISS: That's a problem that I don't have an answer for.

ROGO: I have a quick question and then a more general comment. I was wondering if you have faced any resistance from the parents of students involved in the high school program that you're teaching.

MORRISS: No I have not yet and I don't anticipate any. In fact, I even had the PTA come to me and ask if I would teach a course in parapsychology for the adult education program.

ROGO: Secondly: In Los Angeles, the high schools are very active with parapsychology and during each semester the local *psychic* society does get several requests from high school groups and high school courses asking for people to come up and talk. I have been very active in that over the years. This year it was the first time that I had ever been requested by a junior high school class, and I had very mixed feelings about trying to discuss parapsychology with children that young. The only reason that I did agree to do it was when I found out that the material being covered in a course labeled "Parapsychology," was drawn from *Psychic Discoveries Behind the Iron Curtain,* and the last two weeks of the class had been devoted to pyramid power. So I thought a little hard-headed approach to the subject might be in order. However, the issue that raises is just when do we start educating people about parapsychology? Is it the high school arena? Shall we go to the junior high school level? Or the elementary level? That's an issue which I hope can be brought up during the course of the next two days: just when should we start teaching our kids about parapsychology?

MORRISS: Do you want to know how I feel about that?

ROGO: Yes, please. I would.

MORRISS: I think it should begin very early except that I think that with it you need to have the safeguards of developing critical thinking on the part of the students. There is the problem of chaff with the wheat. As Dr. Schmeidler said, "There's gold in them thar hills, but there's a lot of iron pyrite, too."

BELOFF: I'm very puzzled as to who might have been the guilty person on your Steering Committee. I mean, you mentioned a number of very distinguished names: Hilgard, Bruner, D.O. Hebb, etc. Certainly it couldn't have been Hilgard; it couldn't have been Bruner as far as I could imagine. Was It Hebb? Was it someone you haven't mentioned? Have you any suspicions yourself. Could you enlighten us?

MORRISS: That might make a very interesting guessing game. I'll give you the complete list if you'd like.

BELOFF: You have no concrete suspicions as to who . . . ?

MORRISS: I have no idea. I would certainly appreciate knowing if anyone has any inside information . . .

BELOFF: . . . no idea who would want to veto it?

MORRIS: . . . I would love to know what went on behind those closed doors. I think it might have been a very interesting session . . . .

VAUGHAN: Mr. Morriss, do you think that if the colleges were to incorporate parapsychology programs on the undergraduate level that this would be sufficient recommendation for putting the course into secondary schools? Do you feel that that is probably the main difficulty? That we don't have a standard parapsychology course on the college level.

MORRISS: I'm not sure that the same type of curriculum needs to be designed for the two. I think that the teenagers need a far more critical approach. They are tremendously gullible and they are, I think, in need of becoming far more cautious than the college age group who are perhaps more mature in their thinking.

VAUGHAN: It's been my impression that the college students in California could benefit very much from your course because they're just as gullible.

FRANKLIN: I'm wondering about the senators. I understand that Senator Proxmire and his aides listed some topics that they didn't deem were really supportable. I'm wondering whether it was Senator Proxmire and other people that you know of who may have influenced the support of parapsychology. A number of proposals for grant support have been turned down this year in the field of parapsychology research. I think it's a disservice to society, and I was wondering if you know who in the Congress and who in the Senate, are associated with Proxmire and his attitudes.

MORRISS: No, I can't give you any names now. I don't recall which senators were involved.

PALMER: I was very interested when you mentioned this survey that was conducted in various high school classes. I was wondering if you would summarize briefly what you learned from the survey about where high school students seem to be getting their information about parapsychology, and what kinds of attitudes, etc. they have.

MORRISS: This varied, depending on the part of the country. For example, I was quite surprised that in the East, the major source of information was radio, whereas, in the mid-West, more information came from reading, on the West coast I believe it was TV. If any of you would like to see the survey, I do have a copy of it with me and you are welcome to see it. I haven't had time to analyze the results. I'm presenting them because I'm hoping somebody will find it interesting and carry it further. The results include a good deal of information about the students themselves; their religious affiliations, their parental backgrounds, their education, their interests, and things of this nature, and I imagine somebody could do an interesting study with the questionnaire results, but I myself haven't had the time.

PALMER: I just wanted to add something in relation to Dr. Franklin's question. There's a Congressman, I believe his name is Borman, from Maryland, who was or seemed to be on the side of Proxmire, who actually sponsored an amendment to a bill that would have required a congressional review of all topics for any science proposals submitted to, I believe, the NIMH—so he would certainly be one individual.

FRANKLIN: Thanks.

MORRISS: One of the questions on the survey was, "Have you had or has someone in your family—had an experience that you think could only be described as an ESP experience?" Close to 50 per cent of the students surveyed had. I asked them, those that wanted to describe this experience, to do so. We categorized their responses and tried to determine what categories the experiences would fit in. What surprised me was the fact that precognition was the most common experience, and usually precognition in dreams. Responses such as, "I dreamed that my aunt died, and then we heard the next day that she did." Or, "I had a dream and I met a character in it the next day." This was very very common in the high school students' reports of their personal experiences.

FRANKLIN: I was wondering about the scope of your course. Do you include, or do you think it's appropriate to include things like numerology, astrology, and witchcraft, together with things in the realm of telepathy, precognition, and psychokinesis? Where do you draw the line—if you draw any?

MORRISS: I steered entirely in the other direction. I know that many courses offered on the high school level do go into these things, I used parapsychology as a vehicle for exploring scientific methodology and history. Its content may change over the years as it is taught but this is the way I designed it.

STANFORD: I have just a brief comment regarding some question-naire results you have there. When I test subjects individually in the lab, I routinely ask them about possible psychic experiences they have had, and I have a distinct impression, as you got from your survey, that most of them were reporting precognitive experiences—at least that would be the greatest proportion of cases. However, in probing those, particularly where they have said they were precognitive dreams, I have found that perhaps 80 percent of those cases are what I would call inferential, a person has had what we would call a déjà vu experience and immediately interprets that as having come from a precognitive dream and often reports it as that and you don't know that unless you probe and find out the nature of the relationship.

RHINE: Mr. Morriss, many years ago a publisher that puts out books and materials for high schools came to us with the idea of developing such a module—at least it sounds much like yours—for commercial use in the high schools. There was quite a bit of interest among the high schools in the country, promoted somewhat by the school publications reporting some of the experiments going on. We went so far as to try to see who could do this thing for them; they were ready to go, but it wasn't carried through because we didn't have the right person to design what was wanted, so it fell through. The point is you don't have to get the funding from just one source if you're ready.

MORRISS: Yes, that's true. As I said, at this time I'm more excited about the possibility of exploring sources of funding for developing a course like the one I've just given to teachers which explored some of the new research in the mind sciences. In our course we went into biofeedback, left-right hemisphere function, hypnosis, meditation, and, of course, parapsychological research.

MORRIS: I'd like to mention one thing that happened recently which may help to focus attention on just what was bothering the APA here or perhaps what is not bothering it. At our next APA convention there will be two symposia, I believe, on parapsychology, and there were two last year and one the year before. Also, Joanna Morris just recently got a letter addressed to her as editor of the *Proceedings* of the Parapsychological Association accepting that publication for abstracting in *Psychological Abstracts*. So, it's okay for believers to be editors of publications to get abstracted, but not to interact with, perhaps, high school students. In other words, there is no global discrimination on the part of the APA as an organization. There may really be something highly specific about the high school situation here.

DOMMEYER: I'm going to ask, I think, a kind of gadfly question here. I know that there has been a tendency to push back, say, college subjects into the secondary school level. They've been doing it to some extent in my field, which is philosophy. They have been attempting in some cases to put logic back into the high school situation. I just wonder how wise it is to do that kind of thing, and I'm raising the question as to whether it is wise actually to put parapsychology back on the high school level. I know the experience that I have at the college teaching level and it's this: Most of our students—and I'm willing to say *most of them*—don't know how to write and don't know how to read, and I'd rather see them come up to the college or university level with an ability to read and write than with a knowledge of telepathy or clairvoyance. And I'm just wondering whether the high schools shouldn't put their efforts into giving students the basic tools in English and mathematics instead of trying to teach them Aristotelian logic or the logic of Whitehead and Russell or parapsychology.

STANFORD: It may be I'm the only one in the whole group who has had the unique experience of living in a part of the country where there's a great deal of religious fundamentalism, and it's sometimes dubbed the "Bible Belt." I've had some experience in regard to this. I vividly remember when we had a parapsychology foundation that was established down in Texas and someone there who had some money was proposing to set up a building. We actually selected the lot. But there was actually some talk about burning down the building if it was established. The rumors in the neighborhood were that we were going to put people in that building and cause them to become spirit-possessed and things of this kind. Now this sounds utterly impossible to us, perhaps, but I really believe that parapsychology introduced particularly through government funding in the public schools and high schools could be one of the sorest political spots we've come across in a long time. I now think you're probably right, Jim, about some of the implications of this, and I really wonder, if you're going to pursue this kind of work, whether it may not be a good idea to try to get some other funding than government funding, because this could conceivably, if there's a furor, reflect back on funding for parapsychological research, from the government.

MORRISS: I agree with you. Of course, I didn't suggest the topic as part of their curriculum; they suggested it themselves.

STANFORD: I know.

ROGO: I meant to bring this out earlier. Mr. Morriss said there might be some specific resistance to parapsychology at the high school level. Again, to bring in a little bit of local politics, in Southern California there is a problem with occultism getting on the campuses. Along with parapsychology we have a lot of astrology courses, we have a lot of numerology courses, and a lot of witchcraft courses. This has caused such a tremendous problem with parental objection that last year the state legislature held hearings about the possibility of banning anything dealing with the occult from the high school campuses, because this had caused a considerable problem. I think that to resolve the problem, we might think in terms of educating not only for instance, the students, and the teachers as well, but to hit the high school administrators with education about what is responsible parapsychology. Then those administrators can keep occultism off the campus and make the situation a little easier for us and parapsychology to get on.

MORRISS: This is at the high school level?

ROGO: Yes.

FRANKLIN: In my opinion, at this stage, we should try to make the advance and I think it's very good to see the potential for that taking place. As you say, there are genuine areas of the occult and parapsychology which we can advance and my comment, I guess, is if we don't begin to make that advance, then it just will not be made. We have a fifth grade in which parapsychology is taught in the Kent school system and we have one teacher there who does the experiments in ESP with the children. She's done these experiments for years and it's accepted, and everybody approves of them. So I think it's probably the manner in which it is handled, the individual that handles it, and the manner in which it is tackled, which is the important thing. It's good to see that some progress is being made.

MORRISS: Well, Wilbur, my concern is not that they're going to get exposure, but it's what they're going to get exposure to, and if it's going to cause confusion about what is valid and what is not; what is pseudoscience and what is science. There is this confusion today and that's why I'm very concerned that we have the kinds of experiences in the educational process very early—maybe before the secondary school level, which will help students develop the kind of critical thinking and judgment that they need to deal with the exposure they're already getting in the media—whether we give it to them in the classroom or not.

PARAPSYCHOLOGY IN THE LIBERAL ARTS CURRICULUM

Irvin L. Child

On what grounds might a place be claimed for parapsychology in the liberal arts curriculum? Certainly the place cannot be argued for on the grounds that its propriety is universally acknowledged, as might be true of a few subjects, such as the study of the national language or of mathematics. This argument is obviously not applicable to parapsychology, a field the very existence of whose subject matter is far from universally recognized. It is easy to forget that the argument from universal recognition is also inapplicable to the other sciences. It might be reasonable to expect unanimity about the value of including science in a liberal arts education, but opinion is more diverse than reason would allow. We think of astronomy as including in its subject matter the study of the solar system and of other physical bodies and events stretching out to vast distances in all directions. Yet I remember that as a child I had schoolmates who knew that most of this subject matter did not exist; in their view, the earth was a flat rectangle, because the one completely authoritative book says that the angels went out to the four corners of the earth. A much less authoritative book by Charles Fort presents a different view of the universe, which has us living on the inside of a hollow sphere. I heard of this when I was in college, and was no less amazed at the idea than I was at the fact that some people appeared to take it seriously. It was after I had reached adulthood, too, that one of our country's major religious leaders stated that evolution and relativity theory were both passing fads; his statement, like Charles Fort's, seems to imply rejection of much of the subject matter of the natural sciences. That such opinions had survived so long suggests to me that they survive somewhere still, and this opinion is confirmed now and then by newspaper reports—for example, about actions by state legislatures in recent years on the teaching of biology in public schools. Unanimity of opinion about the status of a science cannot provide the criterion for its acceptance in a liberal arts curriculum, for none would meet it.

For some of the sciences, a place in the liberal arts can obviously be justified on the grounds that they include a body of well-established general knowledge, useful for sound thought and practical action about a variety of problems. The same fact about the sciences, of course, justifies even more thoroughly their inclusion in practical education; the student of engineering will employ very directly in his later work some of what he learns in science courses, and will indirectly employ a great deal more. Some students in liberal arts may find similar practical rewards in the study of the sciences; I have often found my study of physics practically useful in coping with unexpected problems of plumbing and motors. But the justification for including the sciences in a liberal education must lie in their contribution to understanding rather than to mastery of specific practical techniques. Especially does it lie in the possibility of a student's developing an understanding of the scientific process or mode of thought. Only in this way can he appreciate the kind of activity that has transformed human life in recent centuries and upon which may depend, in part, the future changes that will permit human life to continue.

Even for physics and biology this argument based on the practical implications of scientific knowledge would be rejected by some people, especially in recent years. Viewing the practical consequences as generally undesirable, they might feel the world would be the better off the more that study of the sciences could be prevented. But this is surely a deviant view. In Western European civilization generally, and perhaps in the many other countries that have welcomed the technological developments issuing from a scientific mode of thought, a consensus would probably be that the practical consequences of scientific knowledge justify including in a liberal curriculum the main outlines of scientific knowledge about the world. If scientific knowledge has transformed society through its practical consequences, from machines of all kinds to effective contraception, some direct sharing in this knowledge might be an essential part of individual preparation for living effectively and maintaining freedom of action in the new environment science has created. And it might be especially essential for attempts to change unwanted features of this environment; one need not like the effects of science on human life to agree that an understanding of science and its effects is important for anyone who wishes to live a conscious and reflective life in the present world.

I think it is obvious that no such claim derived from practical relevance can reasonably be made for parapsychology itself as it has developed up to the present. It has not thus far produced any body of well-established general knowledge on which sound thinking and practical action may be based in order to solve social problems or modify human life. What knowledge it has developed is not securely general, and its practical application is at best uncertain.

But parapsychology is easily defended as an important part of a liberal-arts curriculum, on grounds related to the general need for understanding scientific modes of thought. The modes of thought are very similar throughout science and they may be best taught with the subject matter that especially engages the particular student's interest. For some students, parapsychology may well be the most effective introduction to science. It provides a valuable example of how science works, of how it progresses, of how errors arise and are eventually eliminated. What can be seen in parapsychology will illustrate only a part of the story of science, but a part especially valuable for a liberal education, because it concerns the early stages of development of a science, and these stages are those whose problems and modes of thought most closely resemble many of everyday life.

That a science may have a value in liberal education disproportionate to the substance of the knowledge it has established may be seen in the case of psychology. In exaggerated form, the point is made by some students' comparison of what they learn from psychology with what they have learned in physics, chemistry, or biology. Psychology is not distinguished among the sciences for importance or novelty of its discoveries, for the elegance of its theories, nor for the adequacy with which theoretical disagreements are resolved by evidence. Yet many a student seems to learn more about scientific thinking by studying psychology than by studying physics, chemistry, or biology. The complaints I occasionally hear from some students about their work in the basic sciences sound strangely like the complaints one might hear from neophytes in some religious discipline. Committing to memory the formulae for various compounds, or the names of the bones that make up the human skeleton can be not unlike committing to memory the required words of a standardized prayer or other religious ritual, and it may be done without coming at the same time to understand the long process by which the compounds came to be known, or the human skeleton came to be placed in an evolutionary sequence. Many students—let us hope it is most students—bring to their memorization tasks a prior understanding that gives them, all through the acquisition of conceptual tools, adequate insight into the origins and the use of those tools, or they are led to this insight by skillful teaching. But some are caught in the tedium and difficulty of the momentary task and come to think of science as a demanding authority, a body of revealed knowledge so definitive and precise that it must, like the ritual forms for addressing the deities, be rehearsed even in the absence of understanding. These students are among those for whom psychology seems to be especially valuable as a way of learning scientific modes of thought.

Psychology is thus far relatively free from this kind of barrier that may lead a student to see science as a rigid authority rather than as a liberating mode of thought. A student may understand much psychological research, and participate actively and creatively in some of it, with a minimum of special mental equipment to be built up through long discipline. Good general intelligence, and ingenuity in using it, seem to be the main requirements. A student may better understand how science has developed if he is able to take part in its development himself. He may even, if he sees how short a way psychology has yet gone, develop a new appreciation of the role played in the physical and biological sciences by the complex and at times tedious framework of previously established and organized knowledge. Nothing can so generate a respect for intellectual discipline as can a realization of just where one's own activities could profit from more discipline.

Parapsychology resembles psychology in these respects. I think it is even like psychology in not being distinguished for the novelty of its discoveries, at least up to the present time. In finding evidence for the reality of telepathy, clairvoyance, etc., parapsychology may startle many people whose view of the world has been shaped by Western science, but it is only confirming what a majority of people in many societies, and many individuals in our society, already take as a commonplace observation. Great and novel discoveries may be made in the future, as study of psi processes advances; some may even have been made already without being definitely enough established for us to assign them the importance they will eventually have. For the most part, parapsychology appears to be at an early stage of development and has—not surprisingly, in view of the small scale on which it has always existed—much less to show than most branches of psychology.

Parapsychologists may regret, as they go about their work, this quality or primitiveness; it is a constant source of frustration in their research. But to their teaching it may bring great advantages. One advantage is suggested by the history of J. B. Conant's attempt to develop science courses for liberal education, courses that would promote an understanding of the scientific enterprise rather than wide information about its findings. A recent account says that toward this end Conant

". . . initiated a course entitled Case Histories of Scientific Discovery in which the tactics and strategy of science were illuminated by extensive quotations from original papers. Although such courses were taught at Harvard and elsewhere for a number of years, they have not survived in general. Opinions differ, but it seems likely that they failed intrinsically because students could not convincingly take up the mental state of the early investigator and share his discovery when their own fund of modern scientific knowledge put them far in advance of the historical era in which the case had taken place. Extrinsically, such procedures isolated students from contact with current science . . ."*

In current parapsychology, students can see the problems confronted by a science that is now at a very early stage of development, problems for which no solution has yet been found. They may become interested in how other sciences have solved similar problems and this historical information can have a livelier meaning when they bring it to bear on their own confrontation of psi phenomena.

A second advantage lies in the educational use of laboratory work. A student who does not know in advance the outcome of his laboratory project may take it more seriously than one who can anticipate the results before he starts. And if he can withstand disappointment he may learn more from the experience. If his mode of thought is changed at all by his laboratory practice, the change may be useful to him in facing the uncertainties of the ordinary world of human interaction. The student doing an experiment in a physics lab, seeing how closely his precise measurements of the length and the varying temperature of a metal bar fit the quantitative law he has learned, may develop a mode of thought useful in making out his income tax return. But will it help him with the perennial problem for which lovers idly pluck petals off a flower: "She loves me, she loves me not, she loves me . . ."? Perhaps experiments which in themselves give no definitive answer, which lead to a conclusion of "Yes, but . . ." or "No, but on the other hand . . ." or just "Maybe . . ." could be more useful training for facing uncertainties which must be tolerated and worked with to maximize and maintain one's interactions with other people who like ourselves are complex creatures with no simple equation.

---

* Paul Doty and Dorothy Zinberg, "Science and the Undergraduate," pp. 199–200, in Carl Kaysen (Ed.) *Content and Context: Essays on College Education.* New York: McGraw-Hill, 1973.)

Especially may an open tolerance of uncertainty be useful in facing the general problems of world citizenship in the current era of accelerating crisis. Undergraduate training in physical and biological sciences, however necessary and valuable in many of its effects, may have one undesirable effect on students, that of encouraging the expectation that world problems have some single and simple solution, comparable to a physical law, and that until this has been discovered there is nothing to do. Experience with research in parapsychology, which muddles along and moves only gradually through the years, might encourage the expectation that peaceful co-existence, like truth, is the product of many separate encounters—no one of them decisive, but each worth making because it contributes something to a complex totality.

For the sake of realizing the values of liberal education, it is appropriate to stress in a college course the controversy about the reality of psi phenomena. For parapsychological research, the controversy has mixed implications. As a warning of the effects of sloppiness, the existence of the controversy is a very useful influence on the care with which parapsychological research is done. When the controversy becomes the major focus of attention, however, it distracts severely from the principal business of parapsychological research, that of seeking to understand psi phenomena. If there really are no such phenomena, this fact should eventually emerge from the attempt to understand them, perhaps more surely and swiftly than if test of their reality had been the sole aim. But if there really are such phenomena—and that is the premise ordinarily involved in motivating research activity in parapsychology—research concerned only with testing their reality will not make much contribution to understanding them.

In recommending attention to the controversy about the reality of psi phenomena, of course, I am making recommendations specifically for the American scene, and I do not know in how many other countries they would be pertinent. In a country where psi phenomena are taken for granted as a common fact of experience, the controversy might seem alien and unreal. Its educational value, if any, might seem to be as an eye-opener about cultural differences among nations in the modern world. In the United States, I imagine, most college students would come to a course in parapsychology with a belief system consistent with the presence of controversy. Many would be uncertain, and eager to become informed about claims and counterclaims. Some would be already convinced of the reality of psi phenomena. For those convinced because of personal experience, knowledge of the controversy should help place their own experience in an appropriate framework. For those whose conviction follows from adherence to a religious doctrine, knowledge of the controversy should be useful, like many other incidents in the history of Western thought, in stimulating critical self-exploration.

There are disadvantages and dangers, too, in expanding the role of parapsychology in liberal-arts education. I would like to discuss three in particular. The first of these is the danger of giving students less than they deserve, by giving them only a one-sided methodological training and not providing the substantive knowledge they may be looking for. Many students might come to the study of parapsychology because they are trying to resolve for themselves some of the philosophical issues recurrent in Western life. Is a human being just a biological organism or is a human being also something different, a spirit or soul? If there is this something different, can it exist and function independently of the organism? If so, what sort of consciousness does it have and what are its experiences? All these questions are of intense interest to many people and can well lead to their studying parapsychology. Under its earlier name of psychical research, parapsychology arose out of the quest for answers to just these questions. Now, as in the 19th century, we are all exposed in the public media to accounts of messages purporting to come from the spirits of dead persons, of some people's seeming to remember a previous life they led in another body before the beginning of this present life, of the supposed temporary possession of a living person's body by some intruding spirit. If these accounts merit belief, acquaintance with them is very important for anyone trying to resolve for himself the issues I have mentioned.

In a parapsychology course with a strong methodological orientation, the student might never read any of these accounts. His only encounter with their existence might come through his studying how objective, quantitative techniques of content analysis can be applied to studying them. Since these techniques have not been extensively applied, and studying the techniques does not necessarily bring one into direct contact with the limited materials to which they have been applied, the materials most relevant to his initial interests may be quite absent from the course. Instead he may spend most of his time learning about experiments in transmission of information about numbers and patterns, experiments that may seem entirely irrelevant to his initial interests and at any rate are not likely to give him very direct help in resolving the philosophical issues with which he is grappling. Disappointed with what he finds in parapsychology, the student may conclude this discipline is boring and meaningless. Conceivably he may draw the same conclusion about science generally, so that a course intended to develop understanding of the scientific approach and an ability and inclination to use it may instead have an opposite effect.

I don't know how generally teachers of parapsychology will encounter this sort of problem, but I am sure teachers of psychology often do. The difficulties encountered by psychology in the past may well provoke thought about future teaching of parapsychology. Psychology courses and textbooks have often had a strongly methodological orientation. The introductory section has often been largely devoted to discussing the nature of science, why psychology is to be classified as a science and how as a science it differs from other efforts to understand or influence human beings. Later in the book, an occasional chapter may give more attention to how its topic may be approached scientifically than to what conclusions have been reached by doing so. Special stress is often laid on methods of special elegance—for example, procedures for psychophysical scaling—even though it is not apparent that those methods are involved in any of the substantive findings reported in the book. Some topics of great interest—love, for example, or mystical experience—may be altogether omitted because they have never been studied with methods the author approves. These features of psychology courses have greatly diminished through the years. But they are still there, and are echoed in student complaints that psychology is too much concerned with proving it is a science and too little devoted to being one.

Can parapsychology as a subject of undergraduate instruction be spared a similar period of insecurity and over-concern with proving its scientific worth? One way would be to forget, in teaching, the scientific orientation that is essential in research. A course might be built around the same varied material whose appearance in popular books on the paranormal suggests it is what most people want to hear about—exciting accounts of purported personal experiences with hauntings and apparitions, of strange coincidences and unusual runs of good or bad luck, of messages from beneficient guiding spirits, and of apparent answer to personal prayer. It may sound absurd to suggest that such material would be presented as the content of a college course, unless it be in a college which conceives its mission as religious indoctrination rather than training in mental skills. The number of books and magazine articles of this character, however, suggests that if standards were relaxed, teachers would be found eager to teach such courses. The courses could certainly be pertinent to the interests I have suggested motivate some students to want a course in parapsychology.

Some students would doubtless be influenced toward acceptance of world views which could easily accommodate the supposed facts in which they were being indoctrinated. Others, bringing a critical eye to their reading and seeing the inadequacy of the material as evidence for anything, might be influenced against those world views, on the supposition that any doctrine for which such flimsy evidence must be offered is probably false.

I don't see any satisfactory way to introduce parapsychology as a liberal-arts subject without running the risk of alienating students by methodological emphasis. For the methods of study are the heart of the matter. That scientific methods can be applied to these topics, that their application is productive of knowledge, even though the knowledge thus far gained is small in quantity and weak in certainty: this, and the mode of intellectual approach represented in this work and perhaps engendered or encouraged in the student are what parapsychology has to contribute to a liberal education. And intrinsic to its contribution in the present state of knowledge is the state of uncertainty and suspended judgment that will lead many students to feel there is no substantial subject matter, just methodology.

I do think a parapsychology course should consider the religious and philosophical questions out of which the discipline grew, and should see that students are acquainted with something of the variety of personal experiences that many people find relevant in answering those questions themselves. This is an important background for under-standing the discipline, its origins and its possible long-term values. But there is nothing very distinctive of parapsychology in a mere account of such experiences. More distinctive is a critical examination of their value as evidence and a comparison with the varied procedures and results of the broader discipline which grew out of pioneering examination of such material by the early psychical researchers.

So much for the danger of the student's being bored, discouraged and alienated. Suppose now that he subjects himself to the critical discipline of learning about parapsychology. A second danger may be seen ahead. Some of those who take a course in parapsychology will emerge with a heightened sense of the reality of psi phenomena. Will this bring about an unwarranted change in the way they think about a variety of events? Will it break down some of their habits of critically evaluating events around them? In particular, will it lead them to see psi operating where in fact events are purely random?

There appears to be a real danger here, already present in the limitations of human functioning and ready to be exacerbated wherever parapsychology leads people to assume psi events to be real.

The danger is made especially apparent in some research that has been done quite outside the context of parapsychology, on human judgments about randomness and non-randomness.

Some of the most relevant research on randomness is that by Amos Tversky and Daniel Kahnemann of Hebrew University in Jerusalem. The people taking part in their research as subjects have generally been college students, though some of the research has been done with high-school students and some with fellow psychologists. Their subjects have been asked to make various judgments about randomness or likelihood and Tversky and Kahnemann have sought to identify some of the conditions that exert an inappropriate or unrealistic influence on those judgments. The conditions they have isolated are extremely pertinent to understanding distortions of thought that may be produced by believing in psi processes and assuming their probable ubiquity.

Techniques of statistical inference provide us with objective rules for assessing the likelihood that a particular set of events could have arisen by random sampling from some specified population of potential events. In parapsychology, experiments are usually arranged so that if we are led, by these rules, to infer deviation from randomness, it is reasonable to attribute the deviation to so-called paranormal processes. Now, Tversky and Kahnemann have found that ordinary judgments of randomness and of deviation from it do not conform very closely to those objective rules. Other and very powerful subjective rules influence our ordinary judgments. For instance, the rule Tversky and Kahnemann call *representativeness:* we tend to reject the hypothesis of random origin for any sample that is not in itself representative of the population which we have in mind as possible source of the random sampling. If in tossing a coin, for example, we immediately get five tails in a row, total absence of heads makes us suspect the coin of bias, much more strongly than would be justified by accurate calculations of probability. In a similar manner, a would-be psychic is likely to be influenced, much more than is warranted, by the variations in his success; from an excess of hits at some times and an excess of misses at other times, he is likely to conclude he is at both times getting information psychically, sometimes systematically hitting and other times systematically missing, whereas the sequence of hits and misses may in fact be completely compatible with the hypothesis of randomness. I have repeatedly seen exactly this mistake made by people who are or would like to be psychic.

This mistake is encouraged by a favorable attitude toward psi, by wanting to be psychic and welcoming apparent evidence of psychic performance. Tversky and Kahnemann offer us a second principle that is pertinent here: the principle of availability. Hypotheses alternative to that of randomness are the more likely to be adopted the more available they are to the person, the more vividly and convincingly he can imagine their operation, for instance. General acceptance of the reality of psi processes, talking about them as though they were some clearly identifiable processes we really understand, in short a whole climate of opinion that might result from widespread knowledge of the positive side of parapsychological findings, could make the psi hypothesis much more generally available than at present as an alternative to accepting random phenomena as genuinely random.

Several experiments have recently been performed by another psychologist, Ellen Langer, that provide other reasons for expecting such an effect. She used various situations where an outcome was to be determined at random and ordinary realistic knowledge would indicate that only random processes would be involved. She systematically varied the extent to which accompanying circumstances resembled those which ordinarily accompany events whose outcome is determined by individual skill and is thus to some extent under the control of the person himself. She found, as she had predicted, that resemblance to skill-relevant situations consistently increased people's unrealistic belief in their own personal control over outcomes that were in fact determined by chance. Perhaps this finding is appropriately to be considered as an instance of the principle of availability, since the idea of personal control comes to mind more readily in situations which resemble other situations in which we have in fact been able to exert our own will. The finding has a distinctive value for us, though, in calling attention to additional specific features of a student's experience in parapsychology that might encourage an unrealistic interpretation of experience. In the very rational act of planning and carrying out experiments to assess the possibility of small and irregular psi effects, a situation similar in many ways to normal testing of skilled performances, some students might unwittingly fall into the trap of believing a random performance to exhibit a massive and continuous influence of psi processes.

This danger is real and important, I believe, and may lead some to feel parapsychology should not be included in a liberal arts curriculum for fear it encourages a loss of the rationality the curriculum aims to encourage. My own conclusion would be that the danger requires us to be watchful, and to try to prevent or minimize it, calling our students' attention repeatedly to how small the maximum psi effect is in these experiments, and how large the effect of random variables, and the need for realistic appreciation of this great difference. To leave parapsychology out of liberal education will, on the other hand, leave students and the general public to gain their knowledge of it largely from everyday life and the public media, isolated from the cautious and critical attitude which can accompany an academic introduction to it.

The third problem likely to arise if parapsychology is more generally given a place in liberal education is that of personnel. Where are the people who could give, at many colleges or universities, a course based on adequate knowledge of parapsychology, calculated on the one hand to make available what it can add to a liberal arts curriculum, and on the other hand, to present it in a way that avoids such difficulties or dangers as the two I have described?

I hope that some of the gap might be filled by people who gain, as I did, the minimum background necessary. Some psychologists, that is, in a summer or in a term's leave, might study parapsychology intensively enough to give an undergraduate course in it. A few psychologists, of course, may already have obtained that level of preparation gradually over a period of years, and need only become aware of student interest in order to consider including parapsychology among their course offerings. Some might have difficulty persuading their institutions of the desirability of offering a course in parapsychology, but I should think any difficulty of this sort must be steadily decreasing.

Eventually, a department's need for undergraduate teaching, or for a combination of that and graduate teaching, might be sufficient to justify a new appointment from outside on the primary basis of qualifications in parapsychology. In some intermediate stage, of course, a person trained primarily in parapsychology might be brought in from outside if he could also serve other teaching needs of the department. In all this I refer to a department of psychology because that seems the most likely of existing departments for the kind of undergraduate teaching I have been proposing. But departmental location of functions, like division of subject matter among disciplines, is partly whimsical and accidental and I think that at some universities possibilities similar to those I have sketched for psychology would arise or would reach fruition in other departments instead.

If there is a great increase in the demand for undergraduate instruction in parapsychology, and it is judged to be lasting, then of course the demand for graduate instruction will increase as well—for the double reason that many students would want to embark upon it and that many institutions would want to employ them after they complete it. And here the topic of undergraduate education merges with that of graduate or professional education, to which I believe a majority of the participants in our conference are principally addressing themselves.

DISCUSSION

HASTINGS: You said that methodology often is boring and dull. Would you comment about methodology as applied to case studies and controlled observations? I think these often have much more intrinsic excitement since they're closer to personal experience rather than the more experimentally-oriented research. That's my first question, and my second one again relates to method, and that is, if we do emphasize methodology, then we're pretty much bound to accept the results. Experiments generally present support for the psi hypothesis so that seems to me a further advantage of the emphasis on methodology.

CHILD: Well, on the first question, I agree with you wholeheartedly that it would be very desirable in methodological discussion in a course on parapsychology to spend a good deal of time on the methods that have been used and could be used in dealing with spontaneous occurrences with case material. I'm not very optimistic, however, from the history of teaching in psychology, that many teachers will spend very much time on that. Consider psychology. It has always been to some extent in a position of inferiority in relation to some of the other sciences, and eager to demonstrate its rightful position among the sciences. A result has been exaggerated on the experimental method—so extreme, indeed, that many courses are taught as though no other methods were conceivably adequate for any purpose. I suspect this exaggerated stress on experimental method will tend to appear in any discipline whose people feel insecure about their status as scientists. If the parapsychologists are more alerted to this danger at the outset and more determined to avoid it than psychologists were, then maybe they can avoid it. The second thing you asked about was . . . ?

HASTINGS: Oh, well, I was thinking that if we do emphasize method, don't you think the method we've used already pretty well indicates that psi phenomena exist?

CHILD: But it seems to me that bears only on the controversy about the reality of psi phenomena, and I don't think that alone is very interesting to many people once they've gotten well into the topic. It doesn't make the substance of a course to me—the question of whether some phenomena exist, when you don't have any idea what they mean. I've found in teaching parapsychology to undergraduates that many feel a lack of subject matter or substance. They find little comparable to what they expect to learn in a course on science—that is, a knowledge of the processes by which certain kinds of events occur, and the influences on these processes. Parapsychology has hardly even started this kind of study. It's very difficult to do, for lack of ways to evoke psi phenomena dependably enough to go about studying what influences them. Many students would feel some sympathy with the point that Edwin G. Boring made in greatly exaggerated form and surrounded by error, in his introduction to the Hansel volume—that parapsychology is often satisfied with negative knowledge. It has been at times content with trying to demonstrate a mystery instead of insistently pushing on toward dispelling the mystery. I think the emphasis in teaching ought to be on the attempts at penetrating the mystery though they haven't gotten very far as yet.

RAO: Dr. Child, you have mentioned that one of the dangers of teaching a course in parapsychology in a university or college is that it may make people uncritically accept certain things and perhaps develop a sentiment of anti-rationality or anti-intellectualism. On the other hand, I have a feeling that teaching of a course in parapsychology as it emerged historically would give them a better appreciation of the application of scientific method to an area where one would think scientific method has no place. And second, I think, it also would reveal the limits of rationality or limits of reason given as a method of science. I think it is just as important for the student to know that there are certain things which might occur even when they contradict certain accepted world views, and this kind of openness is basic to any progress in science; and a conventional science tends to kill this kind of an openness which I think is essential for any growing mind. If this is true, then I would feel it would encourage a greater commitment to true science than discourage a student or encourage a student from taking an anti-scientific stance.

CHILD: Well, I certainly hope that you are right and I certainly have some tendency to agree with you about that point. Yet I would be worried about the extent to which the mere presence of a course in parapsychology would—especially in students who do not even take the course—encourage substitution of astrology for some understanding of personality processes, and generally dependence upon pseudo-sciences rather than on science. I would fear this not only in people who were merely influenced by knowing parapsychology was a respectable subject while misconceiving its nature through lack of contact, but also in people who might take a course in parapsychology taught by somebody who really is basically anti-scientific and is teaching the occult tradition rather than the scientific approach. This seems to me a real danger to be watched for.

TART: Let me make some confused comments because I'm struggling to come to grips with some of the issues you've been raising. One of these is the issue of the pseudo-sciences and their place in a course on parapsychology. I share this feeling; I don't want to be associated with astrology or numerology, because I basically think they're bunk. At the same time the university traditionally includes all sorts of courses in other departments on subjects which, by similar criteria, are probably bunk. For example, how subjective is English literature and art appreciation? We don't raise that question about these kinds of things because they're traditional parts of our education; yet people are looking for belief systems and the students, particularly at this stage (ignoring the more conservative ones coming in) are very much personally involved in these. I teach a course in altered states of consciousness at Davis; it's the most popular course in the psychology department, and yet the main objection that I get from students is that I'm often too abstract, talking about the *research* on the issue, and all that. They're having personal experiences day in and day out with meditation and drugs, etc., and they want things that are more immediately relevant.

Now I mainly take an attitude of trying to teach them some kind of critical attitude toward these things—"Yes, it's a mysterious world and lots of things happen"—and we believe most things on the worst kind of evidence. A course on parapsychology certainly does present the danger of making people much more open to unorthodox belief systems, which is a mixed blessing. It might make them more genuinely open, in the sense of personal growth, and might make them question common beliefs which really ought to be questioned, and it may also make them buy the most ridiculous sorts of nonsense as a belief system. I don't know how we can separate these two things. I've been sitting here thinking: "How can you teach a course on parapsychology without getting into a course on states of consciousness and the limitations of conventional belief systems," and I'm wondering if we're operating in too much isolation, in a sense. I'd appreciate your reaction to that.

CHILD: I agree that we want, in teaching parapsychology generally, to encourage people in openness and the feeling that rationality may have its limits. But the extreme anti-rationality and anti-scientism of many people today make it very difficult to teach parapsychology. How many faculty members would willingly have in their university courses that they felt were primarily encouraging occultism? There are certainly students who would like to be influenced in that direction. The first time I gave a course in parapsychology, despite my warnings at the outset, I think a lot of students really expected a course in occultism and they were greatly disappointed; evidently I'm not able to provide the approach that will lead people whose orientation is primarily toward the occult tradition, to come in and absorb something of the scientific approach. I think the students who stayed with the course and those who came next year, were primarily those who really shared a scientific orientation. Some of the best students were majors in the basic sciences, for example.

STANFORD: On the basis of my experience in teaching parapsychology, I really think it is possible to teach this subject matter in a way that has a special advantage for students. You can say to them that in parapsychology our findings illustrate the importance of keeping an open and inquiring mind about subject matter that sometimes seems, perhaps, to contradict rationality. Another very important thing we can learn from parapsychology, is that what appears to us to be rational may be rational only in the framework of certain implicit assumptions, paradigms, etc., and I think this can have value for students. It can keep their minds open about things which may appear rather odd; and at the same time it can cause them to recognize the necessity of making a rational approach to investigating and drawing conclusions about this particular subject matter or any particular problem area.

Now, my second, and perhaps related comment is that I can't see parapsychology as being a subject matter-less area. I do think that over the century of inquiry we have had, that we have learned, in a tentative way, some things about our subject matter, some specific conclusions which, in some instances, are at least as strong as many of the conclusions we typically hear about in psychology courses. So I want to put on record the opinion that a parapsychology course should not stray away from subject matter; should not stray away from discussing the evidence behind the hypotheses that I think most parapsychologists hold as some of the substance of our field, and if a course is presented in another way, so that it's totally negative, I think we'd be misleading our students.

BELOFF: I would simply like to endorse what Dr. Rao was saying previously. I feel that our task as teachers of parapsychology must always be to try and find the middle way between the occultism and pseudo-science on the one side, and what I would call "scientism" on the other. I think that what worries somebody like Dr. Tart is that the scientistic attitude is one completely encapsulated in its own thinking and it has no room for open-mindedness and therefore, leans towards the credulous, occultist side. We've got to cultivate these critical attitudes that are part of our subject matter. As you were saying, "What can you do with a mystery if it has no explanation; you can't make sense of it." But even if it does no more than inculcate a certain amount of humility in the student—his realization that perhaps we don't know as much about the world as he might be led to suppose from his scientific education, that again, is a gain of some kind.

DEAN: May I just make a brief personal comment on the science and anti-science discussion? I taught a course in Introduction to Parapsychology at State University of New York at Buffalo and it was monitored by some psychologists from the Department of Psychology; then they took me into the Dean's office to have the fight banning parapsychology from the campus at Buffalo. The argument was that for every positive statement I made about parapsychology, giving the results of some experimental data that were collected, I had to make a negative statement saying it was not so; it did not exist. Now probably the reason why they were demanding this was what Dr. Child mentioned to us—that we don't have a meaning for it. Now I don't think that's important. There are many areas in science where we don't have a meaning and the one that comes to mind for me is the square root of minus one. There is no such thing in arithmetic which multiplied by itself will give you minus one, yet the square root of minus one is at the heart of physics and electronics and electrical engineering. I think we can still present our data of parapsychology even though we don't yet have a meaning.

FRANKLIN: Dr. Child, I was interested in the background of your students and the use they might have made of the material they received from your class. Did you have any students that were from the physical sciences, chemistry, physics, math, and can you comment on how they've used the material from your class in further professional work? After they've taken your class.

CHILD: I don't know whether any of the students from the basic sciences went on with it later, but some of the best students I had with the most interesting projects in the course, were majors, advanced majors, in physics and engineering.

NOVILLO: When I started to lecture in parapsychology at my university in Cordoba, 1973, the attendance was more than a 100 people: students and grown-ups alike. There is frequent misinterpretation of parapsychology by older persons. They think it deals with occultism, some spontaneous cases and special practices. A lot of them, as well as persons without scholarly training, abandoned the course after a week or ten days when they realized that I was focusing and discussing the subject in a different way. They are not interested in studying a science. I am lecturing in parapsychology as it really is: a science, if we look at its aim, method and results. Today, a natural selection of the attendance is taking place every year; the scientific level is improving and university students from different schools are coming and persevering to the end of the course. Now you can understand why I was surprised when you said that your students were waiting for occultism.

CHILD: It may be that in Argentina you do not have the current fad of occultism among university students that we do have in this country.

NOVILLO: We suffer from the great influence of spiritism and its magical practices in Brazil; nevertheless only one lecturer in para-psychology I have listened to affirms that the aim in the future for parapsychology is to study the so-called "out of the body experience", satanism and reincarnation.

ROGO: I'd like to introduce what may be a very unpopular point of view. I think all of us know that college students enter courses in any field for a variety of reasons. I'm wondering whether we can afford to allow parapsychology courses to be attended, in much the same way as English and history courses which are just open to anyone to wander in who wants to. In sitting and talking to students taking parapsychology courses, you learn they are often there for legitimate scientific reasons or legitimate philosophic reasons. But also they come in for a lot of psychological reasons that are pretty aberrant such as trying to under-stand certain occult traditions. They want to be taught the occult; they want to be taught astrology, so I'm wondering if we really shouldn't be very very careful in our courses about selecting our students and screening students before they come into our classes and try to get at the root of their motivation. And if the motivation is legitimate we can allow them to take the course. But if their motivation is something that we might consider aberrant or based on psychological need—perhaps we should discourage them from taking that course.

DOMMEYER: I wanted to think in terms of what Charles Tart was saying some minutes ago. He seemed to be concerned about students coming into classes who had interests just in the occult. If parapsychology were to develop in a liberal arts program on college campuses, I wonder whether there could not be a special course in the pseudo-sciences where actually one would apply scientific method to the hypotheses of these pseudo-sciences and demonstrate to students that they don't work out. In other words, let's have a course that includes a study of phrenology and let's have some guy come in and feel the bumps on the guys' heads and say, "You've got such and such capacity," and then let's give that guy some intelligence tests and what-not and find out that the hypothesis of the phrenologist is incorrect. Now I don't say that should be the only course in parapsychology, but if we had several courses in parapsychology, I don't see why one course couldn't address itself to the pseudo-sciences and actually prove scientifically the falsity of the hypotheses. Now you said they're bunk, and I think you've got pretty good reasons for saying that, but I think you'd want to be able to demonstrate that that's so. Let's have a course demonstrating that, and if that won't cure occultism on the campus, why nothing will.

SCHMEIDLER: Let me come back to a couple of points that were mentioned earlier, and the skepticism about the occult with the use of case studies. My experience, too, has been that case studies in isolation don't impress the students favorably. If I cite many cases that seem to me to be good, at first the students are interested but soon they get more and more restless, and respond by pointing out what's wrong with each case, and say that at best each may be only coincidence. It taught me that we can use individual cases to push a group toward a skeptical attitude—which is just what we want for this problem of accepting the occult or accepting false evidence. Lately I've been using just a few of the cases that I thought were good as a provocative introduction to the experiments, but then also bringing up lots of incidents of people who made extreme claims that had been debunked. Then later on if a student describes an isolated incident that seemed to argue for astrology or numerology or whatever the group that heard lots of flawed cases is likely to begin pointing out the difficulties of using a simple incident as a basis for generalization. Citing both the good and the bad cases may be a way to prevent over-acceptance of occult phenomena.

KRIPPNER: I think the points that Mr. Rogo brought up are worth considering from another vantage point. It's true that students will take parapsychology courses for a variety of reasons, from the research-oriented to the outright pathological. I think that one way to control this is through a selection process which would involve the way a course is set up. If a course has a reputation of being a scientifically-oriented course, many of the students who would otherwise take it for less than academic reasons, are not going to sign up in the first place. I've often thought that maybe it's not too early for the Parapsychological Association itself to consider whether it could not have some sort of an Educational Standards Committee that would actually pass upon the content of certain courses at various universities. This would put the Parapsychological Association into a function it's never assumed before, but I think that the PA, as time goes on, is going to have to be more aggressive and more visible, and this might be a very useful function. Now the type of course to which the PA Committee would give some sort of approval, would simply not be the sort of course that would appeal to people who want to develop their own psi abilities or who want to find some rationalizations for certain bizarre experiences that they're having. I think that the issue of motivation for taking a course is a critical one. I think that not only can interviews and some sort of screening be done by the instructor, but when this is not possible, that the course content itself and the reputation of the course will be a screening technique.

TEACHING OF PARAPSYCHOLOGY IN INDIA AND THE ANDHRA EXPERIMENT

K. Ramakrishna Rao

TEACHING OF PARAPSYCHOLOGY IN ANCIENT INDIA

Yoga and tantra are two disciplines that were taught for centuries in India. These disciplines are regarded as *sastras* or sciences and are believed to produce states of consciousness where *siddhis,* i.e., various kinds of supernormal phenomena, manifest. Thus, it can be said that parapsychology has been a subject of teaching from the early beginnings of Indian thought. Not only was the possibility of paranormal communication and supernatural powers extensively discussed in almost all schools of Indian thought, but various kinds of practices believed to be related to the acquisition of these abilities were also traditionally taught in Brahmanic as well as Buddhistic schools. For example, the University of Nalanda, which flourished between the fourth and twelfth centuries A.D., was a great center of tantric studies. Kamalasila was a Professor of Tantras at Nalanda. Citing epigraphical evidence, Sankalia points out that "Tantra was, perhaps, a very popular subject with the students as well as professors in the Nalanda University."[1]

In the heyday of Nalanda there were as many as 8,500 students and 1,500 teachers, all residing at the University. It is interesting to note that education at Nalanda was not confined to Buddhistic learning alone. It is stated, for example, that "Hiuen Tsang himself became a student of Nalanda for the study of yoga-sastra, in which the Nalanda Chancellor, Silabhadra, was the highest living authority."[2]

Tantrism, according to Buddhistic tradition, was introduced by Asanga (fourth century, A.D.). The most important and probably the earliest Vajrayana tantric text, *Guhyasamaja-tantra* is attributed to Asanga.[3] From the time of Asanga down to the time of Dharmakirti (seventh century A.D.), tantric practices were transmitted to trusted disciples by the *gurus* in a very secret manner because some forms of tantra violated the rules of conduct prescribed by the Buddha. But by

the seventh century such men as Indrabhuti, Saraha and Padmasam-
bhava made no secret of these practices.

According to *Guhyasamaja-tantra*, the sole aim of tantra is to obtain
siddhi or "the attainment of superhuman powers of the mind, body or
the sense organs".[4] The Buddhistic tantras are divided into four
subdivisions, viz., (a) *Kriya-tantra*, (b) *Karya-tantra*, (c) *Yogy-tantra* and (d)
Anuttara-tantra.

It should be mentioned that tantrism is not an exclusively Buddhistic
preoccupation. As Eliade points out: "It is a pan-Indian movement, for
it is assimilated by all the great Indian religions and by all the 'sectarian'
schools. There is a Buddhistic tantrism and a Hindu tantrism."[5]

Students are not freely admitted to tantric classes. We are told: "the
prospective Tantric must be properly initiated into the Tantric
practices through the right channel—viz., the guru. And no ordinary
guru would do. He, in fact, must possess all the qualifications laid down
in the Tantric works. His duty was to initiate the *sisya*, to give him
different kinds of *abhiseka*, and then instruct him how to achieve the
Siddhis. Likewise only that student could approach the guru for the
knowledge of the Siddhis and Tantric practices who had the requisite
qualities."[6]

The belief that many physical and psychical powers not commonly
found in men can be secured by practicing yoga is a very old one, and
certainly older than Patanjali. *Katha* and the later Upanishads like
Svetasvatara and *Maitrayani* speak of yoga. In *Katha* Upanishad, yoga is
described as restraint of the senses. "When the five instruments of
knowledge stand still together with the mind, and when the intellect
does not move, that is called the highest stage. This, the firm holding
back of the senses, is what is called yoga."[7]

Svetasvatara mentions for the first time *dhyana* or meditative yoga,
and speaks of postures, breath control and the different psychical
states emerging out of yoga practice. As Radhakrishnan points out:
"the *Upanishads*, the *Mahabharata*, including the *Bhagavadgita*, Jainism
and Buddhism accept yogic practices . . . Patanjali's yoga is the
crystallisation of ideas on asceticism and contemplation extant at his
time in a more or less hazy and undefined way."[8] Eliade also states:
"Patanjali is not the creator of the yoga 'philosophy' just as he is not and
could not be—the inventor of yogic techniques . . . And in fact yogic
practices were known in the esoteric circles of Indian ascetics and
mystics long before Patanjali."[9]

There is no agreement on the probable date of the composition of
the *yoga sutras* by Patanjali. Some authorities, like Woods, assign
Patanjali to the fourth century A.D.[10] But Dasgupta assigns him to the

second century B.C. arguing that the fourth part of the *yoga-sutras* in which Buddhistic references are found is of a later interpolation and therefore does not support the opinion that *yoga-sutras* could not have been written before 300 A.D.[11] *Yoga-sutras* are in four parts. The first part deals with the nature and aim of *samadhi*. The second describes the method of reach the *samadhi* state. In the third part, an account of the supernormal powers that can be obtained by practicing yoga is given. The fourth part expounds the nature of *Kaivalya* (liberation) which is the ultimate aim of yoga.

Since the time of Patanjali, yoga has been practiced in various forms and taught extensively throughout India. *Yoga Today* lists more than two hundred yoga centers functioning in India at present.[12] The University of Saugar has a Department of Yogic Studies. Yogic exercises are taught in a number of educational institutions. Yoga seminars and conferences are frequently held, several of these under the sponsorship of one or another agency of the government, state or central.

The most recent one, "Yoga, Science and Man," was held at Vigyan Bhavan, New Delhi from March 14 to 16, 1975. The seminar was sponsored by the Ministry of Health and Family Planning and co-sponsored by such prestigious bodies as the All India Institute of Medical Sciences, the National Council for Educational Research and Training, the Indian National Science Academy, the Indian Council of Medical Research, the University Grants Commission and the Shri Aurobindo Ashram. The conference was attended by several hundred yogis, yoga teachers, yoga enthusiasts and educators and scientists interested in yoga. Included among them were Maharishi Mahesh Yogi, Pandit Gopi Krishna, physicist Dr. D. S. Kothari, cardiologist Dr. Datey and physiologist Dr. B. K. Anand. The seminar discussed several aspects of yoga. But the most dominant interest shown was in the possible medical application of yoga and its therapeutic utility. There was hardly any mention of the parapsychological relevance of yoga. I have referred to this seminar because it illustrates the general situation. While one could come across a lot of glib talk about the *siddhis* and their acquisition through yoga practice, it is not easy to find in India a serious *sadhaka* attempting to obtain *siddhis* by yoga practice or a serious scientist (except perhaps a couple of parapsychologists) attempting to verify the claim that yogic practice would enable one to acquire supernormal abilities.

It is mentioned quite often that the tradition discourages the practitioner from seeking *siddhis*, or even forbids it. This of course is true. Therefore, it is argued, we do not come across yogis interested in them. I do not find this reasoning very convincing. In the first place, we find a lot of people, called by various names, claiming to possess supernormal powers. Secondly, the number of those who practice yoga seeking *kaivalya* is disappointingly small. Finally, yoga in its popular form is concerned with such lower functions as body culture, health and therapy.

The debasing of yoga as body culture and its degeneration from the lofty heights of *kaivalya* and *siddhis* to a kind of therapy, the efficacy of which is yet to be established, could be a consequence of either of the following. Yoga does not in fact enable the practitioner to obtain *siddhis*. The claims contained in such texts as the *Yoga-Sutras* are but false promises held out by the authors to coax men into practicing yoga in an age which craved magical gifts to control the forces of nature. Or the yoga path to *siddhis* is so arduous, difficult and uncertain that it fell into disuse. It is difficult at this time to say which of these alternatives is more probable. But what is important to note is that yoga as practiced today in many so-called yoga-centers in India is as remotely related to parapsychology as hypnosis or psychoactive drugs. This is surprising because *siddhis* are traditionally regarded as one of the significant outcomes of the practice of yoga or tantra. It may be concluded, therefore, that the teaching of yoga and related disciplines can hardly be regarded as having any direct relevance to parapsychological teaching in contemporary India.

PARAPSYCHOLOGY AS A UNIVERSITY DISCIPLINE IN MODERN INDIA

Parapsychology as a subject of university study and research is a post-independence phenomenon. Some of the Indian universities are more than a hundred years old. They were established by the British and patterned to a large extent on the model of British universities. Therefore, one could hardly expect them to take interest in the study and investigation of paranormal phenomena. After independence, parapsychology soon found its way through the portals of some universities. In the early fifties, Banaras Hindu University offered courses in parapsychology. Under the leadership of that great pioneer of Indian psychology, Dr. Gopalaswamy, Mysore University started work in parapsychology, and offered a parapsychology course in its Department of Psychology. Professor Atreya of Banaras Hindu University, Dr. Kali Prasad of Lucknow University, Dr. Boaz of Madras University, Dr. Kuppuswamy of Mysore University and Professor Parthasarathy of S.V. University, among others, showed interest in parapsychology and encouraged its study. Theses were written and degrees were granted for work in parapsychology. Powerful patronage from politically important men was forthcoming. Soon a parapsychology unit was started at the University of Rajasthan's Department of Philosophy. Lucknow University held a seminar on yoga and parapsychology. Ambitious research projects were announced. Parapsychology Institutes were proposed. But then Kali Prasad and Boaz died. Atreya and Kuppuswamy retired. Banaras and Mysore stopped teaching parapsychology. The Parapsychology Unit in Rajasthan was closed.

This situation is surprisingly similar to the one on the American scene when psychical research first gained admission into universities. As Dr. J.B. Rhine pointed out: "The ESP invasion of the already well-established departments of psychology was definitely not a success. There was no adequate continuity about any single one of these separate investigations."[13]

The reasons for this state of affairs are not difficult to find. Parapsychology, it would seem, was not simply ready for a permanent place in those universities. Its premature entrance was made possible by the personal involvement of a few influential professors who either felt the importance of parapsychology at a theoretical level and wished a place for it in the academic world or simply responded to extramural pressures. The unfortunate part of it is they failed to provide the necessary research and structural base that would ensure continuity. They were either too busy with other things or simply were not themselves sufficiently equipped to undertake serious investigations in this difficult area. Therefore, with their exit parapsychology was quietly shelved. Public pressure and patronage could give only the initial push. The momentum generated by such a push should be self-sustaining. This was not the case, because these universities did not have men trained in techniques that would test the ideas challenging them. Therefore, their commitment was half-hearted; so was their effort.

Fortunately, this is not the end of the story. About the same time as these things were happening elsewhere in India, a young graduate student at Andhra University got interested in parapsychology. His interest and the fortunate confluence of a variety of useful circumstances all converged to bring about a situation where parapsychology found a permanent foothold in an important university. This story is autobiographical. It is briefly told here with the hope that it would reveal the relevant antecedents necessary for the admission of parapsychology into a university. A comparison of the notes by those of us who are involved in similar enterprises of teaching parapsychology in universities, I think, would give us insights into the problems and prospects of academic parapsychology and, more important, into the ways parapsychologists are made.

THE MAKING OF A PARAPSYCHOLOGIST

Professor Saileswar Sen was a chip off the old block among university teachers. He loved teaching; he loved his students even more. He encouraged students to visit him frequently as his home, gave them delicious spiced tea and engaged them in Socratic dialogue. He was an authority on Navya Nyaya, but his scholastic interests were broader than this narrow area of specialization in Indian philosophy. During one of those informal evenings at his house he talked about extrasensory perception and suggested Rhine's *New Frontiers of the Mind* and Myers' *Human Personality* for reading. One of the students read these books and at once saw the significance of ESP, if it existed, for our understanding of the nature of man. After further discussions and consultations he made up his mind to take up research in this area. Professor Sen agreed to supervise

By this time our student at Andhra University became a lecturer there in the Department of Philosophy, teaching psychology. There was at that time no separate department of psychology at Andhra. Professor Sen died before the research was completed. The burden of guidance now fell on his successor, Dr. K.S. Murty. Finally, in 1955, a dissertation entitled "Paranormal Cognition: An Essay in Survey of Evidence and Theories," was accepted by the Department of Philosophy for Master of Arts Honors Degree. This is a degree awarded for two years of acceptable research after the M.A. The work was entirely theoretical and made no claim to any significant contribution to the advancement of knowledge. However, it gave our young lecturer an adequate appreciation of the scope and relevance of the field, the necessary insights into the problems, and further motivation to undertake experimental investigations.

The early experiments did not cause much excitement. The results did not refute the null hypotheses. The interest was about to wane when a belated reply came from Dr. J.B. Rhine to a letter written about one year before. This letter added the needed fuel for continued burning of the desire to search for an empirical base to some of the most challenging ideas contained in classical Indian psychology. There was also the desire to go to Duke University and work with Dr. Rhine.

In 1957, an attempt was made to go to Duke University. Our lecturer was selected for a Smith-Mundt Fulbright grant, but failed to get a placement for graduate study in Duke's Psychology Department. The following year the same grant was offered and placement was obtained at the University of Chicago. A British Council fellowship to study at Oxford with Gilbert Ryle was also offered. The subject proposed for study at Oxford was "An Analysis of Parapsychological Concepts." It was not easy to choose between Oxford and Chicago. The decision was finally made to go to America.

When our young Fulbright grantee arrived on the shores of the U.S. in July, 1958, he was warmly received by Dr. Fahler, who was then assisting Dr. Osis at the Parapsychology Foundation. He later met Dr. Osis and others at the Foundation. The next couple of months saw him attending the first annual convention of the Parapsychological Association at the City College of New York and then paying a pilgrimage to the Parapsychology Laboratory at Duke University. These events were all important for one who was at the cross roads of his research career, with many different paths open to him. The personal contacts with the luminaries in the field at the PA convention and outside created bonds of professional identity. It is these bonds that were decisive in firmly holding him to the field.

Three months at the Parapsychology Laboratory before returning to India in January, 1961, gave the needed training in psi experimentation and also the confidence of success as an experimenter. One year of part-time work at Andhra gave promise and further motivation to seek a full time research career in parapsychology. This led to acceptance of the invitation from Dr. J.B. Rhine to spend three years at Duke University. These years were crucial in transforming a tender-minded theoretician into a tough experimental parapsychologist.

While at Duke, our parapsychologist received a letter from Dr. D.S. Kothari, a distinguished physicist who at that time was the Chairman of the University Grants Commission, an agency of the Government which provides funds to Indian Universities. In his letter, Dr. Kothari expressed his appreciation of the work done at Andhra (based on his reading of a review of the book *Psi Cognition*) and wished that a research center for parapsychology would be established in one of the Indian universities. This led to further correspondence, two short visits to India and starting of a program to train a few more Indian parapsychologists at Duke. Thus, the stage was set for our parapsychologist to launch his operations on Indian soil.

THE ANDHRA EXPERIMENT

Andhra University is fifty years old. As Indian universities go, it is one of the older and leading ones. Situated on the uplands of Waltair and surrounded by sea and hills, it houses nearly forty faculties on campus and supervises over one hundred colleges located in the various parts of the coastal districts of Andhra Pradesh. Under the leadership of such outstanding man of education as Dr. C.R. Reddy and Dr. S. Radhakrishnan, it has enjoyed a liberal tradition from its very inception. It has been open to new ideas, never hesitant to encourage new areas of research and study. Andhra is one of the earliest universities in India to start such specialized faculties as Nuclear Physics, Geophysics, Applied Physics, Oceanography and Meteorology, each offering full-fledged Masters and Ph.D. programs.

That Andhra University is hospitable to parapsychology does not surprise any one who is familiar with its workings. The call of parapsychology was heard by one of its leading Vice-Chancellors, Dr. S. Radhakrishnan, who was later to become the President of India. Over forty years ago, this philosopher-statesman wrote: "The investigations of the Psychical Research Society into what are called 'spiritualistic' phenomena have begun to shake the hardiest faith in the truths hitherto accepted in the name of science, that intelligence and memory are functions dependent on the integrity of the cerebral mechanism, which will disappear when that mechanism decays. Some thinkers are now beginning to believe that the brain is by no means indispensable for conscious activities. Psychologists tell us that the human mind has other perceptive faculties than those served by the five senses, and philosophers are slowly accepting the view that we have mental powers other than those of ratiocination and memory conditioned by the brain."[14]

When I returned to India in July, 1965, with the hope of finding a permanent place for parapsychology atAndhra University, there was of course no Radhakrishnan as its Vice-Chancellor, but Dr. D.S. Kothari still continued to be the Chairman of the University Grants Commission. His interest in parapsychology did not slacken. His commitment to provide a place for parapsychology in an Indian university stood. The UGC gave us money to hold a seminar on parapsychology. This seminar was attended by a number of top psychologists in the country. The seminar also had the benefit of the participation of Dr. J.G. Pratt and Dr. Milan Ryzl. It was the forerunner for the formal entry of parapsychology into the university.

Dr. K.R. Srinivasa, Iyengar, who was the Vice-Chancellor when the Department of Psychology and Parapsychology was inaugurated on December 28, 1967, told the story of the establishment of the Department thus:

> It was in January 1963 that, at the instance of the University Grants Commission, one of Professor Rhine's close collaborators, Dr. J.G. Pratt (who had conducted as early as 1933 the Pearce-Pratt Series of

experiments), visited India along with Dr. Ramakrishna Rao, and went round the Universities and met philosophers, psychologists and educationalists interested in parapsychological research, and came to the conclusion that India offered "a tremendous scope for fundamental scientific work in this field." In their Report to the UGC, Dr. Pratt and Dr. Rao recommended the establishment of a Centre of Parapsychology and added:

"There is so much interest in the country, there are so many parapsychical claims that are made, there are so many people eager to work, and there are so many Universities eager to sponsor, we think the Centre is bound to have a great future." Soon afterwards, in March, 1963, the Chairman of the UGC asked my predecessor, Dr. A.L. Narayan, whether the Andhra University would be prepared to establish a Centre of Parapsychology in terms of the Pratt-Rao Report. After some correspondence, the University Syndicate decided in January 1964 to organise "on a modest scale" a Centre of Parapsychology. But things were delayed, partly because Dr. Rao had gone back to the Duke University, and partly because the University and the UGC could not agree about the exact manner in which the proposed Centre or Institute was to be financed. While the University expected assistance on 100% basis, at least for a 5-year period, the UGC only offered to finance the Centre on a sharing basis. In the meantime, on Dr. Rao's return to the Andhra University, he was appointed by the Syndicate in July 1965 as Honorary Organising Officer of the proposed Centre. After further delays, the UGC sent Dr. J.N. Kaul in January 1966 to hold fresh discussions with the Vice-Chancellor and Dr. Rao, and in their report they recommended the establishment of a Composite Department of Psychology and Parapsychology. The UGC, however, having considered the Report, advised the University in March 1966 to include the proposal for the establishment of this Department along with other IV Plan proposals for the consideration of the Visiting Committee. This was the situation when I took charge as Vice-Chancellor.

When the UGC Visiting Committee came to Waltair in December 1966, they considered this as well as our other proposals, and agreed to include it among their recommendations. But the financial climate in the country was far from bright, and several months passed before the UGC accepted most of the Visiting Committee's recommendations, subject to the drastic proviso that we were to count upon only 70% of the originally assigned allocation for the IV Plan period. . .

We have since been able, in spite of the necessity for pruning our earlier IV Plan Schemes, to retain practically intact the proposals with regard to the establishment of the Department of Psychology and Parapsychology. . .

Although there have been exasperating delays and harrowing uncertainties, and although 5 years have passed since the proposal

was first mooted, still I am glad it is now at last taking a definite shape
and the Department of Psychology and Parapsychology is being
inaugurated today. It is always wise and profitable to function on a
wider basis, and I feel that Parapsychological studies stand to gain by
being linked with Psychology from the very beginning.

Parapsychology, as it finally emerged at Andhra in partnership with
psychology is different from what was envisaged when a parapsychology institute was proposed. Admittedly, this was a retreat from the
original grandiose vision. But this retreat was deliberate and carefully
thought out. It was not forced on us; we chose this way. Why this
choice? The memories of the shift from Duke to the Foundation for
Research on the Nature of Man were fresh. It appeared that a research
center with no teaching base has difficulty surviving permanently on
university grounds. Parapsychology as a discipline is not yet ready for
complete independence on campus. For the present it needed to grow
under the shelter of a more firmly rooted discipline. Also, the training
needs of the profession call for an academic program that is noncon-
troversial and acceptable to the academic community as it exists today
and yet one that could serve the peculiar demands of the field.

It was indeed gratifying to read later that Dr. Rhine held similar
views, even though the solutions he suggested were somewhat different. Dr. Rhine wrote: "as for a permanent section or a department of
parapsychology, I am hesitant to think that either the *subject* [italics
mine] or the universities are yet prepared."[15] His solution is "that the
separation be regarded as a permanent one; that the independent
status parapsychologists have already learned to live with be accepted
in all good grace."[16] The Andhra experiment, however, attempted to
effect an integration of psychology and parapsychology. Such an integration appeared possible at Andhra. This seemed also to be the
obvious step if the prefix "para" were to be dropped eventually.

So, the strategy was to build an academically acceptable and noncon-
troversial teaching program which would be a permanent base for
training and research in parapsychology for the interested student,
leaving others free to pursue conventional courses in psychology.
Therefore, it was decided to keep the department open to
psychologists from other institutions for inspection and involvement
and to recruit to the faculty only those who compared favorably in their
psychological training to their counterparts in the other psychology
departments in the country. The inauguration of the department was
so timed that a large number of psychologists from other universities
would be present. The occasion was the annual convention of the
Indian Academy of Applied Psychology. Our faculty members are

encouraged to involve themselves freely with any kind of psychological activity that interests them. My colleagues and I have welcomed every opportunity for interaction with professional psychologists.

This approach appears to have paid good dividends. We no longer feel an isolated bunch or a persecuted lot. Judging by the usual criteria, we feel we have achieved full academic acceptance not only at Andhra, but throughout the country. We have all but succeeded in dropping the prefix "para." Dr. S.P. Adinarayan, a distinguished social psychologist and the Vice-Chancellor of Annamalai University, who reviewed the work of the Department of Psychology and Parapsychology, wrote in his report submitted to the University last year: "Every psychology department has possibly a line or specialization—should this find a place in the name of the department itself? The work done in parapsychology in the department is of paramount importance and should be continued. Since parapsychology is a branch of psychology, the name as it stands is somewhat redundant. Therefore it may be changed to the Department of Psychology."

THE ANDHRA PROGRAM

At the M.A. level we offer one course in parapsychology. The students get full academic credit for it. However, those who are not interested in parapsychology may take a substitute course. In addition, the interested may opt to write an acceptable dissertation for which he gets credit for one additional course. This teaching course has two objectives: (1) to give the student an understanding of the history, scope and methods of parapsychology and to present a review of the research findings and their interpretation, and (2) to train the students in the skills and techniques of psi research. Accordingly the course is divided into two units—one involving the classroom type of instruction and the other laboratory work, including a research project.

In the formulation of this program, we were guided by what Dr. William McDougall said in his Clark University address on "Psychical Research as a University Study." McDougall spoke of three main functions of the university: "First, the function of educating the young people within its gates; secondly, the function of research, of extending the bounds of knowledge; thirdly. . . the function of exerting a controlling influence in the formation of public opinion on all vital matters."[17]

Our course in parapsychology for M.A. psychology students is expected to serve mainly the educational function. This function has two aspects, as pointed out by McDougall, viz., the imparting of knowledge and giving intellectual and moral discipline. McDougall regarded the latter as more important than the rest. It is in this area, he thought, parapsychology has most to contribute to the training of a psychologist. In its demands for patience and resoluteness in attacking problems, for "selective sagacity" to distinguish the relevant from the irrelevant and for a high level of reasoning acumen to draw conclusions, exercising "infinite caution" and "unlimited precautions," parapsychological discipline is unrivalled. Hence the psychology student who takes a properly given course in parapsychology should be all the richer for it. If we are correct in our assumptions and if this is evidenced by the performance of our students, then sooner or later other universities in the country should follow our example.

In our M.A. program we admit eight to twelve students every year. There has been considerable demand for admission. The proportion of those turned down is nearly ten times those admitted. Every year we receive over fifty requests from interested and eligible overseas students, especially from the U.S.A., for information about our teaching program. Our inability to render any financial assistance almost always stands in the way of welcoming the deserving among them. The minimum eligibility for admission to our M.A. course is a bachelor's degree in arts or science. Nearly all the students when they join the department say that they are interested in parapsychology and would like to study it. But these are largely uninformed. Their notions about parapsychology are usually hazy.

The first year M.A. program is concerned with basic psychology. Students are not required to do any formal reading in parapsychology except when they become familiar with some of the standard psi testing procedures as part of their laboratory work for the experimental psychology course. However, the weekly seminars and review meetings provide sufficient opportunity for them to get a "feel" of the field and its controversial nature. By the time the students come to the second year and are ready to decide if they wish to study parapsychology, we find only a few opting for it. Again, some among them who are found wanting in good scholastic habits are dissuaded from choosing parapsychology and diverted to other specialties. Thus, we have built-in safeguards and an effective filtering system so that only those who are properly motivated and have the necessary intellectual competence and scholastic habits to profit by parapsychological training are admitted. Frankly, we are not interested in numbers. More often we find ourselves discouraging rather than persuading students to take up parapsychology.

In addition to the M.A. course in psychology the Department of

Psychology and Parapsychology offers two research degrees—M. Phil. and Ph.D. in parapsychology. The M.Phil. program is of two-year duration after the M.A. The Ph.D. is three years. One could enroll for the P.h.D. without first doing the M.Phil. The first year program for M.Phil. and Ph.D. degrees is identical. The student makes advanced study of parapsychology and research methodology. These are given as reading courses without any formal lectures. At the end of the first year he is required to pass the pre-Ph.D. written and oral examinations in these subjects. The M.Phil. degree is awarded for an acceptable dissertation presented at the end of the second year. The Ph.D. dissertation is expected to be of much higher standard than the M.Phil. We normally send our Ph.D. dissertations to experts outside India for evaluation. We have had in the past such leaders in the field as Dr. Schmeidler, Dr. Pratt and Dr. Van de Castle as our Ph.D. examiners. We believe our M. Phil. and Ph.D. programs serve, in addition to the educational function, the research function as envisaged by Dr. McDougall.

We have recognized the interdisciplinary nature of parapsychology and have therefore also provided for non-psychologists to join our research courses. Theoretically, any Master's degree holder is eligible for admission to either of our research programs, provided he gives evidence of aptitude in and competence for research in parapsychology. But our research admissions so far have been confined largely to those who have had psychology earlier. Since the basic psychology qualification is essential for recruitment to our faculty positions, we would necessarily have difficulty in providing adequate faculty guidance for any research that calls for knowledge of medicine, physics or biology. This indeed is our serious limitation.

Psi is much broader than parapsychology. I like to limit the use of the concept "parapsychology" only to that part of psi which can be properly assimilated and researched by psychologists. Eventually paraphysics, psi biology and medical psi—therapeutic and diagnostic—are bound to assert themselves in gaining a respectable place in physics, biology and medicine. Dr. Rhine has said: "psi research is obviously of special concern to those who are interested in the full range of the unexplored nature of man . . . . When we come eventually to the stage when the *sciences of man* take a pre-eminent position, we shall find that one of the places around the conference table will have to be reserved for parapsychology."[18] I wish to go still further and say that the implications of psi are much wider and encompass the totality of nature. If psi involves a new form of energy or process there is no reason to believe that it is confined only to man or animals. It may be an important ingredient involved in the various manifestations of matter as well. Therefore, the results of psi research may be just as important to physicists as they are to psychologists.

Having come close to dropping the "para" and integrating parapsychology into the general framework of psychology at Andhra, I fear that, if this does happen, it may have a serious limiting and even distorting effect on our knowledge of psi unless it be augmented by something else. I seem to come back to the institute idea of Dr. Rhine. His quest is for a "bold philanthropic offer to establish an institute for parapsychology at a first-rate university. This should, of course, be done with the approval, and even the collaboration, of that university's department of psychology."[19]I venture to add that Andhra University is ready for such a move, if there is an offer. My reason for favoring the institute idea is that collaborative interdisciplinary research and training are essential for an all round understanding of psi. Such research is possible only at an institute which would have on its staff scientists from all the related disciplines. I would not name such an institute the "Institute for Parapsychology." I prefer the name to be the "Institute for Psi Research." Therefore, the next organizational advance at Andhra should be the establishment of the Institute for Psi Research.

Now, what about the impact of the Andhra experiment on other universities in India? Perhaps it is too early to answer this question. But this much can be said. I know of no psychologist who feels threatened because of our existence as parapsychologists. There is at least one more university department of psychology which proposes to start a parapsychology research center. There are a few psychologists, like Dr. Mathew of Kerala University, who were able to obtain small grants for their research in parapsychology. I believe many universities would now be willing to offer a parapsychology course, if they could find among their teaching staff someone capable of teaching it. Since the financial constraints make it difficult to hire an additional teacher, many universities prefer to have one of their teachers trained in parapsychology. I believe a 10-week summer course in parapsychology to which psychologists from other universities could be invited would serve a very useful function to spread parapsychology to other universities. The faculty for this course may be drawn from the various parapsychological centers around the world.

Finally, what about our resources? Since we are an integral part of the University our maintenance is its responsibility. We depend mostly on the University Grants Commission for any developmental activities. I suppose, no one has all that he needs or wishes. If we had more resources we could use them for the following:

(1) Library and laboratory facilities. There is need to strengthen these facilities. I find considerable gaps in our book collection. We apparently have a lot of difficulty in obtaining books for our library, as several titles are simply not available through our book trade. Also we need to get the parapsychological journals by airmail. We seem to suffer from a good deal of information gap. While our laboratory facilities are adequate for the present, a number of items are still on our shopping list.

(2) Fellowships to research students. These are needed to attract good students to parapsychology. In view of the considerable interest shown by students from other countries, we need to have at least one fellowship sufficient to cover the expenses of an overseas student. Fellowships for Indian scholars would be very useful.

(3) A one-time summer institute and workshop for training psychology teachers in parapsychology. An intensive ten-week course with leading parapsychologists of the world as faculty would enable parapsychology to spread to several universities in India. This requires international collaboration.

(4) Institute for Psi Research. The establishment of such an institute has the highest priority in mind. But I realize that this has the least probability of being realized. Perhaps a beginning can be made if we find resources for inviting specialists in other disciplines to spend a year or so at the Department of Psychology and Parapsychology.

In conclusion, I would like to say, if the Andhra experiment is a success to any appreciable extent it is so because of a number of factors. First and foremost is the rare international collaboration and help received with no strings attached. Second is the academic environment in India that is not hostile but hospitable to parapsychology. Third is the availability to Andhra University of a group of trained parapsychologists who have a healthy commitment to the field and possess academic qualifications and competence comparable to others in the university community.

The Andhra experiment is one of the finest examples of international effort and understanding. In time, we hope, Andhra will become an international center where scientists from all parts of the globe work unitedly for the advancement of knowledge concerning the hidden energies of the universe.

REFERENCES

[1] Sankalia Hasmukh, D. *The University of Nalanda*. Madras: B.G. Paul & Co. Publishers, 1934; p. 86.

[2] Mookerji, Radha Kumud: *Ancient Indian Education*. Delhi: Motilal Banarsidass, 1969. p. 566.

³ Eliade, Mircea; *Yoga: Immortality and Freedom*. London: Routledge & Kegan Paul, 1958; p. 201.

⁴ Sankalia Hasmukh, D. *The University of Nalanda*. Madras: B.G. Paul & Co. Publishers, 1934; p. 91.

⁵ Eliade, Mircea: *Yoga: Immortality and Freedom*. London: Routledge & Kegan Paul, 1958; p. 200.

⁶ Sankalia Hasmukh D. *The University of Nalanda*. Madras: B.G. Paul & Co. Publishers, 1934; p. 92.

⁷ *Katha Upanishad.* I. 3. 13.

⁸ Radhakrishnan, S: *Indian Philosophy*. Vol. II. London: George Allen & Unwin, 1927; p. 340.

⁹ Eliade, Mircea: *Yoga: Immortality and Freedom*. London: Routledge & Kegan Paul, 1958; p. 7.

¹⁰ Woods, James H.: *The Yoga System of Patanjali*. Cambridge (Mass.): Harvard University Press, 1914.

¹¹ Dasgupta, Surendranath: *A History of Indian Philosophy*. Vol. I. Cambridge: University Press, 1963; pp.230 ff.

¹² Yogendra, Jayadev and Vaz, J. Clement Eds. *Yoga Today*. Madras: MacMillan Co. of India, 1971.

¹³ Rhine, J.B.: "Psi and Psychology: Conflict and Solution." *J. Parapsychol.*, 1968, 32, p.101-128.

¹⁴ Radhakrishnan, S. *Indian Philosophy*. Vol. II. London: George Allen & Unwin, 1927; p. 336.

¹⁵ Rhine, J.B.: "News and Comments." *J. Parapsychol.*, 1972, 36, p.325.

¹⁶ Rhine, J.B.: "Psi and Psychology: Conflict and Solution." *J. Parapsychol.*, 1968, 32, p. 124.

¹⁷ *William McDougall: Explorer of the Mind*. Compiled and edited by Raymond Van Over and Laura Oteri. New York: Garrett Publications, 1967, p. 72.

¹⁸ Rhine, J.B.: "Psi and Psychology: Conflict and Solution." *J. Parapsychol.*, 1968, 32, p. 127.

¹⁹ Rhine, J. B.: "News and Comments." *J. Parapsychol.*, 1973, 37, p.232.

DISCUSSION

CHILD: I'm very curious to know to what extent the parapsychology courses at Andhra or the other universities where they are taught, differ in their subject matter or their approach because of the rich background of tradition of the paranormal in India that you mentioned at the beginning.

RAO: Your question, Dr. Child, is best answered by referring to a statement Mr. Angoff made when he visited our department in March, 1970, at a time when we were holding our annual review meetings. He said then: "I will confess to a slight disappointment that more work pertaining to phenomena in the Indian environment is not going on. I will also confess to a little disappointment that the work is along conventional or traditional lines." I'm afraid this statement of 1970 is still valid and that we have not yet succeeded in our attempts to *Indianize* parapsychology. Parapsychology courses we teach at Andhra are basically Western-oriented and drawn mostly from the work done in Europe and the United States. We have as text-books for the first course *Parapsychology* by Rhine and Pratt, my book *Experimental Parapsychology* and Myers' *Human Personality*. We do, however, talk about yoga, meditation, altered states of consciousness, and their possible bearing on psi, but we do not have, for example, *Yoga Sutras* of Patanjali as a text for compulsory reading. We have another elective course, Indian Psychology, which goes rather thoroughly into the traditional Indian approaches to the study of man's nature, including the paranormal.

DEAN: Dr. Rao has just been mentioning the connection between the Yogic thought and our Western thought, but more has been made of this. At the Second International Congress of Psychotronics in Monte Carlo, in the abstracts of the proceedings, there was a paper by Charles Musés, the mathematician. He is playing with very interesting mathematics and of course, it is on the boundaries of brain-storming. It hasn't been proved or anything, but it's very interesting for those of us who are interested in creative ideas on how to solve some of the problems we have in parapsychology. He's come up with some formulae which suggest that perhaps what he's working with is the mathematics of consciousness. One of these equations indicates, and—though he may be interpreting it wrongly—he interprets it as meaning that in order that we can be conscious of our external world, it comes in phases and only on every twelfth phase of the cycle can we be conscious of our universe. He then has looked up the books of Patanjali, and in Book IV, Verse 13, he quotes a statement which seems to connect with this modern mathematics that he's doing. The statement says, "The external manifestation of an object occurs,"—and I'm now adding "to our senses, so that we can be aware of our universe"—"it occurs when its three gunas are in the same phase." Now, he interprets gunas in Patanjali's words to mean "space, time and consciousness." If this is true and if it leads to something that's constructive, it will be very interesting, that Patanjali by Yogic methods of meditation, was able to get at this very deep, profound insight back in 300 A.D.

RAO: I am not sure I would agree with the statement of Mr. Dean. First let me confess that I am a bit allergic to a lot of sanctimonious breast-beating that often is the case when we speak of our past achievements. Historically, it is not true to say that what is contained in the *Yoga Sutras* is "the profound insight" of Patanjali obtained through "yogic methods of meditation." All available evidence suggests that Patanjali simply compiled and systematized the beliefs that were existing at his time. I question also the assumption that the three *gunas*, *satva*, *rajas* and *tamas*, may be interpreted as consciousness, time, and space. According to the *Sankhya-yoga* school consciousness is the characteristic attributable only to the *purusha* and not to the *prakriti*. As you know the three *gunas* are characteristics that belong to the *prakriti*, the primordial matter. I am reminded of a day in the 1950s when the Russians sent their first Sputnik into space and we had a meeting organized in the University to discuss the significance of that event. Our Professor of Telugu at that time, who was one of the speakers, read out a few verses from one of our well known epics in which a reference is made to an elephant being thrown into space by the mighty Bhima. It is said that the elephant is still orbiting the earth. The implication is that the Hindus achieved this feat many, many centuries before the Russians did. I am a proud Indian and very fond of my own culture. But I do not consider it necessary to engage in such excessive and imaginary generalizations to establish the greatness of our ancestors.

KRIPPNER: I was very interested in the discussion about the orientation of the parapsychology course at Dr. Rao's university, because I also was there recently, less than a year ago, and had a chance to discuss with the students the outlook that they had on parapsychology and how they might relate it to the Indian tradition. I certainly found no such thing in India as the so-called occult revival in the United States. In fact, it was just the opposite. The Indian students I spoke to were very much against traditional religion because of the really dreadful things that they thought were being done to their country by religious dogma. They accused religion of holding back progress, exacerbating the population problem, increasing the ecology problem, wasting natural resources, etc. They did not want to have anything to do with that particular aspect of occultism. However, they were interested in scientific parapsychology and very grateful for the opportunities that had been provided to study it at their university. I might also say that Dr. Rao's psychology building is a stunning edifice which would be the envy of many people in this country. It is very tastefully designed and well constructed. You go up to the psychology library and there are a number of very beautiful photographs and paintings—one being a painting of Eileen Garret; furthermore there is a Psychophysiology Laboratory which is very well equipped and which has been named in her honor. And then in the library itself, there is a large painting showing Dr. J.B. Rhine and D. Rao the day that Dr. Rao became president of the Parapsychological Association, and was congratulated by Dr. Rhine. So these are some of the very pleasant memories I have of that beautiful building and the dynamic work that is being carried on there.

WHITE: I'd like to ask you, Dr. Rao, if you're entirely pleased with the name change of the department. It sort of eliminates free advertising, as it were.

RAO: I really wanted to have your suggestions on this question at this time because we now have the choice to change the name. I am at this point unable to make up my mind whether the distinctiveness of the department should be maintained by continuing to call it the Department of Psychology and Parapsychology or whether parapsychology should be dropped so as to indicate the natural and the desired integration of psychology and parapsychology, which seems to have come about in India. I would really like to have your comments on this.

JOHNSON: Dr. Rao, you just touched upon Yoga and Yoga's possible bearing on psi. I know I asked you about this seven years ago. What is your present position? Do you believe that yoga has a bearing on psi ability?

RAO: I am afraid, Dr. Johnson, my answer to you today is not very different from the one I gave you years ago. It is not because of any lack of effort on our part but we simply were unable to obtain the results we hoped. I spent nearly two years going about in search of people who claim exceptional psychical powers. My experience has been more a disillusionment than a significant reinforcement of my hope to find a performing yogi who can demonstrate psychic abilities on demand. While I have so far failed to find one who could do even a moderately significant something for me, I found at least four people using sleight-of-hand which my naked eye could easily catch. I have given up any hopeful search for a psychic yogi. I have not been able, however, to convince any of my American friends who come to India in search of just such people. I find some of them agreeing with me only after they had spent three fruitless months in India.

The other line of research, related to this question, is to do psychophysiological studies of developed yogis under laboratory conditions with a view to discovering any unique patterns that may conceivably be related to psi function. We also have plans for starting a centre for voluntary control of internal states, where students practicing such disciplines as Yoga may be given ESP and other tests throughout the period of their training. On the hopeful side, we have the results of studies made by Mr. Dukhan, one of our doctoral students from the West Indies. He obtained interesting results. His subjects did significantly better in ESP tests taken immediately after they had meditated for at least half an hour in comparison to the ESP scores they obtained before meditating. These results are open to several interpretations, but I have no doubt that Mr. Dukhan's study does indicate an important relationship between psi and meditation which deserves further follow up.

VAUGHAN: I was wondering about your own investigations of such people as Sai Baba. Americans I know have gone there and been quite impressed, yet we've had no official reports from India and I wondered what you might say about it.

RAO: First let me make it clear that I did not study Sai Baba. I simply did not have the guts to take up this very important project. I did not think that studying Baba would serve any purpose unless he is prepared to work under my conditions. I would love to work with him if I could feel reasonably confident about the conditions under which I may be permitted to observe his "miracles." I have carefully read several things written about Baba but I have not been able to make up my mind whether going after him would be worthwhile from a scientific point of view.

I did investigate, though, a number of less-known miracle makers. This work has been mainly fruitless. Some are too clever to permit me to observe them under conditions that reasonably rule out alternatives to psi. Others were too naive to practice sleight-of-hand and other cheap tricks that I could easily discover. I am unable so far to find a miracle-maker whom I could confidently recommend to you as a genuine psychic.

NOVILLO: When I went back to my country in 1973, I lectured in parapsychology and asked that the subject be listed in the school of psychology. At first there was resistance. The name does not have good connotations, it doesn't seem to be a science; then I have suggested the term "dynamic of the unconsciousness" as this really is. After some discussion, it was accepted as a new aspect or point of view of the studies dealing with the dynamics of the unconscious in the school of psychology.

RAO: We really have no difficulty in using the word parapsychology. The question I raised is whether parapsychology should find a place in the name of the department. No one has really objected to calling our course, a course in parapsychology, even though some may prefer other names like paranormal psychology. I must make it very clear that

Dr. Adinarayana did not really object to the name as we have it now. His is only a suggestion. He seems to think that it is redundant to call a department the department of psychology and parapsychology since parapsychology is a branch of psychology.

FRANKLIN: The question of whether or not there's any training that can help in parapsychology performance is an interesting one. In the studies at Stanford Research Institute on remote viewing, they found that the average person could do just about as well as the psychics that they had in their group. And then if you asked the question, whether or not one can do any type of training which will increase one's parapsychological capabilities, I think that's a very interesting question. One of my closest friends graduated with honors from Oberlin and worked at Columbia University for his Ph.D., worked under Skinner at Harvard. Then he was head of a section at Bell Labs, worked at Cornell for awhile, and then studied Yoga in India for a year under a teacher. I was amazed about the things that he told me his Yoga teacher could do. I've also read the books of Sri Aurobindo on Yoga, I've read comments by The Mother, and I find repeatedly things that refer to things that I categorize as parapsychological in nature within those Yoga books. So my question, I guess, is do you feel that there are practices within the framework of Yoga that can increase one's parapsychological capabilities?

RAO: One could make an assumption. But I don't really have any data to suggest that practice of a particular kind of Yoga would enable one to develop certain psychic abilities. This is not to dispute the fact that belief in such possibilities has been held for many centuries in our country.

Regarding the observations of your friend, who may be a good psychologist, I would only like to say that the observations people report are very often personal impressions that are largely determined by one's own frame of reference and belief system. Let me illustrate this by my own experience with a friend who is a well-educated, sensible and level-headed man who has two university degrees. He told me once that a Swami had materialized certain things in his hand and his wife's while he was watching. He was apparently very much interested and persuaded me to visit him. He also arranged for an appointment with him at Madras. A senior psychologist, formerly a university professor, and I in the company of my friend observed the Swami "materialize" a few things. We had no difficulty in agreeing among ourselves that the Swami was playing not even a clever trick. I asked my friend, "Why on earth didn't it occur to you that he could have done this to you and your wife?" He said wistfully, "Yes, come to think of it, why didn't it occur to me? I never thought that a Swami would cheat. Why should he cheat? I can understand a magician using a sleight-of-hand. Why should a Swami cheat?" So, you see, the frame of reference of the observer is extremely important. Most people who go to these Swamis and Babas have a frame of reference which accepts these men as holy—and a holy man cheating is a contradiction in terms.

WHITE: I have another question. Are you pessimistic about Yoga?

RAO: I did not say that. At this time I am neither pessimistic nor optimistic. At one time I must say I was optimistic. Now I am not so optimistic. But still I have not reached the point of skepticism.

WHITE: O.K. You said you had gotten, or your students had gotten some results with meditation. Now what I want to know is are you distinguishing between meditation and Yoga?

RAO: These people went through a course of Yoga in an *ashram* in Pondicherry. The ESP tests were given every day following a meditative session. But these people were also practicing physical yogic exercises under the guidance of a swami. While these subjects were not expert yogis, they were all practicing Yoga.

WHITE: But that is Yoga, really.

RAO: Yoga, yes, and then the tests had taken place in a situation where they meditated for at least half an hour before they took the ESP test. The meditation is not of one kind. They have practiced different sorts of, shall I say, eclectic meditation. Meditation is of course an important part of Patanjali Yoga.

WHITE: I see. Thank you.

ONETTO: Two small questions; and a proposition. At the beginning of the paper you said that traditional thinking in India considered Yoga and Tantra as science. Would you personally be more inclined to consider them as religious beliefs and aims—really Yoga and Tantra what they'd like to do and what they want to do, as their last aim is Samadhi, and this is not the aim of parapsychology, and not of any positive science? And the second question is, have you planned with your department to make a survey of spontaneous cases in the future or have you done something along this line? And the proposition is definitely that you maintain the name of your department. I think it's a very good name—"Psychology and Parapsychology." We are still not mature enough for any change in that.

RAO: Regarding some of your reactions to the name, maybe you could give them to me later as we go on with the conference and have occasions to meet. Now let me answer your first question. It is true that the ultimate aim or goal for most Indian thinkers is liberation from the earthly bondages to find identity with the ultimate and escape the cycle of birth and death. But at the same time you could quote a number of passages, and I did in my paper, which say that *tantra* is essentially a method of gaining psychic powers. So, it seems to me that tantra was regarded, at least by some, as a way of obtaining paranormal abilities even though the striving for them was discouraged. The religious motivation has always been one of attaining *moksha,* the ultimate liberation.

As to your second question, regarding spontaneous cases, we haven't started any scheme of surveying or actually soliciting, but we do have a small collection that is gradually accumulating. The other day, when I was talking to Dr. Palmer in Charlottesville, I was thinking it might not be a bad idea to do a survey of psychic experiences among Indians similar to the one he did in Charlottesville.

PARAPSYCHOLOGY AND EDUCATION

Martin Johnson

When I first read the title of the topic of this conference my first thought was that I should put the entire emphasis upon the type of research and study program that we are offering at the Parapsychology Laboratory of the State University of Utrecht, the Netherlands. On second thoughts however, I realized that a number of issues which can be discussed under the heading of Parapsychology and Education is very extensive. I chose to consider the following:

1. Some facts about our laboratory;
2. Study program;
3. Research projects in progress;
4. Publications and system of publishing.
5. Parapsychology: Implications for science, and our responsibilities as educators.

The Parapsychology Laboratory of the State University of Utrecht was established in 1974, in connection with the inception of the, at least formally speaking, first regular chair and professorship in parapsychology in Europe. The laboratory has an independent status in relation to the Psychological Laboratory of the University. Our laboratory is nevertheless located within the same building, and we have the privilege of sharing the library, as well as having full access to the equipment and apparatus within the Psychological Laboratory. We have, of course, a budget of our own. Our laboratory has four full-time positions, one of which is intended for a visiting research worker.

Visiting research workers can stay for a maximum of one year, and a minimum period of two months. During the stay, the visiting research worker is free to take up any type of research work, assuming of course, that the type of work can be carried out within our laboratory. There is, however, a certain emphasis on experimental work, but a visiting research worker is also allowed to carry out a theoretical study, or use his or her time writing up an article or a thesis based on data which have been collected previously elsewhere. It is also expected that the visiting research worker take part in some of the educational activities in order to enrich the program. During the first year and a half of our existence we have had four visiting research workers.

EDUCATIONAL PROGRAMS

For post-graduate students in psychology (the majority of whom are working on their Ph.D theses) a study program comprising ten problem-orientated seminars was presented. The main objective of these seminars was and is to introduce the students at this level to selected parapsychological problems. A strong emphasis was put on the methodological aspects of how to approach the research problems. The methodological problems were to a large extent approached from the point of view of the philosophy of science.

During the Fall semester of 1974, the topics of the seminars were mainly devoted to basic methodological issues, illustrated by problems from parapsychological research. During the Spring semester of 1975 stronger emphasis was placed on purely parapsychological matters, but of course involving a strong methodological connection. A list of the topics treated in the two series of seminars may be informative:

Fall-Semester of 1974

1. The Task of Methodology.
2. "Scientific Method" in Behavioral Science.
3. Laws, Functions, Contents, and Types.
4. The Place of the Experiment in Science.
5. The Place of Measurement in Science.
6. The Function of Statistics in Science.
7. The Place of Models in Science.
8. The Use of Theories in Science.
9. Explanations in Science.
10. Discussions of the above Topics, and Evaluation of the Course.

Spring-Semester of 1975

1. Introduction to Parapsychology.
2. Facts and Beliefs in Parapsychology.
3. Spontaneous Cases. A Challenge.
4. A Comparison of Parapsychological and Psychological Journals.
5. Psi and Subliminality.
6. Poltergeist-phenomena.
7. The Psychobiology of Psi.
8. The Survival Issue.
9. The Challenge of Precognition.
10. Models of Control and Control of Bias in Experimental Parapsychology, and Evaluation of the Course.

Prior to each seminar, the participants were given rather extensive reading assignments which they had to complete beforehand. The ideal maximum number of participants in any group should not exceed fifteen. Participants were given academic credit for attending the seminars.

For freshmen in psychology, a three week course was given. This course was very elementary. The participants received a general introduction to parapsychology and research methodology, including some statistics. They had to carry out a variety of small experiments under supervision, the results of which they had to evaluate.

There exist possibilities to do thesis work on a parapsychological topic, but since there is no sub-faculty of parapsychology, the thesis has to be defended within the sub-faculty of psychology (which in turn belongs to the faculty of the social sciences).

As a general policy we would not recommend as a first alternative, that a person write his thesis on an exclusively parapsychological topic; we would rather suggest that the person select a topic which is of interest and relevance to both psychology and parapsychology. This policy is based on considerations concerning the chances of obtaining a position after completing the Ph.D. work.

RESEARCH PROJECTS IN PROGRESS

The notion of a relationship between ESP and subliminal processes is an old one. The controversy about the existence and character of subliminal perception has ceased in recent years, and has made way for psychodynamic interpretations.

Professor Kragh's Defense Mechanism Test (DMT) has now been in use for more than a decade, both in studies of perception-personality and as a predictor of scoring behavior in an ESP task. The test can be described as a projective one. A tachistoscopic technique is utilized and "threatening" pictures like those of the Thematic Apperception Test are presented. The DMT was introduced into parapsychology by the present speaker in 1963, during a stay at the Duke Laboratory. The main discovery, based on results from a number of studies, seems to be that the DMT is a useful instrument for the prediction of a subject's scoring direction. By and large, subjects manifesting a low level of Perceptual Defensive Organization (PDO) in their protocols (thought of as being related to a low level of anxiety proneness) tend to score *above* M.C.E., whereas certain other types of PDO seem to be related to the psi-missing syndrome. Extensive studies are being carried out to try and find out more about these and a few other suggestive relationships.

Attempts are also being made to collect and analyse DMT data from subjects who, on the one hand, have manifested very pronounced extra-chance scoring in a laboratory setting or who, on the other hand, have experienced or performed things in a real-life context which lead them to believe, and perhaps others too, that they possess paranormal abilities.

Another line of research within the subliminal field which has been pursued for some time is related to the so-called Pötzl-effect. Here attempts are made to Pötzl-influence a subject's scoring behavior by means of subliminally exposed "micro-traumatic" stimuli-stimulus concepts which in subsequent ESP experiments will be used as one category of targets in a multiple-choice test situation. It is hypothesized that this procedure of "subliminal induction" will, in one way or another, influence a subject's psi-vigilance. So far the findings have not substantiated this surmise in a clear-cut way.

Recently a new approach has been introduced in which subliminal stimulation is utilized as an independent variable. The experiment has both a cognitive part and an ESP part. Two experimenters take part in the experiment , and the procedure is based upon individual testing. The subjects are given a problem-solving task which is supposed to be rather absorbing. One presumes that the task is interrupted just before the subjects arrive at the correct solution to the problem. After an intermission, a subliminal stimulus is given. Fifty percent of the subjects, this number being randomly determined, are given a subliminal stimulus depicting the correct solution, whereas the remaining fifty percent receive a subliminal stimulus depicting an inadequate solution to the problem. After another intermission the ESP part of the experiment is administered by the other experimenter. The subject is instructed to use "his intuition" to pick out the envelope which he thinks contains a target depicting the correct solution to the problem-solving task. In this multiple-choice "pick-out" test p is $1/5$; $q = 4/5$.

Each subject carries out 50 trials. His degree of success is not evaluated during the test session. During the course of the experiment neither of the experimenters is aware as to which type of subliminal stimulus a certain subject has received. So far a pilot-study involving 54 subjects has been carried out. No clear-cut overall outcome was observable.

Does distance affect paranormal communication? For a long time this challenging question has been asked. One of the weaknesses of almost all the studies which so far have been carried out in order to test such a distance-in-space effect, is the fact that either the experimenter or the subjects, or both, have been cognitively aware at least of the fact that a distance parameter has been involved in the experiment. Hence the expectancies of the experimenter, the subjects or their combined working may have exerted an influence upon the outcome of the experiment (here I am supposing that extrachance scoring occurred and that that scoring was attributable to the operation of psi).

For a couple of years now, I have been working on the outline of what is both a complicated and a rather sophisticated ESP-Distance Experiment, which under favorable conditions may yield important and informative results. The experiment will be carried out in close cooperation with Mr. Einar Sverre Pedersen (E.S.P.), well-known for his pioneering work on polar navigation, which made it possible for Scandinavian Airlines to be the first airline to introduce the Polar Route into their schedule.

A few of the main features of the study should now be briefly mentioned.

a) the subjects will not, by means of normal cognition or in-ference, be aware that they are taking part in an ESP experiment involving the distance parameter;

b) the person (E.S.P.) who will be responsible for the assignment of the target sequences for each of the subjects will not be aware of the identity of the subjects; nor will he be aware of their location;

c) the administrator of the study (myself) will not be able, except by means of ESP, to trace the location of the above mentioned Mr. Pedersen and the targets at the announced time of the experiment;

d) the target sequences, with a special coding for each of the subjects, will be sent by Mr. Pedersen, (also responsible for the assignment of the targets), to a computer center, where the information will be fed into a computer. The corresponding sequences of calls made by each of the subjects will also be sent to the computer center, where the information (with the identification code for each subject) will be stored in the computer.

e) by utilizing a certain design characteristic, incorporated in the outline of the experiment, some possibilities will exist to find out if precognition alone could account for a possible overall extra-chance scoring.

f) the computer will be programed to decipher the distance code and to evaluate the possible influence of the distance parameter.

It should be mentioned that the distance between the targets and the subjects (subjects will be located in at least three different countries) will range from a few miles to thousands of miles, and that such a change in distance can be brought about in a few hours. According to present planning, this semi-computerized ESP-Distance Effect Study will commence at the beginning of 1976.

Does ESP function in everyday life without being noticed? How could such a hypothesis be tested? It is reasonable to suppose that the advantages of testing ESP in a laboratory setting are partially offset by factors such as lack of real-life challenge, personal significance for the subject, and decline of the subject's motivation, etc. Dr. Rex Stanford and myself have tried to tackle this problem, quite independently of each other, and to outline test-situations which retain the control advantages of the laboratory, while a subject is placed in a real-life high-motivational situation, and is totally unaware that he is taking part in an ESP test. A couple of years ago I carried out three experiments in which university students participated. They were given a written exam in psychology. The exam consisted of eight questions, each followed by a blank space large enough for a short answer. The test sheets were attached to the front and back of a large, sealed envelope. Inside, underneath the appropriate spaces, attached to each side of a piece of cardboard of the same size as the test sheets, were copies of the front and back sheets respectively. On the sheets within, unknown and invisible to the subjects, were correct answers to four of the eight questions. For each subject a random procedure selected which four of the eight questions would have a "correct target."

The object of the investigation was to discover how well the students performed on the "correct" target questions (the ones backed by answers), compared with the "nontarget" questions. Because "target answers" were provided for only half the number of questions, each subject was able to act as his own control. In experiment 1 and 2 the information related to the target answers was correct, whereas in study 3, *incorrect* target answers were used. The evaluation of the answers was made following a rather detailed manual. The ratings were made blindly and independently by two raters. The inter-rater reliability was at quite an acceptable level. In all three studies, the unseen answers seemed to influence the quality of the subjects' own answers in the expected direction in studies 1 and 3 to a statistically significant level.

The findings seem strong enough to warrant replication and more extensive application, and we are now busy developing new types of disguised ESP tests—tests which nevertheless are still accessible to a statistical evaluation.

Recently we designed and carried out a pilot-study in which a test designated as the test of the "Hidden Dutch Cities and Villages" was used. The same rationale was used as in the case of the written academic exam. A subject is given a test sheet attached to a sealed envelope. On the sheet there is a square comprising 567 letters, arranged in 27 lines times 21 lines. The letters are to a certain extent arranged randomly. At the bottom of the sheet there is a list of 18 Dutch cities and villages. The names of the cities and villages are embedded within the square of letters. In this cross-word-like pattern, six of the geographical names are spaced horizontally, six vertically, and six diagonally. The test is presented as both a cognitive and a perceptual one, and each subject is given 10 minutes to try and find as many of the names as possible. Inside the envelope, unknown and invisible to the subject, is a copy of the sheet. For half the group of subjects, the geographical names on the target sheet are encircled and have locations identical to those on the test sheet; for the other half, the names on the target sheet are encircled but displaced in relation to those on the test sheet.

The first study, involving 54 subjects, did not substantiate the hypothesis regarding a general influence from the disguised targets, but the study will be extended and modified, and the subjects who produced extra-chance scoring will be re-tested. By and large we are working hard on the development of this area. A very interesting type of ESP test, disguised as a reaction-time test, is just in the process of being introduced.

Our present visiting research worker, Mrs. Christa Lübke (from Freiburg Institute, Germany), has outlined and will very shortly commence a rather extensive study on the effect of an experimenter's expectancy upon a subject's cognitive, perceptual-motor, as well as ESP performance. She intends to use this study for her Ph.D. thesis in psychology.

Recently, parapsychology has been the object of studies; 1) from a sociological point of view, 2) from the point of view of the history of science. I strongly believe in the usefulness of cooperation between parapsychology and philosophers of science. So far, surprisingly few philosophers of science have indicated an interest in parapsychology. Dr. Michael Scriven and the Swede Ingemar Nilsson seem to be exceptions here. It is my impression that philosophers of science are, on the whole, not very familiar with our field and its findings. Even such a distinguished philosopher of science as Mario Bunge seems to be very ignorant regarding modern research standards in parapsychology. In his well-known textbook entitled *Scientific Research* (1967) he claims that parapsychology is a good example of a pseudo-science, as according to him we do not use open hypotheses. I do not believe that we have really succeeded in propagating our findings in a clear and informative way. Here I see an educational responsibility and a challenge. I feel too, that this would pay off well. We, on our part, would benefit very much from a feedback of constructive criticism of our field from philosophers of science. Mr. Nilsson, at the University of Gothenburgh, Sweden, is well acquainted with the history of parapsychology and the present picture of problems and results, with their claimed implications. He is a well-trained psychologist, as well as a historian of science, although his special field is the philosophy of science. Because of this background and his keen interest in parapsychology, we decided to invite him for a couple of months as a research associate. He chose to write a couple of articles on the topic "The Paradigm of the Rhinian School", articles which are just in the process of being printed.

The main reason to start anpsi studies lies in the potentials which are offered by this research for studying brain processes associated with psi activity. Before this stage is reached some conditions have to be fulfilled. Electro-physiological research requires a heavy investment in money and time, so before commencing with such experiments one should be fairly certain that during the experiments the subjects will show psi activity. Therefore our research is aimed, in the first place, at finding a set of experimental variables which will enhance psi vigilance, or finding a hereditary effect that will enable us to breed "gifted" subjects. Up till now our efforts have been concentrated on manipulating experimental variables. However, although some experiments show significant results, the total outcome of all these experiments is disappointing, as regards finding a consistent pattern in experimental conditions associated with psi activity. Nevertheless, Dr. Schouten is continuing his studies and hopes, by exploring new techniques, to be able to obtain more satisfactory results.

A second line of research carried out by Dr. Schouten concerns psychophysiological studies. These studies are based on either a "transmission" of emotions, or on arousal effects. A major problem encountered in these experiments is, that a subject reacts to an emotionally stimulated "sender" by showing a rise in his arousal level, which lasts much longer in time than the specific arousal effect induced in the sender. Besides this, some methodological problems, concerning the definition of what exactly constitutes an ESP response in this experimental situation, have still to be solved.

Mr. Henk Boerenkamp, one of our staff-members, is carrying out a rather extensive study on selected subjects or "paragnosts." There are parapsychological as well as psychological aspects which are considered in this study, among other things including a micro-analysis of the perceptual as well as social interaction between the sensitive and the sitter. The study is intended for a Ph.D thesis in psychology.

In addition to the more elaborate research projects just mentioned some preliminary work has been carried out, on a strictly methodological basis, in the two following areas:

(1) Attempts to try and outline new types of "detectors" to illustrate that something is "out there" in the vicinity of a target, when a subject reports an OBE related to the target;

(2) Development of methods by means of which alternative hypotheses articulated in "survival research" can be tested.

PUBLICATIONS

Closely related to the carrying out of research programs is the communication of the results. Here I take pleasure in drawing your attention to the fact that we have recently established a periodical identified as the *European Journal of Parapsychology*. The journal will appear twice a year. The main emphasis will be on experimental articles, but theoretical articles will also be welcome. The latter category should be concerned with issues such as definitions in parapsychology, or design of experiments, or with the development of useful methods for the evaluation of parapsychological results or observations. It should be stated that theoretical must not be viewed as antithetical to experimental, since theories are just as important for scientific understanding as experimental data are for theories. It should also be understood that experiments are no more and no less than observations made under rare and special circumstances, which we ourselves choose, or at best "only experience carefully planned in advance," as R.A. Fisher put it.

When it comes to the ideal of science to which we adhere, we have to admit that we are rather strongly influenced by Karl Popper's school of thought, although one should always recall that no single current approach to the philosophy of science is free from serious and fundamental objections. At any rate, we sympathize with the idea that it should in principle be possible to put a theory to a severe test of falsification before one adopts it as a useful tool in science. I personally share Sir Karl's view, that the more complicated a theory is, the less it says, for the harder it becomes to falsify and the easier it becomes for those who defend it to "immunize" the theory. Another hallmark of the *European Journal of Parapsychology* will be the avoidance of selective reporting, that is, the tendency to bury negative results and only to publish studies that "turn out." For one thing, we believe that there may be a chance to learn something important even from negative findings; for another, the policy of only accepting "supporting" findings may very well exert a strong temptation to "doctor" one's data. As a practical rule, we suggest that the acceptance or the rejection of a manuscript should take place prior to the phase when the experimental data are collected. The quality of the design and methodology, and the rationale of the study, should be judged as *per se* more important than the level of significance of the outcome of the study. We also believe that this editorial policy should save the journal from becoming a graveyard for all the studies which do not "turn out." We shall work hard to enlarge our editorial staff in such a way, that most European countries will have a representative on it.

The main objective of the journal, as we see it, is to stimulate and facilitate the furthering of European endeavors in experimental and allied fields of parapsychology. However, contributions from authors outside Europe are also warmly welcomed. We would like to think that the quality of the articles will maintain such a standard that they can match those appearing in the leading American contemporaries. In this way we may be able to establish a sense of friendly competition with the American journals and our colleagues there, to the benefit of our field in general.

The establishment of a *European Journal of Parapsychology* is hopefully one of the first steps in bringing about a closer cooperation between parapsychologists in Europe. Cooperation between Edinburgh, Freiburg, and Utrecht has been initiated, and I am convinced that a pooling of our know-how and resources will be helpful in improving the quality of the research programs, as well as the educational programs. We also propose to reinforce this cooperation by arranging regional meetings at least once a year. I believe there exist possibilities for establishing a European Parapsychological Association, although I am not quite certain how such an organization should be formally affiliated with the Parapsychological Association.

Besides educational responsibilities within the framework of the University, there are also extramural ones. A strong public interest in parapsychological matters is shown by individuals, organizations, and mass media.

I am afraid that representatives of the press, radio, and TV, are too often biased in favor of the sensational and appealing news, rather than the releasing of subject-matter information in its popularized form. At least during the development phase of our laboratory we have had to curtail our extramural activities rather severely, to be able to manage what we consider as the high priority tasks.

Finally, I would like to make a few statements in my capacity as educator in parapsychology. I must confess that I have some difficulties in understanding the logic of some parapsychologists when they proclaim the standpoint, that findings within our field have wide-ranging consequences for science in general, and especially for our world picture. It is often implied that the research findings within our field constitute a death blow to materialism. I am puzzled by this claim, since I thought that few people were really so unsophisticated as to mistake our concepts for reality. I am, of course, just as puzzled by the attempt to unify science and religion based on parapsychological findings. Here I am thinking of Dr. Mitchell's bold enterprise. I deeply respect his learned involvement and his beliefs, but his position, viewed from an epistemological point of view, is not convincingly strong. He seems to believe in the so-called physio-teleological proof of the existence of God, a way of viewing Man and his Universe which has a long and venerable history, but its weakness is commonly recognized among theologians, philosophers, and philosophers of science.

I am sure that it is not of any great help to say that Dr. Mitchell enjoys the company of many respected and distinguished men of science such as Eddington, Einstein, Jeans and Lundmark, to mention a few names. It is hard to deny however, that the motivation behind parapsychological research has, from the very beginning, been religious rather than purely scientific. I would not like to go as far as to say that parapsychology will not perhaps provide us with knowledge relevant to the understanding of some religious phenomena, but I believe that we should not make extravagant and, as I see it, unwarranted claims about the wide-ranging consequences of our scattered, undigested, indeed rather "soft" facts, if we can speak at all about facts within our field. I firmly believe that wide-ranging interpretations based on such scanty data tend to give us, and with some justification, a bad reputation among our colleagues within the more established fields of science. These critical words do not imply that I am not aware of the fact that almost every theoretical system involves some aspects of a particular world picture.

This is the case, even in fields which are well established and enjoy the reputation of being "pure" sciences. Even there, you will find presuppositions and traditional ways of viewing. These presuppositions are not necessarily articulated, but taken for granted, and transmitted via the educational process.

As an educator in parapsychology I would also like to create suspicion among my students for all types of scientisms. Scientisms are no more and no less than pernicious exaggerations of the function and status of science, or of a scientific paradigm, at a certain time in a certain cultural setting. The risk of relying too strongly on a scientism is highlighted by the much quoted case of the French Academy towards the end of the eighteenth century, when it declared that the idea of meteorites sometimes falling from the sky was a superstition, unworthy of their enlightened times. We are no less dependent on theory and presuppositions for distinguishing between facts and superstition.

And then let me just touch upon the concept of repeatability! May I remind you of the highly stimulating dialogue on this topic by Dr. J.B. Rhine and Dr. John Beloff! I certainly agree with Beloff that we, in the present situation, are lacking a highly repeatable experiment, and that our situation would be somewhat better off if we did happen to have such a thing. (Note that Dr. Beloff does not inform us about what kind of requirements he has in mind as to the level of reproduceability he considers as acceptable, as opposed to non-acceptable.) As I see it, Beloff highlights the fact that experimental parapsychology is still a rather "immature" science. (According to Imre Lakatos "mature" science consists of research programs, whereas "immature" science consists of a mere patched-up pattern of trial and error.) As an educator however, I would like to make a rather pedagogical point related to the doctrine of repeatability being a sine qua non in experimental research.

May I remind you of the phlogiston theory! With this theory *accurate predictions could be made*; different scientists could *replicate* each others results. In other words, *a high degree of repeatabiliiy thus existed*, and nevertheless it turned out that the theory was false, since it was based on erroneous propositions as to the nature of matter! What I here want to say is, that not even the joint criteria of *repeatability,* and having a *theory* by which they could make rather adequate *predictions,* was enough to constitute a reliable line of demarcation between what was "scientific" and what was not.

At any rate, I would like to suggest that we, as parapsychologists, strive to keep an open mind on every issue, no matter how baffling or incredible it may appear at first glance. As scientists, we have to take certain risks, for instance in choosing certain statements and data as the starting points for our work, and temporarily at least, we have to ignore and live with conflicting findings, until such a time that our research projects have reached a certain level of development. At the same time as I am asking for a certain persistence and endurance in our work, I see it, however, as a duty to protest against the regrettable habit of using parapsychology as a kind of trash can for all mysterious and occult ideas, no matter how poorly validated they are. We should not be afraid to confess that we are badly lacking a consensus as to what is paranormal and what is not. Based on previous experience, I suspect that the readers of our articles will be easily led to believe, that there really does exist a consensus on the "paranormal" character of all the peculiar and disparate effects reported in our publications; effects which may not have more in common than the fact that they are hard to explain. What I would here like to stress is that intellectual honesty does not consist in trying, by any means, to prove one's position; rather it involves trying to specify the conditions under which one is willing to give up one's position.

I have been pleading for a mixture of open-mindedness, self-criticism, endurance, and flexibility, in our behavior as research workers and educators. Further, we should avoid thinking that everyone who disagrees with us and rejects our claims, is an ignorant, unsophisticated being. I adhere to Popper's view that there is a certain need for dogmatism in science: "the dogmatic scientist has an important role to play. If we give in to criticism (and wild ideas) too easily, we should never find out where the real power of our theories lies".

In this closing section, I have to make a confession which may sound paradoxical. One of the reasons why I am interested in parapsychology is the cryptic character of the data. My position, simply stated, is that sometimes data however "odd" they may look, may provide a point of departure for very fruitful research and for significant theoretical advances. At the same time, one should remain very much aware that some "odd" out of place data may turn out to be an artifact, depending on errors of observation and interpretation. In other words: data may seem to be cryptic because there is really nothing to be explained except the artifact. I suggest that we, as parapsychologists and educators, should be courageous enough to admit that we often may be dealing with mere artifacts.

For quite a time it has been the popular view that the natural sciences are the paradigm of knowledge. This view has been systematized in various types of positivist philosophy. I suspect that my way of appreciating the paradigm of knowledge shows me to be a child of my time. There are moments, I confess, when I tend to think that paranormal phenomena cannot be properly understood until we have been able to create new ideals of science.

I am far from certain how one might be able to initiate such a process. At any rate, it may be of some educational value to dwell upon the following statement by Paul Feyerabend: "the sciences after all, are our own creation, including the severe standards they seem to impose upon us. It is good to be constantly reminded of the fact that science as we know it today is not inescapable, and that we may construct a world in which it plays no role whatsoever".

DISCUSSION

RAO: Dr. Johnson, I don't know if I understood correctly the point you are making. If I am wrong, please correct me. You seem to think that we should not exaggerate the implications and significance of parapsychological findings and that they are not as terribly important as several of us seem to think. If this is what you said, I'm afraid I have to disagree with you and I will tell you why. Now, if a person is making exaggerated claims in terms of reaching beyond the results he has, I agree with you, and I think we have to be humble enough to limit the impact of our findings in terms of their range to very specific and narrow limits that judgment would allow. But I would not be involved in research in this field, where the possibility of finding the phenomena is so minimal and the percentage of its manifestations so minute, unless I'm convinced that this, when found, is going to have enormous implications. I feel it does. For one thing, parapsychological findings raise serious doubts of the adequacy of the dominant paradigms in current science. This to my mind is more important than anything else I know in psychology. I recall reading Dr. Beloff's book *The Existence of Mind*, in which he considers parapsychology to be "the ultimate battle ground on which the mind-body controversy must be fought out." If what I am saying makes any sense, the implications of parapsychological findings are extraordinarily important to anyone whose business it is to deal with ideas, and I think man's business is, to a significant degree, to deal with ideas after he learned to fill his stomach. So I must very respectfully disagree with you, Dr. Johnson. Parapsychological findings, if true, are tremendously significant to our understanding of man.

JOHNSON: Thank you, Dr. Rao, for your viewpoints. I think that it's partly a misunderstanding because I had to abbreviate what I had written. I think that very often, just as in psychology, we have very scanty data and we should be very careful when it comes to the interpretation of the data. Personally I wouldn't be in the field if I didn't think that it's important and that the findings are important. But sometimes I think that we have too much popular writing and too wide-ranging interpretations. Well, I have nothing against it, even when scientists themselves do it, if they are using "if," or "maybe," or saying "this is a kind of science-fiction which you are allowed to carry out," if you declare these are not facts but possibilities. That's my attitude.

ROGO: I'm very happy to hear about the *European Journal of*

Parapsychology, and probably like many others here, I have many questions about the editorial policy of the journal. First of all, is it going to be devoted exclusively to experimental work, or will it also publish papers on theoretical and historical aspects? Will American parapsychologists be allowed access to publishing in this journal? Do I take it that the journal will be in English and when will it start to appear, and will it be a PA affiliated journal?

JOHNSON: Well, I'll try to answer your questions. There will be, I believe, a certain emphasis on experimental work, but it's not exclusively on experimental work. If you have a theoretical paper, you can publish it. Everything is relative in this world and the criteria can always be discussed. I'm very pleased to announce that Dr. John Beloff will be on the editorial board, as a British representative; Dr. Bender will be a representative of Germany. You can write a theoretical paper and I think you could also use case studies if you are interested in that and the journal is open; American contributors are welcome, of course. I don't know yet if it's possible to affiliate this journal in some way with the Parapsychological Association. These are matters which we have to discuss later. Now, the first issue will appear in October, and there will be two issues a year, published in English.

RHINE: Dr. Johnson, about the journal, in which I'm very interested, as I am in your whole policy and program—just a little question bothers me. Are you going to be open to publication of all the chance reports that come from around the world?

JOHNSON: I beg your pardon, sir?

RHINE: Are you going to accept for publication all the reports of chance results (I call them failure reports)? Are you going to be open for that, because if you are, I want to know where we can advise people to send such reports. You see, we had the idea for the *Journal of Parapsychology* many years ago that in this field if you don't get any evidence of psi you have nothing to experiment with; you have nothing but your failure to report. We settled on a simple program of agreeing to publish a short abstract, not ignoring the fact of the failure. The editors furnish a copy of the complete paper on request.

JOHNSON: Well, as I put it, by using the editorial policy of basing the acceptance or rejection of the manuscript prior to the phase when the experimental data are collected, we thought that we could avoid turning the journal into a graveyard of all the studies which didn't turn out. That means that one should, beforehand, if possible, if feasible, decide whether one should accept or reject a manuscript, try to acquaint the authors with this policy and just see how it works out. We may have to surrender. That's quite possible.

PALMER: I am, like Mr. Rogo and Dr. Rhine, very happy to hear about this new journal and wish it a great deal of success. Also, I very strongly endorse your policy of trying to accept or reject experimental papers prior to knowledge of results. I don't know how it will work out; I certainly hope it will work out, and perhaps it will be a precedent for other journals. Just a brief comment about this problem of publishing only positive results. It seems to me selecting only positive experiments for reporting is in principle the very same thing as selecting only the positive runs in an experiment, selecting those out and reporting them—we certainly never do that for runs and I don't see why we should do it for experiments either. But I do have one question I'd like to ask you about policy, and that is, whether the editorial decisions will be based solely on methodological adequacy, or on the likelihood of the experiment coming out, being successful. I know this kind of criterion has been used by certain review committees for government agencies. I was wondering whether that kind of a criterion will be applied at all, or whether decisions will simply be based on methodological adequacy?

JOHNSON: Well, Dr. Palmer, I'm afraid I can't give you a very specific answer. I believe one could say that there are different rationales for a hypothesis put forward in a paper, and if it's a very unlikely one, I suspect that the editors will be prejudiced against it. I'm using the word "prejudice," but at the same time, I hesitate a bit because sometimes, but very rarely, you may miss something very important when it comes to unorthodox hypotheses.

NOVILLO: We are talking about the mind, its dynamics and effects. The proper subject of parapsychology is the mind and thus, we must ask ourselves: "what is the mind?" To plan a program of investigations, to research correctly, to lecture properly, we must understand what the mind means to us.

JOHNSON: My answer is rather short. Because I don't know very much about what constitutes the mind, I can't speak much about it. That's my answer.

TART: A comment on your editorial selection policy. It sounds a lot like the procedure used to review grant applications, looking at the methodology alone. It usually works out well. There are some apochryphal stories around, however, about investigators who first do the research, and when it's done, then they apply for the grant for it, and spend the money on their next research project. This gives them a great deal of freedom. Unfortunately, the story goes that every once in a while a grant committee will turn them down, saying this research can't possibly work out, even though these people have already done it successfully. You might consider a two-phase policy, where you'd review studies without results, and then give the reviewers a second chance with the results.

SCHMEIDLER: I want to congratulate you on that brilliant editorial policy. I particularly like it because it gives the editors a change to suggest the changes which it's just not practical to ask for after research is completed but which so often an investigator will gladly put in when the change is suggested in advance. I was particularly interested in the possibility of using the standards of dissertation committees, of having the author state in advance the hypothesis that he wants to test, which would make a nice clear distinction between the post hoc conclusions which sometimes are the strongest ones, and the initial hypothesis. If you could have somebody looking over the investigator's shoulder, making sure that the subjects are run after the proposal is put in, I think that you might have very constructive input into parapsychology. And I hope it would spread into other fields too.

STANFORD: I simply want to congratulate you on the journal and also what sounds like a very fine broad-range constructive program at the Utrecht center. Now, I want to comment specifically on the editorial policy which sounds to me to be a good one, and just simply to add some reinforcement behind that. I think one of the things that the willingness to regularly publish negative results can accomplish, is something very useful for future research. Aside from the fact of not attempting to replicate an experiment that has already failed in replication, it can also aid the ability of a person who is familiar with the literature, to estimate the possible strength of the effect that he may wish to study in an experiment. He can get an idea of the statistical parameters of the population that he's studying and therefore can design his experiment, including sample size, more intelligently and stand a better chance of replicating someone's results or extending those results, etc. If you don't have the total picture of results, this is very difficult.

John Palmer has beautifully exemplified this in one of his sheep/goat reviews, in which he showed that much of the work that isn't statistically significant on the sheep/goat effect, is, nonetheless, in line with the idea that there are population differences between sheep and goats. But if we didn't have the non-significant experiments available, we wouldn't know about the strength of the effect, and couldn't apply that in future research on that topic.

Now the second point is that the publication of negative results, so-called, allows not only the elimination of certain sorts of artifactual findings from the supposed findings of the field, but it also does something else. I think it may encourage cross-experimenter replication, which is good—and it's particularly important, I think, because we all know that there is an experimenter effect in the psi area; possibly one that is psi-mediated as well as one that is socially-mediated.

RAO: As an investigator in the field, I would warmly welcome the opportunity to publish papers incorporating experiments that did not yield significant results for at least one reason, viz., I would have a few more to add to the list of published papers. But, thinking of the field as a whole and in the context of making certain policy recommendations for the consideration of those who are in charge of journals in our field, I would like to make a few suggestions, especially concerning the reporting of negative results.

The implication of Dr. Palmer's comment that nonpublishing of an experiment is equivalent to selection of data in a given experiment is valid, it seems to me, only if an experimenter who, let us say, did three experiments to test a variable, chose to report only the results of a single experiment which alone yielded significant results. I do not think this implication holds good in a number of other cases when the investigator chooses not to publish his data. I will explain why this is so.

The phrase "negative results" is an ambiguous one and means several things depending on the context of its use. Firstly, it may mean that the results obtained are insignificant in the sense they do not give evidence of psi. Secondly, it may also mean that the results do not confirm the hypothesis that is being tested, even though there is evidence of psi manifesting in the experiment, or that the results indicate a significant relationship opposite to the one expected. We find our journals publishing a number of reports which provide overall evidence of psi even though they fail to support a stated hypothesis or give significant results in the direction opposite to the one expected. Therefore, there is no issue on the second point.

It is reasonable to assume that a number of experiments which contain no significant data are not published because either the experimenter himself chooses not to publish them or the editors of the journals do not accept them for publication. This may happen in a variety of contexts. The experimenter may be attempting (1) to test a new variable or idea which has not been reported to have been examined or tested by others, (2) to try out a novel design or method,

(3) to confirm the finding of his pilot study, or (4) to replicate (a) his own finding which he reported earlier, (b) a finding reported by another investigator or (c) a study that has become for some good reason controversial in the field.

With regard to (1) and (2), I believe, the investigators as well as the editors of the journals should have freedom to publish or not to publish. The decision should be based on the importance of the idea tested or the significance of the method described. With regard to (3) it is a good thing that we no longer publish in our journals pilot studies which have not been confirmed, unless the pilot study itself is considered to be important for some special reason. When this happens, the failure to confirm a pilot study should be reported. With regard to unsuccessful replications, all that would be necessary is to publish the abstracts of the studies. It would be desirable if the investigator writes up a complete report of the experiment and supplies a copy on request to those interested. Concerning item (4c), which involves attempted replication of some important study which is the center of a continuing controversy, e.g., a reported significant relationship becomes questionable because some new circumstances have arisen, like the unreliability of the experimenter, I believe, there is a good case for reporting insignificant results. Thus I see a number of occasions which do not call for the publication of a full report of an unsuccessful experiment, an experiment which gave no evidence of the occurrence of psi.

The argument that all insignificant psi results should be reported comes from two quarters. First, there are those who are not yet convinced of the reality of psi and wish to evaluate the overall case for psi. They argue that they cannot be expected to come to a reasonable conclusion if the results of all the ESP experiments that have been so far conducted are not available. What are reported may be only the selected best and a large number of experiments which gave only chance results may not have been reported. Therefore, they demand that all experimental results should be published. This is an understandable position which is partly based on misunderstanding of the scientific method and partly due to the ignorance of the work done in our field. I shall not attempt to go any further into this because I do not think there is anyone here who is still in that state of mind.

The second group comprises those who are convinced that psi exists and that it can be measured in terms of test results. They plead for the reporting of all controlled experiments for two reasons. Firstly, if the journals publish only reports of experiments yielding significant results, this may encourage the investigator to select only parts of his data and report a paper that meets the requirements of significance, ignoring the rest. Secondly, non-publication of experiments yielding insignificant results may result in a situation where the true strength of the relationship between variables may not be known in a field like parapsychology, where one cannot be very confident about replication. I believe the first argument is unjustified. It is in a sense as ridiculous as the accusation, which is sometimes made, that encouragement given to those obtaining significant psi results puts pressure on those who are less successful to fake their results. Selection of data is professionally unethical and it must be made known to be so to any one entering the field. It would be naive to think that publication of reports of insignificant results would be a sufficient condition to ensure against unethical selection of data.

The second reason has some face validity. It would be helpful to have information about all attempts to test a particular variable. But this is better served by the publication of an abstract than a full length paper. The abstract would be valuable for the reasons Dr. Stanford has already mentioned—for the assessment of the strategies of research and for arriving at a dependable judgement on the strength of the assumed relationship between variables.

I am afraid, however, there is still a confusion in the minds of some of us as to what an ESP experiment which gives essentially chance results really means. You will agree with me that psi research is somewhat different from other kinds of research that go on in psychology. This difference is in the very nature of the phenomena we study. When we attempt to study a relationship between two variables, such as personality disposition and psi-hitting, we make the assumption that in a given test psi would manifest so that we can examine whether the relationship holds. Unfortunately, our assumption sometimes is not fulfilled, because our results do not give any evidence of psi. I do not see how in such an experimental situation, where there is no evidence of psi, one can reasonably talk about a relationship between psi and another variable. It is like a psychologist attempting to relate creativity to a particular personality characteristic by correlating the scores on a personality test with a test of "creativity" which is not known to be valid. Evidence within an ESP experiment that psi is present in the data ensures the validity of the psi test without which no meaningful conclusions about psi can be drawn. A psi experiment which gives only chance results, is often without any value for an inference because the validity of the test employed is conditioned on the results obtained. Unlike in psychology, where a test once validated can be used on comparable samples without further validation, a psi test needs validation within each experimental study. The validation in each case is the evidence that psi has manifested in the experimental situation. Therefore, for those who accept the reality of psi, a study that yields only chance results is often without much value. This makes the case for publishing chance results less defensible.

JOHNSON: I, at least, partly agree, and already financial reasons may make it turn out that way—that papers not giving significant results will be abbreviated a bit. But of course, then we have the difficulty with the fact that the procedure must be described adequately enough, I believe, to make it justified.

RHINE: First of all, on your last point, Dr. Johnson, you sound very reasonable. I think it's the way it will go. There is another point to add to this: When the editors of the *Journal of Parapsychology* publish an abstract of a paper they offer the reader a copy of the full paper on request. This policy enables the editors to avoid publishing pages and pages of empty results which probably no one will read when they see in the abstract that the data were due to chance.

In 1957 Pratt and I proposed in our textbook the pilot-confirmation technique, a program in which a person may do as many preliminary tests as he likes with no responsibility to anyone. When he discovers a successful procedure and gets evidence, then, and only then, does he see to it that all his controls, etc., are tight enough that he can draw a conclusion when results are secured. He will then see if he can follow up that pilot experiment with a confirmation experiment under these conditions. By this approach we can save both the experimenters and the editors a lot of useless negative reports; we are all spared the cost, the time, and the discouragement of pre-pilot test efforts that did not yield anything. (To be sure, there are strict rules about this pilot-confirmation; for one point, it is understood that the conclusion, if any, must rest only on the confirmation, not on the pilot.)

There are times of course when we do need to know about chance results. This is too obvious to need any discussion. For the most part today the non-significant results (or P. value) ideally belong to a subordinate section of an experimental design, in which, as planned the psi function was not *expected* to operate. Or again chance results may be anticipated where the internal conflict of scoring trends tends to cancel the deviations if they are in opposite directions from mean chance expectation. But chance results in simple pre-pilot exploration or training exercises can best go to the wastebasket.

TART: I'll throw a bit of quantitative data in here. About ten years ago, Burke Smith and I did a survey of members of the Parapsychological Association. Among other things, we asked them approximately how many unpublished experiments they had done versus how many published experiments. This sample does not include beginners, as Dr. Rhine pointed out, but people who are presumably at least occasionally successful enough to go on as parapsychologists. The ratio was about three unpublished experiments for each published experiment. Now most of the experimental articles appear either in the *Journal of Parapsychology* or the *A.S.P.R. Journal.* There are eight issues a year between them. With a three to one ratio we could estimate that you already have 24 journal issues a year filled with what are presumably negative results. So I think you're going to have to use a more feasible editorial policy, such as publishing only abstracts of the studies that didn't come out but making the full text available by Xerox to experimenters particularly interested in that specific problem area.

SOME CRITICISMS OF EDUCATION IN PARAPSYCHOLOGY

D. Scott Rogo

Everyone professionally associated with parapsychology realizes that no science can either develop or win acceptance without some organized attempt to educate both the public and the scientific community, and train students of science in its history, literature and methodology. Education in parapsychology is in its germinal stages and it is of the utmost importance for us to organize education in parapsychology; decide what the pertinent issues regarding education should be; who should educate and who needs to be educated; and how this can be done responsibly and unbiasedly.

These opening remarks may sound rather sophomoric, but I have outlined this problem because I think education in parapsychology has been approached incorrectly. Education should not be messianic in nature, but education in parapsychology has often taken that mode. Max Planck stated it succinctly years ago when he argued that new facts only win acceptance when a new generation grows up familiar with them, and not by convincing opponents. I doubt if many of us would disagree that the resistance to the notion of psi is more often emotional than rational.[1] Should we then try to force the acceptance of parapsychology? Is our attempt to educate the already existing scientific establishment a fruitful way of approaching education in parapsychology?

Biasing my own viewpoints very much upon "Planck's Law" I would tend to believe that trying to convert the dogma of orthodox science, while certainly opening certain inroads, is not the proper way for parapsychology to instate itself in the scientific community. At this time let me also note the writings of Thomas Kuhn.[2] Although citing Kuhn has become almost a cliché in parapsychology, some of his basic propositions support my viewpoint. As is well-known, Kuhn's basic argument is that a scientific revolution is not a startling, dynamic process, but rather occurs when a group of anomalies challenge a science over a period of time. A secondary point, and one not fully explored by Kuhn to the extent I would wish, is that it is usually only when science for philosophical or cultural reasons, is ready for a change that these new facts will be incorporated into its framework via a paradigm clash. I see a natural parallel here to Planck's principle. However, these viewpoints are not only applicable to science. The concept of change as being dictated by cultural readiness has independently been suggested by Donald Grout, a musicologist, who has found a similar process inherent in artistic climates and revolutions.[3] Kuhn's principles then speak not only of the scientific establishment, but also of a very basic constituent of our cultural consciousness.

The epitome of Kuhn's concept is the slowness of scientific change. Our whole educational program—bombarding the media, forcing scientists to evaluate our work, and so on—while efficacious to some degree may be self-defeating. This type of education may be attempting to force a paradigm clash prematurely, instead of allowing the clash to be a natural outcome of science's own dissatisfaction with its generally held notions and models. Today, with so many scientists from outside our field entering our ranks with research projects and claims, we have found that some part of the scientific establishment is open to parapsychology. Yet, from an educational viewpoint, is this good? The work they turn out is often faulty, as witness the furor over SRI's research with Uri Geller.[4] Here we are faced with a deadly problem. These scientists will be getting more publicity for their work in parapsychology than conventional parapsychologists have ever had. Yet, this work will probably be the type of research, with all its inadequacies, based on a low level of understanding of parapsychology proper, that will reach the public. And this work will be most easily "shot down" by the establishment. Again, witness the surge of "key-bending" PK coming out in Great Britain and supported by physicists who have been making ridiculous claims about their work in books[5] and in the media. For example, in a recent issue of *New Scientist* a group of physicists stated that it is well known that PK will not occur under controlled conditions, so conditions must be lax!

To illustrate that we must not be overly eager to allow outside scientists to barge boldly into our field as newborn champions in order to convince their colleagues, let me outline a true incident. A physicist informed me that he would be very eager and willing to carry out a large testing program on ESP. After this announcement, I asked him if he would be just as eager to spend one year just studying the literature and history of ESP research before attempting his experiments. I received a frown in reply. I wonder who needs the education more—this type of scientist, or the die-hard skeptic?

The key point here is that we must not necessarily educate people only *about* parapsychology. We must start educating people *in* parapsychology at the same time. This naturally leads to the type of educational programs and courses being offered at the undergraduate and graduate level on U. S. campuses. While many may applaud the breakthrough of parapsychology into the academic curriculum, I would question if these courses are really not doing more harm than good. I began by stating that trying to educate the scientific establishment may be a lost cause. To me the most important aspect of education in parapsychology is to educate college undergraduates where minds are open and eager. And it is here where our educational status is most deficient.

To begin with, it is rather clear that we cannot expect our university psychology departments to educate students about parapsychology. In 1972 I conducted a survey of five hundred college psychology departments in the U.S. to get an idea of exactly how favorable the academic climate for parapsychology, basically at the undergraduate level, really was. While 61.4% of the departments felt that parapsychology should be given some good coverage, only 50% of those departments which have an experimental psychology orientation were favorable to exposing students to parapsychology. A full 25% of them felt it should definitely not be taught to undergraduates. Clinically oriented departments were more favorable, with only 6% being negative. What is even more disturbing, though, was that the three basic objections to teaching parapsychology were all questionable and two were complete value judgments: (1) that parapsychology is not important to psychology and that (2) parapsychology had no credibility or evidence for it. The third objection, lack of time in the semester, seemed to me a legitimate one. When these departments were asked if they would sanction a course in parapsychology, a full 71.3% were strongly against it. Again, the main resistance came from experimentally oriented departments. The five major arguments against conducting such a class were: not enough content for a course; that other areas of psychology had priority; no faculty qualified to teach it; no evidence for psi; not important enough to psychology. When asked if they would allow graduate students to carry out research in parapsychology to qualify for a graduate degree, 69.1% said, Yes. Once again, clinical departments were greatly more favorable than experimentally oriented departments.

These few statistics point to the inevitable conclusion that although our colleges seem more accepting of parapsychology, we cannot expect any true attempt at education in our field through the existing academic channels. The obvious solution is, of course, the provision of undergraduate and graduate courses specifically in parapsychology. As we all know, a great number of courses are now being offered, but let us not fall into the old pitfall of mistaking quantity for quality. I would now like to take a look at these courses to determine if they really are educationally constructive.

First, consider exactly who are teaching these courses. By the end of 1974 there were 115 courses or very similar educational opportunities in parapsychology offered in the U.S.* For these courses there are 127 instructors. Thus at this present time the entire academic educational effort in parapsychology rests with a little over 125 people. Now, one might ask, what qualifications do these people have to teach parapsychology at the graduate or undergraduate level? I think the statistics are rather a shock. Unfortunately, because of the state of parapsychology today, it is very difficult to make firm commitments about who is and who is not qualified to be considered a parapsychological professional. But for the purpose of this brief report, I shall define any member of the Parapsychological Association to be qualified to present education in parapsychology. As for the statistics: of these some 127 people educating others in parapsychology, only 36 (or 28%) hold PA affiliations as either full or associate members. Thus, we have no assurances that there is any quality in nearly three-fourths of all U.S. courses in parapsychology. These rough percentages are accentuated when one realizes that, according to the last membership list of the PA, 45% of the members have university affiliations (of which 67% are full members).

There are several rather disturbing conclusions one can draw from these general attempts at evaluating the level of instruction in courses in parapsychology. (1) Most college parapsychology courses are being offered by people who very likely have no background in parapsychology, either in its methodology or history. (2) It is doubtful whether such instructors, who have little training themselves in parapsychology, could hope to responsibly train others. This is the dichotomy I drew earlier between teaching people *about* parapsychology and training them *in* it. (3) It would seem to me to be overly optimistic to think that

---

*These statistics are based on the ASPR publication *Courses and Other Opportunities in Parapsychology*, which I have freely revised and amended before making these breakdowns.

education in parapsychology is fulfilling a cogent role in readying students in parapsychology, when indeed we have no way of telling whether or not the majority of these courses are in any way constructive.

Another problem which requires noting is that there seems to be little attempt by the universities to assure the academic legitimacy of these courses. A notable exception to this rule has been the University of California, Santa Barbara, which went through a screening process before choosing a lecturer in parapsychology. Usually, though, courses on our campuses are taught by existing faculty members and neither the administration nor the departments themselves seem at all willing to "police" their quality, nor are they even qualified to do so. For example, of the 100 and more courses presently being listed, several of these, although accredited or adult education, do not cover mainline parapsychology. The Georgia State University's course is devoted to personal psychic development, the University of Kansas undergraduate course is on the "Psychological Future of Human Beings," Oakland University offers a course on "Mediums, Mystics, and Mountebanks," while the University of Nebraska gives a course on parapsychology and dream interpretation. Fairleigh Dickinson's introduction to parapsychology is a course on "Nature and the Occult" and other colleges have offerings on such topics as psychic healing, ESP and the Bible, magic and the occult, and so on. One must remember that in many instances these are the only courses devoted to parapsychology being offered at these institutions. One must wonder what type of distorted view of parapsychology students will get at the hands of those offering these types of courses. None of the above cited courses, I might add, are offered by PA members or associates.

Earlier I asked the question as to whether education is doing more harm than good. In light of the discussion I have just made, I think this question is now rhetorical. Although many parapsychologists are trying to get worthwhile programs underway, these attempts cannot outweigh the potential damage being done by the unqualified, especially at the undergraduate level. Until some sort of quality control is imposed on parapsychology courses in the United States, I feel the entire educational status is dismal despite the superficial evidence that we are progressing on the college campuses. Unless we can be sure that parapsychology is being taught as science, not as occultism or dogma, all of us here should not applaud the new courses in parapsychology that are popping up over the country, but see them as a source of utmost concern.

What of the other 28% of the U.S. parapsychology courses—those being taught by PA members? Even here I cannot end on an optimistic note. I think it is time that every parapsychologist should ask whether or not he really is qualified to teach parapsychology. Because there was little educational training for our generation of workers or those before us, there is very little quality control as to how well one really knows the subject before he is elected to the PA or is classified as a parapsychological professional. Generally, one becomes a PA member by having contributed worthwhile research, usually experimental, on a parapsychological topic before the scientific community or his colleagues. But there is much more to parapsychology than merely a practical program in experimental parapsychology. What about its literature, theory, and history? I am afraid that I have been constantly surprised at how many parapsychologists are deficient in any indepth background not only in the history and literature of the field, but even in those areas of parapsychology not within their own limited experimental interests. For example, one noted parapsychologist, who had published dozens of reports on his ESP experiments, admitted that he did not understand the Quarter Distribution effect in PK research. This example is not cited to embarrass anybody, but only to illustrate the fact that many parapsychologists, while competent experimenters, often have little comprehensive background in anything but very limited areas within the field. These people are really not qualified to teach others.

If parapsychology had good general survey textbooks, the problem of teaching competence among parapsychologists would be less serious. But we have no guiding texts. Before any of us here steps before a class to teach parapsychology, each should go through a self-examining process: Do I know the history and literature of parapsychology, both European and American? Am I versed in all areas of parapsychology from ESP to PK to the survival controversy? Can I present the work of others without biasing it? Can I aid a student in a research project in an area of parapsychology in which I have had little personal experience?

I wish I could say that, on surveying the academic scene, PA members are doing a splendid job in educating a new generation of parapsychologists, but I am afraid that I cannot. I see little evidence that any but a few parapsychologists really have the background *themselves* to give students a comprehensive background in the entire range of topics and issues covered by the subject. Before educating others, perhaps we should spend more time educating ourselves.

I would now like to pass on to an evaluation of another area of education in parapsychology which should be of growing concern to us: graduate degrees in parapsychology. So far there are few institutions offering graduate degrees specifically in parapsychology, but a trend to do so is becoming evident. These degree programs are basically external programs. That is, the student does not maintain residence and education at the campus offering the degree, but carries out his work independently, supervised by a committee. At the present time, two institutions are offering doctorates in parapsychology. The Humanistic Psychology Institute now has an external doctorate program in parapsychology and although the program is accredited in California it does not have national accreditation. The Ohio based Union Graduate School offers a general doctorate and will offer the degree for work done in parapsychology. This program is not yet accredited and at present holds only candidate status. Also, it should be noted, one student at the University of California, Berkeley, is independently working specifically toward a Ph.D. in parapsychology.

Again, instead of applauding these "breakthroughs," I see them as a cause for great concern, because of the public image of parapsychology. Anyone sporting a doctorate in parapsychology is automatically going to have greater prestige before the general and scientific public than any of us who have degrees in related or even unrelated fields. This specialized doctorate will give a rather unquestioned credibility to these people as they are presented to the public and this can lead to certain difficulties. For instance, a few years ago the University of California at Berkeley gave an undergraduate degree to a student in "magic." No sooner was this degree conferred than this young man was paraded before the public in lectures, TV appearances, etc. as an expert on the subject and he eventually wrote a book on it. Anyone with a background in traditional occult literature could see that this student had absolutely no conception of the history and literature of the subject for which he was awarded his degree. Yet, the degree was exploited to the fullest both by the young man, his publishers, and the media. I can only agree with Dr. Bob Brier who in reviewing this student's book stated, "In principle there is nothing wrong with offering such a degree, but judging from its first recipient, the University clearly does not have the faculty for supervising students interested in such a course of study. Under the circumstances, offering the degree was irresponsible."[6] However, the harm had already been done.

Frankly, I fear that we might have to face a similar problem in parapsychology with this wave of interest in granting doctorates specifically in parapsychology. My own trepidations have been even more aggravated by examining the particulars of these programs. I would now like to bring to your attention just what types of programs are being offered at both HPI and the Union Graduate School.

The UGS program is the type of advance degree plan which I feel has practically no method of evaluating the competence of its doctoral candidates. As in all doctorate programs, the student is supervised by a committee of educators who will eventually grant or deny the degree. But who makes up this doctoral committee? The committee consists of six individuals. The first is a core faculty member who should be a Ph.D. but does not necessarily have to be educated in the field of the student's doctoral interests. The second committee member is an adjunct professor who will more directly supervise the student's apprenticeship in his specific area. This committee member is, of course, supposed to be an expert in the subject's field. The third committee member should be a Ph.D. but again need not have any training in the student's area of concentration. The remaining three members are the subject's peers. All are pretty much chosen, in the case of a doctorate in parapsychology, by the student himself. Let us analyze this committee. First of all, of the six members, only three need have any advanced educational training. Further, only one member need have *any* background in parapsychology. Yet this member is chosen by the student, so the additional committee members have little way of judging the competence of the only person who has any right to evaluate the student's work. In other words here we have a group of people granting a doctorate in parapsychology where the majority of committee members need have no familiarity with the field.

After the committee is set, they in turn set up an internship for the student. At this level the student is expected to get practical experience in his field. While this is enviable, there is no set period for this internship. This lack of control severely limits its potential function to equip the student with the necessary skills and knowledge for a doctorate. After completion of this internship, the committee holds a certification examination and if the student passes he goes on to work on his major doctoral project. There, too, the program runs into a snag. The doctorate is granted after the student carries out what is called a "Project Demonstrating Excellence." The project does not necessarily have to be a thesis or an experimental project, but can be anything approved by his committee. If it is accepted, the candidate is given his doctorate.

Frankly, this type of degree program strikes me as a travesty of the Ph.D. There is no quality control over the requirements for the student and even the committee is set up in such a way that it can give a doctorate in an area it is totally incompetent to evaluate. This type of degree is only as good as what the candidate wants to make of it. This is dangerous business and in this type of program there is the potential that UGS will be churning out Ph.D.'s in parapsychology who have no academic or empirical training in the field. It will be easy for us to weed out the incompetents, but again I worry about the credibility these people will have when discussing parapsychology before the media and before the general public.

I am a little more at ease with the HPI program, which attempts to more formalize the Ph.D., although here, too, there are certain criticisms that can be leveled. These, however, are not as serious as my arguments against the UGS degree. Again, awarding the actual degree is under the auspices of a doctoral committee, which includes both a dissertation committee and a special resources committee. The constitution of the dissertation committee includes one home faculty member from HPI with expertise in parapsychology and three field faculty members, preferably within the student's area of concentration, but this is not required. The problem here is that the quality of the degree is based on whether or not, at any given time, there is a qualified HPI staff member with a background in parapsychology. Although, as of now, Dr. Stanley Krippner maintains an affiliation there, we have no assurance that, at some future time, Ph.D. candidates will not be supervised by a home faculty member who is not versed in parapsychology. The three field faculty members are again chosen by the candidate with no assurances that they have the proper background in parapsychology. The special resources committee acts in an advisory capacity to the candidate and it is suggested that this committee include peers much in the same manner as does the UGS program. The same criticisms apply here as I directed to the other program.

The actual degree program for the first year requires the subject to be versed in the following areas of parapsychology and conventional psychology: history of parapsychology; experimental parapsychology; neurophysiology; personality theory; psychophysics; and one elective. (The elective in the case of one of the students enrolled in this program is sleight-of-hand.) This requirement does much to insure some quality control over the student's academic level, but I fear that these requirements are not structured enough. For example, on what basis is it determined if the candidate has a working knowledge of these areas? The program itself is vague as to whether the students must pass a qualifying examination, or merely an oral examination. (One student presently in the program received certification in the psychological areas merely on the basis of having an M.A. in humanistic psychology.) Certification in these areas should be further structured to insure the quality of the doctoral students. This, however, is really a minor point which I feel can be easily remedied. As of now, competence in these areas must be shown before the dissertation committee. But, since the very structure of the committee is rather suspect, this requirement becomes non-operational. After a year's work, the candidate goes through a certification examination and, if he passes, he then goes on to begin his dissertation.

Generally I believe that the HPI program, while flawed, does have potential. If those in charge of the program severely tighten, structure and set up more rigid and clearly defined requirements for the doctorate, the program could be a very useful contribution to education in parapsychology.

This entire presentation has been pessimistic. Perhaps I have overreacted to what I feel to be the potential dangers of unsupervised education in parapsychology—the harm it can cause, not only to the students, but also to the parapsychological community and the general public. There is little clear resolution to these problems. I would hope that eventually the P.A. can act as an organized body to help control the quality of education in parapsychology. Today, the PA has little power academically. However, it seems plausible that, by a strong organized attempt, the PA could be able to clean up much of what passes for education in parapsychology. To reach this goal, the PA should first set up a task force on college education. Secondly, this task force must contact university administrations and departments where education in parapsychology is going on. They must work with these institutions, conveying to them the need for higher quality educational programs. The ultimate goal of this dialogue would be a voluntary form of certification of courses as "PA approved" and, if necessary, "PA not approved." Just as the American Psychological Association lists approved graduate programs in psychology, it is up to the PA to engage itself in certifying parapsychology programs. If there is large scale cooperation with colleges and universities offering such programs, then perhaps the status of obtaining PA approval will force quality control over education in parapsychology.

I would also hope that parapsychologists would hold themselves open to act as trainers or adjunct educators to students at universities, offering education opportunities in cooperation with the students' home campuses, which now do not have a qualified faculty member. In addition, such research centers as the Maimonides Medical Center's Division of Parapsychology and Psychophysics or the Foundation for Research on the Nature of Man could set up educational programs in experimental parapsychology where students could get hard core training in research methods.

In conclusion, it must be apparent that I cannot be very enthusiastic about the educational status of parapsychology at the present time. In fact, with only a few exceptions, such as the wonderful program now underway at the University of California, Santa Barbara, my attitude towards education in parapsychology is that it is very likely doing more harm than good.

REFERENCES

[1] Eisenbud, Jule: "The Problem of Resistance to Psi". *Proceedings of the Parapsychological Association*, #3 (1966)

[2] Kuhn, Thomas: *The Structure of Scientific Revolutions*. Chicago, University of Illinois Press, 1962.

[3] Grout, Donald: *A History of Western Music*. New York, W. W. Norton, 1960.

[4] —— "Uri Geller and Science". *New Scientist*, 64, October 17, 1974, 170–207.

[5] Taylor, John: *Superminds*. London, Macmillan, 1975

[6] Brier, Bob: Review of *Real Magic* by I. Bonewits. *Parapsychology Review*, Jan–Feb. 1972, p. 25

DISCUSSION

DOMMEYER: I thought I might begin by commenting about your suggestion of PA approval and disapproval of courses. What occurred to me was that we don't have that kind of situation in philosophy. We don't have that kind of situation as far as I know in the sciences, English literature, or any of the recognized fields, and I wonder why there should be an exception here in parapsychology. This strikes me as somewhat peculiar. I give what courses I wish to give, and I teach them as I choose to teach them. I have complete freedom, and the reason I have that freedom, I presume, is that someone thinks I am competent enough in philosophy to teach the courses in question. And I wonder, just why, in parapsychology there should be someone looking over the professor's shoulder and telling him whether he is teaching the course properly or not. It seems to me if that is required, you're admitting right to begin with that the instructor is not competent—that he's got to have outside supervision, and it seems to me you put yourself in a very peculiar position under such circumstances.

ROGO: I disagree on several grounds. For instance, the APA does issue bulletins about the level of graduate programs in psychology and they publish a publication, *Graduate Programs in Psychology*, which is meant to dissuade students from going into certain programs and persuading them to go into others.

DOMMEYER: Well, I've been teaching for forty years and I can tell you this: if anybody from the American Philosophical Association told me how to teach a course you can well bet what I'd tell them.

ROGO: Well, in an area like philosophy, which is very old, you have your textbooks.

DOMMEYER: No we don't. We're in a worse situation than you are.

ROGO: But a person teaching philosophy or psychology has credentials in that field. Basically when you have your doctorate in philosophy, you have gone through a very rigorous program. We don't have that type of background in parapsychology.

DOMMEYER: Isn't that the kind of background you should get first before you start teaching courses in parapsychology?

ROGO: Absolutely, but that's not being done!

DOMMEYER: Well, it ought to be done.

ROGO: I agree.

RAO: I have a question to ask you. You mentioned a survey you made, but you didn't tell us what percentage of people had replied. You sent 500 questionnaires. What is the percentage of returns?

ROGO: O.K. We received slightly under 50 percent returns, and I did analyze to see whether there was a bias in those returns. Were people unfavorable or favorable more likely to send back that questionnaire, and also was there a geographical bias? Did certain areas of the country have more of a tendency to respond?

RAO: How did you test that?

ROGO: I gave it to my brother, who is a statistician to check.

RAO: Another question is that you have picked 115 courses that were being taught by these different colleges. What criterion did you use to say that one is a parapsychology course?

ROGO: That was based on an analysis of the ASPR course list that you can get from the ASPR for two dollars. I used that as my source of courses being offered in this country, since Mrs. Nester does try to keep abreast of all currently taught courses at the college level.

RAO: May I ask Mrs. Nester on what basis she had included a particular course as representative of parapsychology? If one is giving a course on witchcraft, somebody might think it is a course in parapsychology, but I don't consider it parapsychology.

NESTER: We've always maintained it was a non-evaluated list and it is partly my own feeling that it is a good course—that it probably has some usefulness. That's all I can say. If I know the instructor and if I have any information about him, of course I use that. I certainly do my best, but nobody has ever pretended that it's evaluated. It's really an indication that there is some interest on that campus—that one person has an interest in parapsychology. It's more that, than a final list of what's evaluated and what isn't.

STANFORD: I first of all want to agree with Mr. Rogo that the PA should, and I believe will take, as time goes on, a larger and larger role to somehow or other augment and improve the structure of parapsychological education. I think it's going to have to do that, or we're going to have chaos. Now with regard to Dr. Dommeyer's remark, I want to respond there. Yes, it's true that nobody literally looks over your shoulder and says, "This must be included; this shouldn't be," but there are certain areas where there is a great deal of filtering of what goes into the training. Now take one example, medicine. Well, your immediate reaction is going to be that medicine isn't relevant because you're working with somebody's body there as a practical application to the individual. But I would maintain that many of the parapsychology courses that are being taught have practical applications for the individual. They're claiming that they can train people's psi abilities—that they can train all kinds of things in them. They're giving them ideas that can feed a paranoid delusion and all kinds of things of this sort. We have an ethical and social responsibility. This is recognized in organizatons like the American Psychological Association, which carefully examines doctoral programs. The APA comes right to the schools and they look at the credentials of every faculty member. They look at the syllabuses for all the courses. The same thing is done by the state organization that certifies programs, and similarly for accrediting organizations. So, while there isn't anyone literally standing over your shoulder, there is this kind of quality control, but we have no institutions to perform this in parapsychology and the only one I can see up in front that could do it would be the PA. We have to take the initiative.

ROGO: I would like to answer Dr. Rao's comments. I should have given you a fuller answer on the analysis of bias in the sample, and I'd like to do that now. On the geographical bias, it was easy to send out an equal number to each part of the country and then judge the statistics on the percentage returned. On the issue of bias in responding, I kept a week-to-week record to see what percentage came in negative and what percentage came in positive each week, and to see if there was more of a tendency to respond immediately or to respond at all. They kept on coming in week by week at the some proportional ratio of favorable-to-nonfavorable, which leads me to believe that there was not a bias of one group answering more readily than the other.

CHILD: I think that Dr. Dommeyer's reaction is one that would be very common, and it conveys a useful warning in connection with attempts to police education in parapsychology in universities. The reaction is very common even in psychology, which has for several decades been used to constraints from outside. As you may know, a number of universities have abandoned their graduate curriculums on clinical psychology and one reason is precisely because in this area of psychology alone a university department does not have the privilege of deciding for itself its own standards and policies. I think that if the Parapsychological Association were to set out on a policy of policing education in parapsychology, it would be a significant influence in causing universities not to offer courses in parapsychology, because that's at least one way that they can avoid outside interference. It seems to me that a program ought to be carefully restricted to offering assistance to universities that want some guidance in a field not yet adequately represented in their faculty.

ROGO: Well, my feeling is that before the program is even set up, the Parapsychological Association should be working with the administration. Now if we can work with college administrations before the programs are set up, then once the programs are set up there would not be any need for any type of outside policing of these courses. I think we really have to work more with the college administrations than with the instructors.

PALMER: Just one quick comment on this business of "policing." I'm having trouble following this discussion because nobody has defined what "policing" is. It almost sounds like you are developing the idea of somebody with a billy club standing over a teacher in a department and if he doesn't say the right thing he gets bopped on the head. I don't think that's quite what the PA has in mind. Maybe somebody else might be able to comment more definitively on this. Just one question about the survey. Were these responses from the department chairmen and how representative of the departments were they?

ROGO: Maybe I asked a very naive question when I sent out the questionnaires. In the covering letter I explained the nature of the survey and I asked them to please speak as well as they could for their department and if they felt that their own bias was against that of their department, to please stipulate that in their returns. This caused some problems. For instance, one was sent back which was very negative, and apparently his secretary or someone got hold of the questionnaire and gave it to somebody else and I had two different answers. I also had one man who proceeded to say he was very pro-parapsychology and that he wanted to use Koestler's *Roots of Coincidence* as a textbook, but he was afraid that his faculty wouldn't believe in physics either. There were a number of comments like that; some of them couldn't be presented before a scientific body nor committed to print.

MORRIS: Dr. Palmer made a comment and raised a question, but I have another comment. It seems to me what would be most useful woud be, perhaps on the college level or the graduate level, something like what we were attempting for the secondary school level, a PA-approved course, or at least guidelines for the development of a syllabus.

ROGO: Well, actually, I thought your high school syllabus would work very well at the college level.

TART: I want to reinforce Dr. Child's comments. You can't police anybody in a negative way. I might want to offer a course on witchcraft myself some time; it might be fun. What you can do is offer help in developing a good, solid, PA-approved course in parapsychology— maybe a video-tape series. You can offer the positive side of it, but I think it's a waste of energy to try to police instructors because the students want courses on witchcraft, etc.

BELOFF: I think there is one point that's being overlooked in this discussion, and that is that people who teach philosophy or psychology—one of these traditional disciplines—have a degree in that subject. As I understand what Mr. Rogo was saying, one of the difficulties here is that the people who are teaching parapsychology today have no professional qualification for doing so, and I think that is where the talk of policing comes in. I mean, what form it takes, of course, is another matter and this is open to discussion, but I would not accept Dr. Dommeyer's point that, because philosophers are free to devise their own curriculum, that anybody therefore can call himself a teacher in parapsychology and get away with it.

KRIPPNER: Well, I certainly have to commend the program committee for placing Mr. Rogo right after lunch. Most other speakers would allow us to fall asleep after that huge meal. One of Mr. Rogo's special talents is to present controversial material, so this was very well timed in terms of the hour of the day.

Now I think that the issue of PA policing of parapsychology is not too difficult to resolve. I feel that the points of view that have been brought forward by several people are not mutually exclusive. I certainly believe that the main emphasis should be positive in terms of helping potential instructors to prepare good courses. Most instructors would appreciate this, as many of them are just grasping at straws; they take what little they know about parapsychology and do the best with it. If there were some place for them to turn to for assistance, I think most of them would do so. I think that the PA would not have to use the word "approval," but it could say "listing of courses in parapsychology," and put on that list only those courses given by people who a PA committee feels have had special training in parapsychology. This, of course, would include PA members and associates and maybe some other people who may have gone through some of the educational symposia the PA has been sponsoring over the last few years.

I think there is one additional process which could be instigated. I would propose that the instructors could submit course outlines, texts, and examinations. Again, a wide latitude should be given in the name of academic freedom for what these people want to teach. But if some blatant example comes up, such as if a Jeane Dixon or Hans Holzer book is used as the main text in a parapsychology course, this would indicate that something is a bit awry in the person's judgment, and that course wouldn't have the best recommendation. So I do see a number of ways in which this can be handled in a very genial way, but still with some greater degree of direction than is happening right now in the field.

The second thing I want to comment on is Mr. Rogo's very thoughtful critique of the external degree programs. The basic facts that he gave you are worthy of your consideration, and they are very fairly stated. First of all, I would say that perhaps the main difference in the Union Graduate School Ph.D. degree and the Humanistic Psychology Institute Ph.D. degree is that we look upon the Ph.D. as representing a research-oriented program. I have no objection to people wanting to give degrees for building a geodesic dome or organizing a commune, or whatever—but we should not call these Ph.D. degrees. I think that the Ph. D. degree has a history and tradition behind it that is worthy of respect. It implies some sort of contribution to academia, some sort of contribution to human knowledge, and also, from the HPI point of view, a contribution to human welfare.

Now, in terms of the name that we give to our degree, we do not call it a Ph.D. in parapsychology. As I mentioned before, only two people are going through a parapsychology sequence among our 250 students. They will receive a Ph.D. in psychology from the Humanistic Psychology Institute. Once the transcript is inspected, it is apparent that the student's program emphasized parapsychology because the transcript covers all of the areas that Mr. Rogo discussed with you.

Also, there is a new development. No longer does the HPI student have sole responsibility for his or her field faculty members. He nominates members. These are approved by HPI, and then letters of invitation are sent to the prospective field faculty members. So now there is more control over that aspect of the program. In fact, some HPI students dropped out of the program, claiming that I refused to let them work with a religious leader who was their first choice as a field faculty member. At H.P.I. we are moving ahead, toward more control and more structure. This, I might add, is also very controversial. Some of the students who advocate "educational freedom" do not want the degree of discipline that we are integrating into the program. On the other hand, for this type of a program one needs to add structure. I think that one can have both discipline and freedom at the same time in this program. I think that without discipline there is a risk that the student will not learn in depth.

ROGO: I'd like to say something very general about that. This may have been one of Dr. Stanford's psi-mediated instrumental responses, but right before getting on the plane, I grabbed the current issue of *Psychology Today*, which has a little article in it reporting on the status of open education. Basically, it reports that there are now some severe problems with these alternative education type of schools at the high school level, and they are finding that students are not responding educationally or even psychologically to this type of unstructured work. These schools are actually closing down as students leave to go back to a more mainline, traditional type of educational program. And I'm wondering if that eventually might not filter in even to the college level when students find that they can't do it by themselves; that they do have to be structured from outside.

WHITE: I would just like to reinforce what Jim Morriss said, and Charlie, and also Stan to some extent. I think, practically speaking, the PA is just not set up or properly equipped, it doesn't have the money, and its people are all full time workers elsewhere and have very little time, and they can't possibly go around the country evaluating courses and programs. But I do think it is within the realm of possibility or practicability to develop a recommended course, recommended readings, and also, as Stan suggested, a listing of schools and courses. I think those are the areas in which we should try to concentrate.

PARAPSYCHOLOGY AND HUMANISTIC PSYCHOLOGY: THE EDUCATIONAL INTERFACE

Stanley Krippner

As one attempts to discern the connection between humanistic psychology and parapsychology, it is tempting to remain at a superficial level of analysis. For example, several parapsychological papers and panel reports appear each year on the annual program of the Association for Humanistic Psychology (AHP). In addition, psychical research has been featured at AHP's international conferences in Amsterdam (in 1970), Würzburg (in 1971), Tokyo (in 1972), Paris (in 1973), Visakhapatnam (in 1974), and Cuernavaca (in 1975). Division 32 (Humanistic Psychology) of the American Psychological Association schedules parapsychological presentations each year at the annual conventions of APA.

Psychologists and psychotherapists who identify their approach as "humanistic" tend to be more open-minded concerning the validity of parapsychological occurrences than psychologists with other orientations. Colleges which include a significant proportion of "humanistic psychologists" on their faculties almost invariably offer courses in psychical research. However, the relationship between parapsychology and humanistic psychology exists at a deeper level (Krippner & Murphy, 1973) and reflects the key theoretical concepts of humanistic psychology outlined by Charlotte Bühler (1971).

1. *The study of the person as a whole*. Psi, the subject matter of parapsychology, can be seen to operate in frequent reported personal experiences which defy an easy explanation. A person may dream of an impending catastrophe before it happens. A "psychic healer" may be involved in the remarkable recovery of a person from a fatal disease. These personal experiences represent a complex configuration of forces, very few of which are taken into account in the typical laborabory experiment with extrasensory perception (ESP) or psychokinesis (PK). Tests with ESP cards and with PK influences on dice reflect the behavioristic influence which dominated American psychology for many years, placing an emphasis on the observed

response of a subject while neglecting intervening variables of "the person as a whole." The studies which have been reported correlating psychic ability with personality traits (e.g., Schmeidler, 1960) are a promising beginning in the task of studying the whole person and investigating some of the variables which are seen to operate in a real-life situation when ESP or PK occurs.

2. *The course of human life as a whole.* There are several clues in the anecdotal and experimental literature which would be worthwhile pursuing if developmental history and longitudinal study approaches were to be applied in parapsychology. One of the most outstanding subjects in J. B. Rhine's early research was a young girl who, at the age of nine, made "hits" on all 25 guesses in a deck of ESP cards (Reeves & Rhine, 1942). It has been suggested that children may be better subjects in psychical research than adults because children's ESP and PK abilities have not yet been stifled by a critical society (Krippner, 1963). The autobiographical writings of Eileen J. Garrett (e.g., 1968) contain considerable material of value to the investigation of psychic development over the course of human life.

Garrett (1970) has recalled how she was often considered a "nuisance" as a child because she could tell when people were lying and when they were telling the truth. She has stated, "As I look back now, I smile over the things I did, but then I was living in a world nobody else understood." Despite the provocative indications that psi may change over the years of a person's life, there are few longitudinal studies of gifted subjects in the parapsychological literature,* nor are there comparative studies which compare ESP or PK performance of people at different ages. K. Ramakrishna Rao (1966:27) has lamented, "Unfortunately, the published experimental reports do not often involve an assessment of the subjects."

3. *Human existence and intentionality.* The parapsychological literature and the writings of humanistic psychologists overlap in the discussion of intentionality, specifically in the concepts of "sense of self" and "free will." A. H. Maslow (1956) has described how the person with a fragile sense of self typically possesses a limited capacity for self-determination. The self-concept of high-scoring ESP subjects was found to be important by Gertrude Schmeidler and R.A. McConnell (1958) who administered the Rorschach technique to subjects in an ESP study. High-scoring subjects differed from low-scoring subjects in that the former displayed more of a readiness to accept new experi-

---

* The work of Berthold E. Schwarz (e.g., 1974) stands as a welcome exception to this generalization.

ences as well as a lack of rigidity in perception and a high degree of "psychological self-sufficiency."

The concept of precognition is thought by some people to threaten the idea of free will, but Rao (1966:182-183) has argued that parapsychological data support free will in several ways: (a) The fact that it is possible to be aware of objects and events that are not in existence now but will exist sometime in the future makes it absurd to maintain that an external event determines or causes everything that comes into our awareness; (b) PK data indicate that human volitions can cause changes in external objects—a reversal of the position that external forces account for the internal processes of the mind.

4. *Motivation and goal setting.* The importance of identifying human goals in humanistic psychology studies is echoed by the attention paid to motivation by some parapsychologists. J. B. Rhine (1964) once investigated the personal motives of seven gifted subjects to make high ESP scores; in each case, there was an "exceptionally strong" drive to score highly. Schmeidler's experiments (1946) with "believers" and "non-believers" in ESP indicate that the "believers" generally tended to make high scores, possible because of their personal motivation. The non-believers tended to produce not merely chance results, but to "psi-miss," making low scores which were statistically significant in the opposite direction; this phenomenon may have been related to personal motives against identifying the correct ESP card.

Rao (1966:59) has summarized the data in this area by stating, "It would seem, therefore, that religious values, the self-confidence of the subject, and the novelty of the test conditions, insofar as they are found to contribute to the success of the subject, may help to raise his motivation." Rao suggests that just about anyone may become a high-scoring subject for a psi experiment if the researcher determines how to maximize that subject's motivation.

5. *The integrative process.* Humanistic psychologists see one's integrative process as a basic human potentiality, a process which orders and unifies one's other potentials. The ordering of values and the search for meaning assist the integrative process; ESP and PK abilities can emerge from this integration. Schmeidler (1960) reported a Rorschach study involving 1,062 subjects rated as "well-adjusted" or "poorly-adjusted." She found that the "well-adjusted" subjects who "believed" in ESP scored significantly higher than the "well-adjusted" subjects who did not "believe" in ESP. There were no significant differences between the "poorly-adjusted" groups. Schmeidler (1960:89) concluded that the element of belief in ESP "will be more pronounced for subjects whose social adjustment is good than for those whose social adjustment is poor."

For many highly developed psychic sensitives, the integration of paranormal events into their personal worldview and behavioral repertoire represents a developmental challenge. In his extensive psychological study of Eileen J. Garrett, Ira Progoff (1964) came to the conclusion that she was a remarkably integrated individual and that her mediumistic "controls" played an important part in this integration. Progoff's study serves as a model for other humanistic psychologists to emulate as they examine psychic sensitives from a scientific perspective.

6. *Creativity and goal-setting*. In the previously discussed basic theoretical concepts of humanistic psychology, two have been presented, representing areas in which parapsychology could benefit from a study of such writers as Charlotte Bühler, A. H. Maslow, Rollo May, and Carl Rogers. Three have been presented in which there are overlapping areas of mutual interest. The remaining three theoretical concepts represent contributions which parapsychology may make to humanistic psychology. Creativity, more than any other human behavior, is seen as a manifestation of Ludwig von Bertalanffy's theory (1966) that the human brain represents an "open system" with certain freedoms of operation and potentials for change. Parapsychological data also support this notion. J. B. Rhine (1935) has written of the mind's occasional ability to function independently of the physical body, a possibility most dramatically expressed by subjects in "out-of-body" experiments (Swann, 1975).

In addition, there are several experiments which demonstrate a relationship between psychic ability and creative ability (e.g., Honorton, 1967; Schmeidler, 1964). A number of anecdotal reports from the lives of gifted people are often cited to link psi and creativity (e.g., Dreistadt, 1971). This idea was followed up by Thelma Moss (1969) who found that artists in an ESP study made higher scores than non-artists.

7. *Person-to-person relationships in psychotherapy*. Humanistic psychologists regard the personal relationship between therapist and patient more important than the specific techniques used or the specific interpretations of behavior proposed. This position is supported by experimental data which show that the person-to-person relationship is important even in behavioristically-oriented therapy which de-emphasizes the therapist-patient relationship (Ryan & Gizynski, 1971).

In taking the positions that they do, humanistic psychologists should be aware of the possibility that their patients may have telepathic experiences concerning the personal lives of their therapists. There is an abundance of psychoanalytic literature on psi in therapist-patient relationships (e.g., Ehrenwald, 1948; Ullman, 1959) that would be pertinent to the humanistically-oriented psychotherapist.

8. *Feeling, experience, and education.* Humanistic education stresses what Carl Rogers (1969) calls "self-reliant learning," which acknowledges the learner's emotional as well as intellectual experiences. A number of parapsychological experiments indicate that successful teaching may have a psi component. For example, M. L. Anderson and R. A. White (1958) found that students who liked their teachers scored higher on ESP card-guessing tests (and received better grades) than students who did not like their teachers. Humanistic psychologists stress experiential education which could well have a psi component. Instead of scoffing at a student who reports an "out-of-body" experience or a telepathic dream, the teacher could deal with the report openly and authentically, using it to help the student enrich the knowledge of oneself. It would not even be necessary to pass judgment on the validity of the report, initially. The elicitation of extraordinary life episodes by teachers is vital if children are to recognize and appreciate "peak experiences." Maslow (1971:170–171) notes, "It looks as if any experience of real excellence, of real perfection, of any moving toward the perfect justice or toward perfect values tends to produce a peak experience." As examples, he cites "peak experiences" obtained through music, mathematics, personal relationships and childbirth. He concludes "We may be able to use them as a model by which to re-evaluate history teaching or any other kind of teaching (1971:178)." To Maslow, learning one's identity is an essential part of the educational process. If education fails at this task, it is without significant merit.

UBIQUITY

An increasing number of colleges are allowing selected students to write Masters' theses on a parapsychological topic. This is often done at the two state colleges most closely associated with humanistic psychology: West Georgia College (Carrollton, GA) and California State College, Sonoma (Rohnert Park, CA). The Masters of Arts' (MA) degree programs at West Georgia College and California State College, Sonoma (CSCS),* include standard psychology courses, introductory courses in parapsychology, and advanced research seminars in parapsychology.

---

* CSCS offers both an "internal" MA degree and an "external" MA degree. In the latter instance, very few courses are taken; the students do a great deal of independent study and supervised research for which they obtain credit.

The program at CSCS is facilitated in many ways by Ubiquity, a campus organization. Ubiquity has been defined (Muehe, 1974) as: ". . . a campus organization dedicated to promoting scientific and scholarly investigations into parapsychological events. It is Ubiquity's philosophy that the crossfertilization of ideas between the physical and biological sciences and the social sciences, humanities, and spiritual disciplines will breed evolutionary, if not revolutionary insights. . . . An information center has been formed in order to compile a directory of researchers and psychics in the area and to gather reference material regarding parapsychological research."

Ubiquity sponsored and coordinated a "Psychic Studies Year" at CSCS in 1974-1975. The "Psychic Studies Year" was described (Muehe, 1974) as ". . . a time for students and faculty to look at psychic phenomena from an interdisciplinary approach. The year will be devoted to parapsychological inquiry from many perspectives. . . . " Among the courses scheduled to include material about psi for "Psychic Studies Year" at CSCS were:

1. *Anthropology Department*: Psychological Anthropology
2. *Astronomy Department*: Cosmology and Extraterrestrial Intelligence
3. *Biology Department*: Human Species
4. *CSCS Extension*
   a. Self-hypnosis
   b. Parapsychology and the Healing Experience
   c. Parapsychology and Psychotherapy
   d. Paranormal Physics
5. *English Department*: The Psychic Journey
6. *Expressive Arts Department*
   a. Psychic Awareness
   b. History of Astrology
7. *Philosophy Department*
   a. Epistemology
   b. Metaphysics
8. *Physics Department*
   a. Descriptive Physics
   b. People's Electronics
   c. Selected Topics in Physics: Paranormal Phenomena
   d. Special Studies: Student-Initiated Research
9. *Psychology Department*
   a. Introduction to Parapsychology
   b. Myths, Dreams, and Symbols
   c. The Psychology of Yoga
   d. Seminar in Za-zen
   e. Introduction to Psychological Research and Basic Statistics

f. Perception and Cognition
g. Neuropsychology
h. Psychopharmacology
i. The Psychodynamics of Energy
j. Psychology of Boundary
k. Psychic Studies Symposia

During "Psychic Studies Year," a psychic counseling service opened in the student health clinic. The psychic counseling service was staffed by psychology students working under the direction of a faculty member in the psychology department. The students who came for counseling consisted of those who felt they had experienced paranormal phenomena (e.g., precognitive dreams, poltergeist phenomena) which were difficult to explain with their model of reality or to integrate with their view of the world. Counseling consisted of offering various explanations of the phenomena, including one in parapsychological terms, and helping the students to determine the meaning of the reported phenomena in their current life situation.

A PROPOSED BACHELORS PROGRAM

A bachelor of arts degree (B.A.) in psychology with an emphasis on parapsychology has been proposed by Ubiquity (1974), the student psychical research society at CSCS. The rationale for the program is presented in the following way:

"The study of parapsychology, one of the frontiers of consciousness, is coming into its own as a legitimate discipline. Parapsychological organizations are expanding, and established research institutes are investigating such occurrences as extrasensory perception, psychokinesis, and unorthodox healing methods. As interest in psychic phenomena increases, the need for well-prepared researchers grows proportionately. Presently, there are about five colleges in the United States that offer undergraduate degrees in parapsychology. The only one of these schools west of Minnesota, John F. Kennedy University, is not accredited. California State College, Sonoma, offers unique advantages—instructors knowledgeable in the field, accessibility to Bay area resources—that render it amenable to a program in parapsychology. Thus, it is reasonable to assume that the majority of prospective parapsychological researchers in California would be interested in participating in such a program at California State College, Sonoma."

The objectives of the major are presented:

1. To prepare the student for further study of psychic phenomena through the development of a well-rounded psychology student who

also has a basic understanding of the physical sciences and is well-versed in experimental procedure.

2. To broaden the perspective of the student of traditional psychology regarding human behavior through investigation of parapsychological events.

3. To enhance a progressive academic environment that encourages research in and discussion of the frontiers of knowledge.

4. To integrate the scientific and metaphysical or religious world views in order to create a synergetic perspective.

The following requirements for the proposed parapsychology major are listed:

1. *Core courses*
   a. Introduction to Psychological Research and Basic Statistics (8 units)
   b. Physiological Psychology or Developmental Psychology (4 units)
   c. Neuropsychology (8 units)
   d. One course in Psychological Theory (4 units)
       1) Perception and Cognition
       2) Abnormal Behavior
       3) Neuroses and Personality
       4) The Psychoses
       5) Personality
       6) Theoretical Systems of Psychology
       7) Seminar in Theoretical Psychology
       8) Seminar in Phenomenology
   e. One course in growth processes (4 units)
       1) Awareness Processes
       2) Dynamics of Human Behavior
       3) Seminar in Myths, Dreams, and Symbols
       4) Seminar in Creativity
       5) Seminar in Psychology of the Mural Process
       6) Seminar in Interpersonal Behavior
       7) Group Processes
       8) Seminar in the Psychology of the Body
       9) Psychology of Yoga
       10) Seminar in Dimensions of Asian Psychology
       11) Seminar in the Psychology of India
       12) Seminar in the Psychology of Asia
       13) Seminar in Za-zen
       14) Seminar in Selected Topics in Self-Exploration
       15) Advanced Group Processes
       16) The Gestalt Process

    f. Introduction to Parapsychology (4 units)

    g. Psychic Studies Symposium (2 units)

    h. One course in introductory physics

        1) Introduction to Physics I, II, and III

        2) General Physics

    i. Selected Topics in Physics: Paranormal Phenomena (3 units)

    j. Principles of Life Sciences

2. *Supporting subjects*

    a. One course in Western thought (3 units)

        1) Advanced Logic

        2) Philosophy of Science

        3) Epistemology

        4) Philosophy of Mind

        5) Phenomenology

        6) Topics in Logic, Epistemology, Methodology

        7) Nineteenth Century Philosophy

        8) Continental Rationalism

        9) Twentieth Century Philosophy

        10) British Empiricists

        11) Greek Philosophy

        12) Topics in the History of Philosophy

        13) Medieval Philosophy

        14) Kant

        15) Philosophy of Man

        16) Seminar in Logic and Epistemology

        17) Seminar in History of Philosophy

    b. One course in non-Western Thought

        1) Afro-American Folklore

        2) Mexican-American Myth and Art

        3) Mexican-American Folklore

        4) Comparative Ethnic Folklore

        5) Asian-American Folklore

        6) Cults and Sacred Movements of the Native American

        7) Native American Philosophy Systems

        8) Psychological Anthropology

        9) Cultures of the Pacific

        10) History of Chinese Thought

        11) Eastern Philosophy

        12) Non-Western Speculative Systems

        13) Psychology of Yoga

        14) Asian Psychology

        15) Psychology of India

        16) Seminar in the Psychology of Asia

       17) Seminar in Za-zen
  c. Three units of independent research (Nemec & Muehe, 1975) or three units in an associated scientific area.
3. *Summary (124 units needed for B.A. degree)*
  a. Core courses
    1) Psychology courses (34 units)
    2) Other courses (7 to 9 units)
    3) Supporting subjects (9 units)
  b. General education courses (40 units)
  c. Electives (32 to 34 units)

Although the number of college courses on the topic of parapsychology is increasing, I am ambivalent about the benefits of this movement to the field. In giving guest lectures at colleges and universities around the country, I am often welcomed by faculty members who teach courses on psychical research, who tell me how popular their classes are and how pleased the university financial officers are to have new money-making courses in evening school, the extension division, and adult education. Unfortunately, I rarely find an instructor who I consider qualified to teach a course in parapsychology. It is true that the instructors are highly motivated, well-meaning people, but they have little awareness of the literature in parapsychology, the history of psychical research, or the basic foundations of scientific method. These instructors frequently include such topics in the course outline as astrology, Kirlian photography, palmistry, pyramids, Tarot cards, UFO's, witchcraft, Yoga, and other topics which, although worthy of study in their own right, are only tangentially related to scientific parapsychology. For texts, these instructors will often select *Supernature* (Watson, 1973), or *Psychic Discoveries Behind the Iron Curtain* (Ostrander & Schroeder, 1970). Further, they often have no acquaintance with curriculum guides in the field such as those prepared by Ashby (1972), McConnell (1971), Rogo (1973), and White and Dale (1973).

I am also ambivalent in regard to the laboratory experiments being conducted in parapsychology by students in these rapidly emerging courses. Psychical research involves a complicated set of procedures, yet many neophyte experimenters blithely go their way without due regard for eliminating sensory cueing, the stacking effect, or other possible sources of artifact that were identified by parapsychologists decades ago. I sometimes think that poor research in parapsychology is worse than no research at all. Poor research, if it gets published, only adds one more datum to the pile of work that someday must be done over again. In the meantime, students are deluded into thinking that they are following scientific methods and advancing the cause of parapsychology.

HUMANISTIC PSYCHOLOGY INSTITUTE

In 1971, a group of psychology professors from CSCS, led by Dr. Eleanor Criswell, formulated plans for the Humanistic Psychology Institute (HPI). It became the educational wing of the Association for Humanistic Psychology (AHP) and its aims have been described (Pokinghorne, *et al.*, 1975) as: ". . . to further research in humanistic psychology and to offer an educational program at the doctoral level in psychology. The Institute grants a Doctor of Philosophy degree. . . to its Research Fellows who (1) demonstrate substantial scholarship and high attainment in psychology, particularly in the humanistic orientation to psychology, and (2) have mastered the ability to accomplish and effectively communicate research in humanistic psychology."

The HPI program has been described (Pokinghorne, 1975) as one which differs from other doctoral programs in psychology in that it focuses on the humanistic orientation toward psychology. This orientation includes a number of understandings and attitudes about the investigation of persons and the means used to promote their wholeness. Some expressions of these understandings and attitudes are:

1. Human life is unique and can best be understood by centering attention on the experiencing person.

2. Knowledge of persons comes from the investigation of individual, exceptional, and unpredicted experiences as well as the regular, universal, and conforming experiences.

3. Knowledge of persons comes from focusing on such topics as choice, self-realization, spontaneity, love, creativity, valuing, responsibility, authenticity, meaning, transcendental experience, and courage, even though these topics do not easily lend themselves to experimental research methods.

4. The understanding of human action needs to include factors such as intentionality and personal values.

Humanistic psychology is concerned with the development of methods which enlarge and expand human experiences and which emphasize the integration of the whole person. Its commitment is to psychology as a science and as an art; it rejects only those assumptions which restrict inquiry and interefere with a total view of human experience.

In its official report on HPI in 1974, the Special Committee on the Approval of Degree Programs of the State of California stated that, "The process of learning in HPI is a fresh breeze in the academic world." Approval to grant degrees was unanimously granted by members of the Committee and HPI is now applying for accreditation from the Western Association of Colleges and Schools. The procedures which make HPI unique are independent study and an absence of residency requirements. The rationale for these procedures has been stated (Pokinghorne, *et al.*, 1975):

1. Most graduate school programs operate with assumptions which make independent, learner-centered education nearly impossible. In these programs, it is assumed that students cannot be trusted to pursue their own scientific and professional learnings.

2. Another limiting characteristic of most graduate programs is residency requirements which exclude many older, experienced persons already involved in professional commitments, families, and jobs. Looking at graduate education as an activity that takes place at a particular time and place is wasteful and elitist—excluding many fertile untapped learning resources that exist outside the university campus.

Therefore, HPI takes the position (Pokinghorne, *et al.*, 1975) that "by establishing set courses, credit and residency requirements through which all must pass, graduate students are often discouraged and punished for pursuing their own interests."

Presently, there are about 250 Research Fellows at HPI pursuing Ph.D. degrees. They devote about 40 hours per week to the accomplishment of their learning goals and dissertations. They live in areas throughout the United States and several foreign countries, using those learning resources and training opportunities wherever they are located, which are most appropriate to their learning objectives. They have been admitted to HPI on the basis of a written application, a personal interview, and completion of a learning contract with one of HPI's five "home faculty members" at a program planning seminar. HPI Research Fellows range in age from 25 to 80; the average age is 38. Presently 60 per cent of the Research Fellows are males and 40 per cent are females, representing a variety of racial and ethnic backgrounds.

Research Fellows work with a doctoral committee composed of one "home faculty member" and two "field faculty members." The "field faculty members" share a Fellow's interests and are able to give time for the completion of specific learning assignments in the Fellow's learning contract. There are four major decisions to be made by the doctoral committee:

1. Each member must approve the Fellow's learning contract as developed at the program planning seminar or as amended.

2. Following at least three semesters in the HPI program, a Fellow may apply for candidacy status. This step must be approved by the committee and indicates that the Fellow has mastered the preliminary knowledge set down in the learning contract and is ready to begin work on the dissertation.

3. Following at least three semesters of work on the dissertation, the Fellow may ask for its approval by the committee. The approval may be granted immediately, upon submission of a revised dissertation, or not at all.

4. The committee recommends to the Institute that the Fellow be granted a Ph.D. degree.

There are two HPI Research Fellows* specializing in parapsychology. The learning contracts of both students specify that the Fellows demonstrate competence in psychology at the graduate level, with special emphasis upon history and systems of psychology (including the humanistic orientation to psychology), developmental psychology, physiological psychology, personality theory, experimental design, and statistics. In addition, knowledge is required of the history of psychical research, experimental approaches in parapsychology, and sleight-of-hand (so that fraud among parapsychological subjects can be detected). Several members of the Parapsychological Association have joined HPI as "field faculty members"; their number includes Robert Brier, Charles Honorton, Thelma Moss, Gertrude Schmeidler, and Montague Ullman. Therefore, a new Ph.D. program exists which allows students to specialize in parapsychology. Of course, a number of programs are already in existence, most significantly those at Andhra University, India, City College of New York, and the University of Freiburg, West Germany.

The State of California's Special Committee on Approval of Degree Programs, upon approving HPI's Ph.D. program in 1974, presented its impressions of the program (Gustler, 1974):

"The student is motivated for excellence by several factors. The project is of his own choosing and he is deeply involved in it. He receives reinforcement as well as criticism from his committee. The aim

---

* E. Douglas Dean and James Terry.

of making a contribution to a humanistic society through demonstration (such as founding a half-way house) or through communicating to others through readable publication (encouraged by HPI) is another motivation for excellence. Some of the projects are much more impressive than the average doctoral thesis.

"The opportunity to select faculty with whom students could work closely was indicated as one compelling motive for entering this institute. Description of projects already in motion indicated much hard work, resourcefulness, and a deep devotion to project goals. The overall impression was one of serious concern to develop a project, not just to 'get a degree,' but hopefully to make a contribution that will help people in some small way, yet at the same time meet the students' own needs and plans. The committee members found the faculty to be enthusiastic and idealistic but keenly aware of some pitfalls, and that they appeared to be dedicated realists. The stated aim of fostering a facilitative, trusting climate of learning has been achieved to a surprising degree."

In conclusion, the Committee stated, "The aim of promoting graduate research of a creative nature and high quality as a contribution to a humanistic society is being achieved through the project method."

PSI SEARCH

A number of students at California State College, Sonoma, as well as some Research Fellows at the Humanistic Psychology Institute, assisted in the development of *Psi Search*. From January 30 to March 30, 1975, *Psi Search* was open to the general public at the California Museum of Science and Industry, the first exhibit on parapsychology to be housed in a science museum. However, two years of planning and preparation had preceded this exhibit, about which the *Los Angeles Times* (January 30, 1975) commented, ". . . most interesting. . . material on psi (has been) accepted at a science museum, an institution that deals in irrefutable fact."

Norma L. Bowles served as the producer of *Psi Search*; Fran Hynds was its director, and Richard Byrne was its designer. I was appointed chairperson of the scientific advisory committee, and was assisted by D. L. Keene, Gertrude Schmeidler, Charles Tart, J. G. Pratt, Jule Eisenbud, Rober Morris, and Robert Van de Castle. Joanna Morris served as coordinator for the Parapsychological Association which decided to cooperate in *Psi Search's* production by decision of the PA executive board in late 1974.

Psi Search was important because it was the first overview of the scientific study of psi to be presented in a science museum. It served an educational function, being designed for the general public to assist it to become acquainted with parapsychological research and to learn the need for supporting the field. The exhibit was divided into two parts:

1. *Psi* touched on the historical and cultural perspective leading to the emergence of parapsychology. It reported on the main areas of 40 years of scientific psi research by describing 15 experiments—all of which had previously been published in referred journals.

2. *Search* explored some of the possible ways in which ESP and PK permeate daily life as well as implications for the future.

Among the California State College, Sonoma, graduate students who worked on the exhibit were James L. Hickman (who served as technical director) and John Hubacher (who served as a writer and researcher). HPI Research Fellows who assisted in the production of *Psi Search* included Douglas Dean, Bam Price, and James Terry.

In February, 1975, J. B. Rhine visited *Psi Search*. He later wrote the producer of *Psi Search* a letter in which he stated:

"I cannot say too often or too strongly that I think the *Psi Search* Exhibit you and your colleagues have developed is a most competent and successful achievement. You have well fulfilled your high aim of broad coverage and good illustrative representation.

"While you have done well in balancing and outlining the progress in parapsychology, you have allowed ample opportunity for future growth and even for later correction if you find reason to alter some item in the wide coverage you have displayed."

"It is a timely event to make available, first, in this distinguished museum, and then, in due course, for all others that may wish to share it, a subject so much in need of this sober, factual photographic display as parapsychology in 1975. There are many signs of this timeliness. The historians are seriously at work on the subject. Sociologists are focusing on its innovative impact. Psychologists and psychiatrists are examining it for its meaning for their fields. It is time for all to have a good look such as you have made possible."

"As it circulates month by month around the leading museums of the country, and grows with the subject it represents, it should, by the time it returns—let us say five years from now—be new enough that all will want to see what progress has been made and what new faces and fresh accomplishments have been added."

"It is surely one of the good educational achievements in this field, and I am personally grateful to those who have contributed so much—first of all, of course, yourself. One of the outstanding features, it seems to me, has been the degree of cooperation you have received."

Later in the year, *Psi Search* sponsored a workshop on "Parapsychology in the Classroom and the Research Lab" for the purpose of stimulating the dissemination of accurate information about psi. In a brochure announcing the meeting, several points of concern to the workshop leaders were outlined (Hynds, *et al.*, 1975):

1. Self-appointed "authorities" have disseminated unsubstantiated data and gross exaggerations about psi as if they were fact.

2. Persons who are associated with psi work in some way, or persons working the the field themselves have different theories about what psi is and how it operates. Unfortunately, sometimes some of these people also present unsubstantiated data on their hypotheses as if they were fact.

3. Results of research done under carefully controlled laboratory conditions have not been easily accessible or available.

4. Anecdotal information about reported spontaneous occurrences of psi is more interesting to most people who wish to learn about the field than is scientific fact, and such information is more easily distorted in the telling.

5. The dissemination of misinformation is perpetuated in that most of the persons who have presented themselves as instructors have no standard qualifications and credentials, but are themselves self-taught by what they think is accurate information.

In August, 1975, the exhibit moved to Santa Barbara for the annual convention of the PA; from there it began a lengthy tour of various science museums around the country under the sponsorship of the Smithsonian Institution.

CONCLUSION

Institutions of higher education which include a humanistically-oriented psychology department present fertile ground for courses centering around parapsychology. However, these courses need to be developed with care and concern or they will often turn into an embarrassment for psychical research rather than an asset. If an instructor insists upon including material in the course which is peripheral to scientific parapsychology, perhaps the word "parapsychology" should be omitted from the course title. Better terms might be "Psychic Studies" or "Occult Studies"; the latter term has been defined by McConnell (1971) as "dealing with psychological relationships whose reality, as manifest, is accepted by a sizeable group of adults but denied or ignored in the orthodox belief systems of the prevailing culture." McConnell includes parapsychology in his list of occult topics, but also includes such areas as mysticism, astrology, black magic, and UFOs.

At long last, parapsychology is making serious inroads into the mainstream of scientific inquiry. As an inevitable result of this development, educational correlates are developing. Because humanistic psychology presents an openness to psychical research lacking in most other psychological systems, a dialogue between these disciplines is essential. Only as each area educates the other, can common progress be made toward a common goal—discovery of the full range of human potentials and their beneficial use.

REFERENCES

Anderson, M. L., & White, R. A.: "ESP Score Level in Relation to Students' Attitude toward Teacher-agents Acting Simultaneously," *Journal of Parapsychology*, 1958, *22*, p. 20–28.

Ashby, R. H.: *The Guide Book for the Study of Psychical Research* (New York: Weiser, 1972).

Bühler, C.: "Basic Theoretical Concepts of Humanistic Psychology." *American Psychologist*, 1971, *26*, p. 378–386.

Dreistadt, R.: "The Prophetic Achievements of Geniuses and Types of Extrasensory Perception," *Psychology*, 1971, *8*, p. 27–40.

Ehrenwald, J.: *Telepathy and Medical Psychology* (New York: Norton, 1948).

Garrett, E. J.: *Many Voices: The Autobiography of a Medium* (New York: Putnam's Sons, 1969).

Garrett, E. J.: Interview, *Psychic*, 1970, *1*, p. 4–7, 32–37.

Gustler, P., *et al.*: *Report of the Special Committee on Approval of the Degree Programs at the Humanistic Psychology Institute, San Francisco*. Sacramento, CA: State of California, 1974.

Honorton, C.: "Creativity and Precognition Scoring Level." *Journal of Parapsychology*, 1967, *31*, p. 29–42.

Hynds, F., *et al.*: Parapsychology in the Classroom and the Research Lab. Los Angeles: *Psi Search*, 1975. Photo-offset.

Krippner, S.: "Creativity and Psychic Phenomena," *Gifted Child Quarterly*, 1963, *7*, p. 51–63.

Krippner, S., & Murphy, G.: "Humanistic Psychology and Parapsychology," *Journal of Humanistic Psychology*, 1973, *13*, p. 3–24.

McConnell, R.: *ESP Curriculum Guide* (New York: Simon & Schuster, 1971).

Maslow, A. H.: "Defense and Growth," *Merrill-Palmer Quarterly*, 1956, *3*, p. 36–47.

Maslow, A. H.: *The Farther Reaches of Human Nature* (New York: Viking, 1971).

Moss, T.: "ESP Effects in Artists Contrasted with 'Nonartists,'" *Journal of Parapsychology*, 1969, *33*, p. 57–69.

Muehe, J.: *Psychic Studies Year*. Rohnert Park, CA: California State College, Sonoma, 1974. Pamphlet.

Nemec, D. W., & Muehe, J. E.: A Student's Guide for Conducting Research Projects. Rohnert Park, CA: California State College, Sonoma, 1975. Mimeographed.

Ostrander, S., & Schroeder, L.: *Psychic Discoveries Behind the Iron Curtain*, (Englewood Cliffs, NJ: Prentice-Hall, 1970).

Pokinghorne, D., *et al.*: *The Humanistic Psychology Institute*. San Francisco: Humanistic Psychology Institute, 1975. Pamphlet.

Progoff, I. *Image of an Oracle* (New York: Helix, 1964).

Rao, K. R.: *Experimental Parapsychology: A Review and Interpretation* (Springfield, IL: Thomas, 1966).

Reeves, M. P., & Rhine, J. B.: "Exceptional Scores in ESP Tests and Conditions: I. The Case of Lillian," *Journal of Parapsychology*, 1942, *6*, p. 164–173.

Rhine, J. B.: *Extra-sensory Perception* (Boston: Humphries, 1935).

Rhine, J. B.: Private communication, 27 February 1975.

Rhine, J. B.: "Special Motivation in some Exceptional ESP Performance," *Journal of Parapsychology*, 1964, *28*, p. 41–50.

Rogers, C. R.: *Freedom to Learn* (Columbus, OH: Merrill, 1969).

Rogo, D. S.: *Methods and Models for Education in Parapsychology*, Parapsychological Monographs, No. 14, 1973.

Ryan, V., & Gizynski, M.: "Behavior Therapy in Retrospect: Patients' Feelings about Their Behavior Therapies," *Journal of Consulting and Clinical Psychology*, 1971, *37*, p. 1–9.

Schmeidler, G. R.: "An Experiment on Precognitive Clairvoyance: IV. Precognition Scores Related to Creativity," *Journal of Parapsychology*, 1964, *28*, p. 102–108.

Schmeidler, G. R.: "Progress Report on Further Sheep-goat Series," *Journal of the American Society for Psychical Research*, 1946, *40*, p. 34–35.

Schmeidler, G. R.: *ESP in Relation to Rorschach Test evaluation*. Parapsychological Monographs, No. 2, 1960.

Schmeidler, G. R., & McConnell, R. A.: *ESP and Personality Patterns* (New Haven: Yale University Press, 1958).

Schwarz, B. E.: "Psi and the Life Cycle," *Journal of the American Society of Psychosomatic Dentistry and Medicine*, 1974, *21*, p. 64–69.

Swann, I.: *To Kiss Earth Goodbye* (New York: Hawthorn, 1975).

Ubiquity. Proposal: Bachelor of arts degree in psychology with an emphasis on parapsychology. Rohnert Park, CA: California State College, Sonoma. Mimeographed.

Ullman, M.: "On the Occurrence of Telepathic Dreams," *Journal of the American Society for Psychical Research*, 1959, *53*, p. 50–61.

von Bertalanffy, L.: "General Systems Theory and Psychiatry," In *American Handbook of Psychiatry*, Vol. III (Arieti, S., ed.). New York: Basic Books, 1966.

Watson, L.: *Supernature* (New York: Doubleday, 1973).

White, R. A., & Dale, L. A.: *Parapsychology: Sources of Information* (Metuchen, NJ: Scarecrow, 1973).

DISCUSSION

TART: I'd like to add a comment based on serving on a couple of HPI committees and one Union Graduate School committee, which has been a mixed experience. This kind of external degree program offers a real possibility for educating some people in parapsychology, but I think you'll agree with this, Stan, that the selection of the people is crucial. For a person who has already shown that he is mature and competent and knows what he wants and how to get it, it's fine, but there are a lot of other people (who might turn out to be just as productive in the end) who really need the structure and the pressure—the examination pressure and the like—of a regular university. If we're not very clear on the selection procedure here and let people who are still sort of drifting into these much freer programs, I think the freer programs are going to be ruined.

KRIPPNER: I couldn't agree with you more, and I think the history of HPI is certainly not one that is of unblemished success. I am aware of many of the problems which existed in the earlier years of HPI. One of them involved some people that were let in but never should have been admitted. Fortunately most of those people dropped out. I think our current admission procedures are much better because now we usually require a personal interview as well as written documentation. But what you say about selection is, of course, important.

NOVILLO: When you were dealing with humanistic psychology, you were considering several aspects of the human being and parapsychology, such as "believers" and "non-believers", but you didn't mention any relation between the sex of the subjects and parapsychological phenomena. I think that the sex factor, male—female, is a very important aspect of human behavior, and consequently it must have specific and direct influence in psi activity. I think you need to take this into consideration. I think that the sex of the subject—whether man or woman—a very human aspect of human behavior—maybe it has a great relationship to parapsychological phenomena. You didn't say anything about that matter.

KRIPPNER: This is a very interesting topic but the reason I didn't say anything is because I don't think we know much about it in parapsychology. There have been a few studies which have shown sex differences. Dr. Freeman did some studies with children and noted sex differences especially in the type of target they best identified. There also were sex differences in studies by Dr. Van de Castle among the Cuna Indians in Panama. Also, in our own work at Maimonides, we found that there were some sex differences in terms of subject/agent combinations. However, I have never seen anything which has convinced me that these sex differences are anything but a product of the experimental design, experimenter effect, and the subject's culture. In other words, I don't think there is anything innate about either men or women which makes them better ESP subjects. Certainly in most cultures of the world, which are sexist, we would expect men and women to respond in different ways to ESP testing situations. One thing that has been noticed, on a cross-cultural basis, is that in England and the United States more women than men typically report ESP experiences. But in India more men than women report ESP experiences. Again, there is a cultural factor here.

NOVILLO: I do not think that man is a better or worse psychological subject than a woman. What I want to say is that their answers are different as Dr. Freeman has shown in his research throughout several years and I too, in PK experiments as I explained before.

KRIPPNER: Favoring which sex?

NOVILLO: The boys or men yielded higher results, if there wasn't an emotional-conditioning situation.

KRIPPNER: This supports my position. In the Soviet Union, just the opposite results have been reported. It's the women who reportedly have more PK than the men insofar as the training sessions directed by V. G. Adamenko are concerned. This is an example of what I said about sex difference being more closely related to the cultural milieu or the experimental situation than to biological factors.

NOVILLO: You are correct. Maybe there is some social conditioning producing different emotional attitudes which influences the results. It is necessary to research this within different cultures and to have the sex of the subjects included as one of the variables.

KRIPPNER: Yes, I think it's very important to find out what these social and educational factors are, because this will lead us to design experiments better and choose our subjects better. Certainly one's belief system is associated with this, and to some extent the world that we believe in is the world that we live in and our abilities, psi and non-psi included, are a result of our belief system. So all of the social and educational parameters are very vital; I appreciate your bringing them to our attention.

HASTINGS: As I was listening to Dr. Krippner's discussion of his many projects, I want to reflect something about his work that I admire very much. He might have some comments on it as an educational matter. In all the years that I have known Stanley, he has served as an inspiration to a countless number of students, both graduate and undergratuate, who have not only gone through his courses, but have also taken active part in his many activities—from the research at Maimonides to working with him on journals and publications, to the *Psi Search*. We heard today that many of them are setting up courses in parapsychology at Sonoma State. It occurrs to me that this is an unnoticed aspect of education in parapsychology. I wonder if you would comment on that.

KRIPPNER: Well, your words are very kind, Dr. Hastings, but you should really pay the compliment to J. B. Rhine because he was the model for me. When I was a student he invited me down to Duke University on numerous occasions, and had me stay at his house with him and his wife. He brought me along to various research meetings, and was a constant source of inspiration to me. I have just followed the model that I learned from him. I know very well that personal interest and personal encouragement are important factors in education. I had such a good teacher myself that I am pleased that I was able to pass the motivation on to a few of my students.

RHINE: I am very grateful indeed to Stanley for his kind remarks.

PALMER: I related to the previous discussion on sex differences and I have a little data to report that might be relevant to that. A couple of years ago we did a survey at the University of Virginia among randomly selected students and townspeople in the town of Charlottesville. We asked various questions about the frequency of occurrence of various kinds of psi experiences, and also dreams and other altered states of consciousness. With regard to sex differences, the only thing we found was that women reported significantly more psychic dreams than men, but this did not generalize to waking ESP experiences. My suspicion is that the reason for this is related to the fact that the women also reported significantly better dream recall and more vivid dreams than men, and I suspect this is why the difference showed up in dreams and not in waking experiences.

KRIPPNER: Dr. Palmer has identified, I feel, the critical variable. The same thing happened in reverse at Maimonides. It's true that we found some differences in that men were the better telepathic dreamers than women in our studies, and yet when we looked at the records, it was the men who reported their dreams more fully and more completely. And this is true of dream research in general; men are the better dream reporters than women. Perhaps this is because so many dreams are sexy and bloody. Sex occurs in dreams frequently and many women in our sexist society, where women first aren't supposed to dream about these things, would hesitate to report this to complete strangers, or even blot it out of their own memories. This, of course, would inhibit the ESP from coming through because much of our target material contains sex, and violence, and very strong emotional material.

FRANKLIN: One comment I wanted to make and that was with regard to the course content in the parapsychology curriculum. I would think that there should be something in the realm of physical science in that regard, and I think that most of you would probably agree with me. In recent history in the Brain Research Lab at UCLA, it was indicated that there are some effects of frequency—FM waves modulated by brain wave frequencies affected monkey behavior patterns—and there's a substantial amount of work that's accumulating in that area now. There are other things, such as electroreception in fish and the body fields that exist around human beings. They're fairly well known, and data is coming forward where it had not existed ten years ago. There's a new body of evidence, and it seems to me that it would be appropriate for any parapsychology curriculum to include something that would be in the realm of electrical engineering with bio-engineering overtones.

KRIPPNER: Let me comment on that because it gives me a chance to make mention of part of my paper I left out because of time, but which will be included in the printed proceedings. I've given a suggested curriculum that is now being debated at California State College, Sonoma, which will probably be implemented if the funding comes through. This is a curriculum for an undergraduate degree in parapsychology, and here are a few highlights:
Introduction to Psychological Research and Basic Statistics.
Neurophysiology.
One course on Psychological Theory.
One course on Growth Processes.
One course on Western Thought; one course on Non-Western Thought.
Selected Topics in Physics is a requirement.
One course in Introductory Physics is a requirement.
Principles of Life Sciences is a requirement.
There are some optional courses in Physics and other sciences.
This curriculum is being developed mainly by the Psychology, Physics and Philosophy Departments at Sonoma State. It has received approval in terms of being implemented, but depends on whether the state budget will have the money and whether such a curriculum is permitted legally. John Vasconrellos, a State Assemblyman, is working on these problems for us, and sees this as a possible model for the State College system. So I basically agree with you that a course in physics would be a very important basic requirement for a parapsychology curriculum. Again, it depends on who would be able to teach it. It would have to be taught properly to be of value.

TART: Stan, let me push you a little bit because we need to bring out an area of possible conflict here. Some days of the week I'm classified as a humanistic psychologist, since I teach a course on it, and I personally find the two fields quite compatible. Your paper, on a theoretical level, makes them quite compatible. But what about some real contrast?

Parapsychology as we know it, stresses objectivity, statistical analysis, and leaving your personal belief system and feelings totally out of your assessments and procedures. Humanistic psychology, as practiced, puts much more emphasis on how you *feel*. You act on the basis of your experience and your feelings and do not let your intellect get in the way. Can you see this conflict? And how do you resolve it?

KRIPPNER: Yes, I see the conflict and I think that the way that I resolve it may not be the way that other people would resolve it. Yet, I will be happy to share my feelings with you. First of all, there is absolutely nothing in terms of experimental procedures which I think runs counter to humanistic psychology. Certainly there are any number of humanistic psychologists who use statistics in their research, and any number that would want to observe phenomena closely and write clearly about them. I think the critical problem comes on the issue of leaving one's belief systems out of the experiment, the way we're told that we are supposed to do in parapsychology. Humanistic psychologists would say that this is a fallacy; one can not leave one's belief system out of the experiment. They would point to such things as the Rosenthal effect, which holds that an experimenter's expectancy can influence one's results. One of the many important things that Dr. Schmeidler did in her second term as PA president, was to bring Dr. Rosenthal to the annual convention, and he gave, what to me, was a very important talk. I think that the Rosenthal effect is of utmost importance, and in parapsychology, perhaps more than in any other area in psychology, what we believe is what we get. This is going to make it very, very difficult for us to actually pin down the critical variables that are dependable and that always lead us in a certain direction. As Dr. Rhine said this morning, there are certain people who are more likely to obtain significant results in psi than other people because of their personalities, their belief systems and their nature. I think it is naive for parapsychologists to feel that they can be completely objective, that they can leave their belief systems out of the experiment, and that what they say to the subject has no impact on how the subject performs. The sooner parapsychologists realize this, the better. It will make research more complicated for us, but it's still one of the facts of life.

PREPARING FOR A CAREER IN PARAPSYCHOLOGY

Rex G. Stanford

Preparation for a career in any scientific field is demanding, time-consuming, and expensive. It can be disappointing and highly frustrating if one is unprepared for the undertaking or is unlikely to benefit adequately from it. It is therefore appropriate to begin a paper such as this by suggesting characteristics of individuals which would likely favor their success in parapsychology or which, on the other hand, might deter it. My advice to the individual contemplating a career in parapsychology is "know thyself." Examine yourself with respect to the following criteria:

1. An individual who has a strong, positive regard for the logic and methods of science, who feels they are essential instruments in the pursuit of knowledge, is better qualified to enter this field than a person who is interested in parapsychology because he finds the subject matter fascinating but who views the methods of science (including those applied to this field) as essential only because they are demanded by a scientistic society which has been indoctrinated into highly rational (as opposed to intuitive) thinking. I have met all too many persons who claim they are deeply excited about parapsychology and who say they wish to enter the field who clearly have a disdainful, condescending attitude toward the logic and methods of science.

2. An individual who has a deep interest in psi phenomena because he sees them as an important scientific problem has the most viable perspective on this area. Contrast that person with the one who wants to enter parapsychology because he is sure it is the way to save the world from its ills or its destruction, or the one who feels he has many profound truths already discovered about psychic events which he will quickly demonstrate through scientific methods to his less enlightened brethren who cannot see the truth for themselves. The person best qualified as a parapsychologist feels that we are only beginning to come to grips with an exciting problem and that part of the excitement of the field lies in its possible surprises and unexpected discoveries. The other types tend to see it as a tool for demonstrating to a hard-headed

generation truths which were long ago fully and clearly revealed by the more effective methods of personal revelation, but which can be re-revealed through parapsychology to save the world. This is not to say that the aspiring parapsychologist should have no hopes that his science might someday provide a basis for making the world a better place to be. We all hope that. The problem lies in having grandiose ideas about the possibilities and linking them specifically to some metaphysical views of what parapsychology is supposed to be proving. Such an attitude often has a messianic flavor and also is chauvinistic. Why should we regard parapsychology as having a greater chance to better the world than all the other sciences?

3. The potential parapsychologist must be willing to work very hard, both in gaining entry into the field and in working in it, without expectation of easy or immediate recognition or social reinforcement from the scientific community at large. The picture in this regard is changing somewhat, but the necessity for the willingness to work hard certainly is not. The field may appear—thanks to TV and movies—to be a glamorous one, but it is not.

4. A future parapsychologist should have at least as much concern for and interest in events which appear reliable and of possible conceptual importance, even though they be weak, subtle, or undramatic, as for those that are sporadic, irreproducible, and seldom seen, but startling and dramatic merely because of their magnitude. He must have a strong resistance to being hypnotized by the purely dramatic. Psi research, in spite of popular misconceptions, is seldom advanced by the "researcher" who has so little useful to do that he waits breathlessly for the next miracle, for which he will travel to the far ends of the earth (and spend research funds proportionately), for the opportunity to ogle. A potential parapsychologist should recognize that the supposed magnitude of an event bears no necessary relationship to its potential value in elucidating our understanding of nature. Indeed our greatest scientists in every field have always been able to see the hidden meaning in undramatic, and even "worthless" or "bothersome" events which would pass by the ordinary observer unnoticed or at least unexamined. In short, if the dramatic events popularly believed to be the province of parapsychologists are what primarily attract a person to the field, he should probably seek a career elsewhere. Very likely he will see few such events, and many or possibly all those might be fraudulent. Even if they are genuine, no scientist can indefinitely retain an interest in simply witnessing uncontrollable, sporadic wonders.

5. Those who prize the pursuit of knowledge far more than personal economic security or societal status will have an advantage in

pursuing parapsychology as a career. I would encourage any bright, eager college student basically interested in research—and in pursuing a doctorate in science—to go ahead with his plans for a parapsychological career (within limits stressed later), but I would be less inclined to encourage the student so concerned with financial security and societal approval that he feels he must (for such reasons) go through medical school hoping to enter parapsychology. Regardless of one's interest in parapsychology, that interest can probably best be served through a bona fide research degree—some form of science Ph.D—than through the scientifically wasteful process known as medical school. This is not to say that medically trained persons have not contributed well to this field, that they will not continue to do so, or that they may not have some unique things to offer us. What I am stressing is that the person wishing to pursue a career in parapsychology had better recognize what he is letting himself in for. If one's personal concerns demand attention to strong financial security and societal status, these are not likely to be found in parapsychology as a career, at least in the foreseeable future. If these are major concerns for a person, he should consider pursuing them and recognize that he may still have some opportunity to contribute to parapsychology, though possibly in a less thoroughgoing way than if he had pursued a Ph.D. in science. One does not have to become a full-time parapsychologist (or even anything approaching that) to make meaningful contributions to the field. Whether one should aim at a full-time position or something less should depend in part on extrascientific, personal values and also on practical considerations. In fact, if we look at the other sciences, most of the persons contributing to them are less than full-time research personnel. There is no reason to think of parapsychology as being any different.

6. A person planning to work in parapsychology would likely benefit during his schooling and later in his career from a broad range of exposure to the sciences in general and to the various areas within his particular science. The person who is broadly interested in and somewhat informed about science in general is likely to be a relatively effective parapsychologist. The overspecialized person, even with fine scientific training, functions more as a technician than as a creative, bold explorer of the vast unknown called psi. The technician type is both useful and necessary, but probably most parapsychologists would agree that we in parapsychology have an outstanding need for creative, bold scientists to enter our field. The technician-scientific type can often be recognized by his overriding conviction that the particular, narrow area in which he is working is the most rigorous, scientific, and

fully justifiable of all the areas in his discipline. He probably has no interest in any other. He probably has disdain for other areas of his discipline and acts condescendingly toward them. If a person does not have a broader interest and knowledge than this, even within his own discipline, he may not have the integrative and broadly informed mind which would seem to be of the greatest value to parapsychology.

7. The person who is to enter parapsychology should have a high level of intellectual endowment. With increased popular interest in this field we are receiving more and more inquiries from some who are intellectually ill-equipped for the job of being a parapsychologist. Ordinarily if a person does not do reasonably well on tests like the general and specialized GRE's and on other tests of intellectual ability and achievement, he should not be admitted to training for a scientific career, including one in parapsychology. I am becoming increasingly concerned that nonresident Ph.D. programs will attract and admit persons for parapsychological degrees who would not qualify for normal Ph.D. programs and who probably lack the necessary intellectual qualifications for doing good work in parapsychology. Later I will return to the topic of nonresident Ph.D programs in parapsychology.

8. Finally, the potential parapsychologist, like any other experimentalist or researcher, should possess an almost obsessive compulsive desire for care and precision in all his scientific undertakings. This point may seem too obvious to mention, but often the aspiring researcher is unaware that without this his other characteristics which might aid him in a scientific career will be in vain. The potential parapsychologist must either bring this to his training or develop it during the course of that training. The person who feels that details are unimportant would be well advised to stay away from any form of scientific career.

One reason for enumerating the above characteristics and asking the possible future parapsychologist to do a little soul searching with regard to them, is that I sometimes have the feeling that persons think they can work in parapsychology quite successfully just because they are so interested in the subject matter, even if they have no interest in science as such and do not regard themselves as being scientific thinkers. The above points might be summarized by saying that the qualifications for preparing for and pursuing a career in parapsychology include the characteristics required for this in any scientific field. Additionally, there are some special qualifications mentioned above.

Persons should be encouraged to enter parapsychology who possess the recommended characteristics listed earlier and who feel a strong desire to pursue scientific study of psi phenomena, even in the face of considerable resistance from scientific colleagues and a lack of adequate funding for this field.

The next major point to be developed here is that the properly qualified person who wishes to do serious parapsychological research would do well to take a Ph.D. degree in some scientific field which has potentially rather direct relevance to the study of psi phenomena (e.g., the behavioral sciences, physics, or the biological sciences). Additionally, he should prepare himself through some form of apprenticeship at a center of parapsychological research and should independently and avidly pursue the study of the parapsychological literature. This apprenticeship might occur during summers while the student is doing his graduate work. There may be risks involved in doing this during, say, a one-year break between the undergraduate degree and graduate work. First, graduate schools may show preference for the student who goes right on from undergraduate to graduate work. Second, it is not impossible that if a department inquires of your activities during the intervening year (namely, in a parapsychology laboratory) they will show conscious or unconscious prejudice against you in their selection procedure. Also, there may be some temptation, if one becomes entrenched at a certain laboratory, to want to stay there and avoid the less secure world of graduate training. But the graduate degree, and the doctorate in particular, is very important to the person who wishes to work in parapsychology. It is important, first, for the training it gives, and second, for the doors it opens.

The recommendation that the future parapsychologist take a doctorate in a scientific area other than parapsychology may not meet the approval of some persons eager to "get into the field," but who could not care less about any other area of scientific endeavor. My feeling is that such persons will not, in the end, make good parapsychologists. Persons with this attitude whom I have encountered often have a disdain for science, its findings and its methods. Thus, no other area of science holds interest for them, and they are typically fixated on getting into parapsychology, not because doing science attracts them but because they believe that parapsychology's subject matter will hold special excitement. While finding the subject matter to be exciting is one requirement of a parapsychologist, it is far from sufficient to make a good one. My experience also indicates that such persons often have a very special, rather occult axe to grind and think that being in parapsychology will help them to grind it! I know of several such persons who plan to enter a nonresident Ph.D. program hoping thereby to get into parapsychology.

Another class of individual who eschews the nonparapsychological Ph.D. route into parapsychology is the person who simply could not make it into or through a normal Ph.D. program and he or she knows it. Such a person, like the type of individual just described, is likely to gravitate toward a nonresident program which promises a relatively easy Ph.D. in parapsychology or a scientific degree within which he can do a parapsychological dissertation. He may very well be able to make it to the Ph.D. traveling this route, but by doing so he really does little credit to himself or to the reputation of the Ph.D. degree or parapsychology. Such programs are likely to be so unstructured and poorly supervised that there is little likelihood that the candidate will get the scientific training required for a career in parapsychology. The good student will be able to succeed in a bona fide residential Ph.D. program and will probably wish to undertake one. For others, I advise a reconsideration of career choice. Either that, or find some alternate route into parapsychology. By all means stay clear of nonresidential programs. They are likely to take your money and leave you with inadequate training, wasted time, and difficulty in selling yourself in the job market as a bona fide Ph.D. I could give specifics regarding cases I know of in which training and evaluation in such programs is inadequate, but I will refrain from doing so in order to avoid embarrassment through possible identification of the students in an area which is still quite small. One hopes that such programs will remain small or, ideally, disappear altogether. Perhaps the Parapsychological Association can intervene to force some adequate quality control or else to shut down the programs. In my opinion, even with sincere efforts at reform, there are intrinsic weaknesses in such programs which make them inferior to residential Ph.D. programs.

There is certainly no crying need for persons holding the Ph.D. in parapsychology, especially from any Ph.D. program, nonresidential or residential, which dilutes not only the quality of parapsychological education but the reputation of the Ph.D degree as well. This brings us to another very important consideration.

When both states and accrediting organizations evaluate graduate programs, one question seems always to be asked, "How do you justify the existence of the program? Does it prepare the student to obtain a position afterward in an area he would not have qualified for beforehand?"

There is nothing even approaching what could reasonably be called a job market for persons holding a doctorate in parapsychology. This may exist at some point in the future, but at present, and for the foreseeable future, it does not exist. Thus, once more, the kind of program I have just described commits an injustice to the student. The existence of such programs seems to imply a job market. If there is no such job market, one cannot justify the existence of such programs.

Further, given the general glut of the Ph.D. market today, the degree awarded by such dubious programs will be next to worthless. Academic and research institutions are well aware that nowadays they can have about as well-trained and qualified personnel as they wish, and they have no interest in persons with dubious credentials. Even well trained, highly qualified new Ph.D.'s in psychology and other sciences often have to take jobs which in years past would have been far beneath their notice.

One final matter deeply concerns me regarding nonresidential Ph.D. programs in parapsychology. There may be some danger that highly capable potential parapsychologists may be attracted into training through that route rather than through a normal, residential Ph.D. program. This would be particularly undesirable from the perspective of the future of parapsychology. Persons entering this field need the very best training possible, and with it they will be able to make important contributions toward our advance of parapsychological knowledge. Without it their contributions will be less. We can only hope that the bright, capable students to which I am referring will be able to see through such sham doctorates, to see them for what they are—something less than the kind of training necessary and less than what they deserve and are capable of undertaking. The reason for concern is that there is always a temptation to take the easiest route toward any desired goal. We can only wish the potential para-psychologist the level of discrimination necessary to understand that there is something much better in store for him in the end if he will accept the challenge of making use of his full capabilities and enrolling in a conventional Ph.D. program. I am happy to be able to report that of the truly outstanding young persons I know with an interest in entering parapsychology, none has expressed the intention to enter such a program.

Many of the arguments listed above apply not only to the nonresident Ph.D programs but to any form of doctorate in parapsychology. In my opinion the person interested in a career in parapsychology should pursue the doctorate in another science. He should do so in an academic setting which provides him with a really solid level of training. This opinion is based not alone upon the job market situation. In fact, that is only a practical consideration, though certainly not a minor one.

Carefully surveying what is happening in parapsychology today, one can easily gain the impression that those making the most meaningful contributions to parapsychology are doing so in part because of their knowledge of areas outside parapsychology, areas with content or methodological relevance. Our building of bridges between parapsychology and the methodology and content of the more traditional sciences has both aided our scientific progress and increased our acceptability among nonparapsychological scientists.

Persons trained to a doctoral level in various of the sciences can certainly make important contributions to parapsychology, but I suspect that a person trained in specific experimental areas of the behavioral sciences is, on the average, best equipped to enter this field. (I have some reservations about this, though, and feel that the picture of who is best equipped to enter parapsychology may be changing, albeit slowly. These reservations will be discussed shortly.) The reason for regarding the behavioral sciences as providing especially good training for the potential parapsychologist derives from the fact that psi events are typically studies in living organisms functioning in a context likely require analysis through behavioral science methods. This may or may not continue to be the case, but that is not the issue here. The areas of the behavioral sciences which a student should especially consider are psychophysiology or psychobiology, experimental psychology (including psychophysics, sensory psychology, perception, and learning), cognitive psychology, and perhaps psychometrics. Work in areas such as personality psychology, social psychology, and clinical psychology have relevance, but are possibly not as useful. Clinical psychology should, in my opinion, rank lowest on the list of advisable specialties. Certain specialties within personality psychology (which can include aspects of cognitive psychology) and social psychology—especially the strongly experimental aspects—might have considerable relevance. A Ph.D. in alternative sciences might be valuable, especially in physics or the biological sciences. It is purely a personal intuition—though an increasingly strong one—but I foresee a much larger role for physicists, especially theoretically-oriented ones, in parapsychology. I say this because I suspect we may be about to make an important move forward which will allow us to break out of the psychobiological paradigm under which we have so long labored.

Anyone seeking doctoral training in a science who plans to enter parapsychology should try to give his education both depth and breadth. He must focus on and thoroughly master both the content and the techniques in a particular area, but he must also gain as much general knowledge of his field (e.g., behavioral science) as he can, and some knowledge of other sciences. Also, he might well devote some time to the philosophy of science.

Effective participation in parapsychology requires that one be able to think in depth and incisively in a special area, but at the same time to range broadly in one's thinking. Proper planning of one's graduate training (and undergraduate before that) can aid in this, though it is really a life-long endeavor.

The potential parapsychologist who pursues the doctorate in another science — and perhaps especially in a behavioral science — may have to agonize over the question of whether to do the dissertation in parapsychology. My recommendation on this account is that the graduate student should not do his dissertation on a parapsychological topic. Let us first look at the facts of life regarding obtaining a postdoctoral position.

The area in which one does one's dissertation labels one (e.g., as a psychophysiologist). This label determines what kind of job one is likely to be hired for and thus how easy it is to obtain a job after finishing school. There are few if any openings in professional circles for parapsychologists. If one has received the academic imprint, "parapsychologist," there is an opprobrium attached to that in the minds of many potential employers. Then if one cannot find a full-time job in parapsychology, there is always the difficulty in selling oneself (opprobrium attached) as something which is not evident in one's academic credentials (which would specify a specialization in parapsychology). These considerations should give serious pause to even the most eager beaver future parapsychologist who is fixated on doing a parapsychological dissertation.

A second general reason for not doing a dissertation in parapsychology is that if one does not do this, one is able to get more specialized training in some other area (e.g., psychophysiology or cognitive psychology) which can have immense value in aiding one's later thinking and work in parapsychology. Additionally, if one does not plan a parapsychological dissertation one probably has a much freer choice of who will supervise the dissertation research, and this enables one to choose a person who can aid one in intensive, high-quality training in another area. If one is in a really good school one is thus free to enlist as a supervisor an outstanding figure in some area. This not only helps ensure a very valuable training experience; it can help one in the job market later.

Parapsychology is really an infant science in terms of having made few real contributions to knowledge and having developed few unique methods. It must and should rely heavily on the better developed sciences. Why deprive oneself of a nice opportunity to explore in some depth an area that is not parapsychology but is germane to it and to do so with the aid of an expert in that area? This is what one does if one opts for a parapsychological dissertation. After all, one may be spending the rest of one's life focusing on parapsychology. In choosing a parapsychological dissertation one may be passing up or at least watering down an excellent and perhaps unique opportunity.

If I may speak from a personal perspective, I am very happy that I did my dissertation in an area of cognitive psychology and that it gave me some concepts and methods which I have fruitfully applied in parapsychology since that time.

A third reason for not doing a parapsychological dissertation relates to the notorious unreliability of results in this field. It has value to be able to speak of one's dissertation as a positive contribution to knowledge and to publish it as such. But nonsignificant results are probably somewhat more probable in psi research than in many other areas of psychology (even given a pilot experiment). Does one really want to risk increasing the probability that one's dissertation will produce null results? Often the dissertation is one's first opportunity for a publication—a very helpful matter in getting a job. Whatever we may think of their publications policy, many journals seem to prefer positive to null results. The chances of getting positive results are probably a bit greater in certain of the experimental areas of psychology than in parapsychology. Also, which journal one's dissertation research finds publication in (if any) can be important to one's finding an advantageous position. You can be reasonably well assured that your dissertation research will not be accepted for publication in a major, prestigious journal if it is concerned with psi phenomena. The history of the outcomes of parapsychological submissions to such journals is not encouraging.

The reason for this emphasis on what kind of job one can get after one's doctorate is completed, is not primarily one of concern about job security. Rather, it is based upon concern that the good student be able to find a place where he can do the kinds of research which will benefit parapsychology. Bright, capable students who stand to make a contribution to parapsychology will have by far the greater chance to do so if they are able to land a good position in a respectable university. The teaching load may be lighter, and they will certainly have available better laboratory equipment and space, more adequate libraries, better qualified colleagues, better graduate students, etc. These are major considerations. I hasten to add that the future parapsychologist should not plan on getting (or if he gets it, keeping) a job in a "para-psychological center." Such jobs are few and far between, funds in such centers are often minimal, and in some instances the freedom to pursue one's own lines of parapsychological research would be much less than, for example, in an academic setting.

Not doing one's dissertation in parapsychology does not imply that one cannot do any psi research in graduate school. Also, one might do it entirely separately, as during a summer sojourn at a parapsychology center, or one might include it very secondarily in one's dissertation research. It would not even have to go into the write-up. It might be possible to include a psi aspect in such research, if it in no way interferes with the approach one is making to another problem area. And, as suggested earlier, one should in any event spend some time (e.g., summers) working with one or more qualified parapsychologists in some context. One could also use summers for getting into the parapsychological literature. Such experiences could provide at least as much depth of understanding of this field as if one did a dissertation in it, and they would not have the costly ramifications of a parapsychological dissertation discussed earlier. In this connection it may or may not come as a surprise that in most universities one would be lucky to have on one's graduate committee even one person really knowledgeable about parapsychology.

There is no substitute for the discipline, the rigorous training, and the knowledge afforded by a valid, legitimate, Ph.D program in preparing the future parapsychologist for a career. The individual student and the field of parapsychology itself will be best served by Ph.D.'s well trained in a related scientific area who have also had preparation in parapsychology.

Incidentally, with the advent of some good parapsychology courses in certain universities and colleges it is sometimes possible to include such a course in one's academic preparation for a degree in another scientific area.

I would encourage the eventual development of Ph.D. programs in parapsychology, provided they have the same standards as usual Ph.D. programs, and provided that they come at a time when the job market for parapsychologists has considerably improved. Additionally, such a program should provide the student with a good knowledge of potentially relevant areas in several sciences. Ideally, it might be an interdisciplinary program, but one carefully structured. Such a program might with profit have certain subspecialties within parapsychology toward which a student could channel her or his efforts (e.g., psychophysiological problems, information processing, or physical-energetic approaches).

As parapsychologists we are obligated to try to ensure that those entering this field have personal, intellectual, and educational qualifications which are as high as those of any other science, if not higher. There is no way to assure continued or rapid progress in any scientific area, but we at least know and can attempt to implement some of the prerequisites.

DISCUSSION

KRIPPNER: I think we're all indebted to Dr. Stanford for a talk which included so many perceptive comments and so many provocative ideas that our question and answer session will be very worthwhile. It was really a model of clear thinking and interesting synthesis. I'm going to comment on the mention that he made of non-residence programs because, in those brief comments, I think there were some assumptions which sound plausible in the abstract, but which do not bear up in the concrete. From a superficial listening to Dr. Stanford's talk, one might get the idea that the few non-residence programs that exist are flooding the field with parapsychology Ph.D.s. This is simply not so. I know of two persons who have been involved in a parapsychological Ph.D. in Union Graduate School, and beyond that, I'm doubtful of any massive movement along these lines. As I said before, HPI does not give a doctoral degree in parapsychology. We do have recommended sequence of work in parapsychology for people who want to consider themselves parapsychologists, to gain admittance to the Parapsychological Association, to present papers at PA conventions, etc. This hardly represents a deluge of doctorates in parapsychology.

Secondly, Dr. Stanford made mention of gaps in knowledge that he has observed among people coming from these non-residential programs, and that he wouldn't mention specific instances because he didn't want to embarrass them. Now I agree that he would not want to mention them in front of our group; it would not really be necessary. But if I had any students or colleagues who were in a doctoral program, and if I felt there was a gap in their knowledge, I would certainly mention it to them and to their professors. Frankly, I think it is inevitable that when you go through a graduate program there are going to be gaps in your knowledge, but you yourself have to be responsible for those gaps. I think that a successful graduate education is more the responsibility of the student than it is of the institution. Of course, the institution should try to make the student aware and responsible. It should stimulate the thirst for knowledge in such a way that these gaps are filled. If any of my HPI students had glaring gaps in their knowledge that I did not find out about, I would want to be informed. Right up to the end of his or her program, we have to observe our students closely. I have a student who is now writing his dissertation. He wrote one sentence in the dissertation on Harry Stack Sullivan, and that sentence so misinterpreted Sullivan that I had him go back and read a number of books by Sullivan before he could proceed with his dissertation. And I received several book reports, indicating that the gap had been filled—perhaps a bit late, but better late than never.

Next is the issue of job opportunity. It would seem with the few job openings there are in the field now, that non-resident Ph.D.s would have a harder time than resident Ph.D.s. In actuality, we have a dozen people who have received degrees from HPI—all of them have jobs. One of my students competed with dozens of people for a job at Franklin Pierce College, and he was accepted above dozens of people who had gone through more traditional Ph.D. programs. Admittedly our excellent record is due, in part, to the fact that many of our people have jobs to begin with. They're older people, they're professional people, and they are often obtaining a Ph.D. more as a process of self-development and self-growth rather than to assist their market-ability in the world of work.

Furthermore, none of us in HPI feel that this is the best program for everybody. However we do think it may be suitable for a very small number of people. Certainly for most people going into graduate education, a traditional residential program is fine. But HPI appeals to professionally-oriented people who cannot pull up family and job and move to a different part of the country to establish residence. For them, HPI often does seem to be a better alternative.

I only knew two people who have gone through a traditional Ph.D. program and a non-traditional program. Both of them preferred the non-traditional program. Specifically, those people are Jean Houston, whom all of you know about as a researcher and writer in the altered states of consciousness field, and J. Schoenberg Setzer, who is an associate member of the PA. Dr. Houston received her Ph.D. in philosophy from Columbia University, had a horrible time—her degree was held up for two years by her major professor for trivial reasons. She had to wait patiently until he was promoted and somebody else came and took his place before she could get her dissertation approved. She did not have such problems at Union Graduate School, and she felt she had a much more profound learning experience. J. Schoenberg Setzer is having, from what he tells me, worthwhile experience in HPI. He has designed a long and extended course of study, which will allow him to understand what he calls "the parapsychology of religion" and how it can be applied in pastoral counseling. The cautions that Dr. Stanford sets out are important ones to consider. Our program at HPI is far from perfect; we make mistakes, and we hope to learn by these mistakes. But I did want to tell you what happens on a concrete basis during the HPI program.

STANFORD: First of all, I want to make it clear, mind you, that I didn't imply in any way and I don't even think that superficial reading would give the impression that I thought that the "yellow plague" was about to take over. I specifically mentioned that there were only a few students in these programs and that was why I didn't want to get into the nitty-gritty—some of which is pretty nitty-gritty—about some of the things I know about the quality of education some of these people have received, and apparently the lack of adequate supervision in certain areas. But I gathered from his remarks that Dr. Krippner agreed with me that, by and large and in the long run, there may be a relative problem as far as the ease with which non-residential people and residential Ph.D. people can get jobs is concerned. But I don't want anyone to think that I'm trying to say that no one should take that route. I'm all in favor of a program of that sort for some people, if the program is adequate, properly supervised. I was pleased today to hear some of the things about changes in the HPI program which sound very constructive to me, and there may be some individuals who can only travel that route. There are some types of discrimination in some graduate schools. There's sex discrimination—or has been in the past in a lot of graduate programs. There's age discrimination. We know that and I'm all in favor of opportunities for these people, and these warnings are intended primarily to urge people to do the best they can with what they can manage, but not to allow themselves to get into a compromising situation if possible.

RAO: I do not want to sound defensive as one who also has a Ph.D. program essentially in parapsychology and accepting dissertations in that area. I endorse the first part of Stanley's statement concerning the perceptiveness and fairness with which you have presented the ideas. You have mentioned a number of prerequisites for a parapsychologist. Now, it is good for a parapsychologist to be highly intelligent. It is very good for a parapsychologist to have excellent training in psychology and physics, etc. It is also good for the parapsychologist not to worry about finances and social recognition. It is very good for him to have all the excellences in life. But where do you get that man? And if you don't get that man, what are you going to do? My own feeling is that your arguments are jumping back and forth between existential realities and idealized expectations.

I feel we have to make compromises all the way, otherwise the field cannot make any impact whatsoever. We have been saying earlier that one of the real values of studying parapsychology is that it's a fine, intellectual discipline. It's a discipline that leads to an appreciation of the nature of science, how science works, and also gives a very diligent training to the enquiring mind. And if that is the case, I would very much like most research trainees to get involved in parapsychological research. If it gives them the training to avoid pitfalls and to see things more precisely than they would otherwise do—a dissertation in parapsychology is something we should recommend to a large number of students. At any rate, I see nothing to be guilty about in recommending a parapsychological topic to a willing student.

So I feel that a Ph.D. in parapsychology could be very desirable if it can be worked out and if it is feasible, and again, if it is not standing in the way of somebody's future prospects. I do not find any difficulty in our country. We have two Ph.D.s in our department and both of them are happily and professionally engaged in their research, and in fact, vocationally they would be a lot happier to get a Ph.D. from me than from physics in my university, because many Ph.D.s in physics have no jobs, and I have three jobs open in my department for those who have a Ph.D. in parapsychology.

STANFORD: Yes, Ram, I agree with a lot of the things that you have said. One of the things that I think is relevant here is that, unless I'm mistaken, people who are ostensibly in training for Ph.D.s in your program are basically trained in psychology with a dissertation in this particular area and it is that sound training in the other areas that helps him to get a job. And as for the relative negative values of the parapsychology Ph.D. or the positive values—there are positive and negative values—I don't mean to deny that a Ph.D. dissertation in parapsychology might not be a very good one to help one bone up intellectually, so to speak.

ROGO: Eight years ago when I started my own college career, I met my first real live parapsychologist, and that was Charlie Tart. The first thing that Dr. Tart told me was to get my doctorate. Now there are three people here in this conference who do not have doctoral degrees, and I, of course, am one of them, which makes me ask this question: If you have a person who has all of the qualities you spoke about at the beginning of your paper, do you think there is necessarily anything wrong to proceeding with a career in parapsychology without getting that doctorate or even planning on getting that doctorate? And what is your attitude towards the charge that I have made and others have made that there is a great deal of snobbery shown by the parapsychologists with a Ph.D. against people who do not have that Ph.D.?

STANFORD: Well, I would say several things. First of all I see absolutely nothing wrong with anybody without a Ph.D. going into parapsychology. There's one person we all know in this field who is very highly respected, who doesn't hold any kind of academic degree, and I think it's just a matter of "paying your money and taking your choice," as, I think, Aldous Huxley said. You're just going to have to take the consequences of your actions. That's all! Some of these people have been in grave difficulties and live with their suitcases packed up on occasions. If you're willing to live with that kind of consequence, more power to you. It's just a matter of what the individual wants to do. I'm just simply pointing out some of the facts of reality.

Now, your second point was about the snobbery regarding Ph.D.s. I think that I myself would advocate, and indeed, I would like to see, for instance, the Ph.D. removed as a specifically stated requirement for membership in the PA. Of course, we know the council can waive this, but I don't see the value necessarily in requiring a Ph.D. for membership in the PA, as long as we're satisfied about a person's scientific ability and his ability to work effectively in parapsychology. I have seen some of this snobbery myself and I'm not sympathetic with it. Note that the Ph.D. is not required for membership in the PA. I believe it's recommended, but if you are nominated by three members of council, then that is waived.

SCHMEIDLER: As I was listening to what you were saying, it seemed to me that you were setting the standards extremely high—so very high that you were drawing rather an ideal figure instead of a real figure. But since you applied the high standards to every one of the characteristics, I kept thinking to myself, "This is self-consistent," until you got to the very end, and then I thought I saw an inconsistency. I'd like to point it out, then end up by suggesting a way of correcting it. The inconsistency came when you proposed doing the dissertation outside of parapsychology so as not to have the opprobrium of being labeled a parapsychologist when applying for a first job. Then you seemed to propose that immediately upon accepting the first job, a person should start to do research in parapsychology. This would label him a parapsychologist before he received tenure and would probably send him, by the time three years were up, looking for another job where being labeled a parapsychologist didn't have all this opprobrium. So there seemed an inconsistency between the self-abnegation of doing a dissertation in another field and the freedom of doing post-dissertation research in one's chosen field. And the way I would suggest correcting the inconsistency is just by adding one word to your title, and that is: "Preparing for a Non-Existent Career in Parapsychology."

STANFORD: I'm not going to say there are many career opportunities in parapsychology.

SCHMEIDLER: I was hoping for disagreement from you.

BELOFF: I would fully agree with Dr. Stanford that aspiring parapsychologists would be better advised doing their Ph.D.s in another field. I think this is true. At the same time, it causes me an awful lot of heart-searching. I get inquiries almost every week from people who would dearly like to make a career in parapsychology and who want to know what their chances are of getting a foot on the ladder, of getting a higher degree, etc. I write to them with the sort of cautions that you've mentioned today, but at the same time, while I sort of warn them off it for their own sakes, I can see very well their point of view. I mean, some of them, for example, already have acquired an interest in parapsychology and a serious one at high school. Then they laboriously go through the psychology degree and take their first degree, etc., perhaps still always, on the side, having their main interest there, and then to be told after that, "No, go away, do a Ph.D. for three or four years (or however long it takes) in something else, and then do your parapsychology," is really expecting a lot from human nature. As it is, of course, we can offer very few places and so more or less in the end they sort themselves out. I mean, we can't take the masses of people who would like to come to us, but I do see it both ways and I agree in principle with what you say.

JOHNSON: Well, I also agree and I think there was much clear thinking behind your presentation, but at the same time, I see several difficulties. It's the ideal you were talking about when you made your listing of requirements. It reminded me of once when I was a member of the board for screening flying officers in the Swedish Air Force, and it ended in a such a way, when we had made up all the requirements, that the Swedish Air Force would have become grounded if we had all those requirements. Then over to reality. It's a kind of problem when you're trying to start up a university-attached laboratory. Being a part of the university, you are in a way a producing unit and the university expects something coming along the production line. If you are not producing any Ph.D.s, they may very well in ten years rationalize, "Well, they are not productive, let's quit it." Consequently, I'm facing the problem of what to do in this instance, and my own feeling is that there are many topics of interest both to parapsychology and ordinary psychology, giving an opportunity for the student to carry out approximately the thing he wants to do, and at the same time keeping the door open for getting a job afterwards. If it takes place within a psychology department and partly is of general interest to the methodology of science or psychology or something like that, the person will not be discriminated against as a parapsychologist in spite of the fact that he has, as far as I see, prepared for a career as a parapsychologist.

STANFORD: I don't know, I guess I had a misperception or a different perception than some of you do about the criteria that I listed. I didn't feel that they were exclusive or that we would have difficulty finding people to meet these requirements. I didn't mean, either, to suggest that this is legislation. It is an attempt to ask people to do a little soul-searching about their real motives for entering parapsychology, more than anything else. With regard to Dr. Johnson's second point, there is the question of whether one is going to do a Ph.D. in parapsychology as such, as a separate topic, or whether one is going to do what is nominally psychology where the parapsychology is a specialty. As long as one has sound expertise in some other area and particularly has some research training in other areas, this increases your job opportunity. What I'm really trying to stress is that I don't like to see people get themselves hemmed in. They may wind up in this day and age pumping gas.

FRANKLIN: I was very happy to hear the comments on physics and especially theoretical physics and the idea of the interdisciplinary Ph.D. versus Ph.D. in various disciplines. I think it's a very important one. I'm a product of an interdisciplinary Ph.D. myself and have an under-graduate degree in biology and one in engineering, and some psychology along the way too. I finally got into physics and sub-sequently into theoretical physics. But I've been exposed to a number of things in graduate programs with Ph.D.s in physics and it's become clear to me that many times the Ph.D. in one discipline such as physics or psychology, is much more useful than an interdisciplinary degree in the sense that the student can do more *in-depth* study. For physics, and theoretical physics in particular, it would be very difficult for a person of that nature to work in an interdisciplinary program. So I would agree that the best route, I think, for much work in the field in Ph.D. programs in parapsychology would be in the discipline itself, in which we can tackle some of the major fundamental problems within a discipline and then do it in a parapsychological way, in other words, bring in parapsychological variables.

I wanted to ask you, Dr. Stanford, if there is a way in which Ph.D.s in physics could work in certain aspects of parapsychology, and what topics in parapsychology in general do you think could be worked into a physics Ph.D. program?

STANFORD: Well, I think that if a person training in physics plans to work in parapsychology, it would be good for him to pick up certain courses in psychology that might be useful, and to pick up some skills perhaps in things like physiological monitoring and certain types of psychological courses. That shouldn't be difficult or prohibitive in and of itself. I think that regardless of what area you get your doctorate in, a little information coming from other areas is going to be very helpful. I really believe that each individual in parapsychology has to be a sort of interdisciplinary person with the focus in one area.

TART: What you said, Rex, that a candidate should really search his own soul and find out why he really wants to be in this field, has reminded me how valuable this conference has been. There have been so many excellent papers bringing up issues, and I want to ask the Foundation to get the *Proceedings* of this out as soon as possible, because I'm going to make it an absolute reading requirement for people asking about careers in parapsychology.

MORRISS: I want to make a prediction. I sense there is a ground swell of interest that is going to open up, a good many career possibilities—at least, avocational possibilities for a lot of people in education and I'm wondering where they're going to come from. Now what I'm basing that on is my own experience. A year ago today, I knew very little about this field. I think the PA convention was about this time last year, and that's where I came upon the scene with my request for support in developing the module. Since that time I've prepared the proposed module in parapsychology for the high school. The teachers in my school district asked me to structure and present a course, and I wasn't really prepared. I would like to have had the opportunity to take courses myself. There are not enough courses that will give a general background to people who don't necessarily desire to go into a research career or teach on the college level, but who may want just enough of a background to make some contribution in education for the general public.

STANFORD: Yes, I very much agree with what you're saying, Mr. Morriss. I think that we're going to have to broaden our perspectives on education in parapsychology; not merely think of educating the researcher, but the teacher, and perhaps counselors and clinical psychologists in special ways related to these problems. There's a whole vast area opening up here and we're just beginning to see the full scope of it.

PARAPSYCHOLOGICAL EDUCATION IN ARGENTINA

Enrique Novillo Pauli S. J.

In general I can say that parapsychology as a real science is taught in only a very few centers in Latin America and specially in Argentina; not only as regards the content or the methodology but the investigations and research work as well.

There exist innumerable centers and people who claim that they teach and investigate parapsychology but in fact what they really do is to present a mixture of confused concepts related to occultism, spiritism, and esoterism. Furthermore, almost everything that is transmitted in courses, conferences, broadcasting, TV, etc. considers historical aspects. They introduce facts which might have happened centuries ago as true, or pay attention to anecdotal, spontaneous events or present several hypotheses which still lack the necessary experimental demonstration. This method of teaching parapsychology has been misunderstood and it requires an adequate trial. Some others repeat what is already known, often misinterpreting without taking care of the variables of the personality and its connection with psi, or they practise occultism and magic in their own way. Apparently all these people ignore the present situation of investigation, its methodology and all the evidence accumulated from research in serious investigation centers, which is afterwards published in their periodicals.

This propagation of a pseudoparapsychology is very well known and it justly provokes rejection among these persons having a certain cultural level. As a result, two universities, the Catholic one in Buenos Aires and that "del Litoral" in Rosario which had included the teaching of parapsychology in its syllabus, decided to exclude that subject from it, although their professors were well informed in the field.

At present two universities have recently begun to teach parapsychology: the John Kennedy University in Buenos Aires and the Catholic University of Cordoba. The former does not have an appropriate plan of studies and investigation on the university level, but the latter, together with the National University of Chile, has the most important center nowadays. Later on I will refer to the teaching of parapsychology in the Catholic University of Cordoba.

There are some private institutions where parapsychology is taught, such as the Argentine Institute of Parapsychology in Buenos Aires, the Institute of Parapsychology of Rosario, Sante Fe and Cordoba. These Institutes include a small number of people and their teaching programs consist of historical aspects, methodology and experimentation. Very frequently in these centers we notice a certain polemic atmosphere and their members attack other people because of their mistakes or wrong orientations.

At present I am teaching parapsychology not only in the School of Psychology of the Catholic University of Cordoba, but in three other cities as well, Mendoza, Santa Fe and Parana, sponsored by their universities.

In my teaching I very specially stress the importance of personality variables to the phenomena. All the states of the subject, emotional, psychological and physiological, affect the manifestations of extrasensory perception and the power of the mind over matter. These variables are, perhaps, the consequence of the subject's psychological states, or of his relation with the experimenter and the target stimulus. These three elements make up a triangle which must always be taken into consideration. All these present the parapsychological phenomenon as it really is—deeply human. It is not something abnormal, supernatural or mysterious at all. Since this was made clear, many professionals (psychologists, physicians, etc.,) stopped rejecting parapsychology and accepted it as another aspect of the human psyche and its dynamic.

In order to interpret accurately the results of the tests, I point out in my classes that apart from the personality's variables, the sex of the subjects must be considered. My basis is the following: if a transitory emotional state affects not only the subject's psyche but also the psi phenomenon, the fact of being a man or a woman is a profound component part of the human being and his personality, and it provides a special feature which in turn determines a different vision of the world and its role in it. Sex is not given by an anatomic and physiological difference only, but also creates functions which differ from each other and consequently the individual in different ways. Through the PK tests on seeds and plants I came to the conclusion that a man and a woman not only achieve different results, but if they work together on the same group of seeds, the result lacks significance. I have done this research work for more than four years and I have checked more than fifty thousand seeds.

During all my classes, I keep the matter open to discussion as to the cause and therefore the nature that provokes the parapsychological phenomenon. While I develop the themes of the courses and explain the experimentation in each of the topics, we analyze the results obtained throughout all the years of investigation, the various conditions of research and the consistency of the results. Therefore, on the basis of this investigation, we analyze the possibility of inferring the factors which provoke the psi activity, the nature of its cause and its properties. According to the nature of the cause we will be able to plan a future investigation and confirm its properties. In this way we try to get to the core of the whole investigation that everybody wants to know. With this purpose in mind, I point out several explanatory hypotheses and the experimentation done to justify them. I bring up the weak aspects, what is still waiting for confirmation and what has already been proved as true. In such a way we analyze the theories of the "effluviums," magnetic and electric forces, the indeterminism of the laws of physics, quantum theory, law of relativity, field theory etc., and the theory of those who attribute the psi effect to communication with the dead. As a consequence of the analysis we can infer that neither physics, nor theories of collective unconscious or synchronicity, not even the communications with the dead, nowadays offer solutions to the problems of parapsychology. It presents difficulties in both its comprehension and interpretation of its way of behaving which demand solutions of their own. It doesn't seem to be necessary or possible, at least at the present time, to find the solution in other sciences, but to look for it within its own field, having in mind the characteristic of acting with absolute disregard of time and space.

We are convinced that in order to carry on a satisfactory investigation many other auxiliary disciplines are needed, that is to say, interdisciplinary work. Therefore it will be very difficult for a private Institute of Parapsychology to recruit all the essential specialists for the investigations. That is why our Institute has been created within the University. Thus we have all the necessary instruments for research and teaching and the indispensable advice of psychologists, psychiatrists, neurologists, general medical practitioners and technicians of all fields: physics, electronics, statistics, biology, agronomy, etc. At the same time there is a spirit of research, of investigation, together with a group of professionals trained for this kind of work. All this provides the necessary seriousness and the level required for a task of this sort. However this is not enough for the teaching-learning process in parapsychology. We think that both knowledge of this field and gradual experimentation should begin in the elementary school when the child first gets in touch with nature and starts asking the first questions, making the first observations and undergoing the first experiences.

During the development of the different topics in the syllabus, all teachers should explain to the children in their course the dynamics in the acquisition of information. That is to say the necessary sensorial response to different stimuli in order to know something.

To carry on an investigation properly, the receptive and trustful relationship between teacher and pupils and the psychological personal and familial situation of the children should be approached simultaneously. Once these conditions have been fulfilled we may plan a test with Zener cards, or its necessary adaptations, according to age and interest of the children so that they themselves can verify the existence of a way of cognition other than the one they are familiar with. In other words, to acquire information without the help of the present physical sensorial stimuli. Likewise we organize experiments with Dr. H. Schmidt's electronic machines fabricated in the laboratories of our School of Electronics.

I have carried out a number of PK experiments with elementary and high school students, the targets being the germination of seeds and the growth of plants. These children have already had information and experimentation on germination of seeds according to the programs. It is then that I suggest a different experiment. Two groups, one of boys and one of girls, are formed; each one has four hundred seeds. There is a third group with the same number of seeds as a control. Those seeds and plants will germinate and grow faster than the ones of the control group due to the children's wish to make them grow faster. This experiment lasts nine days. The results are surprising and the children themselves wonder at the difference.

This way of initiating children and youngsters in investigation, not only contributes to their education but it also allows them to know this other reality of the human being, the psi activity, providing them with the necessary elements to understand and interpret properly a number of facts which are often wrongly attributed to different causes and which they are bound to face in life.

At present a team of teachers and professors who work with me are producing a guide to experiments which together with brief and correct information will help the elementary and high school teachers in the production of tests for school children and youngsters. This has been done as a way of collaborating with teachers in the development of the searching and inquisitive spirit of their students as to the many problems and this one in particular, which they hear about at home or read in periodicals and science-fiction writings.

This gradual acknowledgment and apprehension of phenomena will furnish them with true criteria about this subject theme. It is not something magic, hidden, or a kind of communication with the dead, but the natural potentialities of the human being. In this way they will get rid of the limitations imposed by superstition, misinterpretation, fears and dependence on the so called occult forces, which some people think of as impossible to overcome. This produces psychological states in people which can lead them to the verge of madness. This enlightening plan contributes to social education and mental health. I cannot now explain some of the consequences derived from the cultural and educational aspects.

I would like now to detail how I have planned the teaching of parapsychology in the School of Psychology in the Catholic University of Cordoba, Argentina. I have taken into consideration three main aspects which I think are essential: theory, practice and the Institute of Parapsychology.

Parapsychology at the university level will become a compulsory subject for promotion from 1976 onwards. For the time being the Catholic University has accepted the Institute of Parapsychology on the same level as other Institutes. I have taken over the responsibility for both the teaching and the direction of the Institute. As such I often invite professors and students of the School of Psychology, of the other schools and other universities and different educational centers, to take part in the courses on parapsychology. Some years ago, the attitude of professors and members of liberal professions such as physicians, psychologists, lawyers, etc., was one of skepticism and rejection of parapsychology. It was thought to be dishonorable if a cultured person would care for such a "pseudo-science," one lacking any scientific basis. Nowadays this attitude has changed much but not in full. Those who have had the opportunity of learning of the research done in the last forty years in other centers of acknowledged scientific level consider parapsychology a science. Psi investigation has lost its mythical aspect, it has been stripped of all occultist connotations and can be carried on in laboratories. As I said before, introducing psi as a natural and normal psychic activity has encouraged many people to accept it; thus the number of students of different careers who attend my classes is quite considerable. However, due to the lack of time, many of them ask for the bibliography to get informed by themselves.

Others accept it as a science but are not interested in going deeply into it, as they do not find any connection between it and their profession whatsoever, and others accept some spontaneous cases as something exceptional and sporadic, but which cannot be called a science, as physics or biology, because the results are uncertain and the causes and laws which organize it are unknown.

The students of different university careers, specially psychology, are generally more open-minded and show greater interest in getting information. They experiment and are the ones who have enough time to attend the courses. There is also a large group of employees mainly belonging to the civil service, who are willing to widen their knowledge. A number of them, mainly women, do predictions and clairvoyance, and come to us for an improvement of their natural abilities and so thus acquire a certificate which satisfies the practice of their abilities. The last mentioned group does not generally fulfill the necessary requirements to obtain the certificate issued by the University. The parapsychology course consists of two parts and it lasts two years. Each part consists of three ninety-minute classes per week for two months. A ninety per cent attendance and the submission of original research work are required to obtain the Certificate and the promotion. These rather hard regulations give the course a more serious tone. Most unfortunately, only a few submit this final research work. It is the students' task, mainly psychology students, to arouse the elementary and high school teachers' interest to apply the aforesaid tests to their students.

Extrasensory perception is studied and analyzed in the first year. The second year deals with the power of the mind over matter (PK).

I will explain briefly the content of each one of these parts.

FIRST YEAR THEMES.

1) After an introduction which stresses the remote existence of the parapsychological phenomena and the evolution of the present conception of their causes, there follows a brief study of the metapsychic qualitative phenomenology, what precedes it, and the difficulties of establishing a science with these elements. 2) Then the dynamics of the acquisition of information, sensorial experience and its limitations are analyzed. 3) Later, we analyze three kinds of extrasensory perceptions: clairvoyance, telepathy and precognition. To this we add the techniques for the different tests with the Zener cards and its adaptations; free subject tests, such as drawings and finally the use of electronic equipment. All this is done analyzing quantitative experimentation at the same time. 4) The next step is the study of personality variables, emotional states, stress-causing situations, different features of extroverted and introverted personalities, etc., and the relationship with extrasensory perception. Special emphasis is given to this study so that the research worker is furnished with the necessary conditions to foresee, interpret and understand the different investigation results, both in the high scores and in the systematic losses or oscillations within chance expectation. There exists a special psychological state which seems to be connected with the psi

activity: hypnotism. The characteristics of this state are analyzed: personality dissociation, the pouring of the unconscious through a diminishment or annulment of the conscious, which causes the appearance of possible extrasensory perception latent in the unconscious. The investigations carried on in the state of hypnosis are studied and compared to results obtained in a vigilant state (without the intervention of other variables). 6) There exist other psychological states reached through such chemical procedures as drugs and which are also manifestations of the mind. Together with this, other techniques are studied to produce altered states of consciousness through physical procedures or mental concentration through meditation. We analyze the possible relationship between these states and psi activity through the knowledge and discussion of investigations carried out in these special states, as well as the possible connection with the brainwaves. 7) A widely known subject is extrasensory perception in animals and plants. Being a science we cannot depend on anecdotes; therefore the investigations carried out in laboratories are analyzed. What is under discussion is whether the provoked phenomenon has really been isolated to such an extent that we should attribute the obvious effect solely to the animals, excluding the experimenter. We analyze the parallelism found in many experiments between the experimenter's psychological state and the results of the experiments on animals which would point out the real reason for the results. Besides, if poltergeist cases are the spontaneous result of human being's PK it follow that animals should produce the same results if they had the same PK ability, something which is still unknown. The supposition of the existence of psi in animals would go against the evolutionist conception of the appearance of intelligence when the organism has reached the most complex state, and obviously psi is an activity of the intelligence. On the other hand, the general belief of the existence of ESP and PK in plants is a misinterpretation of certain experiments. 8) Bearing in mind what has been analyzed in the above mentioned sections and the consequences derived from the different investigations carried out, we try to learn the conception of man provided by parapsychology and if the research work done up to now permits a comparison between man and machine or, on the contrary, if the results demand a different dimension to explain psi activity. The different explanatory hypotheses of the nature of the psi phenomenon and its cause are developed and analyzed. We also analyze the possible relationships between parapsychology and religion, if they are antagonistic situations or mutually exclusive or if they have anything in common. 9) Finally we explain some of the mathematical techniques used in the different statistical test analyses, as well as the standard results (CR Test of Variance, Student t Test etc.)

SECOND YEAR THEMES.

1) We first explain the historical antecedents of the known spontaneous cases of PK which show the existence of this activity throughout the centuries, though its effects were attributed to very different causes from the ones we know today. At the same time we analyze the qualitative experimentation of the metapsychical period. 2) Further ahead the quantitative experimentation is studied as the mind acts over movable, static and living targets. We analyze the classical test techniques with dice, discs, and marbles, their changes and adaptations as well as experimentation with electronic equipment, animals and plants. I specially emphasize my investigation on the power of the mind over living targets (rye seeds) as regards sex, age, emotional states, number of subjects, considering as well the distance between targets and subjects, and time. In my opinion this is an unknown field, as no investigation has been carried out regarding these aspects of the PK experiments. As mentioned before, I have been working on this research for four years, which has been partially replicated by the University of Cuyo in Mendoza. I think that it is not only an original investigation but also a very valuable one for the conclusions derived from these experiments. I reported it partially at the XV Annual Convention of the PA held at Edinburgh in 1972 and will also report it at the XVIII Convention which will be held at Santa Barbara. All this information is published in detail in the textbook "Parapsychological Phenomena. Psi in the Lab", Chapter V. 3) In the same way that we have already analyzed the personality variables and their influence on extrasensory perception, we deal here with their gravitation on the PK phenomenon. 4) The following step is the exposition of the most common and acceptable hypothesis formulated to explain the PK effects as telergy, magnetic forces, field theory etc., pointing out the aspects which are still to be confirmed, their weak and strong points. 5) Finally the various mathematical techniques used in the statistical analysis of PK tests are stated.

This is the information aspect of the courses which I teach at the Catholic University of Cordoba as well as in the other universities and educational centers. We realize that information is not enough, so we also have a laboratory with traditional and new elements to carry out different tests and the necessary advice for the psychological evaluations of the subjects. We have issued Zener cards with pertinent instructions and record sheets; we have the electronic equipment designed by Dr. H. Schmidt with the new adaptations planned and carried out by the Electronic Department of the School of Engineering. We also have the necessary elements for the tests with plants, etc.

The lab has a double function: 1) to do the routine work, training those who start or do the courses in investigations so that they acquire the necessary skill; 2) to carry out investigation work in new aspects which is done by post-graduates and students. We bear in mind the fact that both informative and practical teaching would be transient, rootless if it were not given permanence and continuity. That is to say, we need something stable which can be in itself a center for consultation and orientation, to serve the purposes of a permanent guidance for teachers and students of the University of Cordoba and other educational centers and people in general. It is for this reason that the Institute of Parapsychology was created with a staff including professors from the School of Psychology, members of the liberal professions and people acquainted with this subject-matter.

This Institute of Parapsychology started in 1973 in the Psychology Department of the School of Philosophy of the Catholic University of Cordoba. It was officially recognized by the Educational Committee of the University in 1974, as part of the investigation and education activities. This Institute fulfills a double function: 1) to provide the necessary interdisciplinary advice in the different areas, on investigations and problems which may come about in the field of parapsychology and its relationship with such areas as psychology, medicine, psychiatry, philosophy, theology, anthropology, etc.; 2) to take care of the subject matter of these sciences which either have a connection with or derivations in the field of parapsychology. The aim is to provide and look for mutual interdisciplinary guidance specially in the anthropocentric sciences.

The Institute is opened to all serious investigations in any areas related to parapsychology. It rejects no hypothesis; on the contrary it tries to look for and find the appropriate methodology and techniques, efficient and valid for the investigation. The Institute does not accept as true any kind of research work which is still in the stage of investigation or which does not go beyond the limits of a work hypothesis or theory. Both in teaching and research work we are open to what has been scientifically demonstrated in other centers and all creditable publications in this field.

Another feature of our Institute is its dynamic, that is to say, the activity it displays. It has a library which may be consulted by all those who require information. It may be considered the most complete and specialized library in parapsychology in Argentina. Periodical meetings are held to discuss the investigations done at the Institute, their evaluation or necessary corrections plus the discussion of investigations carried out in other centers. Our Institute organizes and teaches courses on parapsychology at the School of Psychology of the Catholic University of Cordoba as well as in other universities. It promotes publications, both general information and the highly specialized. It presents a wide panorama of parapsychology through different media such as radio, newspaper, television, round tables, panels etc.

We have been often consulted by bishops, priests, families, about different cases of poltergeist, bleeding religious images, people undergoing extraordinary phenomena, etc. Some of these cases were fully studied by a specialized team at the institute, others were investigated by psychiatrists and physicians. We also advise educational centers which are willing to get information or do their own experiments. I have not heard of any other center in Latin America which experiments in parapsychology and develops such a wide and coordinated educational activity and on a university scientific responsibility level.

The only periodical on parapsychology published in Argentina is the quarterly journal "Cuadernos de Parapsicologia" which is edited by Mr. Naum Kreiman, Director of the Institute of Parapsychology in Buenos Aires. This periodical publishes experiments carried out in other centers as well as at the Institute, and articles from other publications as well.

What can we think about parapsychology and its relationship with other sciences? Must we consider it as an independent science? According to the aforesaid, its relation to other sciences is clear and obvious. Nevertheless if we consider its specific feature, that of having no physical stimulus up to now, parapsychology is situated in a unique position, different from those which require a physical stimulus. However, some people prefer to incorporate it in conventional psychology, since it deals with human and knowledge phenomena, while others consider parapsychology a science totally independent of, though slightly resembling physics, specially if the PK effect is taken into account. These people have given several names to psi activity such as: psychobioenergy, psychobioelectronics, psychobiodynamics, etc. trying to explain parapsychology through psychology, biology and physics. However, the data provided by the quantum theory, the physical law of indeterminism, the theory of relativity and cybernetics are not enough to satisfactorily explain psi activity. In addition we can say that up to now parapsychology could not be placed in such models especially if we consider its distinguishing feature: the disregard of matter (time and space). What is then the relation of parapsychology to other sciences and their branches?

If, in order to understand this relationship and the placement of parapsychology among other sciences, we consider its effects, such as acquisition of information and action in the physical field by unknown stimuli notwithstanding, we will be focusing on a secondary aspect. On the contrary, it is essential to consider the level at which PK action, knowledge or activation takes place; that is to say, attention must be paid to the level in common of both activities. They are unified by the deepest psychic zone commonly called "unconsciousness."

We are accustomed to act in accordance with sensorial stimuli. However, we meet here something which is not sensorial and in spite of this it is real and will happen with manifestations belonging to the unconscious: hallucinations, convictions, dreams or physical effects. These in turn would be provoked by what underlies the unconscious, such as automatism, and these provoke the spontaneous effects we call a poltergeist. Then psi activity would be the way out for the extrasensorially incorporated, since this is not easily achieved without using the senses or expressing a deeply rooted wish that maybe the individual has never consciously admitted. Therefore, to place psi activity we must turn to human depth psychology and on this level we find that the unconscious dynamic uses these resources to reach the conscious level and deliver its content. Consequently, parapsychology, in its relationship to other sciences, should be placed within the study of depth psychology, of unconscious dynamic, together with all the influences, implications and gravitations it exerts over all activities and the development of the human being and, at the same time, over all sciences related to the human being.

As a result of the above mentioned, we can say that parapsychology is a normal psychological activity, not a strange or magic one; and that man sometimes expresses himself through his senses and other times without them.

Finally I would like to mention a fact which in itself illustrates the genuine interest the Argentine people have, to seriously and deeply know what parapsychology is. Mr. Sobrino Aranda, a National Deputy, introduced a bill in the National Congress in which he suggested that all Universities should include parapsychology in their syllabuses. This bill became law in 1974.

DISCUSSION

BELOFF: I would like to say, first, that I am full of admiration for your tremendous championship of parapsychology in your country. But I couldn't help wondering, while you were speaking, whether you weren't perhaps a little complacent about the educational value of parapsychology in all circumstances, particularly, for example, where young children are concerned. Children's thinking is ordinarily full of magical notions. I mean, children very naturally take to magical ideas, and if you convince them that they have the power simply to make plants grow and such things, aren't they going to have a little bit of difficulty in coping with scientific ideas in school and when they grow up, learning, as it were, the ordinary scientific approach? Won't this produce a certain kind of conflict in their minds? This would worry me a little, but perhaps you have your own solution as to how these many different kinds of ideas can be integrated.

NOVILLO: You are right that there is a danger of misinterpretation since this experiment seems to exercise a kind of magical power. But, on the other hand, it presents a good opportunity to give a proper understanding of this human ability with which they are already acquainted through TV, radio, newspapers, etc. At the same time, it is necessary that the teacher has a clear idea of the psi dynamics. The teacher then can explain later to the children the meaning of the research work. If the subjects are young boys or girls, this explanation is done either by myself or by my assistants.

I started my investigations about the growth of plants at Durham, North Carolina, in an elementary school where the teachers were nuns. They accepted it quite willingly and the children were very enthusiastic. When my experiments were over, the students were given a few days to perform their personal research projects in order to appreciate the scientific method of research. I was greatly surprised when the children spontaneously presented the influence of music in the growth of plants.

Throughout the four years of my research, I had to deal with different kinds of subjects varying in age and culture, and I never heard of any magical interpretations.

MORRISS: What percentage of your results where you worked with the boys and girls separately were significant?

NOVILLO: I have conducted more than forty experiments and most of them were significant. My main goal was to research the relation of

PK ability to the sex of the subjects; and within my experiments, as I have quoted in my paper, I analyzed other variables influencing the results, such as emotional changes in the subjects, the influence of men and women together on the same group of seeds, etc. In general I can say that the results produced by the men in regard to the height of the plants was greater than that produced by the women. In addition, I can say that the results produced by women were nearer to those produced by the control group.

To determine whether the difference in the results had to be attributed to the sex of the subjects, I used mixed groups of men and women to influence the same group of seeds and in this particular circumstance, the experiment lacked significance. It seems a cancellation effect. Looking for the evidence of the influence of the sex in psi ability, I had two groups of girls and a control group in several experiments; and two groups of boys and a control group in others. In the experiments with the boys, the results are significant if we compare the height of the subjects' plants with the height of the control plants; but there was no significant difference in regard to the height of the plants achieved by the two groups of boys. In the experiments with the girls, the height of their plants did not yield any significant result.

I have also conducted other experiments where the distance between subjects and targets was several meters or even hundreds of kilometers, and sometimes the number of subjects in each group has varied. In spite of these changes, I achieved the same significant results as before and thus no relation was found regarding these changes of distance and number of subjects. In other words, to have one boy or girl or several boys and girls in each subjects group; or to be close or far away from the targets exert no influence on the results already obtained from the experiments.

SCHMEIDLER: You said so many interesting things that mostly I was just listening and trying to absorb it. But I'd like to ask about one particular matter, concerning sex and its relation to results. Might you be willing to subsume it under the general topic of attitude and personality? I'm not trying to say that sex is a matter of personality, but that the way sex affects PK results might be through its effect upon a person's attitude. For instance, when you, as an enthusiastic male experimenter, come in and set a scientific experiment to boys, they're more likely to identify with you and with the experiment, I should think, than girls are. It would seem to me that if you could possibly recruit an equally enthusiastic and convincing and likeable female experimenter to come in and present the same material both to girls and to boys, you might find a reversal in sex patterns. And as for the effect you found with mixed groups, I would tie that in, tentatively with the Mihalasky and Dean finding, that where there were groups of either mixed sex or mixed race or mixed professional achievement, the sub-group that was dominant, that represented the great majority, got higher scores at ESP than did the non-dominant sub-group. This is the sort of thing that I've been finding very recently. Just last month it turned up in research. That is, when there were only one or two males in a mixed group, the females had higher scores. When there were only one or two females, the males had higher scores. The sex that was more comfortable and presumably more at home in the situation, did better. Perhaps, in Argentina where there is a mixed group, there is less feeling of comfort in making things grow together, than there would be with the two sexes separated, where each would feel more at home.

NOVILLO: Dr. Schmeidler—your research is about ESP?

SCHMEIDLER: Yes.

NOVILLO: What I want to say is that sex is a fundamental component of a human being. There is a difference between men and women and, consequently, it must affect psi ability in several aspects. Remember, Dr. Schmeidler, that I was not alone in conducting these tests about the growth of the plants. There were female teachers dealing daily with the students, both boys and girls. The teachers were sure that the girls' results would be better but this was not so, despite the fact that there were sometimes fewer boys or a large number of girls. I also had female assistants, but I never talked about my expectations in the results of the tests. I have sometimes anticipated a particular result in the boys' group and nevertheless it was not so. Thus there does not seem to have been my influence on the subjects' attitude. In addition, for the height obtained in the targets, it doesn't matter whether the subject was a man or a group of them, or a woman or a group of them. What I want to say is that the number of subjects in each group does not affect the results, at least, in my PK experiments.

Some people have said that these results could be the hormonal effect of the subjects over the seeds or plants. Nevertheless we have to remember that the subjects who came daily for a few minutes to the laboratory were children eight years of age; and when the subjects were older persons, there was distance between targets and subjects: from meters to hundreds of kilometers.

In the experiments with the children eight years old, the girls yielded higher results than boys, although the boys' number was larger than girls'. But in the adults, it was the men who achieved the higher results.

ROGO: Last night I was talking with Dr. Morris and Dr. Stanford and we were discussing the fact that on U.S. campuses there seems to be a slight tendency for Catholic universities to be a little more open to parapsychology, and I was wondering how you felt the acceptance of parapsychology in Argentine education related to the predominant Roman Catholic tradition and population in South America.

NOVILLO: I think—at least this is my position—in my University, that parapsychology is a science, there is no problem. If it is a science, it is a truth. I am not afraid about truth, and if parapsychology is truth—there is no problem.

KRIPPNER: I'm still speculating on Dr. Beloff's comment, which I thought was very well put, regarding the magical thinking that many children go through and that even emerges from time to time in adults, and how this affects educational procedures. I don't think we've given enough thought to this, in the conference. Furthermore, I don't think parapsychologists have really done much work on this topic. It might very well be that in educating for parapsychology, somewhat different strategies and techniques are going to be used at different age levels. If we examine Piaget's theory on developmental stages we notice that he's proposed a number of terms that display differences in children's thinking. We have the movement from the motor to the motor-visual, to the visual-motor to the visual. We have the shift from concrete to abstract thinking; we also have the shift from pre-operational to operational thinking. It would seem to me that any instruction that we give young people, especially very young people, in para-psychology is going to have to consider these modes of thinking very carefully.

Jerome Bruner once said that any academic topic can be taught to any person no matter what that person's age may be; it just needs to be adapted in accordance with that person's developmental status. Now, of course, I'm sure that parapsychology was the last thing that Bruner was thinking of, but I do think that parapsychology is a proper example in terms of how these adaptations might have to be accomplished. I certainly don't have any answer for this and I'm not even saying that magical thinking is always negative. It might be there are events in the world and events in parapsychology which ultimately are going to have to be explained aside from cause-and-effect thinking. But Dr. Beloff did put his finger on a very important issue here, and those of us who at any point are going to be working on parapsychological issues with very young children, should give this matter some thought, should read the studies of children's thinking, should examine fantasy among children—even altered states of consciousness among children,—and see where these data apply.

STANFORD: I wanted to raise a question, specifically a matter in your course outline. I noticed that in both courses you seem to be placing the matter of statistical evaluation as a last topic for discussion. It seems to me that that should have come earlier in the course so that people could have better comprehended the studies, the adequacy of the evaluation. Perhaps you would like to comment on why you do place that at the end of the course rather than elsewhere.

NOVILLO: I am following my text book in my courses and if you would see it you could realize that from the beginning I am dealing with statistics because the basis of my lectures and explanations are the research work performed in different laboratories where statistics are fundamental. At the end of the courses, I explain in full the meaning and use of the statistics: different techniques for the evaluation of the tests: CR, Test of Variance, Student t Test, etc. Sometimes I do not need to explain very much about statistics because the students are familiar with them, for example, students of psychology, physics, engineering, etc., but for others it is a difficult subject, for example, for law students, liberal arts majors, etc.

Starting the course by explaining statistics would not be a good method especially for the students not acquainted with mathematics. If they want to have a fuller knowledge after my explanation and the use of the text book, they can consult specialized books.

RAO: I have two very brief comments. One is, I think, some sort of a comment on the possible interpretation of your PK results. I have a guess that, probably, you were the subject in those PK experiments and not your students. You also mentioned about long distance PK experiments, and if you, by any chance, stumbled on this hypothesis of sex differences, maybe you are using your PK on these plants all through, so that your own assumptions are getting confirmed.

The second one, as I heard about the legislation in your country in 1974, making parapsychology compulsory . . .

NOVILLO: Not compulsory—recommendation.

RAO: O.K., recommendation.

NOVILLO: Recommendation only. Congress recommended to the universities to include in their syllabus the teaching of parapsychology. *Recommend*, and not one university has accepted.

RAO; Does it mean if you accept you get more money from the government?

NOVILLO: I don't understand. Please repeat that.

RAO: If you accept this recommendation, do you get more money from the government?

NOVILLO: We don't receive any money from the government. Not one penny.

RAO: In our country, the Catholic schools teach Bible to the students, and some Hindu schools teach the *Gita* and I hope parapsychology will never be in that position.

NOVILLO: I don't know what is happening in your country. In my country it is different. In regard to the first part of your question, I think I have partially answered it already. I do not believe I have unconsciously been a subject myself in my research work. Several times the results of my experiments were absolutely contrary to my expectations. If I had been the subject throughout the more than forty experiments (each lasting ten days) I would be exhausted. Nevertheless I have had consistently good results in research. It is also not easy to influence two targets simultanously and get significance; and I was conducting the experiments with blind targets as well. If such was the case, that I was the subject, I find that hard to believe.

THE ROLE OF PARAPHYSICS IN PHYSICS EDUCATION

Wilbur Franklin

A QUANTUM JUMP?

The Chance for Departure

The choice of whether paraphysics has a justified role to play in physics and physics education or, rather, in the newly developing and often criticized pseudoscience is a significant contemporary choice. The question of whether the hierarchies of conservative thought in physics education will restrain the emergence of new findings and educational programs in parapsychology/paraphysics because of conditioned heritage or whether the strength of the chrysalis of advocators will be sufficient to bring the powerful techniques of physics and physics education to the students of the occult fields is a question with holistic significance. In the interesting poem "The Quantum Jump" by Julius Stulman,[1] the necessity for departure into new pathways permeates the composition which begins: "We stand at civilization's impasse, groping for direction . . . seeking unheard symbols to consciousness. We stand in relational constructs, echoes of blinding pages, school-tool designed; education—no education; security seeking—insecurity; fact—no fact; calling for additional steps, a pathway to wisdom. While survival begs a quantum jump toward wholeness . . . Can man—mankind continue emergence?"

The study of human consciousness in the holistic sense by physicists and physical scientists holds, in my opinion, the potential for quantum jumps in the return stemming from inquiry into 1) the role of the observer in the observed universe,[2] 2) the structure of physical theories,[3] and 3) the symbiotic relationship of the mind to educational methodologies.[4] Only through careful, thoroughly planned and executed programs, can the potential for attainment of quality efforts in education and research be fulfilled in this most interesting and potentially useful field.

In a recent listing[5] of courses in parapsychology dated November, 1974, three departments of physics are listed that have taught recently or are teaching courses in paraphysics/parapsychology while a fourth department (not physics) lists a course called "Physics and Parapsychology." In addition, courses have been taught at Kent State University in teleneural[6] physics in the Physics Department. A list of these courses and their physics-related instructors follows. All of these courses received university credit.

Course	*Instructor*	*Department*
Paraphysics and Ind. Study	Dr. Curtis Wagner & Dr. Charles Reinert	Physics Department SW Minnesota State College
Physics 499 & 499G	Dr. James Wray	Dept. of Physics & Astronomy Morehead State College
Physics & Parapsychology	Rochelle Winnett	Course Mart University of Michigan
Nature & the Occult	Dr. Albert Shadowitz & Dr. Peter Walsh	Physics Department Fairleigh Dickinson Univ.
Introductory Teleneural Studies and Teleneural Interactions & Ind. Study	Dr. Wilbur Franklin & Mr. Elan Moritz	Physics Department Kent State University

At Morehead State, the course by James Wray was taught as a pilot course in conjunction with faculty in the psychology and philosophy departments. Two years of physics, psychology, or philosophy or a combination were required as prerequisites. At Fairleigh Dickinson, the course by Drs. Shadowitz and Walsh has had 50–100 students each semester and consideration is presently being given to preparation of the course notes as a manuscript for a text. At Kent State University, the course in Introductory Teleneural Studies requires no prerequisites and is designed for non-science students whereas the course in Teleneural Interactions requires introductory physics, calculus and psychology as prerequisites. More detail regarding these courses is given in Pilot Courses in Teleneural Physics at KSU below. In addition to the introductory courses in paraphysics listed above, two interesting physics courses by Otto Theimer dealing with contemporary physics and society have been introduced in New Mexico State University which include discussions of "all kinds of psychic phenomena" and utilize a text written for the courses by Theimer.[7] There are undoubtedly other courses in physics departments which include discussions of paraphysics which are unknown to the author and their omission in this brief listing is, therefore, unintentional.

Rudiments of a Rationale

Historically, the role of physics in society has been to discover the nature of the physical universe, to develop applications and to propose and test theories. The three fundamental forces of nature, the conservation rules, and symmetries have been discovered and developed, for the most part, within the framework of physics. The scientific method utilized in the development of physical principles and laws involves repeatability of experiments by the same investigator and by different investigators in different laboratories. The charges that psychic events are unique, unrepeatable[7] and, hence, unscientific and that they should reside within the scope of pseudoscience, religion, or witchcraft is, in my opinion, incorrect since those who understand how to treat the most complex variable in teleneural experimentation—the human being—have been able to obtain repeatable results with the same and/or different subjects which do not follow the laws of physics as presently taught. The charges made by others that no reasonable theoretical *approaches* have been proposed for psychic-type phenomena is also untrue, in my opinion, since theories for the propagation of a telepathic signal have been worked out very well for the electromagnetic case by Kogan[8] and checked and extended by Franklin,[9] a theory of short-term precognition has been broached by Feinberg[10] using the advanced potential, and information theory approaches to different aspects of psychic phenomena have been developed over a number of years by Chari.[11]

With these and other developing theories there is, in my estimation, a developing nucleus of theoretical approaches to paranormal teleneural interactions on which to base educational programs in physics and the physical sciences. On the experimental side, there is a much more substantial body of reliable evidence for classroom presentation. It is not the purpose of this article to give a critical review of experimental work, so the reader is referred to the recent work of Targ and Puthoff[12] and references therein, the parapsychology journals, and abstracts of the recent international conference on the physics of paranormal phenomena.[13] While the number of articles written by or agreeable to professional physicists is not large, sufficient evidence of a substantive nature is available to form a nucleus of reliable data for physics classroom presentation.

One of the most interesting articles in recent months by a renowned physicist is that by John Wheeler[2] entitled "The Universe as Home for Man." Many questions are posed in this article concerning the role of the mind and the observer in the nature of the physical universe. Wheeler, who is one of the world's foremost astrophysicists, addresses the problem of black holes and the origin of the universe. He asks "Is the universe deprived of all meaningful existence in the absence of mind? Is it governed in its structure by the requirement that it give birth to life and consciousness? Or is man merely an unimportant speck of dust in a remote corner of space? In brief, are life and mind irrelevant to the structure of the universe—or are they central to it?" Serious questions of this nature are also being asked by paraphysicists groping for an explanation for their repeated observations of paranormal teleneural interactions with matter and with bioinformation transfer at great distances.

The role of the observer in experimental observations has been an integral part of atomic and elementary particle physics and physics education since the initial work by Schroedinger and Heisenberg in the development of quantum mechanics. Since quantum mechanical analogs for macroscopic PK events have proven to be fruitful, at least initially, in the development of theoretical paradigms,[3, 13] the inclusion of quantum mechanics in the contemporary programs of physics education offers one of many possible avenues of serious interplay between physics and the theory of teleneural phenomena. Other avenues of possible interplay exist via elementary particle theories, cosmology and unified field theories. In addition, the student of physics is, perhaps, the best able to distinguish paranormal events from those which can be explained using electromagnetic or other extant theories. What must be done by students of the field of paraphysics is to delineate clearly which laws of contemporary physics are not followed in teleneural interactions, how the interactions differ from those known, and how what we know in physics can be applied to the problem. If there is a quantum jump to be made in a progressive direction in paraphysics/parapsychology then a significant portion of the burden of that advance will be on physicists and on the educational and research backgrounds of the workers involved.

In the courses which are described in the following sections the author assumes a posture, based on his own experimental and theoretical observations and on those of others, that there is something new in psychic phenomena that is most likely not explainable by contemporary physics. This assumption may not be as well-founded as desirable, but there is, in my opinion, sufficient good evidence at this time to hold such a disposition seriously.

PILOT COURSES IN TELENEURAL PHYSICS AT KENT STATE UNIVERSITY

Course Content and Syllabi

Three distinctly different classroom courses in teleneural physics have been taught in the Physics Department at Kent State University for credit. One of these has been taught twice in the two successive academic years 1972–73 and 1973–74. This course was a one-quarter junior-senior level special topics course for two credits. There were no prerequisites and students' backgrounds varied from physics to English and education. Projects by students were carried out and term papers were required. A closed book mid-term and final examination were given. A few faculty and graduate students sat in on this course. In the third year the course was replaced by two four credit hour one-quarter courses. They received a small grant from the Ford Foundation via the Kent State University Venture Fund for innovative advances in teaching. Prerequisites of introductory physics, calculus, and psychology or permission of the instructor were instituted for the more advanced of the two courses. This course was junior-senior level, required a term paper, and offered opportunities for experimental projects for students. The introductory course was sophomore level, had no prerequisites, required a term paper and offered project opportunities. It was taught by a Ph.D. graduate student in theoretical physics, Mr. Elan Moritz. The course content of both courses contained approximately 50% in the realm of traditional physics and 50% which dealt with observations and theories of paranormal teleneural phenomena. In addition to classroom courses, individual investigation projects have been carried out by physics and other science students in the Physics Department in projects involving electrophotography on human subjects and on plants. These projects were done for credit in physics.

A description of the sophomore-level course, Introductory Teleneural Studies, is given by the syllabus which follows.

SYLLABUS—INTRODUCTORY TELENEURAL STUDIES

A. The philosophy of science
  1. Scientific method and past developments in science
  2. Concept evolution and paradigms
  3. Interrelationships between science & society; values & mores
  4. Important developments & paradigms in science in perspective (i.e. relativity, the uncertainty principle, quantum mechanics, cosmology, etc.)

B. The fields of Man—survey of known electromagnetic effects
  1. Electromagnetic spectrum and effects of certain frequencies on living systems
  2. Static electric and magnetic field effects
  3. Electromagnetic theory of bioinformation transfer
  4. Altered states of consciousness and brain waves
  5. Observations which don't fit in with known laws
C. Implications for society and the future
  1. Societal effects of technological developments which affect Man
  2. Effects of developments in paraphysics on society, political science, sociology, mental health, etc.
  3. Value judgements from the perspective of a scientist

Recommended reading: Lyall Watson, "Supernature", and class notes of the instructor; additional references will be given.

Essentially the first five weeks of the nonmathematical ten week course in Introductory Teleneural Studies were devoted to development of the major paradigms of contemporary physics, science and the philosophy of science. Particular attention was given to the growth and emergence of concepts in classical mechanics, quantum mechanics, relativity theory, and electromagnetic theory. The historical development of paradigms in the climate of traditional physics at that time was outlined and comparisons were made with the development and potential development of new paraphysical paradigms today. The second half of the course dealt with definitions, descriptions, and interpretations of various aspects of parapsychological phenomena and their interplay with physics.

The junior-senior level course, Teleneural Interactions, also devoted approximately the first half of the course to traditional areas of physics emphasizing electromagnetic theory and observations relating to living systems. This provided a background for comparison of electromagnetic effects on living systems with paranormal teleneural effects. A syllabus for this course follows.

SYLLABUS—TELENEURAL INTERACTIONS

A. Interactions of electromagnetic radiation with living systems with emphasis on Man
  1. Survey of types of interaction of electromagnetic (em) radiation with living systems from Earth waves to cosmic rays
  2. Energetics—resonance effects
  3. Electrostatic and magnetostatic effects on living systems
  4. Electrophotography, bioplasmas, Kirlian photography, and aura—a comparison

5. Electromagnetic pollution
6. Positive and negative ions in electric fields and effects on biological systems
7. Electromagnetic theory of teleneural projection and reception

B. Psychophysics and signal detection in living systems
1. Mechanisms of overt and subliminal sensation in Man
2. Power law relating psychological response to sensory stimulus
3. Threshold and non-threshold detection of signals
4. Neural networks, signal detection, and information processing

C. Information theory
1. Application to communication, experimental psychophysics, and telepathy
2. Information theory and propagation of negentropy—relationship to telepathy and teleneural interaction with matter

D. Paranormal teleneural phenomena and comparisons with known theory
1. Historical survey and classification
2. Teleneural interactions between living systems
3. Teleneural interactions with matter

In this course it was assumed that entering students would have a knowledge of the fundamental paradigms of physics and physical science. Therefore, most of the background material given in the first half of the course dealt with an exposition of the variety of teleneural electromagnetic effects which are presently becoming known. Then the paranormal teleneural effects, which are probably not electromagnetic, were defined, classified and discussed in depth in the second half of the course.

Projects, Resources, and Papers

Experimental and theoretical projects were explained to students in each class indicating briefly the scope and methodology of the proposed projects. Students were encouraged to develop and/or to participate in projects and were given the freedom to choose one of the suggested projects or to propose an acceptable one suited to individual interests. A small amount of financial support (about $500) was available for equipment and supplies for both classes. The experimental projects which were carried out in the three years of class offerings at Kent State include the following:

1) Kirlian photography
   a) In human subjects as a function of altered states of consciousness and physiology

    b) In rats in the normal state and various drugged states
    c) In human subjects—relationship to health and to acupuncture
       points and meridians
2) Telepathy inside and outside a Faraday cage
3) Effects of human interactions with plants
    a) Effects on Kirlian photographs of leaves in vivo
    b) Effects on resistivity of leaves in vivo
4) Negative ion effects on humans
5) Design of PK measuring devices

The most popular projects in every class were those involving Kirlian photography. For these projects there were Tesla coils, Polaroid and 35 mm cameras, film and other necessary equipment and supplies available. The basic techniques were demonstrated in class and some of the theory given and pitfalls discussed. In addition to Kirlian photography, there was also a great deal of interest in various types of experiments with plants. These were, however, more difficult and less rewarding than the Kirlian photography projects. There was an unexpectedly small number of choices involving experiments with telepathy or PK. The reasons for this were not apparent since experimental techniques and theory were discussed in class and facilities and potential subjects were available. On the theoretical side the following topics were investigated by students.

1) Information and communication theory and teleneural phenomena
2) Biofeedback
3) Teleneural interaction with matter and poltergeist phenomena
4) Paranormal techniques of healing
5) Electromagnetic effects
    a) Effects of low frequencies on living organisms
    b) Effects of microwaves on Man and living systems
    c) Electromagnetic pollution of the environment

From discussions with students regarding their choice of topic it was apparent that early in the course those who were not physics majors were usually unable to distinguish the significance of many topics to the involvement of psychic phenomena nor the differences of paranormal phenomena from well-known theories. For example, many thought that Kirlian photographs were produced "psychically." Physics students and others with good backgrounds in physics were much better able to interpret the significance of paranormal observations and the comparisons with and differences from known theories.

The literature resources available to students for support of their projects and papers included a file of over 100 selected references and files of copies of articles.

In addition to the reference file and file of articles, a small library of books was conveniently available and, in addition, a list of Kent State library books on many pertinent topics was included in the notes distributed to students.

Lectures and Class Notes for Teleneural Interactions Course

A set of lecture notes prepared during the previous two years and consisting of 35 single-spaced pages was distributed to students in the 1974–75 Teleneural Interactions course. These notes deal with the topics in the first half of the course. Notes for the second half are in preparation for the next time the course is taught. The lecture outline for this course, listed chronologically, follows:

1) Introduction
2) Classification of teleneural phenomena & definitions
3) Classification of known electromagnetic phenomena, the frequency spectrum & biological interactions
4) Electrosensation & communication in fish
5) Effects of static electric fields & ions on biosystems
6) Magnetic field effects on living organisms
7) Telepathy, hypnotism, & mesmerism
8) Theories of telepathic informtion transfer
9) More on telepathy—theory & experiment
10) Telepathic overtones: Synergistic effects in groups, automatic writing, invention origins, etc.
11) Teleneural interaction with matter: experimental evidence
12) Clairvoyance, alteration of materials, & information transfer
13) Kirlian photography, acupuncture system, & aura
14) Meditation & altered states of consciousness—a scientific review
15) Plants: known electrical effects compared with new observations
16) Psychophysics—the science of sensation
17) Information & communication theory
18) Information theory applied to teleneural phenomena
19) Unique features of living organisms: origins of life, evolution theory, organization & negentropy
20) Other theoretical constructs & theoretical overview

The intent of the chronological design given was to present a good background of electromagnetic effects on living systems and then to get into paranormal teleneural phenomena. Because of the interest expressed by students in items 13–15 for possible projects, these items, which are mostly electromagnetic in nature, were moved to an earlier position in the course. Then, after lectures on telepathy and teleneural interaction with matter, the interesting topics of psychophysics, information theory, unique aspects of living organisms, and new theoretical constructs were presented.

Rationale

In a field which has been impeded by charlatanism, measurements reported by incompetent researchers, and an historic deep-seated skepticism by much of the academic community, it is imperative to set and maintain a high degree of integrity and honesty regarding the information related to students in classes. It is also important not to omit the reporting of good evidence because of preconceived bias against it, since good physical basis for such evidence may become available at a later date. An operational framework suitable for courses in physics which seems substantial in basis at the present time might include a full discussion of the following paraphysical phenomena:

1) Telepathy, its many different forms & manifestations, and its theories
2) Information retrieval regarding remote inanimate targets
3) Precognition
4) Psychokinesis, bending & fracture of metals, telephotic phenomena, and poltergeist events

This list omits specific reference to things like astrology, pendulum swinging, numerology, psychometry, methods of witchcraft, and similar phenomena because of their largely subjective nature which is often difficult to quantify and to study physically. In addition, other major subfields of parapsychology including healing and paranormal medical techniques, studies of the EEG and biofeedback, and paranormal events in abnormal psychology are more within the framework of psychology and the medical sciences than physics and are, therefore, not covered in depth in Kent State's teleneural physics courses. It seems important for physics and the physical sciences to address the fundamental questions of the nature of the influence fields or forces involved, to distinguish the characteristics of paranormal teleneural interactions carefully, and to develop *new* paradigms for their expression. In this manner, the scope of physics courses in this area can deal with substantive issues and need not infringe on other disciplines. There is, however, substantial opportunity for interdisciplinary effort in paraphysics/parapsychology.

The level of mathematics involved in the Teleneural Interactions course utilized algebra and calculus at the level of an introductory physics course. For example, in psychophysics the power law stems from the integration of $d\psi/\psi = kd\phi/\phi$ to give

$$\psi = K(\phi - \phi_0)^k \tag{1}$$

where ϕ and ψ are the stimulus and psychological level of attainment, respectively, and K, k, and ϕ_0 are constants. Another example of the type of mathematics found useful in the course is based on the information theory equation for the transmitted capacity C in terms of the bandwidth W and signal and noise powers, P and n, respectively.

$$C = W \ln_2 \frac{P + n}{n} \tag{2}$$

Using this equation the critical power P* is derived needed to transmit a telepathic message using electromagnetic theory or not. Then the requisite biocurrent is derived using, simply, $P = I^2R$. This theory, which stems from the work of Kogan[8] and extended slightly by Franklin[9], was presented without the derivation of the antenna equations.

The type of attitudes in academia toward courses dealing with paranormal phenomena is significant in the design of educational programs in this area. Attitudes are initially influenced by the degree of respect in a particular institution for the college, department, and faculty member concerned with the proposed course. Since nothing of significance has appeared in the physics literature on psychic type phenomena it seems important for a prospective instructor of a course in teleneural interactions to spend considerable time speaking personally with members of the department and others about the intended scope and content of the course. For the average scientist the *only information* he has to read concerning paranormal phenomena stems from the popular press and this is hardly the best source of information to prepare a physics department for a course in this area! It is important to note, however, that a new climate of acceptance does exist for the study of paranormal phenomena which is receptive to high level technical work in this field by physical scientists and engineers.

Concepts and Paradigms

One of the most interesting and challenging aspects of these courses to students was the presentation of the historical paradigms of physics and of the application of new concepts and paradigms to observations of teleneural phenomena. The theories of relativity, the uncertainity principle, and cosmology, which were presented and discussed in the introductory course, demonstrated very well to the non-science student how new paradigms in their historical setting challenged traditional structure and heuristic principles. The analogy between the developments of contemporary paradigms of theoretical physics and the recent (as well as historic) observations in psi phenomena which require a new paradigm pointed up the difficulties in surmounting traditional concepts and laying new foundations.

Theories which were broached in the Teleneural Interactions course included concepts of extra dimensionalities such as those utilized in cosmology theory and those postulated to explain certain psi phenomena. The role of determinism in science was discussed and compared with the results of the uncertainty principle in quantum mechanics.

The uncertainty principle, effects of hypothetical hidden variables, and important role played by the observer in quantum mechanics offer excellent topics for discussion as exposition of the principles and domains of possible applicability of each. The possible role of the advanced potential and of determinism and causality in precognition was discussed. Also, tachyon approaches to communication, the role of information theory in the analysis of telepathy, and the seeming inapplicability of the conservation laws and laws of force and motion to certain PK phenomena provided important avenues of teaching both the traditional concepts known to the physics community and the significance of the new observations in teleneural interaction with matter. Care was taken to obviate dogmatism on these issues and to distinguish hypothetical concepts from well-known and accepted paradigms. Discussion was open and the fundamental and intriguing questions raised by the field of paranormal teleneural phenomena were put forth and analyzed for their possible contributions to the field.

FUTURES IN TELENEURAL PHYSICS EDUCATION

The innate and impinging forces acting on the thrust of teleneural research and education give rise to numerous possibilities for the future of the field. The strength of the emergence of education in teleneural phenomena and its acceptance is dependent on 1) the genuineness and scientific validation of the observed phenomena, 2) the availability and style of presentation of the results to the academic community, 3) the strength of opposing forces and alternative explanations, and 4) economic factors. Only through persistent search for the truth in the field and a determined effort toward academic excellence will the guise of charlatanism and witchcraft, in its derogatory sense, be removed from academically enlightened institutions and individuals active in the field in the physical sciences. Even though the word "magic" in its broad interpretation includes the paranormal, there are recent indicators that the field of paraphysics is emerging from the mystique of magic in the minds of many scientists to take a very significant place in physical and medical science and science education.

The distinctly different roles played by the popular press, the occult literature, and the conservative scientific journals of the field of parapsychology/paraphysics are important avenues for the establishment of credence and diffusion of knowledge in the field. Despite many well-known and widely publicized scandals and errors in certain observations in recent years, the popular press has evidently served a useful function in the rapid dissemination of new scientific findings. Workers in the field who could "read between the lines" often had access to laboratory results one to two years before their appearance in journals. Probably one of the most difficult problems facing workers in the field of physics and other sciences at the present time is the conservative attitude of editors and reviewers for physics and related journals. Evidently no article has yet been published in a good American physics journal which deals, in a substantive and positive way, with either theory or experimental observations of psi phenomena. However, an important article by Targ and Puthoff[14] has appeared recently in an engineering journal. Since the diffusion of scientific knowledge in a discipline, material for new courses, criteria for promotion in professional ranks, and outlets for thesis work all depend strongly on journal publications in the discipline, the fields of physics and other sciences will have to find avenues for publication within the framework of the existing discipline if workers in the field are not to be ostracized and segregated into pseudoscientific or pseudoacademic areas. The neglect of the field of biophysics by the mainstream of the physics community for many decades probably slowed the growth of that useful field substantially in comparison to nuclear, plasma, and other traditional areas of physics. The potential of the field of paraphysics/parapsychology for social usefulness, the understanding of information transfer in cellular and neural systems, and the basis of the conservation laws and forces in the physical universe seem to warrant serious consideration of a major thrust into this interesting area by physical scientists and educators at this time.

REFERENCES

[1] Julius Stulman, "The Quantum Jump," *Fields Within Fields 5*, p. 3 (1972).

[2] John A. Wheeler, "The Universe as Home for Man," *American Scientist 62*, p. 683 (1974).

[3] Charles Panati, "Quantum Physics and Parapsychology," *Parapsychology Review 5*, No. 6, 1 (1974).

[4] Georgi Lozanov, *Suggestology*, Nauka Press, Sofia, Bulgaria (1971).

[5] *Courses & Other Study Opportunities in Parapsychology*, Am. Soc. for Psychical Research, $2.00.

[6] The word "teleneural" stems from the Greek word "tele" meaning far or distant and "neural" which has to do with the nervous system in the broadest sense. Teleneural interactions include both electromagnetic and paranormal interactions.

[7] Otto H. Theimer, *A Gentleman's Guide to Modern Physics*, (Belmont, California: Wadsworth Publishing Co., 1973).

[8] I. M. Kogan, *Telecommunications and Radio Engineering 21*, p. 75 (1966); *22*, p. 141 (1967); *23*, p. 122 (1968). Kogan concludes that electromagnetic theory is probably insufficient to explain long range telepathic results.

[9] Wilbur Franklin, *Bulletin American Physical Society 19*, 821 (1974).

[10] Gerald Feinberg, Physics Department, Columbia University, personal communication; also, see Ref. (3).

[11] C. T. K. Chari, "The Challenge of Psi: New Horizons of Scientific Research," *J. Parapsych. 38*, p. 1–15 (1974).

[12] Russell Targ and Harold Puthoff, *Nature, 251*, p. 602, 1974.

[13] "The Physics of Paranormal Phenomena," International Conference, Tarrytown, New York, Feb. 21–23, 1975; Abstracts to be available from Brendon O'Regan, % Stanford Research Institute, 203B, 333 Ravenswood Ave., Menlo Park, CA 94025; the author has personal notes available on request.

[14] Russell Targ and Harold Puthoff, *Proc. IEEE 16*, No. 14 March (1976).

DISCUSSION

KRIPPNER: I was very pleased with Dr. Franklin's presentation. It stimulated my thinking along lines that I haven't considered before, I have three comments and questions for him. First of all, there are two recent articles that you probably know about, but if you don't, I would recommend them to you. One is the paper on "biogravitation" by Alexander Dubrov in the UNESCO Journal *Impact*. Dubrov proposes a theory on psi phenomena which stresses the body's ability to create gravitational fields. The second article is one of a series that Rex Stanford has been writing for the *ASPR Journal*, which I personally think are some of the most important articles to come out in some time. I'm referring to his recent paper where he suggests that telepathy may indeed be a form of psychokinesis. It makes sense to me, even more sense than the older notion that telepathy is probably a form of clairvoyance, and I'd recommend careful reading of that article.

FRANKLIN: Yes, I will.

KRIPPNER: Now I have a question about a term that you used frequently and I'd like to know the rationale for it. You used the term "teleneural interaction," and I'm wondering what the origin of that term is and how you use it in your context. The other question I have is in relationship to Dr. Schmeidler's previous statement—that she thinks that courses should be geared more to developing researchers than anything else. I'm wondering if her comments are applicable to your courses.

FRANKLIN: First of all, I think that any theory that's postulated at this time would have to account for both gravity and electromagnetic effects, and perhaps nuclear effects as well. We're testing that at the present time, or trying to. And then the second comment . . . let me see, what was the second one?

KRIPPNER: Teleneural . . .

FRANKLIN: Oh yes. Teleneural . . . "Tele" stems from the ancient Greek which means far or distant; and "neural" deals with the nervous system even down to the cellular level, and I coined the word so that I wouldn't offend people. I initially had that problem. I actually have on my office doorway, "Liquid Crystal Physics," and "Teleneural Theory," listed. Now with respect to training researchers—most of our Ph.D.s at Kent State go on to college teaching, and I would anticipate that the training I give my Ph.D. students in paraphysics will certainly be reflected in their teaching. In research, I'm hoping that we'll have a couple of Ph.D. students graduate soon, capable of doing research in paraphysics. With respect to undergraduates, two or three have already gone on to professional schools and are very interested in carrying on some of the things they've learned in my courses. A couple are in medical school, and graduate school in the physical sciences, and biology, so hopefully, they'll be useful.

MORRISS: I like "teleneural." It doesn't sound occult.

FRANKLIN: It's not entirely. It includes electromagnetic effects.

MORRISS: With the physicists' interest in parapsychology I think we may witness an interesting phenomena in the next few years. You know, parapsychology has long been the unwelcome stepchild of psychology, and I think we may be about to see what you might call the "salad dog" effect. That is, you have a dog that wouldn't touch salad, but you tell him the cat's going to get it, and he'll eat it. I have a feeling that with psychologists, there may be a new interest in the field of parapsychology once they see that the physicists seem to be taking serious note of what's going on.

FRANKLIN: I think that the role of physics and psychology is a very important one to analyze. I don't think it's necessary to distinguish clearly between the two, but I do think that psychologists can make a tremendous contribution to the theoretical approach as in information theory and cybernetics. Psychologists who know those fields could construct physical theories using those ideas, in my opinion. With respect to physicists' contributions, I think that we are needed to do physical experiments on psychokinesis, and telepathy. Propagation through distance should be analyzed by physicists using mathematical techniques. Action at a distance has not been known. If action at a distance occurs, we mean that you could act at the fringe of the universe instantaneously or retrieve information from the galaxy, at the fringe of the universe, or even beyond the universe. So people who speak glibly about interaction at a distance, and proposed theories in that regard, in my opinion, don't really have a handle yet on understanding physical theory properly. In my opinion, we cannot adopt interaction at a distance yet, probably not at all for paraphysical phenomena, but that remains to be seen.

JOHNSON: Dr. Franklin, I'm very pleased with your presentation and by and large, by seeing physicists coming into the field. I have a few questions of a more general type. Firstly, I thought it was very interesting when you touched upon the problem of repeatability and stated that, if I understood you correctly, that isn't the only hallmark of science. I believe that is correct in a way, especially at an early stage of development of science when you don't know enough about necessary and sufficient conditions for bringing about a phenomenon. That was interesting in itself. One of the many examples of criticism directed towards parapsychology is the lack of theory, and you, in a way, denied this by referring to the existence of certain theories, surmises, perhaps we would say it better. I think you mentioned Feinberg's "Time Reversal." This is very interesting, still it's a great problem not having repeatability because if you have a theory, the theory must have test replication—and my question is, looking back into the history of science within your own field, could you give an example of a situation rather similar to the one in parapsychology? That would be very interesting.

FRANKLIN: Yes. First of all, you're not saying that paraphysical experiments are not repeatable, are you?

JOHNSON: No, no . . . I'm not stating anything myself about them.

FRANKLIN: O.K., I think they're repeatable. As far as repeatability goes, I do believe that there are instances in the past of very good repeatability. Now, with respect to theories, I don't think there are any theories yet that are correct, but I do think there are advances that are beginning. I think it's going to take a genius to come out with the proper theory.

JOHNSON: Yes, but isn't that rather a common thing in the history of science?

FRANKLIN: Yes, it is.

JOHNSON: My second question is a very general one. Almost all of us have tried to make a distinction between science and pseudo-science, and I would like to learn a bit more about the way you are viewing it. What kind of line of demarcation or criteria are you using as a physicist? Trying to distinguish between science and pseudo-science. Could you give just a few examples?

FRANKLIN: Yes, O.K. That's a very interesting question and I'm glad you asked that. What I try to do at this stage is to make a critical analysis of the literature and of people who I know that are doing experiments. I will talk with people. I will try to delineate, in my own mind, whether or not I can accept what they've done within the framework of physical theory, physical understanding. I'm having a hard time delineating because I'm repeatedly finding things that I do not believe in. Subsequently I find substantial information for it, such as the interaction with matter (PK). I was invited in as a scientist without any previous bias to see Uri Geller, and now I've analyzed, I think, better than anyone has, the metallurgical nature of the fractures that he causes in metal and I did it almost entirely on the basis of my metallurgical background. I have a degree in biology; two degrees in metallurgy, and then my Ph.D. in solid state science, so I do have some background to investigate Uri Geller's fractures. I do believe that I now have substantive evidence for the existence of interaction with matter (PK) of a very unusual nature. In other fields we've done things in the laboratory which I can rely on. But if you take numerology, or take astrology, I don't have any substantive basis for believing in those yet.

JOHNSON: Well, I don't think that's exactly an answer to my question. Some kind of criteria must be formulated, wouldn't you agree? Are you familiar, for instance, with Popper's view of science, and the progress of science?

FRANKLIN: Of course, you have to have criteria, and a criterion of scientific method, of course, has been repeatability in different laboratories.

HASTINGS: I was impressed by Jim Morriss' comment that psychologists might suddenly clutch parapsychology to their collective bosoms at the thought that it would be snatched away from them by physics. I don't think that will happen! Actually, I am impressed and stimulated by the potentials of physics to investigate many of the phenomena that psychologists have been somewhat stuck with. I think of direct perception by clairvoyants and sensitives, and awareness of fields of energy. Psychologists have treated these as psychological phenomena with an ambiguous physical status. But physical scientists may be able to investigate physical phenomena that are correlated. So I would see the language and approach of physics as able to do things complementary to the psychological research. Perhaps at a later date if we've learned anything about understanding and cooperation and coordination then we can fill in the blind spots and gaps with a synthesis of the two fields.

FRANKLIN: Yes, I certainly agree. Those are very important comments.

ROGO: I don't think there is any doubt that parapsychology is really heading towards the physical sciences. It's a trend that's been occurring for a couple of years now. Dr. Franklin's presentation, in his opening remarks, were kind of an open invitation for physicists to enter into parapsychology and actively take part in experimentation. Now so far everybody seems to be very happy about physicists entering our field. I'm not so happy about it. Now, in a recent issue of *New Scientist*, three very active physicists in Great Britain wrote to that publication a group letter to the editor, making the statement that it was a well known fact that PK does not occur under controlled conditions. Now that type of remark really shows an enormous amount of ignorance over what's been going on in parapsychology for the last one hundred years, and it seems to me that a physicist who would make a statement like that would know so little about the field that he should not be qualified to carry out research. Now, more than any other group of people, I found wtih these physicists that they are not spending adequate time boning up on this field before they enter it, and they're pulling a lot of soap box routines that frankly are misrepresenting the field very severely and potentially could hurt the field very much.

FRANKLIN: That's an important comment and I'd like to comment on that. As I said in the beginning, I hope that parapsychologists will put up with physicists rattling around for the first few years until they find out what's going on. Physicists are prone to blunder when they begin in a new field, but eventually I think they come out with substantial contributions.

ROGO: Do they have to blunder publicly?

FRANKLIN: Well, let me ask you this: Is there any group of people that can understand physical law besides physicists and physical scientists? They have made contributions in that area.

ROGO: Oh, I agree. But you made a couple of comments to the effect that you didn't think that psychologists or many parapsychologists had this understanding of physical law. But if I were to look at the prime example of a good process-oriented PK project which really showed us something about PK, I would choose Dr. Schmeidler's work with Ingo Swann which did show some very interesting physicalistic principles about PK, and Dr. Schmeidler is not a physicist.

FRANKLIN: Yes, I know Dr. Schmeidler's work very well and I've quoted it and proposed to do work of a similar nature.

ROGO: Maybe you could do some back seat driving.

BELOFF: I merely just want to put on record that where the whole topic of paraphysics is concerned, I find myself a complete skeptic. In other words, I just do not believe that there is a physical explanation for psi phenomena. I just want to make this statement. Now this doesn't mean, of course, that I condemn your enterprise. On the contrary, I'm watching it with acute interest because if I am right, you will not make progress; you will not find a theory and you will not get a physical explanation. If you do, I am wrong, and I shall admit I am wrong, and therefore I am watching the outcome with the greatest of interest.

FRANKLIN: That's a very interesting comment, Dr. Beloff. Two and a half years ago I talked with Julius Stulman and he said the same thing to me and he is a man for whom I have a very high regard. I have received the same comment from many people. I don't know what to say. But we just try and explain what happens in the physical and we try to do it mathematically. That's the ball game of physical scientists and physics, and it is my impression that we will be able to describe mathematically how things move in psychokinesis; we'll be able to come up with a phenomenological type of theory as most of our theories are. Whether or not we'll be able to define what the universe is, or what mass really is, and to define where it goes if it is dematerialized, it certainly is a very deep fundamental question and in my opinion, gets deeply into philosophy and perhaps into a psychological construct.

KRIPPNER: As I said before, I certainly welcome the interest of physicists in the field and their productive interaction with other psi researchers. The one matter that bothers me, though, is something different from what other people have brought up, and I don't know the answer to it. It's been my impression that some of the physicists now entering the field will have nothing to do with the Parapsychological Association. They're not interested in applying for membership in PA; they think that PA has gone off on the wrong track, and they adopt sort of a supercilious attitude toward the PA which I think is very unfortunate, I've picked up this opinion throughout the years from a couple of people, and I'm wondering if you have any reaction to it or what is either in the nature of physicists or in the nature of PA that causes this reaction?

FRANKLIN: Two comments, Stan. One is financial. I have a very limited budget myself. I can't afford to join more than one organization unless I have a very, very good reason for doing it. That's one thing—in today's economic situation especially. The second thing: there is a difficulty if you take a theoretical physicist who is trying to write a highly mathematical theory and you bring him into a group of this nature where he cannot communicate. I think there is a domain for pure physicists to publish both in physics journals and to publish on paraphysics. I think that exists. Now for more interplay between physicists and parapsychology, I believe that those physicists should belong to both organizations and should be active in both. There are physicists, in my opinion, who should have a strong interplay with the Parapsychological Association and the SPR and other organizations worldwide. I think that should be done.

RAO: I welcome the interaction between psychologists and physicists, and I include parapsychologists among psychologists, but this could be a two-way affair, and also could be good and bad. We know from the history of psychology that physics, especially the classical physics influenced psychology, and then we got stuck with behaviorism, which is not changing even though physics has changed. Now, I think, it is time for physics to be influenced by psychology, specifically parapsychology, and if parapsychology could influence speculations of physicists, in turn, maybe it will also affect psychologists as well. I don't think there is anything wrong with physicists dabbling or researching in parapsychology. I think it would bring a great tradition to bear upon the investigation of man's nature. Even if they have not read much about parapsychology, I don't think it would disqualify physicists from investigating parapsychological phenomena. Sometimes I feel that absolute ignorance can be a bliss.

PARAPSYCHOLOGY AND THE TEACHING OF PHILOSOPHY

Frederick C. Dommeyer

A conviction of the present writer is that parapsychology can be of value in the teaching of philosophy. Doubtless, too, some branches of philosophy, e.g., philosophy of science, can be of value to parapsychology, but it is only the former matter that will be considered here.

Peter A. French, in his introduction to *Philosophers in Wonderland*,[1] said:

> "Let us then define *paranormal events* as those events the accounts of which must include sentences which are strictly nonsensical. These sentences cannot be true or false statements because they violate the grounds of our judging truth and falsity."

If French is right, it makes no sense to relate parapsychology to the teaching of philosophy for it would only be to add nonsense to it.

What are French's grounds for this statement? One must present an account of the essentials of his view in order to assess them.

In his *Introduction*, French makes a distinction between C-1 and C-2 certainty. With respect to C-1 certainty, French remarks that it is different for things or events to be certain and for persons to be certain. "In the case of persons, to be certain (C-1) is to feel certain; though, conversely, feeling certain is not always being certain." " 'I am certain of it' (C-1) is not then the equivalent to 'I know it.' " "I know it, " he adds, usually means having appropriate grounds for what is said and having the responsibility of "getting it right." "Being certain" (C-1) is compatible with being wrong. The present writer finds no difficulty with C-1 certainty; it has sometimes been called "psychological certainty."

C-2 certainty is for this discussion the more important kind. C-1 certainty is "supported" by C-2 certainty. "C-2 certainty is only extraordinarily compatible with being wrong." Ludwig Wittgenstein, as French notes, maintained that C-2 "truisms" are not properly true at all. They are the very presuppositions of all of our judging, investigating, knowing, etc. C-2 propositions lie beyond "being justified or unjustified." French claims also that it is "inappropriate to confuse C-2 propositions with things we know." Does everyone share the same set of C-2 propositions? "C-2 propositions might best be described as *our* fundamental certainties." Then, significantly, French adds: "They are *my* certainties only insofar as I share this form-of-life. To a large extent my 'making certain' and my answering 'Why are you certain?' questions is dependent upon our acquiescence or tacit agreement with these fundamental certainties." C-2 certainties are described as "our epistemological mythology." They serve as "the scaffolding of our thought"; the sciences rest upon C-2 certainties. "The real challenge of psychical research is to the C-2 certainties of our form-of-life." C-2 certainties "set the boundaries of sense and mark off those enterprises we accept from those we adjudge to be half-witted or the entertainments of madmen." French asserts that C-2 certainties are not "intuitions." They are "best described as limiting propositions (rules of a sort) which are embedded in our language as its very condition of use."

What are some examples of C-2 certainties? French lists the following: "I am certain that I am alive," "I am certain that I have not existed on Earth for the full span of Earth's years," "I have a body," "I have certainly never been very far from the Earth's surface," "I have two hands," "Trees do not talk," etc. Some additional C-2 certainties, purportedly ones that make psychical research nonsensical, are also listed by French. They are: "Events cannot have effects before they themselves have happened," "Causation at a considerable distance in space in the absence of intermediate causes is not possible," "Events removed much in time (events in the past) cannot cause events in the present unless a sequence exists of other causes linking the first event to the eventual effect," "Each of us knows what another is experiencing only by either observing the other's behavior or by being told what he is experiencing," "One can't experience the future in the present," "Mental processes in a human subject cannot directly bring about effects in the events of the physical world without the agency of the subject's body," "Death is the end of life," and "All men are mortal." This second list is so well tailored to the declaration that sentences in parapsychology are nonsensical that one cannot help wondering if they came to be C-2 statements for this reason alone. How, in fact, does one identify C-2 statements? Is it because they cannot be called true or false, are not objects of knowledge, cannot be doubted, etc.? If those are the reasons, they are indistinguishable from the predicates that apply to the supposed nonsensical statements of parapsychology.

But for all of the epistemological importance attributed by French to C-2 certainties, they are not unchanging. They are not "forever fossilized in our form of life." The suggestion as to how such change occurs is found in French's statement, following Wittgenstein, that "it is as if some of our C-1 propositions have hardened into C-2's so that they form a channel for those propositions which are not hardened but fluid." In a later passage, French asserts:

> ". . . we have maintained that our certainties, even of the C-2 variety, are not permanent fixtures. They do change . . . as the metaphor of the river and its bed suggests, there is shifting. . . . It is not usually dramatic; it is a slow process. Yet the nonsense of today's psychical research might well be the certainty of tomorrow's psychology and even eventually the certainty of our common linguistic heritage."

French then quickly adds that this is a "remote possibility."

The philosopher's function in all of this is to examine the disguised nonsense roundabout him and show it to be patent nonsense. This is what French believes himself to have done for sentences of psychical research.

Such is the view of French and his condemnation of parapsychology. His position is a formidable one and it doubtless reveals why the statements of parapsychologists are often ridiculed out of hand because they are, if French is right, in conflict with C-2 certainties, which are the very foundations of sense.

I do not agree with French's use of the term "certainty," as it appears in "C-2 certainty." To use the word "certainty" in that context is arbitrary and misleading, as I shall endeavor to show. It is also my belief that the distinction between C-1 knowing and what he calls "C-2 certainty" is much less determinate and far more fluid than he supposes.

Let a beginning be made by examining what I shall call his "first-person" C-2 certainties. He illustrates C-2 certainty with several first-person statements, as the list of his C-2's establishes. "I have two hands" is given by him as a C-2 certainty. I am prepared to argue either that his use of first-person examples forces him into a psychological linguistic relativism, which destroys the monolithic character he wishes language to display, or that he must abandon this view that first-person statements are C-2's.

"I have two hands" could very well be taken as a commonplace judgment embedded in French's language structure. Could this proposition, "I (French) have two hands" be a C-2 statement for me? I cannot say sensibly that "I (French) have two hands," simply because I am not French. This is thus a judgment confined to French's language structure. The closest I can come to saying what French has said would be to say: "He (French) has two hands." To say, however, that I can assert this with the same degree of certainty, with which French can assert his first-person statement, is obviously wrong. I do not know French; I have never seen him; his statement in his book that he has two hands could be false. I do not want to say I can be certain about statements that, so far as I know, could be false. Of course, someone might say that French *really* means to say, when he says "I have two hands," is that "All people have two hands." I shall undertake to criticize this sort of claim later when I take an example of such a universal statement under consideration.

The result of this line of criticism is that these first-person statements, which he claims to be C-2's, are not inherent in the general language of all but are confined to the person asserting them. Even if we were to grant, for the sake of argument, that "He (French) has two hands" might become indubitable and a C-2 for the close associates of French, it would still be the case that such a C-2 would not be embedded in the language generally but only in the language of those who knew French well.

The end-product of this discussion is, as was suggested earlier, a psychological linguistic relativism, i.e., there is not a communal use of C-2's in the case of these first-person C-2's and not necessarily in the case of the third-person restatements of them either. There are then "language islands," so to speak, from which each of us approaches his world. For French to declare from his "language island" that the sentences about paranormal events are nonsensical is thus gratuitous. Only if the language structure were monolithic and immutable would French have the right to use it as a means to a categorical declaration that this or that statement in parapsychology is nonsensical.

French can avoid this psychological linguistic relativism only by denying that first-person statements are actually C-2 statements. He, of course, affirms just the opposite.

A further point to be noted is that one can trivialize the notion of C-2's by means of French's own example. If "I have two hands" is a C-2 certainty for me, then "I have ten toes," "I have ten fingers," "I have two nostrils," "I have two eyes," "I have one head," etc., are also C-2 statements, for they are of the same kind of statement as "I have two hands." Yet, C-2's have been declared by French to be the very foundation of knowledge and of science. This claim hardly holds water in the light of the possible multiplication of trivial examples. Being a C-2 would not necessarily cause it to have such a role as French assigns it. There must be some other properties that some C-2's have, when they function importantly as a foundation of knowledge, that French has left unspecified.

Let us turn to another example of French's that will serve to make another point or two. Take his C-2 example: "I have never been very far from the Earth's surface." We can now ignore the "first-person" difficulties noted above. Let us assume with French, for purposes of the argument, that this is a C-2 certainty that has become embedded in the language structure. Edgar A. Mitchell, astronaut and parapsychologist, could both believe and know a C-1 proposition to the effect that "I (Mitchell) have certainly been very far from the earth's surface." If we imagine that space travel becomes commonplace in the future, this C-1 may in its fluidity serve to change the C-2 status of French's example. The new C-2 would have to be formulated, not as French has it, but (taking account of our earlier criticism of first-person statements) in a third-person universalized form, i.e., "One does not get very far from the earth's surface unless he uses some mechanical device, such as a space ship." It is hardly necessary to say that space travel was not so many years ago as much a wonderland notion as French finds psychical research today; it was only in the minds of science-fiction writers—nothing but fantasy and practical nonsense. Cannot one apply this Mitchell example to parapsychology? Can there not be "technological advance" in parapsychology such that numbers of persons may be taught telepathy, and use it? There are some parapsychologists who have created ESP teaching machines (e.g., Russell Targ), and they have had evidence that the use of such machines improves ESP performance. May not the C-2's that cause French today to declare sentences in parapsychology "nonsensical" have to be eliminated from the language structure under the pressures of C-1 knowledge that such researchers as Targ are providing? Happily, for this line of argument, French himself has said, as we saw, that "the nonsense of today's psychical research might well be the certainty of tomorrow's psychology and eventually the certainty of our common linguistic heritage." Even though he says this is a "remote possibility," one can say that so was space travel not very many years ago. Why then do philosophers such as French relate themselves to parapsychologists as they do, namely, by telling them what they are saying is nonsense? Since, on French's own statement, it is possible for parapsychological sentences to make sense, would it not be more helpful for philosophers to use their linguistic skills to assist in that direction?

Not all of French's C-2's are in a first-person form; some are generalized. It will be useful to examine such a C-2 instance, as was earlier suggested. As a case in point, let us take his C-2 statement that

"Each of us knows what another is experiencing by observing the other's behavior or by being told what he is experiencing." This C-2 is of course tailored to make statements about telepathy into nonsense. It is claimed by French to be indubitable in the sense that no one doubts it. I doubt it and many parapsychologists do. I doubt it because I do not believe it to be true and hence it is for me not certain. It begins "Each of us knows . . ." How can French possibly regard this statement as certain except in the C-1 sense of merely believing it or by means of some aberrant meaning of "certainty"? To say with certainty (in any commonsense or scientific use of the term "certainty") that "Each of us knows . . ." would require a complete enumeration of each and every living person with respect to this supposed knowledge—a perfect induction that neither French nor anyone else has made. It is a statement that is only "probable," and not certain, except in a psychological sense or in some aberrant sense of "certain." If it is corrigible, it follows that, under pressures from C-1 knowledge about telepathy, the C-2, "Each of us knows what another is experiencing only by observing the other's behavior or by being told what he is experiencing" may have to give way to a new C-2, namely, "Each of us knows what another is experiencing only by observing the other's behavior or by being told what he is experiencing or by telepathy."

If now a broad commonsense look is taken of French's view, it appears wrong on the face of it. Here is, let us say, a language with its C-2 certainties. It is a means of representing, more or less adequately, the actual world. It is analogous to a map which depicts in abbreviated fashion some part of the Earth's surface. It is not possible to say sensibly that a map is an ultimate criterion for what is in the world. It is rather the other way around; what is in the actual world is the criterion for what gets on the map more or less adequately. Why should French's language-map be used to make nonsensical what parapsychologists formulate about their empirical findings in the actual world by experimental work in the laboratory? One is reminded of the pre-Magellan days when it was doubtless for many a C-2 certainty that "The earth is flat." Philosophical analysts of that day, had they existed, would have affirmed solemnly that it is nonsensical to say that "The earth is round." One is also reminded of the professor of philosophy at Padua who, when invited to look through Galileo's telescope to view the satellites of Jupiter, refused to do so. He said:

> "There are seven windows given to animals in the domicile of the head. . . From this and many other similarities in nature, such as the seven metals, etc., which it were tedious to enumerate, we gather that the number of planets is necessarily

seven. Moreover these (alleged) satellites of Jupiter are invisible to the naked eye, and therefore can exercise no influence on the earth, and therefore would be useless, and therefore do not exist. Besides (from the earliest times men) have adopted the division of the week into seven days, and have named them after the seven planets. Now if we increase the number of planets, this whole and beautiful system falls to the ground."[2]

A major point that French overlooks is that there are parapsychologists who do not talk nonsense. If one says, as Dr. Rao does, that "ESP is guessing with non-chance results," there is a clear operational way of saying when ESP has occurred. We know what guessing is and statistical methods enable the parapsychologist to know when he has got significant scores above or below chance. This procedure is prefectly compatible with modern scientific techniques. Or, take French's view that it is C-2 certain that a future event cannot be in the present. There have been theories of precognition proposed that do not violate this C-2 certainty (if it is that). Such theories do not place the future in the present any more than does an astronomer when he predicts an eclipse of the sun. Let it be admitted that some parapsychologists have made nonsensical statements, but so have many scientists and many, many philosophers. If French wishes to ascertain whether what parapsychologists do is worth doing, let him go to the laboratories of the parapsychologists, note their carefully controlled experiments, their methods of evaluation and their often positive results. How can one judge experimental parapsychology fairly by means of purely linguistic considerations? Perhaps there is a real wisdom in Alfred N. Whitehead's statement that "The history of thought shows that false interpretations of observed facts enter into the records of their observation. Thus both theory, and received notions as to fact, are in doubt."[3] The insight here is that we should be careful not to throw out the hard facts of parapsychology with the bathwater of the false interpretations.[4]

With these criticisms of French's position in mind, it is possible to move into the original purpose of this paper, which is that of showing how one can use parapsychology in the teaching of philosophy.

Epistemology or the theory of knowledge is a branch of philosophy and it is the title of academic courses in philosophy. A number of epistemologists in the past and present time have been interested in the nature of perception. They have elaborated complex theories of perception. All of them propose to explain the manner in which man directly knows his environment. Some of them have been sense-datum theories in which sensing is made primary. One senses ineffable colors, sounds, tastes and the like. Perceiving, in such theories, requires sensing but in addition presupposes conceptual and memorial elements such that one "sees" a table or "hears" a train.

There are other theorists who are critical of sense-datum theories of perception. They may hold that one directly perceives such objects as stars, chairs, and tables. They view sense-data as the abstractions of analysts and not as actual participants in the perceptual process. Others may escape a sense-datum theory by an adverbial notion of sensing ("I see redly").

Whatever may be the variations in the philosophers' account of perceptual knowledge, there appears to be agreement among them that some form of sensory experience is a necessary ingredient. If one is to know objects and events in the environment, the sensory route is a necessary one.

But such a view will not do in the face of claims about extrasensory perception of objects or objective events. Spontaneous cases of clairvoyance are well-known and laboratory experiments have provided reasonable assurance of the reality of this ESP capacity. And clairvoyance reveals the striking fact that a percipient can know objects and objective events precisely without the use of the senses. The fact is that, in well-controlled laboratory experiments in clairvoyance, the experimenter will have done everything possible to exclude the use of the subject's sensing or perceiving in knowing the target. "Sensory leakage" and also inferential knowledge are carefully screened out of the experimental situation. It is true that in laboratory experimentation in ESP the subject does not necessarily know when a call is a hit; it might be claimed that he lacks knowledge of the objective fact in such a situation. In many spontaneous cases of clairvoyance and other forms of ESP, however, there is a breakthrough to the level of consciousness and an awareness that one has knowledge. Many instances of spontaneous clairvoyance testify to that fact.

The epistemologist, then, who sees some form of sensory experience as the only mode of knowing objects and events is apparently mistaken. The reason for his error is his neglect of clairvoyance, which is a non-sensory way of knowing objects and events. Here is a place where parapsychology obviously impinges on philosophy. Clairvoyance, as a way of perceiving, should become a datum for the theorizing of the epistemologist and this mode of knowing should be considered in courses in epistemology, even if only from a logical and critical point of view.

Another common epistemological assumption of philosophers is that it is impossible for Person A to know what Person B is experiencing unless Person A perceives and interprets sensory signs of the experience which are produced by Person B, e.g., a verbal report on an experience by Person B, which Person A hears and interprets. Such a relationship, it is held, is basic to one's awareness of another's experience.

But telepathy is the extrasensory perception of a mental state or activity of another person. It is quite different from the way of knowing just described, even though both involve awareness of what goes on in another's experience. It is different because telepathy occurs without the mediation of a sensory vehicle, which is then interpreted. As with the case of clairvoyant laboratory experiments, so it is in the telepathic ones: the experimenter tries to provide sufficiently rigorous controls so as to insure that the target of telepathic cognition cannot have been known sensorially or inferentially by the subject. In his neglect of telepathy, the epistemologist fails to take into account a datum that is relevant to his theorizing, namely, a non-sensory mode of knowing another's mental state or activity.

It is also commonplace for the epistemologist to hold that one cannot predict future events except by use of data that one obtains directly or by testimony from others. By means of these data and by rules of inference relevant to them, future events can be predicted. Or, one may have a non-inferential anticipation or expectation of future events grounded on associations that had their roots in past experience and which are presently activated.

But this is not how precognition operates. Precognition is the prediction of future events whose occurrence is not inferred from present sensorial or testimonial data. Neither is it an anticipation of future events grounded on associations that had their roots in the past. Precognition is explicable in terms of neither the inferential nor the associative modes of knowing the future. It is knowledge of future events via a hunch, a vision, a dream or some other non-sensory psychic event, having no essential similarity to the common sense or scientific modes of knowing future events—modes which dominate the thinking of epistemologists.

Despite the evidences for belief in precognition, philosophers have generally neglected it. The conclusion to be drawn here is that philosophers, who are theorizing about "knowing" or teaching epistemology courses in which modes of knowing are relevant to their interests, might well turn some of their attention to precognition as a way of knowing future events.

Similar comments can be made about retrocognition, though parapsychologists themselves have given less attention to this mode of knowing past events. The usual view explanatory of knowledge of past events is that such knowledge is dependent on memory or testimony grounded on memory, or it might be based on records of what has been perceived or of memories, or dependent on present data and relevant rules of sequence. But, again, retrocognition does not conform to these requirements of knowledge of past events so that the view mentioned just above is inadequate.

How can one explain this indifference of epistemologists to extrasensory modes of knowing? Many philosophers know practically nothing about the contributions of parapsychology. Others may have some slight knowledge of the field but they view it as a pseudo-science, not worthy of consideration. Others may refrain from relating parapsychology to philosophy for the reason that these four psi capacities, even granting that they exist, are so little understood that it is judged they can better be ignored. Only a few philosophers have considered them and have effectively related them to epistemological issues, e.g., Broad, Ducasse, Price, Scriven, and French.

The philosophy of religion is widely taught in American universities. Though this course can be presented in many different ways, a common approach is that of including in it such topics as the classical "proofs" for God's existence and evaluations of them, ostensible evidences for survival after bodily death, mysticism, the problem of evil, prayer, faith, alternatives to supernaturalistic religion, etc.

If one chooses to include in a philosophy of religion course the question of evidences for survival after bodily death, much use can be made of the contributions of parapsychology. Undergraduate students are usually acquainted with the idea of discarnate survival through religious training. Some of them will occasionally experiment with spirit communication and will succeed in getting messages from a deceased person, or so they believe. Dr. Ryzl and I attended such a student seance at San Jose State University in the recent past and the phenomena generated by these students were remarkable, even though their interpretation of them was naive. These facts are mentioned to show that, though spiritism would interest only a very few present-day parapsychologists, a discussion of it in a philosophy of religion class can be helpful for students. In fact, in the educational matrix, there is no reason why the instructor should not choose spontaneous cases from the remote past if they serve to provide striking instances useful to his classroom purposes. One can call the students' attention to such an unusual medium as Leonora Piper, who was a subject of study by William James from 1885 until his death in 1910, not to mention investigation of her by other eminent American and English researchers. A striking characteristic of her work was the paranormal information she provided under conditions that would make deception practically impossible. Was she obtaining this information from a spirit or was it coming from living persons by means of ESP? This question serves the function of leading students to serious consideration of the ESP hypothesis as, in fact, it led J. B. Rhine and many other parapsychologists from studies of spirit communication to investigations of ESP. One can thus duplicate the historical movement of psychical research in the classroom.

But spiritism is also a useful springboard in a philosophy of religion class for a variety of topics relevant to the question of discarnate survival. Spiritism presupposes the existence of discarnate beings. An obvious question is: can a "soul" or "mind" exist without its body? Is this even a thinkable notion? Such questions can be the opening for a consideration of the body-mind problem. They lead naturally to an examination of a number of body-mind theories such as the Identity theory, Epiphenomenalism, Psycho-physical parallelism, Hypo-phenomenalism, and Interactionist dualism. The student will learn that some of these theories entail the impossibility of a "mind" surviving the destruction of its body and that others leave open this possibility. That each of these theories has had its ardent adherents causes the student to realize that the answer to the question of discarnate survival is not likely to be simple. He will finally realize probably that at the present time no rational solution is possible.

But one can also focus attention on what parapsychology, independently of spiritism, can contribute to a solution of the body-mind problem and that of survival in a discarnate form. One can turn to a variety of spontaneous cases found in the history of parapsychology, examine them and raise questions of their bearing on both the body-mind problem and discarnate survival. Through this approach, the student learns something more about the philosophical issues at hand but also about the sorts of cases that have interested parapsychologists.

Poltergeist cases have been alleged to provide evidence for a discarnate mind's existence, e.g., as recounted in Bishop Pike's book, *The Other Side*.[5] Those familiar with this book will recall that the Bishop, while on a sabbatical leave at Cambridge University and after his son's death in New York City, experienced in the presence of two friends who were staying with him in his apartment a series of events of a poltergeist nature. Some of them were of such a character that they pointed to his son as a cause, or so the Bishop believed. Was his son's discarnate mind the cause of these unusual events or were these physical disturbances caused psychokinetically by living persons? In answering this question, one can point out to students why most parapsychologists would favor the latter hypothesis.

Out-of-the-body experiences or bilocation are *prima facie* relevant to the body-mind problem as well as to discarnate survival. In such cases, the experient-mind seems to be able to leave its body. More than that, this mind is on occasion able to "bring back" paranormal knowledge. If one's mind can leave one's body, as such experiences suggest, there appears to be in that fact a solution to the body-mind problem. The mind is apparently capable of existing independently of its body. A dualism is suggested as the correct body-mind theory. And, if the mind can leave its body while the body is alive, why cannot it leave it at the death of that body and survive independently of it? Unfortunately for this view, the experience of being out of one's body may be an hallucination and the paranormal knowledge that sometimes occurs explicable in terms of clairvoyance or some other ESP capacity. The preference of most parapsychologists for this latter explanation can be indicated to students.

Apparitions of deceased persons suggest discarnate survival, especially in such cases as that of Mrs. George Butler.[6] After her death, "she" returned to her village near Machiasport, Maine, in the form of a phantom. She was seen a number of times over a period of three months by some one hundred persons, including her husband, in groups as large as forty. She gave long discourses and accurately predicted births and deaths in the community. On one occasion, Captain Butler passed his hand through the apparition as though its body were made of light. All of this is based on thirty affidavits collected by a witness, Rev. Abraham Cummings, which he published in a now rare pamphlet, *Immortality Proved by the Testimony of Sense* (1826). It would appear that there is in this case a strong suggestion that a discarnate mind, that of Mrs. Butler, revealed itself through an apparition. The events recorded suggest a body-mind dualism and discarnate survival. Classroom discussion can readily center about such a puzzling case.

Is it possible to explain these events on an ESP hypothesis? The one hundred or so persons who heard Mrs. Butler's discourses and predictions must have heard them clairaudiently, for the phantasm was proved to be without physical substance. The phantasm was seen collectively, i.e., by groups as large as forty. Paranormal information was forthcoming from the apparition. If one tries to explain these events by reference to the living, a very far-out hypothesis is needed. G. N. M. Tyrrell, in his book on apparitions,[7] has pointed out that "collective" apparitions do occur with some frequency. There were also in this Butler case "collective" clairaudient hearings, not to mention the paranormal predictions. The continuation of these sorts of events over a period of three months adds to the strain on credibility. What causal factors among the living could have accounted for these visual and auditory hallucinations that were collectively experienced? What causal factors in these many villagers led to the paranormal knowledge? To explain these events by reference to the living would call for a super-ESP hypothesis. Whether one would explain such a case by means of a discarnate survival hypothesis or by reference to living persons would seem more a matter of the theorist's predisposition than a matter of evidential coercion. This Butler case is nonetheless relevant to the survival issue and its consideration can bring to students in a philosophy of religion class some idea of the complexity of the problem.

There are other categories of spontaneous cases, e.g., "possessions" and death-bed visions, that can be used in a philosophy of religion course in an instructive way. The contributions of parapsychology can thus merge with those of philosophy at the points of impingement noted. *Twenty Cases Suggestive of Reincarnation*[8] by Ian Stevenson can well serve to introduce the philosophy of religion student to his recent investigations. The definition of reincarnation provided by Stevenson raises questions about the body-mind problem in a somewhat different context. His cases raise also the question of an ESP hypothesis as an alternative to that of reincarnation.

Much of the foregoing discussion has involved the notion of a disembodied mind. Is this idea unthinkable, as some have claimed? Professor H. H. Price asserted that it is a conceivable notion and says why he believes that in his article, "Survival and the Idea of 'Another World' ".[9]

The problems of both discarnate survival and reincarnation raise for the philosopher (metaphysician) the question of *personal identity*. How can an investigator of the survival problem be assured that a supposed communicating mind is the same mind as that of the once living person whose mind it is *prima facie* supposed to be? Bodily identity through time will not work, for the discarnate mind is without a body. Neither will it work for reincarnation in that there is not continuity of the same body in reincarnation. It would appear that the personal identity would in both cases require some kind of mental continuity, e.g., possibly memory continuity. Stevenson depends partly on memory continuity in the cases he cites. Besides this problem of personal identity, there is also for the metaphysician the problem of a mind's nature. Is there indeed a mind, or is there only a brain? If there is a mind, how would it be described? These are profound philosophical issues.

Mysticism is frequently included as part of the content of a philosophy of religion course. In such an experience as the religious mystic has, he believes himself to be one with a transcendental being, which may be a personal, an impersonal or a superpersonal entity. William James held that there are four traits that generally characterize mystical experiences: (1) ineffability, i.e., the mystic cannot really describe his experience; (2) transiency, i.e., the brevity of the experience; (3) passivity, i.e., though the mystic may actively seek the experience, he is passive during it; and (4) a noetic quality, i.e. the experience will often bring an illumination, an insight or knowledge. Only the noetic quality will concern us here.

Dr. R. M. Bucke described his own mystical illumination in the third person. He wrote: "He (Bucke) claims that he learned more within the few seconds during which the illumination lasted than in previous months or even years of study, and he learned much that no study could ever have taught."[10]

How does one explain such an illumination? It could have originated within himself, or he may have obtained this mystical knowledge from other living persons by ESP or it may have originated in the transcendental being with whom he felt united. On this latter hypothesis, paranormal modes of knowing also suggest themselves.

Sir Alister Hardy, in his article, "Anthropology, Parapsychology and Religion,"[11] offers support for the latter view. He asserts:

> "If we can get cast-iron evidence that one mind can communicate with another by other than physical means it will at once bring about a revolution in present-day ideas of the mind-brain relationship. It would at once lend plausibility to the possibility that the influence which religious people feel when they say they are in touch with what seems to them to be some transcendental element — a power that affects their lives, whether they call it God or not — may be something within the same field as extrasensory telepathic communication. Could it perhaps be . . . that the element that is at the back of all religion might be some extrasensory shared spiritual experience; perhaps some source of spiritual 'know-how' which may be tapped by those who may have discovered or learnt the way of making rapport with it . . ."

If Hardy's speculation is sound, one can fit much that goes on in religion into it. Religious mysticism finds a ready place within his belief and it can be viewed as an ESP phenomenon, especially with respect to the noetic quality it frequently displays. If one conceives of prayer as communication between a human being and God, such communication becomes intelligible only on an ESP hypothesis — at least if the usual spiritual nature of God is accepted. There are also intercessory prayers in which one prays in behalf of a sick relative or friend. Even if there is no God, such prayers, being the product of a wish and volition, might thereby bring about unorthodox healings by psychokinetic means. How will God answer prayers if He chooses to do so? If the answers were in the form of advice or admonitions, communication could be by ESP means. To the extent that an answer required some action by God in the devotee's body or in the physical world, psychokinetic action would serve His intention. Much in religion can be subsumed under an ESP-PK hypothesis. Prophetic dreams and utterances can be viewed as precognitions. The walking on the water by Jesus (levitation), his unorthodox healings (psychokinesis), his being seen after his crucifixion and burial (apparitions), his foreknowledge of his betrayal by Judas (precognition), etc. can be explained, at least speculatively, by means of the concepts of parapsychology. If the alternative is leaving them as incomprehensible miracles, one can see some advantage in thinking of them in terms of Sir Alister Hardy's speculation.

Causation and its nature have been of interest to philosophers (metaphysicians, epistemologists and ethicists) from ancient times down to the present. Parapsychology offers in this area some puzzling facts and theories that ought to interest philosophers concerned with the cause-effect relation.

Psychokinesis is itself a puzzling phenomenon. How mind can interact with body *within* the human being, e.g., wanting to raise one's arm as a causal condition of it being raised, is a difficult enough problem. Psychokinesis, however, presents the far more difficult one of knowing how a mind can directly move or otherwise influence objects *outside* of its body, e.g., influence the fall of dice. A great many philosophers would consider this kind of psycho-physical causation an impossibility, usually without looking at the evidences for it. If it exists, however, there are philosophical implications of significance. One of them is that a physicalist view of nature must be abandoned and some place provided for a nonphysical causal intervention in the course of nature. A second form of energy has been suggested by some parapsychologists in order to explain psychokinesis.

Precognition also presents a philosophic challenge to those who would understand causation. J. G. Pratt asserts that precognition is "a direct perception of a future event which is beyond the reach of inference or which is not brought about to fulfill the prediction."[12] If, as Pratt says, precognition is direct and does not depend upon inference from present or past remembered data or recorded data, and if the precognized event is not intentionally brought about to fulfill the prediction, then it would appear that the future event itself is left as the only conceivable cause of the precognition. This appears to be the reasoning of E. Douglas Dean when he asserts:

> " . . . in the precognition case, there is involved a further test of logic—where logic breaks down completely. This occurs in the fact that someone gets information from the future. Thus, instead of a cause preceding the effect, it seems that the effect precedes the cause. Logic has broken down— . . . Effects coming before causes are not forbidden in nature; they are only forbidden in our brains, which work with logic circuits composed of neurons like computer logic circuits. Thus, we should not flinch . . . to use breakdowns of logic if they explain precognition."[13]

Dean's view of precognition is philosophically a startling one. It has been taken as axiomatic by philosophers that a cause must temporally precede its effect. But Dean's view is that man's brain, limited in its structure, is incapable, in some instances at least, of understanding nature, i.e., when nature is not in line with the brain's "circuitry." Interesting epistemological and metaphysical problems are raised by the position he takes. Here are some puzzles calling for a solution. Can Dean's view be avoided by a new theory of time, say, a multi-dimensional concept of it? Can one avoid it by the concept of the "eternal now" along with a theory of how the "specious present" operates at an unconscious level? Is there some way of saving the causal relation from Dean's view of it and reconstituting the view that a cause is necessarily prior to its effect? Dean's view seems to imply either (1) that a future event, which does not now exist, can be a cause, which raises the question of how something that does not exist can do anything at all; or (2) that a future event does have some kind of existence now in that it can presently function as a cause of a precognition. This is probably Dean's view. It would then be interesting to know in what sense he would hold that a future event does have some kind of existence now. His view poses a whole host of philosophical issues.

There are doubtless other uses for parapsychology in the teaching of philosophy, but those mentioned in this paper will show that teachers of philosophy would do well to know something about parapsychology, both because of the purely philosophical issues concerning its nature and the knowledge that it can add to the content of courses in philosophy.

REFERENCES

[1] *Philosophers in Wonderland*, edited with an Introduction and Comments by Peter A. French. Saint Paul, Minn.: Llewellyn Publications, 1975. xii and 376 pp.

[2] *A History of Western Philosophy* by W. T. Jones. New York: Harcourt, Brace and Company, 1952. p. 622.

[3] *Process and Reality*. New York: The Macmillan Co., 1930, p. 13.

[4] I am much indebted to my friend and colleague, Professor Whitaker T. Deininger, who discussed at length with me the issues taken up in the above section of this paper. He has no responsibility, of course, for any errors that are there.

[5] With Diane Kennedy. Garden City, N.Y.: Doubleday & Co., Inc. 1968.

[6] *The Belief in a Life after Death* by C. J. Ducasse. Springfield, Ill.: Charles C Thomas, 1961. p.21.

[7] *Apparitions*, with a preface by H. H. Price. London: Gerald Duckworth & Co. Ltd. 1953.

[8] New York: American Society for Psychical Research, 1966.

[9] *Proc. of the SPR.*, Vol. 50, Jan., 1953.

[10] *Cosmic Consciousness*. New York: E. P. Dutton & Co., Inc., 1905. Pp. 7–8.

[11] *Parapsychology and Anthropology*, edited by Allan Angoff and Diana Barth. New York: Parapsychology Foundation, Inc., 1974. P. 137.

[12] *Parapsychology, An Insider's View*. Garden City, N.Y.: Doubleday & Company, Inc., 1964. P. 167.

[13] *Psychic Exploration*, edited by John White. New York: G. P. Putnam's Sons, 1974. P. 171.

DISCUSSION

RAO: I think we are all indebted to Dr. Dommeyer for his very fine presentation and excellent focusing of the topics involved. Certainly this has aroused my dormant interest in the things he's talking about. Dr. Dommeyer is a favorite person around here and I was hoping to find some disagreements with him, but I didn't succeed. I am not going to give up. For there can't be a better person to disagree with than Dr. Dommeyer.

Now, I do not see anything in what French is talking about that is very startling or new. These things are being said time and again by a number of people. Several psychologists expressed their opposition to psi research for almost the same reason. What French now calls the C-2 statements are what Broad described many years before as "the basic limiting principles." I cannot accept the view that the key parapsychological statements are sensical but perhaps false. I believe, on the contrary, they are perhaps nonsensical but essentially true. Whether something is sensical or nonsensical, it seems to me, is a function of one's frame of reference. I have no doubt that within the frame of reference of Mr. French the parapsychological statements are nonsensical. I myself feel that a good many of parapsychological findings make no sense. But the evidence is so overwhelming, I accept them as true even if they do not make sense to me. On the other hand, what makes sense need not necessarily be true. The primitive man accepted the existence of the spirits. So they became sensical to them even if false. It seems to me, therefore, the main difficulty with people like French who attempt to clarify for us the meaning of concepts is that they themselves end up confusing their own limiting frames of reference with reality as it essentially is.

DOMMEYER: Thank you for your comments, Dr. Rao. I would respond to them this way. I believe we have an ambiguity here with the word "nonsensical." I would take it in the strict meaning of making no sense from the standpoint of asserting or not asserting a proposition. In other words, I would say any proposition is true or false. We would say in a two-valued logic that any proposition has to be true or false. If it is a genuine proposition, it then makes sense. Now there is another meaning of nonsensical which I think is the one you were utilizing: that in your frame of reference, psychologically, a proposition might be true and yet nonsensical. I would say a true proposition cannot in my use of the term "nonsensical" be nonsensical, because to be true, it has to make sense. You wouldn't know it was true unless it did make sense. Now it might be nonsensical in a second meaning of the term—say that it's fantastic. I'm not accustomed to accepting this truth; it's esoteric, etc., but if it's a true proposition or a false proposition, it seems to me that in my use of the term "nonsensical," and "sensical," that it has to have sense; otherwise we wouldn't know it to be true or false. That's the reason I would say in my use of the term "nonsensical" here, I would have to disagree with you that something could be nonsensical and true at the same time. So I think we have an ambiguity there, but I do thank you for your comment.

TART: French's comments remind me that too many philosophers have been talking so long that they mistake *talking* about reality *for* reality. What French seems to be saying with his C-2 statement is something we already know—that people make assumptions, and those assumptions tend to become implicit and not questioned at all. So when French says "Parapsychological phenomena are nonsensical," he's making a statement about *his* mind—*he* can't grasp them. But that doesn't have anything to do with whether that statement makes any sense about the real world or not.

Now, it was Korzybski who gave us the famous statement that "the map is not the territory." I find in my own experience that while that statement is true, it's not descriptive of most of our actual thinking. For most of us, we prefer the map and give it much more reality than the territory. This is frequently even true in science. We don't really care about the territory. There are untold millions of facts that, in a sense, nobody cares about. There are three hundred thousand four hundred sixty-two cars in San Francisco at the moment, so what? We care about the facts, the data as they aid our *understanding*, so science is really a map-making business. The thing that saves science from going off into nonsensical things is the requirement that you constantly check your map back against the territory. If you've drawn a wonderful map and it says you can get from here to there, you have to try actually *going* from here to there; if it doesn't work, that's too bad for your map.

The philosopher has a lot to tell us about our logic system. What are the assumptions we've made explicitly; what are the hidden assumptions that go along with that, and are we using that system accurately? But this requirement of always checking our conceptual system back against the territory is where I differ with French, and what I think gives science its unusual power. Make up any conceptual system you want. Use it logically: there's no point in saying one and one equals three if you're trying to prove a point unless you want to come up with a very different mathematical system. But constantly check it back against reality. I think French is just telling us about his own limitations and they have nothing to do with the territory, with reality.

DOMMEYER: Thank you, Charles. I have no disagreement with anything you say, and I think that is so—that what we have here is a language system which just happens to have embedded in it a certain body of limiting principles, if you will, and the fact that this exists within the language system entails nothing about what the real world is.

TART: In fact, Fred, sometimes instead of talking about paranormal phenomena, I've simply called them "paraconceptual" phenomena.

DOMMEYER: Sure. I agree wholly with you, Charles.

ROGO: I just have one quick question about the book. When it first came out, I thumbed through it, and it is an anthology, is it not?

DOMMEYER: Yes, it's a collection.

ROGO: And it seems to me that the contributions that cover parapsychology, cover it quite favorably. I was wondering how French comes to grips with many eminent philosophers whose works are included in the volume and are quite favorable to parapsychology and its assumptions.

DOMMEYER: Well, of course, Dr. Rhine had a selection in the volume at the end of it, for which I was very happy, so you're quite right in suggesting that the book does include people who are not unfavorable to parapsychology. I think we do have to credit French with that degree of fairness. Indeed, French sets up a criterion that he obviously doesn't follow. The criterion that he sets up is that he is going to include authors who are of a philosophical analytic persuasion. In other words, linguistic philosophers, but it's obvious that he doesn't stay with that formula because I certainly don't think Dr. Rhine would fit into the category of being one of these philosophical analysts, for which I'm very happy. So I think French was quite fair, indeed. I have more complaint over the book in terms of its demeaning title and some of the things of that sort. "Philosophers in Wonderland." You see, the "Wonderland" is the land of psychical research and it's a demeaning title, and actually it's a bad title as I'm going to point out in my review, because he has a lot of philosophers with their selections in here and they don't go into the "Wonderland" at all. They're just papers that he took out of the journals of philosophy on dreaming, etc., and these fellows . . . well, take O. K. Bouwsma, at the University of Nebraska. There's a paper here by Bouwsma, who is one of these ordinary language people, and I don't think Bouwsma ever got into "Wonderland," and I don't think he even knows that this "Wonderland of Psychical Research" is around to enter. So it's just a faulty title, and I think the book would have been so much better had it not had all of these implications of this demeaning sort. Actually, the papers in the book are excellent; they're good papers. They're very thought-provoking papers, even though some of them don't seem to me to be on the topic of psychical research at all, and as I have indicated, never get into "Wonderland," but are just purely philosophical papers. There's only one paper I thought perhaps should not have been there, and that was the paper that was in the same section as Dr. Rhine's. There was a paper by George Price. And he pens a little note after some asterisks, that he really essentially libels parapsychology, except that he phrased it in such a way that the law couldn't get at him. When the author now, many years later, admits this fact, I don't see that that paper should have been included at all, because it was certainly written from motivations, it seems to me, that seem to be totally out of harmony with what we would expect such a book to have in it.

KRIPPNER: Well, I also would like to pick up on some points in French's Introduction, and I wish that French were here so he'd know about all the time we're spending on his book. Certainly, Dr. Dommeyer has cut through a lot of the problems in that Introduction when he differentiates between nonsensical statements and sensical statements on the one hand, and true statements and false statements on the other hand. I see an additional problem with French in that he apparently is not really acquainted with types of logic systems that one gets into in altered states of consciousness or in other cultures. What is nonsense in ordinary consciousness could be completely different if he were having a dream, if he were stoned, if he were tripping, if he were meditating, if he were making love, or if he were in the middle of a desert or a forest. Then it might be clear to him that an effect could come before a cause. Or as an alternative, he might go to a different cultural system and visit people in some of the back mountain passes of Nepal whose religious system doesn't foster the type of causality that we hold, or he might go among the Hopi Indians or certain other indigenous tribes, and he might find a logic system that presents different cause-effect relations in perfectly sensible terms.

DOMMEYER: Thank you for your very good comments. I think everything you said certainly holds, and it again reveals what one might call the provincial position that he takes—that somehow or other since his linguistic system has such embedded C-2 statements as those he mentions, this must be the criterion in terms of which all reality is to be sketched out. It could well be the case—I don't know from my own personal knowledge—but it could well be the case that another culture might have a language system that would not have very many of these C-2 statements or even necessarily any of those C-2 statements he mentions at all. And yet he has this linguistic orientation, provincial linguistic orientation, by means of which he categorically states that parapsychology is nonsense, and I agree wholly with what you've said and I thank you.

CHILD: In agreement with the other comments, I find Dr. Dommeyer's suggestions about the role of parapsychology in philosophy far more constructive than the opinions of Dr. French's that he cites. In case the argument against Dr. French's position is worth pursuing for the sake of the role of parapsychology in philosophy, I'd like to add a couple of other ways of countering his position that I think are in agreement with what several others have said. French seems to me extremely ethnocentric and apparently unaware of the fact. His reasoning appears to be dominated by assumptions of a small subgroup within our society, and he naively generalizes it without justification. As I understand his reference to "linguistic system," it seems to be a gross misuse; it seems to imply that there is something in the English language that makes it reasonable to call some statements nonsensical. It seems to me it's not in the language, but in the particular set of beliefs expressed in this language by him and certain of his peers. I wouldn't be surprised if some of the things he calls C-2 statements would actually be disagreed with by a majority of speakers of English; I think his argument does not proceed from the language itself, but only from what he and some of his fellows say in that language.

It might be constructive to point out, too, that while his statements apparently have the trappings of an intellectual discussion, they seem actually to be an extreme example of magic. He is wrapped up in the use of words and purports to dictate what reality is on the basis of his own utterances which is exactly what a traditional magician is trying to do.

DOMMEYER: Thank you for your comment. I would just make this point in agreement with you, Dr. Child. It seems to me also that one might regard some of his so-called C-2 statements as questionable. For example, though I don't think I quoted it here—he regards as a C-2 statement the proposition that all men are mortal. Now if one were to think of medieval times or possibly some time when religion was very dominant, it might very well have been the case that his C-2 statement of that time or culture might have been that "all men are immortal."

CHILD: It was not many years ago that a senator, I believe, said that Eleanor Roosevelt was unfit to represent the United States at the United Nations, because in her magazine column she implied some doubt about personal immortality.

BELOFF: It was recently my privilege to spend a morning talking to a distinguished Oxford philosopher who is very much in the central tradition of Oxford analytical philosophy. He had never given any thought to parapsychology until he woke up one morning to find that first his young daughter and then his young son, were starting to produce "Geller-type" phenomena. He now has a completely different attitude. He doesn't quite know what to do with it philosophically, yet. I think that like Dr. Franklin, he is rather hoping that the quantum physicists will sort of come to his rescue and make some sort of sense of it in physical terms. But to me it illustrated beautifully what Dr. Tart was saying, that reality can be stronger than talking about reality.

MORRISS: I just wanted to remind you that in the seventeen hundreds at a meeting of scientists, Lavoisier made the statement that meteorites could not exist because there were no rocks in the sky; everybody knew that, so it was not possible for rocks to fall from the sky.

FRANKLIN: A couple of comments on the pitfall of causality. I got interested in the field of parapsychology a few years ago and found out from my reading that causality itself is not a fundamental pillar of physics. I was a bit shocked by that because most of my background had indicated causality was necessary, but since the introduction of quantum mechanics, of course, the uncertainty principle has given rise to the breakdown of the principle of causality and has had proofs in physics' journals as late as 1972. People here at Berkeley did experiments which prove that causality is not a fundamental pillar of physics. Another interesting thing is that the fundamental pillars which we seem to espouse in physics, and others have adopted, such as conservation of mass—energy, evidently is not a fundamental pillar of physics in curved space.

If you look back at the paradigms of physics, curvature of space was introduced by Einstein and there were tremendous traumas intro-duced in philosophical thinking at that time as to why space and time should be connected. As for parapsychological phenomena, if we go now to five dimensions, and some thinkers are progressing that way, try to characterize a fifth dimension as being different from space and time. Then I assume that will also introduce some very intricate problems to explain. With respect to the fundamental ideas in physics, I think it's important at this stage to try to maintain a close contact with *modern* theoretical physics thought, rather than stuff that is thirty or forty years old in this regard.

DOMMEYER: Thank you for your comments.

RHINE: There is a question that I have often been asked in the years since George Price wrote his apology in *Science* regarding his earlier article criticizing the work in ESP back in 1955. People asked why Price changed his mind. Why did he feel like apologizing? Price has added to this paper, as it appears now in French's book, a good bit of information which he had written me years ago, but he had written it in confidence. He wanted to save it until he got a certain article written giving a fuller explanation, and that has never happened. But this explanation is here and it seemed to me that it might serve to illustrate one of the points under discussion here. It seems to me, that as an explanation, it is neither true nor false; I am just not able to make sense of it.

DOMMEYER: I might just read this little statement if you would be interested. George Price says, "My paper is extremely unfair to J. B. Rhine and S. T. Soal, because I simply assumed, without making any slight attempt to find evidence to support my assumption, that they had faked ESP results for the purpose of promoting Christianity, and I suggested this in a way that made clear what I meant while cleverly avoiding libel. During correspondence with Rhine in 1971, it became obvious to me that he really was, after all, concerned with the scientific question of whether ESP occurs, and not at all seeking to promote religious beliefs through fraud. Undoubtedly the same is true of Soal, and as for the question asked by several correspondents whether I now believe that ESP occurs, I'm afraid the answer is that I have myself become guilty of accepting and trying to follow, in a rather radical way, that strange system of beliefs that I accused Rhine and Soal of trying to promote, and consequently I now believe in much worse things than ESP."

TART: Two brief comments. One on the Price article. I was very angry about that article at the time it came out, but in the years since, I've actually come to appreciate it. Here is a man who simply said, "I know what reality is and no amount of evidence will make me change my mind, so phooey on you." At least he's being very honest about his prejudices.

On promoting philosophy teaching through parapsychology, I think this is exceptionally valuable. As a psychologist, and especially looking at altered states of consciousness, I've become more and more overwhelmed by the degree to which people's mental functioning is limited by their belief system, and the degree to which the belief system is usually used very sloppily. We like to believe that our ordinary state is rational, but I think it's primarily rationalizing. So philosophy has something to teach us about actually being rational instead of just pretending to be. But even more important, parapsychological data provide a splendid example of how a conceptual system that we've come to believe in simply cannot handle certain kinds of data, and it could be used to illustrate to people how much we need to be careful not to mistake our conceptual system for what's out there.

THE ROLE OF THE LIBRARY IN EDUCATION FOR PARAPSYCHOLOGY

Rhea A. White

INTRODUCTION

It is obvious that in the transmission of knowledge about parapsychology to students parapsychologists are the starting point, for initially they must provide reliable information about parapsychology to teachers who in turn will inform students. But librarians, particularly reference librarians, should also be considered as having an important role in education for parapsychology, for they serve as middlemen between the parapsychologists, on the one hand, and the teachers and students, on the other.

Although some who will teach parapsychology have learned about the subject firsthand through visits to research centers and perhaps even from actual experimentation, most teachers will get their information from secondary sources. And although teaching courses and workshops may be held, or films and tapes on teaching parapsychology prepared, the most important medium will still be the written word. The chief repositories of our knowledge about parapsychology are now, and I think will remain, journals and books. These will serve as the basis for what is taught on parapsychology. And although, hopefully, teachers will encourage their students to do research, conduct field trips to local laboratories or other places of parapsychological interest, and provide thorough and reliable lecture notes, students will doubtless also be asked to do reading on parapsychology outside the classroom. In addition there will be many independent learners who are not enrolled in courses but who will be seeking to educate themselves on parapsychology. So from the point of view of both teachers and students, the librarian will be called on to play an active role.

But how is the teacher, let alone the student, going to know which books of the hundreds of titles available provide reliable information? Where will they find out what the important journals are, and having found out, how will they know what specific subjects are covered, and in which issues? And if they get *that* far, how will they get hold of a copy of the book or article they need? Although in the past a handful of parapsychologists and parapsychological organizations have borne the brunt of this educational burden, the demand today has gone far beyond their means to answer it. But the answers to these questions may be found at the library, although not necessarily by the teacher or student looking for information solely on his own.

Most people assume that the key to the resources of any library is its card catalog, and if they don't find what they are looking for under the first heading they try in the catalog, they give up. But the catalog is a very imperfect index and if a patron cannot find what he needs on his own, he should never leave the library without first consulting a reference librarian. Even if he does find some information himself, it is likely that a librarian can help him find additional, and perhaps better, material.

A reference librarian is someone who is professionally trained to help people find the information they seek. If the information exists anywhere, theoretically a reference librarian can find it. In actual practice, of course, there are limitations such as time, language barriers, and possibly financial considerations. For example, if the only source of an answer is a book in a library in the Soviet Union which is for reference use only, and the parton needs it the next day, obviously a librarian cannot get it for him. But for materials in English, given enough time, a good reference librarian should be able to answer nine out of every ten questions put to him.

Upon being consulted, a librarian may first go to the card catalog even though the patron protests he has already tried it. This is because the patron may not have looked under the right subject heading, and if not, the library could contain many books of interest to him but he would not know it. A good catalog would contain cross references from all synonymous headings to the one actually used, but catalogers are human and do not always include all relevant terms. So a librarian who is familiar with the use of the catalog and aware of its imperfections can often find books listed there, after some perseverance, which the patron was not able to locate for himself.

But even when used properly, the card catalog is only one means of finding information in a library. The reference librarian is aware of many other approaches to information and is being paid to help people find what they are looking for.

As I see it, the librarian has two functions to perform which are central to education for parapsychology. First, even if he knows little about parapsychology, by using specialized sources he can help the student and teacher find the information they need. In my daily work as a reference librarian I am frequently confronted by patrons who say something like, "I don't suppose you know anything about marketing procedures, but do you think you could help me find information on automation in marketing"? Or, "do you know anything about organic chem? I need a particular formula." And I reply, "No, I don't know anything about marketing—or organic chemistry—but that doesn't matter. I know where we can find the answers." With the proper reference tools, librarians can help people find the information they need, including information on parapsychology.

You will note I just referred to reference "tools." I will be using the term throughout this paper. By "tool" librarians refer not to hammers or saws but primarily to books: not just to any kind of book, but to a particular class of books which tells where to find information on a particular subject. Such books are truly the tools of the librarian's trade, and when he has the proper tools, he can help people find information on parapsychology or any other subject *even though he personally knows nothing at all about it*. This is important, and so is being emphasized, because although we as parapsychologists must provide teachers of parapsychology with the knowledge of what to teach, we must provide librarians with the proper tools. Much of the remainder of this paper will be devoted to describing and evaluating existing reference tools and pointing out what additional tools are needed.

The second function which librarians can perform on behalf of teachers and students (and for that matter, parapsychologists) is that of obtaining copies of specific books, periodical articles, films, technical reports, or whatever else is needed. Here the question is not what book or magazine will answer the patron's needs. Rather, what he wants has been determined and the problem is to find a copy. Sometimes the needed item is in the library but the patron doesn't realize it; or else he knows it, but still can't find it. More often, especially as regards parapsychological materials, the item will not be owned by the library, but library service today is not confined to the walls of one's own library. Any librarian worth his salt can obtain 90% of what has been published for his patron and in regard to nine percent of the remaining ten, at least tell the patron where actual copies may be found even if, for whatever reason, the library cannot get a copy.

The process of obtaining a book from another library is called "interlibrary loan," or "interloan," for short. Periodical articles also may be obtained in this way. (However, in the case of an article, usually a photocopy of the original is obtained, rather than the periodical itself. This service is usually free, but occasionally a nominal fee is charged, especially for articles longer than 20 pages.)

Since at the present time the most important sources of parapsychological information, the periodicals of the field, are not owned by many libraries, as the volume of parapsychological research increases so will the demand for interloaned articles from these journals. This points up another reason why it behooves parapsychologists to see that the proper reference tools in their field are produced. When interloaning a book or periodical article for a patron, a librarian simply cannot take the patron's word that the author and title are correct as he has given them. Moreover, the publisher and date of the publication are required, and rarely does the patron have this information available. Even if he has it written down somewhere, invariably he leaves it—and for that matter his library card—at home when he comes to the library! In interloaning a periodical article, not only the author and title are required, but also the name of the journal, the volume, the year, and the inclusive pagination.

So before interloaning an item, a librarian must "verify," as it is called in the trade, the bibliographic information on the book or article the patron wants. (A librarian spends a good many hours each week verifying interloans, some searches taking close to an hour or even more.) Books are checked against *Books in Print, Cumulative Book Index,* the *Library of Congress Catalog of Books*, and other general reference tools. Books on parapsychology may be checked in these same works just as books in any other field, so they are not a special problem. But articles in parapsychological journals are. The only indexing and abstracting service that presently includes significant runs of parapsychological periodicals is *Psychological Abstracts*, and one problem is that only large libraries are likely to own it. Second, even if a library owns it, it may not own a complete run. And third, the *Journal of Parapsychology* is the only parapsychological periodical with complete coverage in *Psych. Abstracts*. There is only scattered coverage of the SPR, ASPR, and Parapsychology Foundation publications, and inclusion of even one issue of a foreign language parapsychology periodical is a rarity. On the surface this may seem a small matter, but I assure you its ramifications are far-reaching. This is a weak link in parapsychology's chain of information and it will certainly slow down the educational process if it is not soon strengthened.

The remainder of this paper will be devoted to descriptions of some general sources of parapsychological information, some specifically parapsychological information sources, as well as some areas of parapsychology lacking bibliographic control and some specific reference tools which are needed in parapsychology.

GENERAL REFERENCE TOOLS CONTAINING
PARAPSYCHOLOGICAL INFORMATION

There are a number of general reference tools which provide information on parapsychology and are to be found in most libraries of any appreciable size. The first tool, of course, is the card catalog, as has been mentioned. This may be used not only to locate books under the name of the author or title but also by subject. In order to use the card catalog productively, one must know the right subject headings under which to look. Most libraries use Library of Congress subject headings, or modifications of them. The subject headings of primary relevance to parapsychology are as follows: APPARITIONS, ASTRAL PROJECTION (for out-of-the-body experiences), CLAIRVOYANCE, DIVINATION, EXTRASENSORY PERCEPTION, FAITH-CURE (for unorthodox healing), FUTURE LIFE (for survival), GHOSTS, OCCULT SCIENCES, PSYCHICAL RESEARCH (for parapsychology), SECOND SIGHT (for precognition), SPIRITUALISM (for mediumship), and THOUGHT TRANSFERENCE (for Telepathy).

Having exhausted the library's store of books on parapsychology, one may look for additional titles in the *Subject Guide to Books in Print* which also uses Library of Congress subject headings. The books listed in this annual publication are taken from U.S. publishers' catalogs of in-print books. A more exhaustive listing, by author, title, or subject, may be found in the *Cumulative Book Index*, which attempts to list all books published in the English language. If a paperback book on parapsychology is wanted, *Paperbound Books in Print* may be consulted. It is published twice a year and lists books on parapsychology under the heading PSYCHOLOGY—OCCULT SCIENCES AND PARAPSYCHOLOGY. New books that have been published since the annual *Books in Print* are included both in a supplement to *Books in Print* which is published between editions, and *Forthcoming Books*, which includes newly published titles as well as books about to be published. Parapsychology books are listed again under the heading, PSYCHOLOGY—OCCULT SCIENCES AND PARAPSYCHOLOGY.

If biographical information on persons associated with parapsychology is needed, *Biography Index* is a useful guide to material in whole books, parts of books, reference sources, and magazines. It uses the unfortunate heading of PSYCHISTS for both parapsychologists and psychics.

The names and addresses of parapsychological organizations as well as brief descriptive information about them may be found in Gale's

Encyclopedia of Associations and its supplement, *New Associations*. Reviews of books on parapsychology other than those published in parapsychological journals may be located through *Book Review Index* and *Book Review Digest* and to a lesser extent, *Index to Book Reviews in the Humanities*. For general magazine articles on parapsychology, *Reader's Guide to Periodical Literature* is invaluable. The relevant subject headings in *Reader's Guide* are CLAIRVOYANCE, EXTRASENSORY PERCEPTION, FAITH CURE, FUTURE LIFE, GHOSTS, MEDIUMS, OCCULT SCIENCES, PARAPSYCHOLOGY, PRECOGNITION, PSYCHOKINESIS, SPIRITUALISM, AND TELEPATHY. More specialized articles may be found through *Psychological Abstracts* under the headings of CLAIRVOYANCE, EXTRASENSORY PERCEPTION, PARAPSYCHOLOGICAL PHENOMENA, PARAPSYCHOLOGY, PRECOGNITION, PSYCHOKINESIS, AND TELEPATHY. The *Social Sciences and Humanities Index* and the new *Social Sciences Index* (which includes the *Journal of the American Society for Psychical Research* and *Journal of Parapsychology*) are also useful and generally use the same subject headings as *Reader's Guide*.

Definitions of terms may be found in the unabridged dictionaries and in psychological and psychiatric dictionaries, especially those by Drever, English and English, Eysenck, and Warren.

A number of general encyclopedias, as well as specialized ones such as the *McGraw-Hill Encyclopedia of Science and Technology,* the *Encyclopedia of Philosophy*, and the *International Encyclopedia of the Social Sciences*, contain considerable information on parapsychology. The contents of these encyclopedias as regards parapsychology are reviewed and evaluated in *Parapsychology: Sources of Information*.[35]

These are just a few of the general reference tools which a large percentage of libraries are likely to own and which provide basic information on parapsychology. They are especially helpful in libraries which do not carry many specifically parapsychological tools. Any reference librarian will know about all these sources and of course many more.

SPECIFIC REFERENCE SOURCES IN PARAPSYCHOLOGY

When I was invited to this conference, I was asked to describe a basic reference collection in parapsychology. Accordingly, in this section I will review the reference books that exist in the field, but will conclude the paper with a more extensive list of what we do not have.

There are two major kinds of reference works in any field: those that are in themselves compendiums of information, such as handbooks, almanacs, encyclopedias, dictionaries, yearbooks, atlases, and so forth;

and those consisting of works whose purpose is to provide bibliographic control, or listings of existing sources of information in a particular subject, so that access may be gained to any part of it. In other words, this type of tool will tell you what is available and where to find it, but unlike the first type, it does not contain the actual information. In a sense, the second type is more important than the first, for without access to the complete file of information on a given subject, the first type of reference work could not be compiled. I will therefore begin with a description of our bibliographic reference works.

Bibliographic Tools in Parapsychology

A major means of obtaining bibliographic control of the books in a given field is through catalogs of the collections of large libraries specializing in that subject. This type of tool serves the dual purpose of providing bibliographic information on what has been published, as well as indicating what library owns a copy. Our field already has several library catalogs. One of the first was Harry Price's *Short-Title Catalogue of Works on Psychical Research, Spiritualism, Magic, Psychology, Legerdemain and Other Methods of Deception, Charlatanism, Witchcraft and Technical Works for the Scientific Investigation of Alleged Abnormal Phenomena from circa 1450 A.D. to 1929 A.D.*[17] (It may be a "short title catalogue," but for a catalog, it certainly has a long title!) It lists 6000 titles. Price also compiled a supplement[18] to his catalog containing 2500 additional items acquired between 1929 and 1934. The College of Psychic Studies, when known as the London Spiritualist Alliance, published a title and author catalog[11] of their library in 1931 which was updated by supplements in 1939 and 1950. The published catalog of a smaller collection is the *Catalogue of the John William Graham Collection of the Literature of Psychic Sciences*, published in 1950.[30]

Unfortunately none of the above catalogs contains information on books published since 1950, yet for the most part the more recent books are also the more important ones. This situation is soon to be rectified for G. K. Hall has announced the publication, next year, of the *Catalogue of the Library of the Society for Psychical Research*. It will contain listings by both author and title.*

A second type of bibliography is the standard subject bibliography which lists titles on a given subject by author, or under a number of subsidiary subject headings, or both. This is one of the most important

---

* This has now been published. It may be obtained from G. K. Hall & Co., 70 Lincoln Street, Boston, Mass. 02111.

types of reference tool for parapsychology, since it is essential to obtaining the requisite background information on any aspect of the field, but unfortunately we do not have adequate coverage.

Zorab's *Bibliography of Parapsychology*[38] is notable for two reasons: it is a subject bibliography which includes both books and periodical articles and it lists works in several languages. Unfortunately it is highly selective, and even with the supplement which was published in 1960, it is now outdated.

Probably the most important bibliographic attempt we have in parapsychology is Techter's *Bibliography and Index of Psychic Research and Related Topics*[32] which was published for the years 1962, 1963, and 1964. It consisted of an author list of practically everything published on parapsychology for each of those three years, with a subject approach through an index. Had funds been available to continue its publication, many of our current bibliographic problems would be much less acute.

The Naumov and Vilenskaya *Bibliographies on Parapsychology*,[13] which was translated into English and published by the Joint Publications Research Service, provides a selective listing of publications on parapsychology in all languages, with emphasis on Russian materials (with English titles).

Some useful bibliographies, which are important because they emphasize periodical articles and cover recent material, are compiled by Mrs. Babusis, the librarian of the Eileen J. Garrett Library of the Parapsychology Foundation. These bibliographies vary in length from 4 to 8 pages, and each is devoted to a specific subject, for example, unorthodox healing, out-of-the-body experiences, and auras. Unfortunately these bibliographies are not published, but photocopies are available upon request.

Two bibliographic guides to the literature of parapsychology, both of which appeared in 1973, are Ashby's *Guidebook for the Study of Psychical Research*[1] and *Parapsychology: Sources of Information*, by Laura Dale and myself.[35] Although there is considerable overlap in titles, they by no means cover the same books. Annotations are included in both, although Ashby only annotated a portion of his titles. His bibliography is in two main sections: books for the beginning student and books for the advanced student. The arrangement of White and Dale is by subject, but each title is rated according to whether it is suitable for a beginner, an intermediate student, or an advanced reader. Book review citations are provided for each title.

Finally, although not intended primarily as bibliographies, *Extrasensory Perception after Sixty Years* compiled by J. B. Rhine and others[22] and

Rao's *Experimental Parapsychology*[19] include extensive bibliographies (361 items in the former and 1251 in the latter) and are especially important because most of the references are to articles in parapsychological periodicals.

Indexes

My definition of an index is a tool that enables you to do in seconds what otherwise would have taken hours or even days. In fact, a good index can make it possible for one to do what otherwise one might not even attempt. And yet, even though indexes are probably the most useful reference tool of all, we have virtually none in parapsychology. The Society for Psychical Research has published an index to its *Journal* and *Proceedings*[23-26] which is in four parts. This is useful in narrowing down a search, but unfortunately the index does not tell you the author or title of the article you are being directed to, and so after troubling to find it, you may learn you already have that reference! The last issue[7] of the *Proceedings of the Parapsychological Association* (before it became *Research in Parapsychology*) has a useful cumulative index. Most parapsychological periodicals have their own indexes for each volume, but when a title such as the *Journal of the American Society for Psychical Research* has been published since 1907, it means that 68 separate indexes must be consulted.

Lacking a cumulative index, it is quite useful at least to be able to scan a table of contents listing. Here again the SPR is a pioneer, having compiled lists of the major contents of both its *Proceedings*[28] and *Journal*.[27] My September, 1953, issue of the *Journal of Parapsychology* is very dogeared and worn, because it contained a contents listing of the JP[31] from 1937 through June, 1953. But it only covered 17 volumes of the 38 that now exist. Surely it is time for a new *Journal of Parapsychology* table of contents listing! An index to the ASPR publications was compiled by Fraser Nicol, but it is at least ten years behind the current volume, and only exists in the form of a card file in the ASPR library.

An attempt at indexing in detail the contents of books of importance in parapsychology was made with *Parapsychology: Sources of Information*.[35] Each of the 282 books included is not only classified by subject but the index of subjects at the back of the book contains several index terms per book. For example, the Ciba Foundation Symposium, *Extrasensory Perception*, which is classified under Interdisciplinary Works, contains a few papers on anpsi, and this is indicated in the finer subject index. It also includes the first index we have to illustrations, but it is limited to those found in the 282 books, the encyclopedias, and the periodicals described in the book. This is only a fraction of the illustrative material which exists, and which is in demand for use in teaching, in displays, and in audio-visual materials.

Abstracts

As has been pointed out, *Psychological Abstracts* provides some coverage of parapsychological periodicals, especially the *Journal of Parapsychology*. Gaining access to these abstracts, however, is not easy, because the indexing of *Psych. Abstracts* is poor.

"Parapsychological Abstracts," a section of the *Journal of Parapsychology* since 1958, contains useful summaries of articles in other parapsychological journals, of articles on parapsychology in non-parapsychological journals, of books which otherwise would not be reviewed in JP, and of some foreign articles or books as well. An author and title listing of each abstract is included in the annual table of contents listing of JP, and the abstracts are included in the annual JP subject index.

Specialized Encyclopedias

For older material we have Spence's *Encyclopedia of Occultism*[29] which, however, does not contain much material of direct relevance to parapsychology. Fodor's *Encyclopedia of Psychic Science*[8] covers terms, publications, events, and persons associated with psychical research and spiritualism. However, because it was published in 1933, it necessarily contains nothing on modern experimental parapsychology, which was then just beginning. A more up-to-date encyclopedia is the 24-volume *Man, Myth and Magic* edited by Cavendish.[6] It is lavishly illustrated and covers parapsychology along with magic, witchcraft and occultism. Cavendish has recently edited another encyclopedia, independent of the first, which is entitled the *Encyclopedia of the Unexplained*.[5] It is a one-volume work and is quite useful as a reference. Rhine served as an advisor for it on parapsychological material and wrote some of the entries himself. Long articles are signed and contain references to further information.

Terminology

If definitions of terms are needed, older terms associated with spiritualism and early psychical research may be found in Fodor[8] and Spence.[29] Some of the terms associated with experimental parapsychology may be found in the Cavendish encyclopedias as well as in glossaries which have appeared in recent books such as Ashby,[1]

Mitchell et al.[12] and White and Dale.[35] The best glossary we have for research-oriented terms is the one published in each issue of the *Journal of Parapsychology*. An even more inclusive glossary including both older terms and experimental terms will appear in Wolman's *Handbook of Parapsychology*.[37]

Directories

A directory is a listing of organizations, persons, or publications associated with a particular field or other subject area. Although parapsychology is still small enough so that everyone in it knows almost everyone else, as well as the major organizations in the field, even we could use a directory to serve as a handy source of addresses! And of course the first thing needed by a newcomer to the field would be a directory.

Most of the directory-type information we have is very scattered. The leader in providing this sort of information is the Parapsychology Foundation. From time to time the *Newsletter of the Parapsychology Foundation* and now *Parapsychology Review* contains an "International Directory of Parapsychological Associations,[9]" the latest one having been published this year. It is arranged geographically and lists the name and address of each organization and the name of the person to contact.

Another useful directory published in *Parapsychology Review* is "A Selected List of Periodicals in Parapsychology and Related Subjects, Currently in Print, and Received by the Eileen J. Garrett Library."[2] It is also arranged geographically, and gives the title, publisher, editor, price, and a brief description of 53 periodicals.

A description of the major parapsychological research organizations and English-language periodicals is given in *Parapsychology: Sources of Information*[35] and Ashby's *Guidebook*[1] includes descriptions of research organizations, libraries, periodicals, and bookshops. Directory-type information on organizations, publications, lectures, and libraries is included in Chapter 8 of Mitchell, et al.[12]

An annual directory entitled "Courses and Other Study Opportunities in Parapsychology"[14] compiled by Marian Nester is published each year by the Education Department, American Society for Psychical Research. Each issue is usually updated by a supplement. It is a non-evaluative list of credit and non-credit college courses. For each college or university included it provides information on the department giving the course, the instructor's name, the name of the course, requirements for taking it, if any, and the name of the person to contact for details.

The best current source of directory information is *Parapsychology Review*. Also useful is the *ASPR Newsletter*, the "News" section of the *Journal of Parapsychology*, and the "News Ambit" section of *Psychic*.

However, there is a wealth of information that never gets published, due to lack of space and the ephemeral nature of much of this material, which nonetheless, for the moment at least, has considerable importance. A new organization has been formed in New York for the express purpose of disseminating reliable information. It is called Information Services for Psi Education, or ISPE. Its purpose is to serve as a clearinghouse for parapsychology and related information. It hopes to make available, particularly through its publication, *Psi News*, information on sources and resources in parapsychology. It is specifically aimed at educators, but will assist anyone interested in information on organizations, services, products, publications, and events in parapsychology. For further information, write to ISPE, Box 2221, New York 10001.

Audio-Visual Materials

Although an increasing number of movies, tapes, and slides on parapsychological subjects are becoming available, there is no master list of them, nor is there any easy way of compiling one. However, the ASPR Education Department has an unpublished list of films as well as a list of educational materials, which includes sources to contact as well as a highly selected list of tapes, a filmstrip, and a slide collection. Additional tapes of parapsychological interest may be found in the Spiritual Frontiers Fellowship's list of tape recordings for loan to members and the catalog of Big Sur Recordings.[3]

In the space that remains I would like to describe some types of information and specific reference tools which parapsychology lacks.

AREAS IN WHICH BIBLIOGRAPHIC CONTROL IS LACKING

Experimental Data

It seems to me that parapsychology more than most fields needs to preserve the data on which its reports are based, whether it be transcripts of mediumistic trances or token object readings or dream protocols or experimental studies of ESP and PK using cards and dice. This is needed in part because of the many criticisms of our claims. Presumably we have nothing to hide from our critics and the sooner they realize this, the better off we'll all be.

But critics are not the only ones interested in examining the data on which published reports are based. Many psi effects have been discovered in later investigations which were then noted also in the data of earlier experiments when they were reanalyzed in the light of the new findings. Displacement is a notable example. There is always the possibility that as we become more sophisticated in recognizing the presence of psi, later analyses may turn up evidence of it even in what are now considered to be chance results.

Fortunately, in the past most of the experimental work was done in one laboratory—the Duke University Parapsychology Laboratory—and so the data were readily accessible for reanalysis. However, with the spread of parapsychological research to many other centers in recent years, maintaining control of data becomes a problem. It would be helpful if, after an investigator has finished with his data, he could voluntarily place them on file in a central data archives where the material would be preserved, cataloged, and made available to anyone wanting to review it, with the investigator's permission.

Moreover, the question is frequently raised in the literature as to what percentage of parapsychological experiments never get published because insignificant results were obtained. It would be to the credit of parapsychology if data and reports of unpublished experiments, if available, were also kept on file.

Technical Reports

Occasionally an experimental report or paper on parapsychology is published separately, i.e., not in book or periodical form: for example, "Testing for Extrasensory Perception with a Machine," by W. R. Smith, E. F. Dagle, and others, which was published by the Air Force; or the Parapsychological Association's "Techniques and Status of Modern Parapsychology," the transcript of the first PA American Association for the Advancement of Science symposium; or the Myers Memorial Lectures, which are published by the SPR but not generally as part of their *Proceedings* or *Journal*. Some of these independent papers are quite important and certainly may one day be of historical interest, but they tend to get lost after a period of time because they do not lend themselves to storage in a particular file nor are they likely to be indexed. Parapsychological libraries, at least, should pay particular attention to the cataloging and storage of these elusive items.

Foreign Language Materials

Another area in which bibliographic control, in this country at least, is almost entirely lacking is that of materials published in languages other than English. We do not have a record of what has been published, either in the form of books or periodicals, nor a subject or author approach to this material. Perhaps the European Parapsychological Association can do something to rectify this situation, at least for the languages represented among its members.

Translations

For those who can only read English it would be helpful to have English translations of at least the titles of all the foreign language material. Then those that are of particular interest could be selected for translation. We also need a listing of translations already in existence. At present there is no record of what has been translated nor where it exists. Many of these translations are not published. The ASPR library, for example, has several unpublished translations on file.

SPECIFIC TYPES OF REFERENCE TOOLS NEEDED

In addition to the need to control certain types of material in parapsychology, there are several specific tools which the field requires.

Handbook or Manual

The fields of chemistry and physics have many handbooks which contain tables and formulae and other such tabular information. Parapsychology's needs in this area are different due to the nature of our subject matter, but we could use something like the *Psychology Almanac* recently compiled by Wilkening.[36] It contains the APA's "ethical standards for psychologists," descriptions of journals in psychology and related fields, terminology, some symbols and notations used in statistics, and 34 statistical tables. It seems to me that the Parapsychological Association ought to sponsor the publication of something similar which would contain information on the P.A., basic ESP and PK tests, including methods of obtaining targets in precognition tests, special test booklets such as those developed by Freeman, and psychological tests used in parapsychology experiments such as the Betts Imagery Scale, the Knapp attitude toward time questionnaire, the Taylor Manifest Anxiety Scale, Stuart's interest inventory, and the "mood" questions used by Nielsen and Osis, to name a few which come quickly to mind. There are many others of course. It would also bring together descriptions of all the analyses used for evaluating various psi effects such as the reinforcement effect, salience ratios, variance, etc. I think that such a tool would be of immense practical importance to students and to researchers and in itself would be a stimulus to carry out research. It would not only save time in planning research but it would encourage more sophisticated designs and it would aid in standardizing research methodology. (A handbook of such tests in psychology has recently been compiled by Lake et al. called *Measuring Human Behavior*.)[10]

Union List of Parapsychological Periodicals

A "union list of periodicals" is a listing of the periodical holdings in a group of libraries. It would be very useful to know what specific libraries have which issues of what parapsychological journals. For example, in an index I am preparing, I would like to include all issues of the *Newsletter of the Parapsychology Foundation*, but neither the ASPR Library, FRNM Library, or even the Eileen J. Garrett Library has certain issues. Does anybody? A union list would tell us. Such a list should include all parapsychological journals that have been published in any language and it should include listings for large public, college, and university libraries, parapsychological libraries, and perhaps even some individual libraries. The *Union List of Serials* and its supplement, *New Serial Titles*, put out by the Library of Congress, already supply this information for a number of large libraries in the United States and Canada. I am simply proposing that to its listings we add the holdings of parapsychological libraries the world over.

Biographical Dictionary

Although the Parapsychology Foundation's pioneer *Biographical Dictionary of Parapsychology*[4] was an excellent first step in providing a source of biographical information on persons associated with parapsychology, it is time for a new edition. For example, only a third of the current members of the Parapsychological Association are in the *Biographical Dictionary*. Ashby's *Guidebook*[1] is much more recent and has a biographical section, but it only includes one person not in the *Biographical Dictionary* (John Beloff, I am happy to say, has this honor), but the entries of the *Biographical Dictionary* are much more complete than those in Ashby.

Union Catalog of Books on Parapsychology

In many fields, a means of providing increased bibliographic control is the compilation of a "union catalog." A union catalog is a listing of the combined book holdings of a number of libraries in a particular geographic location or a specific subject area. For example, the library where I work is located in Nassau County, New York. There are 53 libraries in the county. The Nassau Library System maintains a union catalog of the books in all the libraries in the county so that if we do not own a book or our copy is out, we may find out from Nassau Library System what other libraries own the book, and borrow it from them for our patron.

A useful means of obtaining bibliographic control of the books in our field would be to compile a union catalog of the books in the major parapsychological libraries. This would not only tell us what has been published but where copies may be found.

Encyclopedic Compendium

Another reference tool we lack is an authoritative encyclopedia which includes information on experimental parapsychology and other developments since 1930, as well as the older material covered in Fodor[8] and Spence.[29] The multi-volume Cavendish set[6] and the one-volume *Encyclopedia of the Unexplained*[5] are useful, but much more coverage is given in them to the occult, magic, and witchcraft than to hardcore parapsychology. We need a work which deals extensively with psi missing, position effects, dual targets, the psychic shuffle, experimenter effects in parapsychology, doctrinal compliance, the "psychic pathology of everyday life," and so forth.

However, perhaps what we need at this stage more than an encyclopedia is a compendium of review articles on where we stand, what we know, how we know it, and what we need to find out, in all the major areas of parapsychology. I mean review articles aimed at parapsychologists, rather than surveys directed at laymen or specialists in other fields. It would be the sort of article psychologists write for other psychologists in *Psychological Bulletin*. We have some papers that would qualify in this category, such as the two-part review of the sheep-goat work done by Palmer,[15, 16] or Rhine's reviews of psi missing[21] and position effects,[20] or Ullman's review of psi and psychiatry in a recent psychiatric textbook.[33] I have recently brought together for publication 19 of these review articles and have updated their bibliographies, but in compiling this work[34] I became acutely aware of the many subjects for which we do not have state-of-the-art reviews. I think we need this sort of job done not only for students and teachers and librarians but for parapsychologists themselves. I am hopeful that Wolman's *Handbook of Parapsychology*[37] will serve this purpose, but it is too soon to tell.

Periodical Index

Finally, I would like to conclude this list of the types of reference tools we need with what I think is the most important one of all: a detailed index to the periodical literature. This is what we need more than anything else in order for students to be able to locate the work that has been done relevant to their own interests and also so that we ourselves do not spend more hours than necessary of precious time in reviewing the literature. But what is a student, or for that matter, a research worker, to do who wants to review research on, say, the decline effect? We have no review articles on the decline effect. He could check the annual indexes of the *Journal of Parapsychology* and the *Journal of the ASPR* and the four indexes to the SPR publications— if he had access to them, and that is very unlikely. But say he did, then would he still have enough time? Done properly, it would take literally days. What is needed is a detailed index to periodical articles so that all one need do is look under "decline effect" and find references to all the articles that have anything significant to say about the decline effect. Sometimes I think we forget that most people in the field grew up with knowledge of the decline effect, the question of whether ESP is diametric, the fact that multiple tasks invite the preferential effect, and so forth. This information was absorbed by osmosis as we went along. But in the expanding world of parapsychology today, we have reached a new stage where a more formal and standardized approach to information is needed. There is no virtue I can see in having to spend hours or days on a search that could just as easily be accomplished in minutes. Time enough will be spent in getting hold of the material and in actually reading it.

The only alternative, and it is increasingly evident from reference lists at the end of articles that this is the road we are being forced to take, is to be concerned mainly with what has been done in approximately the past ten years, and not attempt to pay attention to what was done earlier, except for what spontaneously comes to mind or is encountered by serendipity. This too is foolish. The *Journal of Parapsychology*, for example, is a goldmine of information and has been since the very first issue. But at the present time only those may make full use of it who possess complete runs *and* have the time to search it anew with every question that arises.

Unless, of course, one had an index.

I am happy to say that, with the assistance of the Parapsychology Foundation, I am at work on two such indexes, one to articles on parapsychology in English in non-parapsychological journals and one to the major English-language parapsychological periodicals. The first will cover general periodicals such as *Atlantic, Life, McCall's, Science, Time* and specialized journals such as *American Anthropologist, English Journal, Physics Today,* and *Psychological Bulletin.* The second one will cover the 13 parapsychological periodicals described in *Parapsychology: Sources of Information*.[35] However, I am not equipped to do the same job for periodicals in languages other than English. I hope the European Parapsychological Association or some other organization or individual will see the value of such an index to periodicals in other languages and will undertake to compile one.

CONCLUDING REMARKS

Some may consider this discussion of the role of the librarian and the use of reference tools far removed from the core of parapsychology which is research. Others may feel that having to consult a reference librarian or to turn to reference works is not for parapsychologists themselves but only for those who know little about the subject. Throughout this paper I have tried to show that both of these ideas are incorrect. For one thing, in a field as small as ours, with so few workers actively engaged in research, it is as if each person must do the work of three. What we lack, among other things, is man hours. And I want to stress that what adequate reference tools and professional library service can provide us with is *time*. And second, no matter what the field, whether it be parapsychology, physics, or philosophy, the aim is *completeness*—to leave no stone unturned in the quest of extending man's knowledge. No man can remember everything in his field, let alone be exposed to all of it to begin with. But a good index can quickly provide him with the information he would have had if he had read everything and had a photographic memory of every detail. A competent bibliography or directory or handbook can save many precious hours and insure completeness of coverage as well. This is true both for literature searches required by those engaged in research and those involved with the process of teaching parapsychology or learning about it. Everyone in parapsychology is called on from time to time to provide information of an educational nature—a list of publications, certain names and addresses, a bit of historical information, or a survey of a certain type of experiment. I wish I had back the many, many hours I have spent looking for a name or an address or a bit of information I knew existed but not exactly where. Or, even if I knew something had been published in a particular publication, say the *Parapsychology Bulletin*, I still would have to look through each issue until I found it. If I had an index, I not only could find it quickly, but I would probably also find references to related information with which my memory alone would not provide me.

So I would like to close by urging all parapsychologists to do whatever they can to see that our field gets the proper reference tools it needs. We would probably get where we are going without them, but with them, it will be a lot faster. In the same way, those of us who did not have to cross an ocean to get here could have walked to San Francisco. But it certainly saved a lot of time and shoe leather to be able to fly!

REFERENCES

[1] Ashby, R. *The Guidebook for the Study of Psychical Research* (N. Y., Samuel Weiser, 1972).

[2] Babusis, G. "A selected List of Periodicals in Parapsychology & Related Subjects, Currently in Print, & Received by the Eileen J. Garrett Library," *Parapsychology Review*, 1974, 5(5), 23–27.

[3] Big Sur Recordings (2015 Bridgeway—Dept. T, Sausalito, Cal. 94965).

[4] *Biographical Dictionary of Parapsychology with Directory and Glossary: 1964–1966*. Edited by H. Pleasants (N. Y., Garrett/Helix, 1964).

[5] Cavendish, R. (Ed.). *Encyclopedia of the Unexplained: Magic, Occultism and Parapsychology* (N. Y., McGraw-Hill, 1974).

[6] Cavendish, R. (Ed.). *Man, Myth & Magic; an Illustrated Encyclopedia of the Supernatural* (N. Y., Marshall Cavendish, 1970). 24 vols.

[7] Cumulative index to Numbers 1–8 (1957–1971). *Proceedings of the Parapsychological Association*, 1971, No. 8, 161–206.

[8] "Directory of Parapsychological Associations." *Parapsychology Review*, 1975, 6(1), 22–28.

[9] Fodor, N. *Encyclopaedia of Psychic Science* (Secaucus, N. J., University Books, 1966). (First published in 1933).

[10] Lake, D. G., Miles, M. B., and Earle, R. B., Jr., (Eds.). *Measuring Human Behavior: Tools for the Assessment of Social Functioning* (N. Y., Teachers College Press, 1973).

[11] London Spiritualist Alliance. *Catalogue of the Library of the London Spiritualist Alliance* (London, The Alliance, 1931).

[12] Mitchell, E. D., and others. Edited by J. White. *Psychic Exploration* (N. Y., Putnam's, 1974).

[13] Naumov, E. K., and Vilenskaya, L. V. *Bibliographies on Parapsychology (Psychoenergetics) and Related Subjects* (Arlington, Va., Joint Publications Research Service, 1972).

[14] [Nester, M.] *Courses and Other Study Opportunities in Parapsychology* (N. Y., American Society for Psychical Research, 1974).

[15] Palmer, J. "Scoring in ESP Tests as a Function of Belief-in ESP. Part I. The Sheep-goat Effect," *Journal of the American Society for Psychical Research*, 1971, 65, 373–408.

[16] Palmer, J. "Scoring in ESP Tests as a Function of Belief in ESP. Part II. Beyond the Sheep-goat Effect," *Journal of the American Society for Psychical Research*, 1972, 66, 1–26.

[17] Price, H. *Short-title Catalogue of Works on Psychical Research, Spiritualism, Magic, Psychology, Legerdemain and Other Methods of Deception, Charlatanism, Witchcraft and Technical Works for the Scientific Investigation of Alleged Abnormal Phenomena from circa 1450 A.D. to 1929 A.D.* (London, National Laboratory of Psychical Research, 1929).

[18] Price, H. *Supplement to Short-Title Catalogue of Works on Psychical Research, Alleged Abnormal Phenomena, Spiritualism, Magic, Witchcraft, Legerdemain, Charlatanism and Astrology from 1472 A.D. to the Present Day.* (London, University of London Council for Psychical Investigation, 1935).

[19] Rao, K. R. *Experimental Parapsychology: A Review and Interpretation, with a Comprehensive Bibliography* (Springfield, Ill., Thomas, 1966).

[20] Rhine, J. B. "Position Effects in Psi Test Results," *Journal of Parapsychology*, 1969, 33, 136–57. Also in White, R. A. *Surveys in Parapsychology* (Metuchen, N.J., Scarecrow Press).

[21] Rhine, J. B. "Psi-missing Re-examined," *Journal of Parapsychology*, 1969, 33, 1–38. Also in White, R. A. *Surveys in Parapsychology* (Metuchen, N. J., Scarecrow Press).

[22] Rhine, J. B., and others. *Extrasensory Perception after Sixty Years: A Critical Appraisal of the Research into Extrasensory Perception* (Boston, Branden, 1966). (First published in 1940).

[23] Society for Psychical Research. *Combined Index to Phantasms of the Living, vols. I & II. The Proceedings, vols. I –XV. The Journal, vols. I –IX & The Proceedings of the American Society for Psychical Research. With Table of Contents of "The Proceedings"* (London, R. B. Johnson, 1904). [Part 1]

[24] Society for Psychical Research. *Combined Index to The Proceedings, vols. XVI –XXVI & The Journal, vols. X –XV. With Table of Contents of The Proceedings* (Glasgow, Maclehose, 1914). [Part 2]

[25] Society for Psychical Research. *Combined Index to Proceedings, vols. XXVII –XLVII, 1914 –45, and Journal, vols. XVI –XXXIII, 1913 –46* (London, Society for Psychical Research, n.d.). [Part 3]

[26] Society for Psychical Research. *Combined Index to Proceedings, vols. XLVIII –LIV, 1944 –66, and Journal, vols. XXXIV –XLV, 1947 –70* (London, Society for Psychical Research, 1973). [Part 4]

[27] Society for Psychical Research. *List of the Principal Contents of the Journal from 1949 to 1969* (Available from the Society, 1 Adam and Eve Mews, London, England W8 6UQ).

[28] Society for Psychical Research. *List of the Principal Contents of the Proceedings from 1882 to 1969* (Available from the Society, 1 Adam & Eve Mews, London, England W8 6UQ).

[29] Spence, L. *An Encyclopaedia of Occultism: A Compendium of Information on the Occult Sciences, Occult Personalities, Psychic Science, Music, Demonology, Spiritism, Mysticism, and Metaphysics* (Secaucus, N. J., University Books, 1960). (First published in 1920).

[30] Swarthmore College. Library. *Catalogue of the John William Graham Collection of Literature of Psychic Science* (Swarthmore, Pa., John William Graham Fund for the Study of Psychic Science, 1950).

[31] Table of contents (volumes 1– 16). *Journal of Parapsychology*, 1953, 17, 231–46.

[32] Techter, D. *A Bibliography and Index of Psychic Research and Related Topics for the Year 1962* [Also for 1963 and 1964] (Chicago, Illinois Society for Psychic Research, 1963 [1964 and 1965]).

[33] Ullman, M. "Parapsychology and Psychiatry." In Freedman, A. M., Kaplan, H. I., and Sadock, B. *Modern Synopsis of Comprehensive Testbook of Psychiatry* (Baltimore, William & Wilkins, 1974).

[34] White, R. A. *Surveys in Parapsychology: Reviews of the Literature with Updated Bibliographies* (Metuchen, N. J., Scarecrow Press).

[35] White, R. A., and Dale, L. A. *Parapsychology: Sources of Information* (Metuchen, N. J., Scarecrow Press, 1973).

[36] Wilkening, H. E. *The Psychology Almanac* (Monterey, Cal., Brooks/Cole, 1973).

[37] Wolman, B. B. (Ed). *Handbook of Parapsychology* (N. Y., Van Nostrand Reinhold).

[38] Zorab, G. *Bibliography of Parapsychology* (N. Y., Garrett/Helix, 1957). (First supplement published in *Les Cahiers de la Tour Saint-Jacques*, No. 9, 1960.)

DISCUSSION

KRIPPNER: I'd like to compliment Ms. White on her very excellent review of libraries, periodicals, reference problems, etc. It is something that certainly expanded my horizon to some of the opportunities and also some of the needs. The main thing that I would support is the need for some kind of archives in experimental parapsychology. During the years that I was at Maimonides, we compiled masses and masses of data which, in retrospect, I think could still be useful to people making various types of analyses. It got to the point where we simply didn't have storage space and we had to throw away material. If somebody in the field had any sizeable basement or warehouse or better yet, filing cabinets, this is the sort of material that could be filed away.

The articles that these data appear in could be indexed and these could be microfilmed. Photocopies could be made available to people who wanted them. The notion of archives appeals to me very very much. I don't know how practical it is, but this might be something the PA could discuss at a future meeting to see if there is any way this could be started or initiated.

The type of proposal that John Palmer has been making, that many of you are aware of, involves filing away a protocol for the experimental before it actually starts. It seems to me that not only could the protocol be filed away, but maybe also the supportive data could be filed after the experiment has been published. I can see many, many advantages of an archives.

The other matter I wanted to mention is the information services for psi education that Marian Nester and her group have initiated. It is an excellent addition to the field, one especially useful for the colleges and universities now offering courses. I urge all of you who are not familiar with her newsletter and with the organization, to contact Ms. Nester some time before you leave tonight.

WHITE: I couldn't agree with you more.

BISAHA: There is a small point that bothers me, but I want to also compliment you on the fine and extensive work you've done in this area. It could be just a mid-west phenomenon but I know it bothers my students. Going into a library, doing research, and looking in the card catalogue, and if they do have a reference under parapsychology, there are very few volumes; but if you look under "Occult," you will find definitely Rao, Rhine—all these people under that particular reference. Now, the first place that any student goes, of course, is the library to get information, and I think that this is definitely misinformation. Is there anything we can do about this?

WHITE: Well, here again, it's useful to consult a librarian, because the librarian is there in part to interpret the catalogue, which is practically in another language, and it takes a lot of work to learn the ins and outs, which you never really do. The way it all came about is there's a lag in subject headings and when subject headings are changed, I believe new books by Dr. Rhine would be listed also elsewhere, but libraries require a lot of money to go back and recatalogue and change the cards and everything else, and usually they just don't do it. They start off with a new heading, and when that changes, they'll have a third heading perhaps, and this is why it's very important, even if you think you've helped yourself and found something, it's a good idea to also ask the librarian.

MORRISS: I also want to compliment you, Rhea, on what I think is a very, very important presentation. I can't wait to get my hands on all these resource materials that haven't quite yet been completed. I wonder if you would comment on how long you think it would be before the indexing that you're working on now will be completed, and if you would suggest, in your own estimation, what some of the other more important things are that should be focused on.

WHITE: You mean other than the ones that I mentioned?

MORRISS: Yes, other than the ones you mentioned.

WHITE: Well, as far as how long it's going to take me to complete the indexes, I really can't give an accurate estimate. I would think at least five years. I have a full time job and a part time job and the index has to be worked on after those are done. As far as the most important ones are concerned, I think the handbook sort of thing, where we would pull together really research methodology, all the different tests—this has been done to some extent but never really for, say, graduate students or for new research workers, or all research workers for that matter, if everything were included. I would give that high priority. For myself, I would very much like to see a union list of periodicals and I don't think it will be that difficult to compile. There aren't that many parapsychological libraries, and as far as the university and college libraries and the public libraries are concerned, that's already been done by the Library of Congress in their *Union List of Serials* which is updated by *New Serial Titles*, so we would just have to get the information on what libraries have there, and get our own.

MORRISS: So then the real problem is personnel, time, money?

MORRIS: I'd like to make two comments. Number one, just to back up what Stan said about the backlog of data at Maimonides and its usefulness. One of the kinds of studies that we would like to do is to examine the role of judges in free verbal response material. One of our intentions eventually is to try to get the original classical dream study data and do sheep/goat studies with judges and look at a variety of parameters affecting the judging art itself. We would very much like to use old data from which we could make a comparison, so that's a general statement in support of your point. Now a question to you, Rhea, concerns the origin of the rather curious filing system of the Library of Congress. In our library, right after BF 1000, we have the journals, and then we have a batch of parapsychology books, and then hypnosis, and then another batch of parapsychology books, and then all the dream books, and then another batch of parapsychology books, and those three totally separate clusters of parapsychology books, as near as I can tell, are completely overlapping in content. It's not survival here, and experiments here and something else there. Do you have any idea of the origin of this? It's a fascinating system.

WHITE: I'm not an expert on this classification system. We don't use it in the library where I work, but I would guess that again it's a matter of recataloguing, because I know that recently LC reclassified its schedule, and probably some books are in the old number that they used, or letters, and now they're putting them in the new one, and they haven't put them together, and they may never do it.

MORRIS: Is there any way we could have an input into that?

WHITE: They know it. This is just a constant problem in libraries—recataloguing; and they don't have the time, the money, or the staff to do it.

ROGO: I have two comments. One is on reference sources that I think should be mentioned. In the *Journal* of the *SPR* George Zorab does a review of continental periodicals. He also does a similar review of the European Press for the *Parapsychology Review*, and these are very valuable because they abstract a lot of Italian, French and German periodicals. Secondly, there's another need that was not mentioned which to me is very important and usually overlooked. Both the SPR in London, and the ASPR in New York have very extensive archives and to someone such as myself who is primarily interested in historical research these archives are very important. Yet there are no published lists of holdings for either the SPR or the ASPR archives. Now these archives have been set in order. In England, they have been put in order by Mostyn Gilbert who worked in the archives, and the ASPR archives were put in order by Thomas Tietze a few years ago. I think there is a real need to get someone to do "holding lists" of the materials that are in these archives, because they contain some phenomenal things. For instance, in the ASPR archives there is the entire Hyslop-Hodgson correspondence with some very valuable information which, of course, has never been published. Also, the Institut Metapsychique in France has an archive holding of extreme value which I don't think has been placed in order, much less catalogued, and this I think is one of the preeminent needs right now in the field.

WHITE: Yes, I certainly agree with you, Scott. There again it's a matter of priorities and not enough money and not enough staff and not enough time. The ASPR library was roughly put in order by Tom Tietze, but he had a lot more work to do and it's by no means been catalogued. He just made rough headings that would stand for maybe a whole catalogue drawer, and right now I don't think the ASPR has any plans to go forward with this job at this time.

BELOFF: I'm glad that Scott Rogo mentioned George Zorab because quite recently in correspondence we were talking about bibliographies and he told me that he would very much like to compile a new bibliography that would be up to date and comprehensive. It struck me that he's an ideal man to do this sort of job, you know, speaking many languages, and having great knowledge of the field, etc., so that if anyone has any money for this sort of enterprise there is somebody who would be very well equipped to tackle it.

WHITE: That's good to know.

STANFORD: I notice you mentioned the current parapsychological journals, I believe you said that only the *Journal of Parapsychology* is abstracted completely in *Psychological Abstracts*, and I was wondering if you could throw any light on why this is the case and how, and under what conditions it could be rectified.

WHITE: Well, I think currently almost all of the English language journals are in *Psych Abstracts*. It's the old material I was referring to. I think the *ASPR Journal*, for example, has been in for the past fifteen years or so. Before that, it was in sporadically, and the SPR *Proceedings* was in early issues and hasn't been in recent ones—just the *Journal* has. I don't think *Psych Abstracts* has any program for going back and doing old material. I think they'll pick up new material just as they decided to recently abstract *Research in Parapsychology*, but I don't think their policy covers retrospective material, unfortunately.

FRANKLIN: There are two problems I want to bring up. One is the professional journal of non-parapsychologists and the other is unpublished manuscripts. Within the professional journals, I'm finding a number of allusions in articles to parapsychological matters and it's very, very difficult for the people working in the field of parapsychology to keep in contact with all of those. The one thing I'm hoping to do is maybe send Rhea and the Parapsychology Foundation Library, articles that I find that would deal with parapsychological type things. Namely, there was an article by Anninos on electromagnetic communication between nerves; it's a very, very interesting thing. *The Journal of Psychosomatic Medicine* is another journal in which I find interesting articles. The *T.I.T. Journal of Life Sciences* also has some interesting things. I think that the traditional professional journals are going to have many allusions or many references which will be small; there won't be many major articles on parapsychology, but professional people will have comments.

Another thing which I see as a problem is unpublished manuscripts. I have many on my desk that have not been published and which probably will not be published, but which include some new ideas which I think are important to know about and again, I think it's probably worthwhile to submit those to libraries so that other people have reference to them.

WHITE: Are these in parapsychology? The unpublished manuscripts?

FRANKLIN: Yes, definitely on parapsychology.

WHITE: Because you could always send them to the *Journal of Parapsychology* because in their *Parapsychological Abstracts* they do publish an abstract and then they will make the full paper available in photocopy upon request.

HASTINGS: I would like to comment on, something at this point in the conference, and Rhea's material, I think, makes it more visible. We are not talking only about education and how to educate students, for parapsychology, but we are also talking about how we are going to create a professional field. Many people here, I think, assume that they are part of a professional field of parapsychology, but it may be that only now is the field beginning. Most of us here do not have degrees in parapsychology but in some other field. Parapsychology has developed out of our personal and professional work. What's happening now is that we see we are going to be educating for parapsychological research, teaching, administration, and bibliographic work. We're really discussing education in a broad context of how the group of professionals is going to become a professional field—a discipline with researchers and educational programs; with relations to institutions and other disciplines, and as Rhea has pointed out, with professional communication including indexes and up-to-the-minute state of the art material, handbooks, continual bibliographic development, etc.

This is an extremely important thing we are talking about here, and it is not what we have done in the past. Whether we like it or not, we are having to face a new professional situation, and what Rhea is talking about is how we can interact with each other so we can make this productive? There is no other experience in science, in my awareness, where the researchers and scholars are consciously discussing this—

well, maybe Michael Faraday did when he was talking about putting words to electricity. What Rhea White has pointed out is something that we should given conscious attention to in order to develop a coherent discipline.

VAUGHAN: I think that as parapsychology becomes more interdisciplinary, it creates a much greater bibliographic problem. How long can we rely on two or three journals to contain all the material of importance to us? Perhaps the PA could set up bibliographic committees, so that each discipline would have a representative, as Wilbur Franklin volunteered for physics, to send to a central location perhaps, or to the Foundation either copies or abstracts of articles which may be of importance to other parapsychologists. I think in the same way that it might be advisable to set up an "expert" index—who knows what—because our various fields of expertise are sometimes quite precise and unexpected. For instance, someone asks me for reseach on animal psi, and I tell them to see Bob Morris. For research on magic, now I know I must tell them to see Arthur Hastings. People are a very valuable bibliographic resource. Yet there's no central index for them.

WHITE: I think probably Mrs. Nester at the ASPR Education Department is making a beginning in doing that sort of thing, aren't you, Marian? Names of people to contact for specific purposes?

NESTER: I haven't done that particular thing, but I certainly am aware of the need myself. I think it's terribly important when students come in and want special references in a field and I want to say, "Write to so and so," and I think if that kind of information came to me, I could certainly include it in the pages that the education department puts out. Incidentally, if anybody wants to see these pages, the education department does have pages that cover some of these questions that all students ask, and if anybody wants to look at them, they can; but I think this is the kind of thing the education department can do, and we would be very glad to have this kind of information come in so that we can collate it and have it available for anybody that wants it.

ROGO: Just a couple of comments. About funding: I don't think it's generally known, but publishers are getting terribly interested in this type of material for publication purposes. This year I made three trips to New York during which I met with several publishers over publication policy in parapsychology and during these talks, on two occasions, I was asked about my doing a combined glossary of parapsychological terms. I turned down both offers for various reasons, but the fact is that commercial publishers now are getting interested in promoting this type of bibliographic work and that they might constitute one source of publishing.

Secondly, there is another very good reference source list that no one really knows about and it is compiled by Mrs. Babusis at the PF. She has been compiling lists of papers and publications on all sorts of different areas of parapsychology and I would hope that eventually the *Parapsychology Review* would run a list of these compilations that Mrs. Babusis has made. When I was in New York, she showed them to me. She showed me one which had pages and pages of references to literature and periodicals on "out-of-body" experiences, and I would hope that these would become widely available to students.

My third comment is rather a personal one to Miss White. In 1965 you did a paper on "The Library and Psychical Research," in The *Journal of the ASPR*, and it was listed as Part I. For ten years I've been wondering, is there going to be a Part II?

WHITE: I doubt it. You can consider this as Part II.

THE RESPONSIBILITIES OF INSTRUCTORS
IN PARAPSYCHOLOGY

ROBERT L. MORRIS

There are two sources of input into this paper which I should clarify at the start: my preconceived notions about how to teach parapsychology to a diverse group of students, developed while I taught the topic to honors students in psychology in small seminars at Duke University and as Research Coordinator for the Psychical Research Foundation; and what happened to me during the past year when I attempted to apply these notions to the teaching of parapsychology to undergraduates at the University of California, Santa Barbara.

Each quarter I have offered three full-credit courses in parapsychology through the Tutorial Program, a separate interdisciplinary department. *Introduction to Parapsychology* is designed to expose students to the general problems and complexities of present-day parapsychology. *Research Methods in Parapsychology* provides a detailed look at the research methods presently used and the reasoning behind them, from a critical perspective. Students are encouraged to participate in the design and conducting of research projects. *Internal States and Parapsychology* examines in detail the recent research which relates the internal state of the receiver to psi success. Included are discussion and readings on the general problems of investigating complex human experiences, "altered states of consciousness," and so on, without hopelessly interfering with them. Students are also encouraged to participate in the design and conducting of research projects. In addition to these three courses, several options for independent research credit are available.

There are several major groupings of students who are likely to sign up for courses in parapsychology, each with somewhat different needs.

(1) Those who are unaware that parapsychology as a research area even exists, and who may or may not have beliefs about the nature and validity of psychic experiences. At least two students who signed up for my courses admitted later that they had expected to receive training in

how to assist psychologists in their therapy sessions, much as paramedical training does for medical assistants. Both completed the course and seemed none the worse for wear. They were pleased to learn that we do exist and were collecting information that might eventually contribute usefully to their daily lives.

(2) Those who are aware of parapsychology, but have no firm opinions, and who are simply eager to learn more about it.

(3) Those who wish to pursue active careers in parapsychology, either full-time or as part of their other chosen profession. They need an accurate picture of the present state of the art as well as its likely future, when they have finished their education and are competing for funds and jobs. They also need special training in the most modern parapsychology research tools, and in the related areas of physics, biology and/or psychology that are most germane to their potential and intended careers. Finally, they need an accurate and honest assessment of their own likelihood of success. The parapsychology instructor should be prepared to serve as a vocational guidance counselor and should not be afraid to dampen enthusiasm, if that seems fairest and in the best interests of the student.

(4) Those who readily accept far more psi phenomena than they should, as a result of inaccurate media-disseminated information. Such students are often hard to deal with, because they must be taught how to judge for themselves and why their present judgments are premature, without hurting their feelings or insulting their intelligence.

(5) Those who place psychic phenomena within a firm religious context, to be validated by science but not to be studied and understood (and thereby profaned). These students are often very hard to communicate with, and are probably more inclined to drop my courses than any other group. To be effective with them it is necessary to understand their approach to religion and what needs are being served by their specific approach to psychic phenomena. This is a tall order in a one-to-one discussion, and is impossible within the context of a classroom of a hundred students, unless the students in question feel free to approach the instructor outside of class. It is easy for me to say that the real need of such students is to be given a more objective perspective on the validity of various psychic claims so that they can conduct the rest of their lives on the basis of more solid and reliable information; such a position could readily be debated, however, and will be touched upon again below.

(6) Those who follow a specific set of occult practices and order much of their lives according to astrology, Tarot, I Ching, voodoo,

demonology, and so on. Such people are often playing a game, which they either continue or abandon according to social circumstances beyond the influence of any parapsychology course; or, they may be pursuing a practice which really seems to work, in their opinion. In the latter case, they are often disappointed to learn that they won't be given further instruction in the latest occult practices. The instructor has the difficult task of trying to show such an individual the difficulties of validating the efficacy of such practices in a way that will seem to make sense, and not just be an academic, perfunctory dismissal. This is a message, of course, that such a student is not particularly eager to receive.

(7) Those who are skeptical about the research in parapsychology and feel it is poorly done. Often such students are very sophisticated science majors and desire detailed information about experimental procedures and results, and general research strategies. The instructor must find ways to address those needs specifically, yet without going beyond their classmates' expertise and boring them.

Thus the instructor is faced with an extraordinarily diverse group of students with equally diverse needs. Some instructors may prefer to screen students to weed out some of the above groups, but this is not always feasible or desirable, and essentially leaves the excluded students high and dry. In my opinion, general instructors in parapsychology share three major interrelated responsibilities if we are to be effective.

First, it is our responsibility to the student to present parapsychology in a way that is genuinely meaningful to the instructor. Otherwise we will be hesitant and insincere in a way that is readily picked up by today's students. They will then be thrown back on their own uncertainties, having learned that even the professed expert has doubts and confusions which he/she is unwilling to admit.

Second, we must do the above in a way that allows us to communicate effectively with a wide variety of students having diverse backgrounds, areas of expertise, and emotional needs, rather than just those whose specific way of looking at the world resembles our own.

Third, we must accomplish both of the above with accuracy, reflecting as best we can the true present state of the art in parapsychology. This means resisting the temptation to push any form of strong belief system personally held. A corollary of this is that the instructor must be able to communicate with and get along with other faculty and administrative staff within the instructional institution, many of whom may be concerned about the impact of parapsychology instruction on campus.

Success at all three is difficult. If the third is sacrificed for the first, or first and second, the program will probably fail because it will either be terminated or will be so severely restricted as to be ineffective. Unsuccessful resolution of this problem may have led to the termination of some programs in the past.

The problem of interfacing with one's colleagues within the administration, faculty and staff is an issue often acknowledged but rarely addressed, and yet an instructor who fails to establish good relations with those around him essentially deprives himself of one of the major values of college-level parapsychology, namely the opportunity to interact intellectually about the problems of parapsychology with peers from different disciplines. It is well known that Duke University's identification with parapsychology was not always advantageous to Duke in general and to the Duke Psychology Department in particular.

The personnel of any school worth its reputation should be realistically concerned with the caliber of any parapsychology program that develops on campus. They must understand and be in reasonable sympathy with the philosophy, goals and practices set forth by the parapsychologist(s) involved. This means that such philosophies, goals and practices must be well thought out and communicable upon demand to a variety of academics who may have radically different world views and language systems. Research procedures advocated should be clear-cut and airtight.

Parapsychologists are very accustomed to viewing themselves as a maligned minority group, the victim of intellectual prejudices. Yet in truth many of the attacks against the field do have some solid basis. Many of us still do very sloppy work and indulge in naive theoretical meanderings in public places. This must be acknowledged from the start in academic interactions, or the instructor/researcher's credibility with peers and students alike will disappear swiftly.

Last quarter I required a term paper from my introductory students. One option was to read and write a critique of any experimental article from the *Journal of Parapsychology*, the *Journal of the ASPR*, or the *International Journal of Parapsychology*, finding at least two major flaws in procedure. Over forty of them chose to do so, and none had any difficulty. In summary, to set up a program of instruction in a college is to request to be taken seriously; to be taken seriously one must be quite serious oneself.

My own approach to these problems and perceived responsibilities has been to develop and present an interdisciplinary construction of psi that uses the simple language of communication theory in a way that can be related to a variety of disciplines. Psi is construed as implicit communication between organism and environment through means other than presently understood channels.[1,2] In each case we have a source, receiver, and message, but no specifiable channel by which the message is propagated.

In ESP paradigms the target is source, information about it is message, and the subject is receiver. In PK paradigms the subject is source, the content of a goal-directed intent is message, and the target is receiver. In neither case can a channel be specified, and communication must be inferred through observed correspondence between source and receiver.

The goal of parapsychology now becomes to find the channel(s) and understand the entire communication system in detail. Such a conceptual system makes few assumptions and provides a set of terms that can be easily understood by mathematician, physicist, biologist, psychologist, anthropologist, and so on, all of whom can understand and use the concept of communication systems. Each discipline is still free to translate these terms into its own vocabulary when needed. The study of communication systems and the development of new systems is a very commonplace occurrence today and is well within the rubric of one or more interdisciplinary programs as well as individual departments on most major campuses today.

In presenting such an approach to the student it first becomes important to insure that the student well understands all the presently known modes of communication, the explicit systems for which we can identify channels. Only then can he understand why under certain conditions we are willing to infer that, because we have eliminated the known modes, a new mode may be at work. To get this across, I generally devote two lectures near the beginning of the introductory course to demonstrating various techniques for simulating psi, such as musclereading, trick blindfolds, stacked card decks, telepathy codes, audience stooges, various seance-room techniques, modern electronic communication and detection systems, how to phrase and time public predictions, and so on. Most students soon learn that impressive psychic demonstrations can be faked surprisingly easily, and this starts them reevaluating the processes of logic by which they infer communication in the world around them.

Next the students are given a relevant overview of sensory and cognitive psychology, emphasizing the range of ways we can take in information and process it; and a bit of biophysics, emphasizing various nonbehavioral ways we can put information out into the world around us (e.g., by modifying the intensity of the electrostatic field around us, and so on).

With this information in hand, we consider the early history of parapsychology, the problems of interpreting individual spontaneous experiences, and the uses (and misuses) of large collections of thematically related spontaneous cases for generating hypotheses about how psi works.

Once this beachhead has been established intellectually, the student can be confronted with the complexities of experimental research in parapsychology. Such research is described within a communications context. In order that we may infer that a new system of communication is in operation, two things must take place: (1) we must eliminate all known systems; and (2) we must show that there is sufficient correlation between source state and receiver state, i.e. that a message of some sort actually did get through from source to receiver.

These two elements of parapsychological research are the keys by which communication along specific channels of any sort is inferred. The student learns to confront any experiment (or personal experience) by asking what channels of communication, if any, are open between the designated source and receiver, and how much information, if any, really did get through to the receiver. In this way the study of parapsychological research designs and procedures can teach the student general principles of communication that he can use in daily life as he interprets his own experiences and how they relate to the world around him. Thus the course has value above and beyond formal parapsychology training, an important point when it comes time to justify the presence on campus of parapsychology in its present state of uncertainty and infancy.

The remainder of the course is divided into three main sections: (1) what are the consistent findings in parapsychology research; (2) what are the main kinds of hypotheses about how psi works, and how do they relate to the empirical data on hand; and (3) if psi is for real, what are its implications for our daily lives. The last section includes cross-cultural studies of psi, and an examination of the ethical issues presented by psychic development courses, professional psychics and psychic counselors, as well as other related topics.

Throughout such a course I have used two texts, one positive and one negative, assigning comparable readings from each. This helps the students to retain a balanced view and also serves as a constant reminder that gifted writers can be emotionally persuasive without necessarily being factually accurate.

As an additional part of such training students can be shown in detail the logic behind adequate studies of psi and the differences between adequate and inadequate studies. Useful illustrative studies for student learning by participation include: standard card-guessing and dice-throwing procedures; sensory deprivation free-response studies involving relaxation tapes and Ganzfeld procedures; remote viewing; stable system PK studies using thermistors; Schmidt machines; and plethysmograph studies. All involve equipment that can be purchased or constructed at relatively little expense. My students and I have used these procedures, among others, and found it a valuable experience.

This also helps to keep up the interest of students, as both subjects and experimenters, and helps them to develop a good feel for the interdisciplinary teamwork needed in any serious psi project. By being both subject and experimenter they learn to appreciate the problems of each role and the delicate relationship of each to the other. Intensive critical examination of specimen studies can be a valuable tool for instruction in advanced experimental parapsychology courses, and can also provide an opportunity for independent replication of some of the most important studies. Additionally, most good students are capable of coming up with occasional creative insights about how to investigate a given area.

There are many additional issues that can be raised, depending on the expertise of the instructor and the interests of the students, most of which involve the relationship of parapsychology to other disciplines. Physics becomes involved in any discussion of "paraphysics" and hypotheses involving energy fields around our bodies, bioplasma, psychoenergetics, and so on.

Cognitive and humanistic psychology, as well as philosophy, become involved when the discussion turns to currently fashionable notions of "alternate realities," the epistemology of personal knowledge, and so on. Anthropology and religious studies become a part of any discussion of occult practices and psi, spirit hypotheses about the functioning of psi, and so on. The issues in these areas being raised today often seem to be a rehashing of old problems, that are recurring without benefit of genuine scholarly expertise in the relevant disciplines. An ideal solution is the use of team-taught courses involving someone knowledgeable about parapsychology and a friendly faculty member in the associated discipline.

By setting up course work in this way I think we can satisfy the responsibilities outlined earlier as well as appeal to a wide variety of students in ways that will be deemed genuine education, rather than sensational education, by one's colleagues.

An additional set of responsibilities of parapsychology instructors involves a complex set of ethical issues related to the needs of today's average naive but intelligent student. If psi is taken seriously, one can easily acquire an exaggerated view of the permeability of the boundary between oneself and one's environment. David Rogers[3] cites a client of his in North Carolina who, after taking some card-guessing tests and being told he seemed to have ESP, began to assume that psychic interactions were taking place all the time. Soon he lost his friends because of his "weird" behavior and his life became very painful.

This individual was somewhat unusual to begin with, and his response is obviously not typical. This does not absolve us of the responsibility to confront intelligently others like him when they come along. One of the first things I did on the UCSB campus was to give a talk at the student counseling center and establish ties with a community relations center, making clear who I was, what my goals were, and asking for feedback if students started pouring in with psychic complaints. To my knowledge none have.

A second ethical obligation is to help people avoid being easy prey for "psychic ripoffs"—superpsychics who charge to tell you how to conduct your life or diagnose and heal all illnesses; and courses that purport to teach you how to be a superpsychic yourself. A favorite final exam question of mine asks the students what they would investigate and how they would do it if they were members of a Nader's Raiders task force assigned to parapsychology. This helps them think for themselves, organize the material they've already received, and come up with general principles which they can then apply to specific situations.

A third responsibility in this area is to describe in detail the methodological complexities involved in investigating spirit-related and energy-related hypotheses about how psi works. These two lines of thought have had strong adherents for hundreds of years, and today are frequently offered as ready explanations for psi. Without detailed knowledge of the problems involved, we can readily find one or the other quite persuasive, such that we are tempted to build the rest of our lives around a set of concepts that may well be patently false. As mentioned earlier, a good approach is to bring outside expertise from related disciplines, perhaps as guest speakers, to deal concretely but fairly with the issues. Since many students may have acquired emotional adherence to one of these viewpoints, it thus becomes doubly important that the material be presented fairly, without insulting the people involved.

A fourth responsibility is to orient students towards critical consideration of the implications of psi for present-day society. This means focusing attention on the potential creative uses of psi in interpersonal communication, teaching, child development, and so on, as well as its potential misuses. Some people with apparent psychic ability are very happy, others very unhappy. What is the difference, and how does it relate to the individuals and to the larger social context within which these individuals find themselves?

A final responsibility, covered in part earlier, is to insure that students are fully aware of the ethical issues that have been raised in general over experimentation on living organisms.

At present I don't think we instructors can completely fulfill all of these responsibilities; they touch on many issues that are not about to be resolved satisfactorily for some time to come. Nevertheless, by raising them now among ourselves, and by discussing them openly in the classroom, I think we can keep open the kind of dialogue that will have to take place in order for us to be prepared to deal with these issues ourselves. Also, we will hopefully place pressure on those who close off these issues and refuse to discuss them. Our message to students now must be one of enlightened uncertainty; to claim otherwise is to go considerably beyond our present experiential and empirical data base.

REFERENCES

[1] Morris, R. L.: "Building Experimental Models," *Journal of Communication*, 25, (1975), 117–125.

[2] Morris, R. L.: "Tacit Communication and Experimental Theology," in *Research in Parapsychology 1974*, Morris, J., Roll, W. G., and Morris, R. (eds.) (Metuchen, N. J., Scarecrow Press, 1975), 179–198.

[3] Rogers, D. P.: "Driving Subjects Crazy," in *Research in Parapsychology 1974*, Morris, J., Roll, W. G., and Morris, R. (eds.) (Metuchen, N. J., Scarecrow Press, 1975), 165–170.

DISCUSSION

KRIPPNER: This was a very exciting presentation about some of the things that can happen when the opportunities and the finances and the administration combine to make them possible. Hopefully, this is something that will emerge on other campuses over the next half-dozen years. I'm just curious about all the paraphernalia and equipment that you brought in. Which did the students find most motivating? Was it the thermistors, the polygraphs, or what? Is there anything that really intrigues them more than anything else?

MORRIS: I don't really think there is. I think there are a great many individual differences involved and that's one of the values of this sort of approach. I'm quite surprised sometimes at the people who get very wrapped up in certain kinds of experiences. I must say that the remote viewing procedure has been especially useful as a heuristic device because it is a new area of research; most of the good thought about it hasn't been done yet. It involves exciting and interesting and yet very complex targets to analyze. In our research methods class through the summer quarter, we had two separate teams—one of which was involved in collecting the data through the remote viewing procedure, and the other, all three of them, focused almost exclusively on the problem of what it means to be a judge and how one develops adequate judging techniques.

KRIPPNER: Have you been able to use the same orientation procedure that the Stanford Research Institute uses for remote viewing?

MORRIS: We took a field trip up there with six students. Russell Targ and Hal Puthoff put us through a session right there and we were able to bring back a good feeling for their procedure. The part of the SRI orientation that emerged as most salient to us was that they really build up the confidence of the person involved in the beginning. They've estimated that they work for a minimum of an hour with anybody before they actually start the experimental session, describing all the past success they have had and they make the statement that basically they have yet to find someone who can't do it. By the time we actually got into the remote viewing study, we had done a rather intensive methodological hashing through of their procedure, etc. So we were not necessarily quite so confident that the effect was consistently statistically demonstrable. We said to the students "Look, we're using this as a device to work out methodological problems, so be aware of that; however, when you actually get into the testing situation itself, try as best you can to approximate what went on up there, including the air of confidence they built up."

ROGO: The Santa Barbara program is in its second year, and I'd like to ask Dr. Morris a question. After having run these courses now for a considerable length of time, what do you feel is the greatest area of educational success and what do you feel is the greatest area of educational failure during your period of time at Santa Barbara?

MORRIS: The second question is a lot easier. I'm not sure what successes I have had, because I wouldn't want to measure them for another year or two. I guess the greatest problem really is finding good source material. There is no textbook that really gets into all the topics that I feel should be covered. At least a third of my course is non-parapsychological material. It is background material and I'm badly in need of getting my own notes in these areas organized and some sort of reference material out. And, of course, some of you, I'm sure, will find the communications approach inappropriate. It's just simply one that I feel good about and that I found I could communicate to people from religious studies through mathematics, and all the folks in between. I would say, as a matter of fact, that that may well be the strongest personal success that I've seen there; I am able to put people together from quite different disciplines in the same room and have them, somewhat imperfectly, still at least able to talk with each other. Afterward you can run off to your own department and use what language system you're most comfortable with, but in the meantime you've at least been able to share some sort of conceptual integration with members of other disciplines. I try to get my advance students to form small teams from different areas so that they can help each other and complement each other. Ideally, they get a feeling that when progress is being made, it's being made by an interdisciplinary team and not by the isolated researcher.

PALMER: I have never actually taught in parapsychology, but I have had the experience of students dropping into my office and asking me about it, and one of the problems I found, and which I think might generalize to the teaching situation, is usually that the first question someone asks me is, "Have you read such and such?" And "such and such" being a piece of "trash." I won't get into the names of books, but I'm sure most of you know what I have in mind. More often than not my answer is "no," because frankly it's hard enough to keep up with the good material without getting into the trash. But on the other hand, I find that often as soon as the student realizes that I'm not up on this—here's someone who is supposed to be up on parapsychology and he hasn't read this great book—I find I'm tuned out, I can't criticize this particular book because I haven't read it and if I try, the answer is, "Well, how do you know it's a bad book if you haven't read it?", even though I would know something about the author. My question is, from your experience, is it important to have grounding in this literature? Should an instructor in parapsychology be up on the occult trash, so that he can deal with it when he's asked about it?

MORRIS: I think you've raised a really important issue. I think that to the extent that we can, we either should ourselves, or we should know people who have specialized somewhat in that area. I have some students who have read extensively in some of these areas, who have now come into my classes and become much more methodologically oriented. They often are now able to go back and re-interpret the systems that once had captivated them and then they can do the job for me that I can't do.

But one term paper project that we did one quarter was kind of interesting—what I call "The Airport Project." I had everybody sign up for a separate paperback of the kind you'd find in airports on the newsstands—that's why it was called "The Airport Project." They were told, "Take one that emphasizes techniques for psychic development; do a book report on it; review in detail as much as you can the exact procedures for becoming a psychic as outlined in that particular book, and then criticize it with respect to what we've covered so far in class. About 47 different books were reviewed in that way and we were able to come up with about seventeen common themes that were present in almost all of those books. The fascinating thing was that the same great advice for how to show psychic ability, is probably excellent also for developing sensory hyper-acuity, and so it is not necessarily surprising that these books worked. Almost all testing procedures offered to validate the methods were extremely weak and generally amenable to sensory cue alternative explanations. With respect to Dr. Palmer's original question, now I can offer this to people as a completed study and say, "All right, now you're into a specific system. Let's look at it and analyze it." The one thing I try never to do is to assert that astrology or whatever is junk, because I truly, of course, cannot prove that. I can opine it, but I cannot assert it and I will eliminate myself as an intelligent human being very quickly if, in fact, I claim I can disprove astrology. I ask students what kind of source material they're familiar with and what kind of documentation they have that a procedure such as astrology works. Are they familiar with research literature suggesting alternative possibilities? For instance, if people are born during summer in temperate climates, they start to crawl when it's winter time, and are kept off the floors, bundled up, etc. People have argued that personality differences depend in part on what time you first start to crawl. If you're born in the winter time, then come the summer you have much more freedom to move around unhampered and thus develop quite different attitudes. Such suggestions are always in a reasonable friendly way. Your system may be fine; let's just get down to the details. Sometimes the people come in excited, do reports and get guided a little bit further. Sometimes the battle continues; sometimes I just simply never see them again.

FRANKLIN: I was very happy to hear about the involvement of students with experiments in SRI. I've found a similar reaction. I've had students involved in my own personal experiments—students from my classes that have come in and helped me with experiments. Their own positive attitude—their positive thinking comes forward then. We've had exposure of films in an experiment with Olga Worrall and one of my pre-med students took some Kirlian photographs and got some very interesting results.

Another thing I wanted to comment on was the course content—rather, I wanted to ask you about it. Were you able to include anything on electromagnetic effects on living systems, or anything on nerve physiology or physical theories—anything of that sort?

MORRIS: The physical theories, some that you've outlined, I'm not competent to give. Sometimes I can get somebody in the electrical engineering department or in physics as guest lecturers on that point. As far as these biophysical influences on human tissue that you were talking about, are concerned, I certainly make clear to them that those exist. I am limited in my capacity to give them the exact research details, but I can draw from animal sensing systems to illustrate a lot of the work done in that area. I try to make it very clear to them that there's a lot of physical interaction we have with the world around us. I detail maybe three or four and say, "Look, there's a lot more. This is just an area we haven't gone into; it's been taboo to a large extent itself for a variety of interesting reasons," and that generally opens them up enough to say, "Okay, from now on we'll bear that in mind," especially in interpreting phenomena involving close interactions between an organism as evidence for some new form of communication.

RHINE: When I listened to Dr. Morris' talk about what teaching parapsychology means to him, I can't help but think back to my own efforts forty years ago which offer a contrast. There is so much today that has happened since then; that is evident in what all of you are teaching on the subject today. I think the conference has been an education in itself. If now anyone could make a composite course—a course based on all of these offerings at least it would make a splendid educational beginning.

But I want to add a word about those who, like Rhea White, are not doing formal teaching, because it was in our laboratory that she first crossed the threshold of parapsychology. As she spoke I was mentally reviewing her career. It struck me that there ought to be some way to recognize this quiet, back-in-the-corner and largely volunteer work that she's been doing, which has been so basic for the field in a broader educational way. There ought indeed to be some kind of a special sainthood for people like that—librarians, editors, statisticians,—a suitable award perhaps.

ANGOFF: That is the last paper of this conference. All the papers and all the discussions have been recorded and will be transcribed, and the entire proceedings of our three days of meetings will be published in book form next year.

The officers and trustees of the Parapsychology Foundation thank all of you for your contributions.

Ladies and gentlemen, this conference is adjourned.